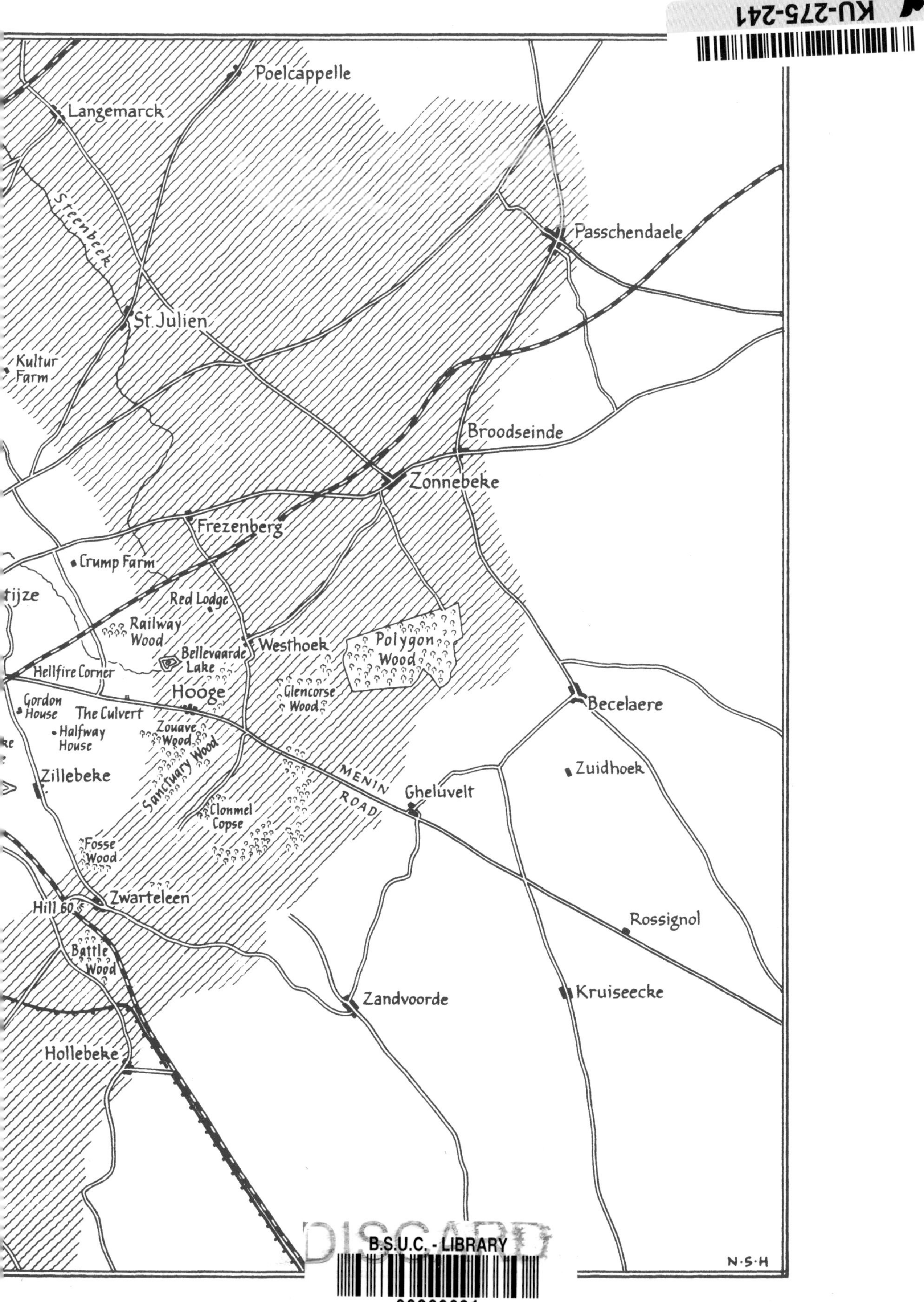

Poelcappelle
Langemarck
Steenbeek
St. Julien
Kultur Farm
Passchendaele
Broodseinde
Zonnebeke
Frezenberg
Crump Farm
Red Lodge
Railway Wood
Westhoek
Polygon Wood
Bellevaarde Lake
Hellfire Corner
Hooge
Glencorse Wood
Gordon House
The Culvert
Zouave Wood
Halfway House
Sanctuary Wood
Becelaere
Zuidhoek
MENIN ROAD
Gheluvelt
Zillebeke
Clonmel Copse
Fosse Wood
Zwarteleen
Hill 60
Battle Wood
Rossignol
Zandvoorde
Kruiseecke
Hollebeke
N·S·H

THE WIPERS TIMES

THE EDITOR OF *THE WIPERS TIMES*

THE WIPERS TIMES

THE COMPLETE SERIES OF THE FAMOUS WARTIME TRENCH NEWSPAPER

FOREWORD BY
IAN HISLOP

INTRODUCTION BY
MALCOLM BROWN

NOTES BY
PATRICK BEAVER

This edition published in 2006 by Little Books Ltd,
48 Catherine Place, London SW1E 6HL

10 9 8 7 6 5 4 3 2

A CIP catalogue record for this book is available from the British Library.

ISBN: 1 904435 60 2

Printed and bound in Great Britain by William Clowes Ltd, Beccles, Suffolk

CONTENTS

FOREWORD

'Oh, to be in Belgium now that winter's here.' This is the unmistakable voice of *The Wipers Times*, and ninety years since it first appeared I am delighted to see the complete collection back in print. This extraordinary magazine was written, printed, distributed and read by British soldiers serving in the trenches of the Western Front during the First World War. It was produced on an abandoned printing press salvaged from the ruins of Ypres – hence the title with the classic British mispronunciation – and was an immediate success from its first edition. It continued to appear throughout the war and was subsequently reissued in the following years of peace. Its extraordinary mix of jokes, sarcasm, black humour and sentimental poetry make it a unique record of the period. It is quite literally laughing in the face of death, with jokes about flame-throwers and gas attacks from the troops who were facing them. It is also very rude about senior officers, the home front and the organization of the war. It is *Blackadder* for real and an obvious forerunner of magazines like *Private Eye*.

I have long been an admirer of *The Wipers Times*, and once made a documentary about it for BBC Radio Four called *Are We As Offensive As We Might Be?* This was a question which staff officers from headquarters used to ask troops in the front line when they thought that they were insufficiently keen to go over the top and attack the Germans. It became a sort of catchphrase for the writers of the magazine, who would ask each other, 'Are we as offensive as we might be?' I thought that this was very British – as was the fact that the editor, a very talented man called Captain Fred Roberts, was working on the copy for an edition of the magazine called *The Somme Times* during the Battle of the Somme. He was correcting proofs in the trench and yet he went on to win the Military Cross for bravery in that very battle. That's an editor who commands respect.

Roberts wrote that war was mostly about 'wallowing in a ditch', but he and his fellow writers managed to create something finer, funnier and more life-enhancing from their grim situation. I think that *The Wipers Times* has often been unjustly ignored and that it is actually firmly in the great tradition of British comic literature. The authors would probably have laughed at that idea, too.

Ian Hislop

To John Billham

in memory of good days

from the Editor

JP Roberts

Dedication reproduced courtesy of the Imperial War Museum

INTRODUCTION

The British first entered the Belgian city of Ypres in October 1914. The name baffled them; the Tommies didn't know how to pronounce it. They had the same problem with many of the names they came across in their travels around France and Belgium. Etaples, near Boulogne, where the British Expeditionary Force (generally known as the 'B.E.F.') rapidly established a large training camp, became 'Ee-tapps', even 'Eatapples'. Ypres became 'Eeps' or 'Eepray'. Another version, which was widely taken up by the press back home, was 'Wipers'. When in early 1916 a trench magazine appeared, devised and printed inside the battered walls of a city which by then had become almost iconic to the soldiers of the B.E.F., there was a name ready and waiting with which to entitle it. It was called *The Wipers Times*.

Ultimately the magazine ran to twenty-three numbers, all of them produced by the same two-man team: Captain (later Lieutenant-Colonel) F. J. 'Fred' Roberts as editor, and Lieutenant (later Major) J. H. Pearson as sub-editor. Of necessity its title changed as the editors migrated around the Western Front. After publishing four editions in Ypres, they moved to Neuve Eglise, just short of the Franco-Belgian border, where they produced *The New Church Times*. Subsequently they moved back north to the vicinity of Kemmel Hill, where they produced *The Kemmel Times*. They then transferred to the region of the Somme, where they produced *The Somme Times*. Posted subsequently to a range of destinations, they settled for the catch-all title, *The B.E.F. Times*. Wherever they went, they could use that title with equanimity. Additionally, there was no give-away to the Germans, should copies fall into their hands, as to where they might be based.

Finally, at the war's end, eager to catch a mood of sudden optimism – or, arguably, sudden deliverance – they settled for *The Better Times*. It was almost as though they were concluding a kind of literary symphony with an ode to joy, with the rider that by this juncture there was less exultation than sheer gut relief. That the better times they hoped for turned out to be not as good as they were meant to be was not their fault. Yet they caught that moment with all its ambiguities and encapsulated it. I think there was something of greatness in all this.

What was the point of this gesture – this attempt to cope with the squalors and challenges of war by producing a kind of military *Punch*? Even, as has already been suggested, almost a prototype of *Private Eye* several generations ahead of its time? If there was a closer actual role model, it is implicit in the title, echoing that of Britain's most famous national newspaper, *The Times* of Printing House Square, London. 'Our paper was started as the result of the discovery of an old printing-house just off the square at Wipers,' wrote the editor in a lively thumbnail history hurriedly put together in 1918, adding, in what can only have been a conscious bow to the greater publication: '*Some* printing house and *some* square.'

The 'point' was, above all, humour: to find and to celebrate the funny side of a deeply unfunny war. Lord Plumer, a general of the Great War whom many soldiers genuinely admired, put the point perfectly in the brief foreword he wrote for the first collected edition of the newspaper, published in 1930: 'This book is not a serious narrative of the events which took place during the period 1916 to 1918, but a perusal of its numbers will give the reader a vivid and correct impression of the cheerfulness which prevailed, notwithstanding all the sacrifices, hardship and privations the troops were called upon to undergo.'

In one of his most powerful poems about the war of the Western Front, Siegfried Sassoon wrote of 'the hell, where youth and laughter go'. In not dissimilar vein Wilfred Owen once wrote: 'Merry it was to laugh there/Where death becomes absurd and life absurder'. We have become so convinced of the hell that we have forgotten there could also be laughter. Indeed, it was the laughter – the mockery, the jokes, the cocking of the snook at authority, the leg-pulls, the puns, the catchphrases, the songs and snatches, the limericks, the earthy wit – that made the hell tolerable: perhaps even made it not quite the total interminable hell we now assume it to have been.

Leading the van in this fight for hearts and minds were the trench newspapers, of which *The Wipers Times*, it should be emphasized, was one among legion. In a sense they were school magazines revisited, remakes for a new kind of academy in which the masters were commanders, no one knew when the terms would end and the playing fields were lethal ones where the blow of a whistle meant not the start of a match but the launch of an attack, with not everybody trooping back to the pavilion when the 'game' was over.

They appeared in every war theatre. The Royal Naval Division produced *Dardanelles Dug-Out Gossip* while based in Gallipoli, but when transferred to the rain-soaked terrain of France they re-titled it *The Mudhook*. *Barrak* (so named from the throaty expression 'BRRRRK' used to make camels kneel) came from the Imperial Camel Corps in the Middle East; revived by enthusiastic survivors fifty years later, it ceased publication as recently as 1989. *The Moonraker* emanated from a Wiltshire battalion in Salonika, though its humour could have sprung from any of the fronts in which the British were engaged. A particular favourite, in this as in many other such publications, was the gently risqué limerick, such as the following example:

I know a blithe blossom in Blighty
Whom you (I'm afraid) would call flighty
For when Zepps are about
She always trips out
In a little black crêpe de chine nightie.

A damsel who dwelt on La Tortue
Said, 'George dear, do you think we ortue?'
George replied: 'My dear girl,
My head's in a whirl
Ought or ought'nd be hanged – pull the dortue.'

Salonika also produced *The Balkan News*, which in one edition printed an item to the effect that a large vessel had recently been unearthed (not entirely incredible in an area where digging trenches often brought up archaeological remains) bearing the curious inscription:

ITIS APIS POTANDA BIGONE

Clearly meant to challenge an army not without its classically educated members, the meaning of the riddle was not disclosed. Readers seeking assurance that they have correctly understood this curious item of service wit will find the solution asterisked* at the bottom of the page.

The genre produced a whole range of titles, especially on the Western Front. *Clickety Click* was a late arrival on the scene, courtesy of the Royal Air Force. *The Bird* was the product of an anti-aircraft unit. *Behind the Lines* explained itself as 'The (Unofficial) Magazine of No. 10 Stationary Hospital'. The 23rd Division boasted a particularly successful annual publication called *The Dump*, another magazine with a penchant for the pungent limerick:

I once asked a Choleric Colonel
To write something short for this jolonel.
But I'm sorry to tell
He replied, 'Go to ???' – well,
He confined me to regions infolonel.

Another standard feature was the parody. *The Fifth Glo'ster Magazine*, in its edition of February 1917, adapted W. B. Yeats's famous celebration of quietness and serenity,

* It is a piss pot and a big one.

'The Lake Isle of Innisfree', to the circumstances of a particularly unserene and noisy war. (Note: a Lewis G. was a Lewis gun, and a Minnie was a *Minenwerfer*, a German missile-thrower much loathed by the Tommies):

I will arise and go now and go to Picardy
And a new trench line hold there, of clay and shell-holes made;
No dug-outs shall I find there, nor a hive for a Lewis G.
But live on top in the b. loud glade.
And I may cease to be there, for peace comes dropping slow
Dropping from the mouth of the Minnie to where the sentry sings,
There noon is high explosive, and night a gun-fire glow
And evening full of torpedoes' wings...

Aussie was, unmistakably, 'The Australian Soldiers' Magazine'; often teeming with caustic wit, it offered this moving poem, in honour of the fallen, in March 1918:

When the last barrage has lifted,
And the dawn of Right breaks thro'
And back we trail to the Bushland
We will drink, dear friends, to you.

We will drink a toast to our comrades
Who fought with us side by side,
And fell as the barrage lifted
And the dust of battle died.

That hope for the ceasefire and the silence that would surely come was also powerfully expressed by the Royal Naval Division's *The Mudhook*, in the first weeks of 1918:

It's a long road that has no turning
It's never too late to mend:
The darkest hour is before the dawn
And *even this* war must end.

It was this culture, of which the foregoing is the merest glimpse, that produced *The Wipers Times*. Well-written and edited as so many other trench publications were, it is *The Wipers Times* which has emerged as the undisputed leader of this extraordinary pack. It has become a cult classic, but, as has arguably been made evident, out of a field not without sturdy competitors.*

* Extracts from trench magazines other than *The Wipers Times* are printed courtesy of the Imperial War Museum's Department of Printed Books.

What was it that made it so special? For one thing, there is the heroic story of the way it was produced. Some magazines, such as *Clickety Click*, were typewritten; *The Bird* was hand-drawn. Most of the publications here quoted had necessarily to be printed in Britain. As already indicated, Roberts and Pearson, the creators of *The Wipers Times*, found an abandoned printing press somewhere in Ypres and acquired it in what was perhaps the most inspired piece of looting in the Great War. When their press suffered from enemy action, they topped it up by yet more judicious looting. Their first editorial den was a rat-infested cellar that was part of the ramparts of Ypres as constructed in the eighteenth century by Louis XIV's great expert on fortifications, Vauban, located not a stone's throw from the Menin Gate (though the gate at that time was merely an exit from the city, not the memorial arch of today). They produced their first editions under fire, and throughout their frequent changes of location and of title, and in spite of certain interruptions – some of them major ones owing to the exigencies of war – they kept going determinedly to the end, never far from shot and shell until the guns at last fell silent.

And then its editors went their way and did nothing like that ever again.

Who were they, this remarkable duo, to whom we are all so much in debt? They were both officers of 24th Division, one of six new divisions whose formation was ordered by Lord Kitchener, as Secretary of State for War, in September 1914. The 24th, together with its fellow division, the 21st, was thrown into action almost totally unprepared in the Battle of Loos in 1915 and thereafter fought in every Western Front campaign until the end of the war. Both were 'hostilities only' officers, as opposed to regulars, who had 'good wars'; Roberts ultimately became commanding officer of his battalion with the added distinction of a Military Cross, while Pearson won both an M.C. and a D.S.O. (Distinguished Service Order). Without in any way compromising their military commitments, and with the practical help of certain equally committed 'other ranks', they produced one of the great literary phenomena of what has been often described as a literary war.

What is more impressive is that *The Wipers Times* did not emerge from a gilded unit full of highly educated and well-connected glitterati, but from the 12th Battalion of the North Midlands Nottinghamshire and Derbyshire Regiment, generally known as the Sherwood Foresters. As if that were not enough, the 12th Sherwood Foresters was a pioneer battalion – by long tradition going back to Elizabethan times, a unit consisting of labourers rather than fighters. In this case a large number of the personnel were former miners; Roberts himself, in his early thirties, was a pre-war mining engineer. If there was a pecking order within army divisions, pioneer battalions came distinctly low in it; not for them the cachet, even in a regiment of modest reputation, of a battalion of the line. Unworried by such considerations, the editors followed their star and achieved a triumph that came to be respected and valued across the army.

And they did so with the lightest of touches while achieving a standard of consistency that never wavered. Although they could occasionally call on the skills of such distinguished writers in the making as Gilbert Frankau, they (especially Roberts) kept the pages filled with a remarkable stream of wit, humour and, at times, hilarious invention. And, it should be noted, they did so without vulgarity. There was bravura in plenty but no bawdiness; in the context of an army which knew, and used, every expletive and excoriation in (or not in) the dictionary, this is a fact worth recording.

There was, however another reason why this was an outstanding member of the genre. It was not just light entertainment. It had *gravitas*. It had style. And it included evocative, even inspirational writing, such as this passage, on page 5 of its first issue, describing the impact of Ypres by night, already by this time a city of gaunt ruins:

> Like the figures of ghosts they seem to point importunately to heaven, crying for vengeance. It is a city of ghosts, the city of the dead. For it and with it the sons of three nations have suffered and died. Yet within that city, not many days ago, a little maid of Flanders was found playing. That is an omen. Ypres has died, but shall live again. Her name in the past was linked with kings: but tomorrow she shall have a nobler fame. Men will speak of her as the home of the British soldier who lives in her mighty rampart caverns or in the many cellars of her mansions. And even when the busy hum of everyday life shall have resumed its sway in future days, still there will be heard in ghostly echo the muffled rumbling of the transport, and the rhythmic tread of soldiers' feet.

The authorship of this eloquent meditation, entitled 'Reflections on Being Lost in Ypres at 3 a.m.', is assigned (in inverted commas) to 'The Padre', with the signatures of the two editors appearing below. It has been suggested that the Padre in question might have been Revd. P. B. (Tubby) Clayton, forever associated with the 'Everyman's Club' at Talbot House, Poperinghe, founded in December 1915, which ultimately gave rise to the famous Toc H movement. But Clayton was a member of 6th Division, as was the officer killed in July 1915, Lieutenant Gilbert Talbot, after whom Talbot House was named. Moreover, Tubby Clayton's club was barely launched when Roberts and Pearson began plying their typefaces in the first weeks of 1916. It seems most unlikely that the editors would have called upon a contributor from another and far more senior division to grace their first number. The probable solution is that the editors devised and wrote it themselves. But essentially the matter of authorship is irrelevant. It is the quality of the piece, of which the above is merely an extract, that is important. Effectively the editors were setting a benchmark in their first edition: 'Watch this space. Don't expect just larks and jokes. We can also be serious.'

And having shown their seriousness, they breezily mocked the same phenomenon – of a city in ruins – with a *Times*-style letter to the editors by a correspondent signing himself 'Well Wisher':

> 'May I through the medium of your valuable paper call attention to the disgraceful state the roads are getting into. What, what, I ask, are our city fathers doing to allow such a state of things to come to pass?'

One important subject that merits exploration is the attitude of the magazine to the Ypres Salient, which was effectively its birthplace. This was arguably the most hated battleground of the whole war in the eyes of the British Tommy. To remind present-day readers, this zone of Belgium to the immediate east of Ypres was fought over in every year of the war; it saw – literally – the first use of poison gas in 1915, and in 1917 was the setting for that undeniably dreadful three-month-long battle generally known as Passchendaele. It can seem unthinkable to later students of the phenomenon of the so-called 'Immortal Salient' that someone as free with their opinions as the editors of *The Wipers Times* did not fulminate in the most outspoken manner against the British determination to hang on to this piece of torn and battered territory.

But this is where it is all too easy to visit the past with facile hindsight. Not yielding ground to the enemy was part of the ethos of the time. Additionally, the Belgians had lost so much of their homeland to German occupation that to concede even more – and by so doing to allow the Germans to advance to the very walls of Ypres – would have been not just a geographical adjustment, it would have been a psychological one, indeed almost a gesture of defeat. The subject was not, however, one that *The Wipers Times* would ignore. It would deal with the issue, but do so in its own way. One of its standard features throughout publication was a regular slot entitled 'Things We Want to Know'. The following appeared under that title in the second issue (*see* page 17).

> 1. Who discovered the salient.
> 2. Why.

This was the perfect riposte. The matter was raised, but deftly, subtly, without bombast.

So with other later references, such as the half-page advertisement in issue number 4 (21 March 1916; *see* page 46) offering for sale 'The Salient Estate' with, among its attractions, 'Shooting Perfect!! Fishing Good!!!', and the invitation to apply for particulars to 'Thomas, Atkins, Sapper & Co, Zillebeke and Hooge': the last names being those of two villages which had been the focus of much savage and sacrificial fighting.

Another regular feature was 'People We Take Our Hats Off To'. In its third issue, dated 6th March 1916, among those to whom the magazine raised its hat were: 'The French at Verdun'.

It has long been the case that we in Britain tend too often to see the Western Front war in British terms only. In fact, essentially the war in this theatre was to a substantial degree the war of our coalition Allies: Belgium, almost totally occupied and with a seriously depleted army; and France, with ten of its ninety departments under German rule, and, what is often overlooked, by far the greatest part of the Western Front to maintain. The prime motivation behind Britain's commitment to the war in Western Europe was to assist our allies in the task of defeating the enemy and forcing him back to whence he had come. Thus, when in February 1916 the Germans launched a massive attack on the fortress city of Verdun in faraway Lorraine, this produced a crisis which demanded Allied solidarity and support. It is therefore to be applauded that the editors of *The Wipers Times*, almost 300 miles away at the extreme other end of the Western Front, were sagacious enough not to make easy jokes about the French but to express admiration for their determination to resist whatever the cost.

The prolonged battle for Verdun, which dragged on (if with substantial breaks) until December, materially affected the long-planned Allied attempt to take the war to the enemy in 1916 by a major joint offensive in Picardy. Because of Verdun the French could give only limited support to the long-awaited 'big push' which became known as the Battle of the Somme. For this and a range of other reasons, the first day of that battle, 1 July 1916, was an almost total disaster. We look back on it now with horror, even anger. Yet turning to *The Somme Times*, published on 31 July 1916, a whole month into the battle, we find that it singularly failed to express the views which hindsight might now expect of it. Surely, at the least, we think, its reaction must have been deadly serious. Surely the Somme could never have been seen as a laughing matter. No jokes, no limericks. On the contrary, we find this immediately after the editorial:

> There was a young girl of the Somme
> Who sat on a number five bomb.
> She thought 'twas a dud 'un
> But it went off sudden –
> Her exit she made with aplomb.

There is also a limerick mocking the German emperor, Kaiser Wilhelm, a favourite target of soldierly wit from the outset of hostilities. In this case it suggested (which we now know to have been the case) that it was not only the British who were suffering on the Somme; the Germans, too, were not finding matters to their liking, having underestimated the determination and sheer guts of the British forces opposed to them:

The Kaiser once said at Peronne
That the Army we'd got was 'no bon'.
But between you and me
He didn't 'compris'
The size of the job he had on.

Yet at the same time the edition includes what has the look of a daringly seditious advertisement offering help for anyone who thought himself a victim of the prevailing doctrine, emanating constantly from high places throughout the campaign, of 'Optimism'. Thus:

> Do you suffer from cheerfulness? Do you wake up in the morning feeling that all is going well for the Allies? Do you consider our leaders are competent to conduct the war to a successful issue? We can cure you. Two days spent at our establishment will effectually eradicate all traces of it from your system.

For the full text of this jewel of tongue-in-cheek martial wit, *see* page 123.

However, *The Somme Times* does have at least one moment of editorial anger, not directed against the conduct of the battle but against one of the members of the media reporting on it. If anything got up the nose of the fighting soldier it was the lurid, self-congratulatory despatches by certain journalists who lauded themselves more than the men whose efforts they were meant to record. A figure under frequent attack in the publication's pages was William Beach Thomas of the *Daily Mail*. To Roberts, he was 'Our Special Correspondent Mr Teech Bomas', whose 'Message' datelined 'No Man's Land 20/7/16', appears on page 119 and of which the following are keynote sentences:

> I write from the middle of the battlefield. There are a lot of bullets but I don't mind that. Also the air is thick with shells. That I also don't mind … Let me tell you of the gallant dash of the Umpshires: into the pick of the Prussian Guard they dashed. The few of the Guard who remained cried 'Kamerad' and surrendered. That rush was epic. I then walked over to the German lines to have a look at them … A correspondent must always see to write. This may appear unnecessary to the cognoscenti, but it is so … I return now to the battle.

At a time of high daily casualty lists and sustained sacrificial fighting, this was for the editors, as for their readers, an arrogance too far.

In a sense, however, to concentrate on controversial aspects of this remarkable publication, as seen from ninety years on, is to miss the central point. *The Wipers Times* merits, above all, not deconstruction for its attitudes, but celebration for its wit, its gusto, its inventiveness and its sheer high spirits. The trench magazines' affection for parody has already been mentioned. Nowhere were there such parodies as those which graced this publication's pages. A very popular poem of the time was Edward Fitzgerald's translation of *The Rubáiyát of Omar Khayyám*; although published as far back as 1859 it still had huge appeal. *The Wipers Times*, in yet another crack at the Kaiser, offered its readers *The Rubáiyát of William Hohenzollern* (*see* page 193). Rudyard Kipling's *If*, a national favourite today, was also hugely popular then. *The Wipers Times*, almost inevitably, came up with its own cleverly crafted version, of which the following are the first, tasty lines:

> If you can drink the beer the Belgians sell you,
> And pay the price they ask with ne'er a grouse,
> If you believe the tales that some will tell you,
> And live in mud with ground sheet for a house…

For the full version *see* page 241: note, too, its title, avoiding any reference to Kipling or to *If*, but clearly showing the editors' addiction to the parody as a genre: 'With the Usual Apologies'.

There is, however, one important element in this story not yet disclosed. The magazine won so high a reputation during the war that its first twenty-one editions were actually published for general release before the war was over, in two facsimile editions, *The Wipers Times* and *The B.E.F. Times*, by the London publisher Herbert Jenkins. If nothing else, this effectively made the magazine an instant classic, a status confirmed by its continued and growing reputation over the following decades.

Roberts contributed a fascinating foreword to the 1918 printing of the first of these two collections, entitled 'How It Happened' (already quoted on page x above for its description of how the printing press was found). It is a breezily exuberant piece of writing which shows him relishing what had been achieved and confident that his account of how the magazine had braved and overcome the challenges of war would be hugely appreciated by his readers. He shares with them the fact that at the time of writing his beloved printing press is temporarily out of action.

> At present it is marooned in the care of an amiable town major at a dorp not far behind the line. There it must stay until we can commandeer a tank as a travelling printing works, as the red-hats [*i.e.* the Army Staff] are most unsympathetic at present, and awfully keen on fighting.

In fact it was the heavy and successful fighting of 1918, finally breaking the stalemate of the trenches and putting the enemy into retreat, which had stayed his editorial hand

and made him question whether he would be able to bring his self-appointed task to a satisfactory conclusion. 'Whether we shall have a chance to print again before the fast approaching finale,' he writes, 'is on the knees of the gods.' Fortunately, as we know, the gods were kind, and the work was subsequently completed in two memorable final editions: one published in November, the second in December.

It was a triumphant conclusion. But after the success, what then? It is clear (*see* page 324) that the editors had hoped to carry on until everybody concerned had received 'the order of the bowler hat' (*i.e.* had become civilians again), but this was not possible, since most of the printing staff were miners due for immediate demobilization. So the editors offered their readers best wishes for Christmas and the future, thanked them for their aid and support, and, effectively, made their farewells.

After that, nothing. A resounding silence. The question has inevitably been asked: Why? Why did this brilliant voice from the trenches have no continuing echo in the postwar years?

Notably, the final issue of *The Better Times* contained a brief item entitled 'The Horrors of Peace', (*see* page 326) which began:

> We have had a good look at the horrors of war, and now we are undergoing another sort of frightfulness. What a life! Can anyone tell us of a nice war where we can get work and so save our remaining hair from an early greyness?

The text meanders on through several sentences, then returns to the same basic point: '...if anyone knows of a *nice* war, or if one can be arranged, we hope we shall be allowed first call'.

The tone is deliberately ironic, yet perhaps there was an undertow of genuine anxiety, even the tiniest hint of panic, behind the questions here posed. Could it be, therefore, that the silence of both these outstanding talents in the immediate postwar years is best understood in terms of the reaction that affected so many men who had given their all to the war: a failure to find a role in a world in which the simple verities of wartime had given way to the complex confusions of a less than happy peace? It is a very plausible explanation. In the case of F. J. Roberts, apparently his attempts to continue in journalism were not successful; at one point he was alleged to be compiling, with difficulty, crosswords for the *Daily Mail*.

His silence thereafter is arguably more understandable. He contributed a specially written foreword to the first complete edition of *The Wipers Times* published in 1930. Entitled 'Twelve Years After', this essay, still buoyant but subtly different in tone from the piece he wrote in 1918, includes, I believe, a number of clues as to why this was the end of the road for F. J. Roberts.

Between the first editions, in 1918, and the collected one in 1930, a revolution had taken place. The mood had changed. The euphoria of a war won had given way to an increasing sense of a victory thrown away. Too many heroes of the trenches, finding the world unfit for them, had become the gaunt sellers of bootlaces on street corners. The gush of instant heroic memoirs that had appeared in the 1920s slowed as a new generation of anti-war writers seized the agenda. The old doctrine of belief in the cause, of confidence that, whatever the sacrifice, the end justified the means was being overtaken by the new doctrine of disenchantment. In particular such publications as Erich Maria Remarque's *All Quiet on the Western Front* and Robert Graves's *Goodbye to All That*, both published in 1929, had effectively remade the image of the war. Siegfried Sassoon's *Memoirs of an Infantry Officer* added its insights in 1930. Wilfred Owen's powerful posthumous voice would be heard in 1931. The war had been a betrayal, a massive deception, a pointless waste of young men's lives; it should never have happened, or, having been found for the ghastly thing it was, should have been abandoned. Cry, not havoc, but futility.

It was at this point, I believe, that Roberts bowed out. He had satirized the war, mocked and joked about it in every possible way, but he had supported it. Whatever the faults and the failures, he and his kind believed it should have been fought and won. He would not now be persuaded that the whole business was a misguided act of folly. There *had* been ideals worth fighting for, even if they now seemed to a new generation to be tarnished and unworthy.

In this context the dedication of the 1930 volume is worthy of note. Doubtless devised by Roberts himself, it reads:

> TO THE SOLDIERS OF THE SALIENT
> AND THE TRUTH ABOUT THE WAR

The 'truth about the war' was, clearly, *his* truth as he saw it – not the new truth now being promulgated to the disadvantage of the old.

His 1930 foreword, however, is far from being an act of surrender. There is a last, rousing foray of *Wipers Times*-style wit, harking back to the time of the great German attack of 21 March 1918, which was the event that was most responsible for taking his magazine off the presses for much of the war's final year. In it, far from yielding ground to the best-selling titles commanding the literary field in 1930, he takes a deliberate, brilliant lunge at them:

> Hastily taking two aspirin and placing helmet, gas, in position, I looked out of the door, only to find the beautiful March morning obscured by what seemed to be one of London's best old-style November fogs. Shouting for batman, Adjutant, Sergeant, Sergeant-Major and the Mess-Waiter, I emerged into the chilly air, which was being torn and rent in the most

> alarming way. All was *not* quiet on the Western Front, the Sub-Editor and I drank a case of whiskey, shot the Padre for cowardice and said "good–bye to all that". (The influence of these modern War Books is most insidious.)

This is in the body of the piece; the final paragraphs contain the clearest indication that, for both Roberts and his sub-editor colleague, the world was not as they had hoped it might become. 'Talking things over two or three months ago,' he writes, 'we came to the conclusion that Peace of the 1929 vintage is nothing to write books about.' He then adds, pointedly: 'In the days of *The Wipers Times* we had some bad times, but – well! we had some good times, too. Thank Heaven that friendships made in those days have held in these after years.'

It is a potent statement, but, by chance, we have access to a parallel gesture that is perhaps almost equally telling. The library of the Imperial War Museum has on its shelves a copy of the second impression of the 1930 version of *The Wipers Times*, autographed on its pre-title page by Roberts himself, the dedicatee being very possibly a fellow officer who might well have been a wartime reader. The message reads:

> To John Bilham
> in memory of good days
> from the Editor
> F. J. Roberts

For this dedication in facsimile, *see* page viii of this volume. Surely, not only in the words he used but in the very flourish with which his message was written, Roberts was making a gesture of pride and protest: pride in what had been achieved in the war, protest against the way that the efforts of his generation were now being diminished and downgraded. I think this was Roberts' last word, and explains his later, total withdrawal from the literary scene.

Attempts to find out what happened to the editors have not been very productive. In his pre-war career as a mining engineer, Roberts had prospected in the diamond fields of South Africa. At some point he resumed prospecting, emigrating to Canada where he died in relative obscurity in 1964. Sadly, he never had an entry in *Who's Who?*, nor did he receive what would have been the most appropriate of accolades for this most remarkable of soldier-writers: an obituary in *The Times* of Printing House Square. Yet it can be argued that Roberts needed no such memorial. For his real memorial, and that of his fellow editor, J. H. Pearson, is here, in the pages that follow, still as eye-catching and entertaining, and also as thoughtful and challenging, as they were when first set in print not far off a century ago.

Malcolm Brown

THE WIPERS TIMES.
OR
SALIENT NEWS.

No 1. Vol 1. Saturday, 12th February, 1916. Price 20 Francs

WIPERS FISH-HOOK & MENIN RAILWAY.

—o—

DAILY EXCURSION TICKETS ARE ISSUED TO

MENIN.

Trains will Leave Daily at 8 a.m. & 1 p.m., Commencing Feb 1st, 1916. For Further Particulars See Small Bills

———

Until further notice trains will not go beyond Gordon Farm Station, line beyond that closed for alterations.

UNDER ENTIRELY NEW MANAGEMENT.

—o—

HOTEL DES RAMPARTS.

—o—

NO EXPENSE HAS BEEN SPARED BY THE NEW MANAGEMENT IN THE RE-DECORATING AND RE-FITTING OF THIS FIRST-CLASS HOTEL

———

SPECIALLY RECOMMENDED TO BUSINESS MEN.

———

New Electric Installation. 5 Private Lines. Tel Pioneers, Ypres.

Cloth Hall
YPRES.

This Week 

THE

THREE DUDS

WORLD'S BEST KNOCKABOUTS

—o—o—o—

BOUNCING BERTHA

THE LITTLE MARVEL,

Only 17ins. high.

—o—o—o—

THE

JOHNSONS

A Shout. A Scream. A Roar.

This Season the Johnsons' have carried all before them.

ETC., ETC.

—o—o—o—

Entire change of Programme Weekly.

BEST VENTILATED HALL IN THE TOWN.

—o—o—o—

PRICES : 1fr. to 20frs.

MENIN GATE.
CIN'MA
Nightly

◁O▷

GREAT SENSATION THIS WEEK ENTITLED

THE ROAD to RUIN

15,000 Feet Long

EVERY FOOT A THRILL.

People have been so overcome when the final stages are reached as to necessitate help being given to enable them to reach home.

BOOK AT ONCE.

Other Items △

THE RUINED HOME.

—o—o—o—

SOLDIERS AT PLAY.

—o—o—o—

ETC., ETC.

THE WIPERS TIMES. OR SALIENT NEWS.

No 1. Vol 1. Saturday, 12th February, 1916. Price 20 Francs.

Editorial.

Having managed to pick np a printing oufit (slightly soiled) at a reasonable price, we have decided to produce a paper. There is much that we would like to say in it, but the shadow of censorship enveloping us causes us to refer to the war, which we hear is taking place in Enrope, in a cautious manner. We must apoiogise to our sucscribers for the delay in going to press. This has been due to the fact that we have had many unwelcome visitors near our printing works during the last few days, also to the difficulty ot obtaining an overdraft at the local bank. Any little shortcomings in production must be excused on the grounds of inexperience and the fact that pieces of metal of various sizes had punctured our press. We hope to publish the "Times" weekly, but should our effort come to an untimely end by any adverse criticism or attentions by our local rival, Messrs. Hun and Co., we shall consider it an unfriendly act, and take steps accordingly. We take this opportunity of stating that we accept no responsibiliiy for the statements in our advertisements. In conclusion we must thank those outside our salaried staff who have contributed to this, our first issue, and offer our condolences to those who have paid 20 francs for a copy. The latter will at least have the comfort of knowing that proceeds have gone to a worthy cause.

The EDITOR.

The Editor takes no responsibility for the views expressed, or the thirst for information on the part of our subscribers.

The Ration Carriers.

1.

On the road from Pop. to Bosinghe
And from Bosinghe down to Ypres,
Where the pavé's rent with Johnson
And the mud's just ankle deep
Where you darsn't light a fag up
'Cos the Boche's eyes are skinned
Ah, that's the place to be boys,
If you want to raise a wind.

—:0:—

2.

When the road's all blocked with transport
Taking rations to the dump,
And they're shelling Dawson's Corner
With shrapnel and with crump,
When the word comes down the column
"A stretcher bearer, quick!"
Then your mouth goes kind of dry boys,
And your stomach's awful sick.

—:0:—

3.

When you hear a sort of whistle
That swells into a roar,
And yer ducks, yer ducks like Hell, Boys!
'Cos you've heard that sound before.
There's a crash that echoes skywards,
And a scream of mortal pain.
Then you curse the blasted Kaiser
And just march on again.

—:0:—

4.

So you chaps back in Blighty
Who have'nt got the grit
To go and take the shilling,
And to come and do your bit.
Just now and then remember
At night time, 'ere you sleep,
The men who carry rations
On the road from Pop. to Ypres.

D. H. R.

Reflections on Being Lost in Ypres at 3 a.m.

I wish I had been more studious as a youth. Then I should not have neglected the subjects I disliked. Then I should not have failed to cultivate the sense of geography. And thus I should not have contrived to lose myself so often in Ypres in the small hours of winter mornings.

Lost in Ypres. it is an eerie experience. Not a soul to be seen not a voice to be heard. Only far out on the road to Hooge, the quick impulsive rattle of the British machine guns answers the slower more calculating throbbing of the Hun variety. If a man would understand what hate means, let him wander along the Memn Road in the evening, and then let him find some poet, or pioneer, or artilleryman to express what he feels concerning the Hun operator in that concrete, machine-gun redoubt.

Lost in Ypres at night: in the daytime it is a difficult feat to accomplish Transports and troops pass and re-pass along the ruined streets. From almost every aspect, throngh gigantic holes torn in the intervening walls, the rugged spikes of the ruined cathedral town mark the centre of the town. From time to time, too, the heavy thud of a "crump," (like some old and portly body falling through a too frail chair with a crash to the floor), is an unerring guide to the main square.

But at night all is different. The town is well-nigh deserted. All its inhabitants, like moles, have come out at dusk and have gone, pioneers and engineers, to their work in the line., Night after night they pass through dangerous ways to more dangerous work. Lightly singing some catchy chorus they move to and fro across the open road, in front of the firing line, or hovering like black ghosts, about the communication trenches, as if there were no such thing as war. The whole scene lights up in quick succession round the semi-circle of the salient as the cold relentless star-shells sail up into the sky. Here and there. a "grouser" airs his views, but receives little sympathy, for the men are bent on their work, and do it with a will.

All this while, however, I have been standing lost in Ypres. I cannot steer by the star-shells, for they seem to be on every side. And at night, too, the jagged spires of the cathedral are reduplicated by the remains of buildings all over the city. Like the fingers of ghosts they seem to point importunately to heaven, crying for vengeance. It is a city of ghosts, the city of the dead. For it and with it the sons of three nations have suffered and died. Yet within that city, not many days ago, a little maid of Flanders was found playing. That is an omen. Ypres has died, but shall live again. Her name in the past was linked with kings; but to-morrow she will have a nobler fame. Men will speak of her as the home of the British soldier who lives in her mighty rampart caverns or in the many cellars of her mansions. And even when the busy hum of everyday life shall have resumed its sway in future days, still there will be heard in ghostly echo the muffled fumbling of the transport, and the rhythmic tread of soldiers' feet.

By "THE PADRE."

◁O▷

EDITOR

[signature]

SUB-EDITOR [signature: J. H. Pearson]

People We Take Our Hats Off To.

—o—

The person who re-introduced the sale of whisky in Pop.

The gallant C.O. who has just got his Brigade.

The officer in charge of the costume department of the Fancies.

The person who introduced the order forbidding Company Commanders to go beyond their front line trench.

The Editor of this earnest periodical.
(Thank you SO much. ED.)

Things We Want To Know.

The name of the brunette infantry officer whose man got hold of the carrier pigeons, (sent to this celebrated Company Commander when his communications in the front line had broken down) and cooked them. Also who were his guests?

—o—

The name of the M.O. who attended one of the leading lights of the Fancies, and was overcome by her many charms.

—o—

The celebrated infantry officer who appears daily in the trenches disguised as a Xmas tree.

—o—

Why the dug-out of a certain Big Man is so much affected by subalterns of tender years, and if this has anything to do with the decorations on his walls.

—o—

The weekly wage bill at the Fancies.

R. B.

Agony Colnmn.

E J. N. and L. S. P. Meet us at the Clock, Popperinghe Station, at 6 p.m. Wear red carnations, so that we shall know you.—Plymouth.

WILL any patriotic person please lend a yacht and L10,000 to a lover of peace. Size of yacht immaterial.—Address Lonely Soldier, c/o Editor, Wipers.

WILL anyone lend Car to gentleman impoverished by the war. Rolls Royce preferred —Address Mishap, P.O., Box 21, Hooge.

FOR SALE, cheap, Desirable Residence. Climate warm, fine view. Splendid links close by, good shooting Terms moderate Owner going abroad.—Apply Feddup, Gordon Farm, nr Wipers.

DEAREST, I waited two hours on the Menin Road last night but you didn't come. Can it be a puncture that delayed you ?—Write c/o this paper.

Occasional Notes.

—:o:—

We regret to report a further rise in property to-day.

—:o:—

The culinary department at the Hotel des Ramparts is temporarily out of action, and the emergency kitchen is in use. This should not deter intending guests from putting up at this fine old hostelry, as the prices are as heretofore, and no new cooks were necessary as a result of the accident.

—:o:—

May we ask how it is that street noises are becoming a bigger nuisance daily Several noted residents have complained that their rest is seriously interfered with. We should like to see this nuisance put a stop to immediately.

—:o:—

It has been reported to us that there is a crack visible in the cathedral spire. We should like to start a subscription list to have this repaired. Will some well-wisher head the list ?

Poem.

The Night Hawks.

—o—

Talk not to me of vain delights,
Of Regent Street or Piccadilly.
A newer London, rarer sights
I visit nightly willy-nilly.

—o—

When daylight wanes and dusk is falling,
We start out clad in gum boots thigh.
To wander through the gloom appalling
Through crump holes deep in mud knee-high.

—o—

From Gordon Farm to Oxford Street
(These duck boards are the very devil).
Where strange concussions fill the air.
(I wish they'd keep the—CENSORED—things level).

—o—

Through Oxford Street we gaily slide,
And call at Batt. H.Q. to see
If there be aught that we can do
For them. (Well, just a spot for me!)

—o—

Then on through Regent Street, and thence
To Zouave Wood, where plain to see
That " Spring is Coming," hence the change
From winter's gloom to verdancy.
(For authority see D.R.O.)

—o—

Here Foresters make nightly play,
And in the mud hold revel high.
Recalling fancy stunts performed
At Shoreham, and at Bletchingly.

—o—

Should you but care to journey on
You'll reach, by various tortuous ways,
To Streets named Grafton, Conduit, Bond.
Where memory ever fondly strays.

—o—

And each in some peculiar way
Has charms not easy to define.
So thus the London which we knew
Remembered is along the line.

By A PIONEER.

Correspondence.

—:o:—

To the Editor,
"Wipers Times"

Sir,

As the father of a large family, and having two sons serving in the Tooting Bec Citizens' Brigade, may I draw your attention to the danger from Zeppelins. Cannot our authorities deal with this menace in a more workmanlike way. My boys, who are well versed in military affairs, suggest a high barbed wire entanglement being erected round the British Isles. Surely something can be done :—

PATER FAMILIAS.

—o—

To the Editor.

Sir,

Whilst on my nocturnal rambles along the Menin Road last night, I am prepared to swear that I heard the cuckoo. Surely I am the first to hear it this season. Can any of your readers claim the same distinction?

A LOVER OF NATURE.

—o—

To the Editor.

Sir,

May I draw your attention to the fact that lately the lighting by night in Oxford and Regent Street has been terribly neglected, star-shells being sent up at very irregular intervals. Cannot someone move in the matter?

PRO BONO PUBLICO.

—o—

To the Editor.

Sir,

May I thrrough the medium of your valuable paper call attention to the disgraceful state of repair the roads are getting into, What, what I ask are our city fathers doing to allow such a state of things to come to pass.

Hoping you will give this letter the publicity that I consider it merits.

I am a
WELL WISHER.

Answers to Some of Our Many Correspondents.

—o—

JOCK. (Zouave Wood).—No, when on patrol work and you hear the words—"Ach Gott! ich bin gauz fed-up gerworden"=issue from an unknown trench, this does not necessarily signify that you have worked too far over to your left and stumbled into the French lines.

—o—

MOTORIST. (Popperhinghe).—Yes, we have had other complaints of the suspected police trap on the Menin Road, and advise caution on the stretch between "Hell Fire Corner" and the Culvert.

—o—

WIND UP. (Hooge).—Certainly not. A "Whizz Bang" does not leave the gun *after* it hits your trench, but just before.

—o—

T. T.O. (H 23 B 56).—We sympathise, but when unknown females write to you with requests for photographs, it would be safer to send for references first.

Stop Press News.

As we go to press we hear from our esteemed contemporary the "D.C.C." that a German was seen in I 4 B 2-1 wearing red braces, this is awful.

Addition to "People We Take Our Hats Off To" The R.B.

Our original estimate of day of pnblication was rather optmistic. As a certain liveliness has delayed us, for this and the errors made in our haste we apologise.

Borrowed Plumes.

—:o:—

EXTRACTS FROM OUR ESTEEMED CONTEMPORARY "D.C.C."

—:o:—

1st iust.

No. 7 informs us that a German band was heard playing at abont 11-30 a.m. This new terror leaves us cold, as we take it to be only another phase of frightfulness.

—:o:—

The following gem comes from the issue of 28th ult.—

. . . "They climbed into the trench and surprised the sentry, but unfortunately the revolver which was held to his head missed fire. Attempts were made to throttle him quietly, but he succeeded in raising the alarm, and had to be killed." . . .

This we consider real bad luck for the sentry after the previous heroic efforts to keep him alive.

Sporting Notes.

—o—o—o—

We hear that there are one or two greatly fancied candidates for the Spring Handicap, in training way back. We shall get some more information shortly, and will keep our readers posted,

—o—o—o—

The Hooge Course is now in great trim for 'chasing, and this sport promises to be a great success since the new management took it over.

—o—o—o—

There is some good shooting to be had in Railway Wood. but game is getting wilder.

—o—o—o—

The fishing in the Moat and Zillebeke Lake is falling off, as the fish is getting shy.

Golf Notes.

—:o:—

The Sanctuary Wood course was opened on Saturday, under delightful climatic conditions, and before a large and representative throng.

—:o:—

A match had been arranged by the enterprising Committee between the two well-known players Tom Sniper, the Wipers professional, and Wilhelm Bos chun, that champion of Hollebeke.

—:o:—

The course, which has many natural advantages it has been planned almost entirely on the pot-bunker system so that straight driving and an accnrate knowledge of all the hazards one is likely to encounter is essential, and our two experts found trouble rather more frequently than they are wont to do.

—:o:—

The first hole is not particularly interesting, and has no noteworthy feature, being of the ordinary drive and pitch variety, and was halved in 4.

—o—

The second hole, is a short one, bordering Zouave Wood, was also halved, and was noticable only for extraordinary pungent odour which assailed the nostrils near the green, and which affected the putting of both players, as they each took three putts for a short distance.

—o—

The 4th, 5th, 7th and 8th holes were halved again in the proper figures, but at the 6th Tom Sniper was hit by his opponent on the elbow and this seemed to worry him somewhat, and he consequently lost the hole.

—o—

However the Wipers pro got his own back at the 9th. He hit his second—a brainy shot—clean and hard. hitting Boschun in the neck. He claimed the hole in a dignified manner which much impressed his supporters, and the players thus turned all square.

—o—

Going to Culvert the Hollebeke representative was unfortunately stymied by a whizz-bang which cost him the hole.

Both were bunkered in the new breast-work in Cambridge Road, and a half in 7 ensued.

—o—

The 12th and 13th were won by Boschun and Sniper respectively through the other finding trouble. The 14th. known as the Fish-hook, was won by Boschun through a perfect nfblick shot stopping dead. The 15th was halved in par play, but Tom Sniper took the 16th through his opponent topping his second into the stables.

—o—

The 17th saw the end of an exciting match. This hole, known as the Appendix, is a long one shotter, and blind from the tee. Boschun had gone forward to see his line, and Tom played a beauty, which caught Wilhelm full in the mouth and finished him.

—o—

Tom was met with the usual request to stand a bottle for holing out in 1, and this was promptly disposed of in the Clnb House at Gordon Farm.

The world wasn't made in a day;
And Eve didn't ride on a 'bus,
But most of the world's in a sandbag
The rest of it's plastered on us.

OUR NEW SERIAL.

Herlock Shomes at it Again.

SHOT IN THE CULVERT.

CHARACTERS:

BILL BANKS—A Corpse.

LIZZIE JONES—A Questionable. Person Living at Hooge.

HAROLD FITZ GIBBONS—Squire of White Chateau. (in love with Honoria.)

INTHA PINK—A Pioneer (in love with himself).

HONORIA CLARENCEAUX—The Heroine, (in love with Pink).

HERLOCK SHOMES.

DR. HOTSAM, R.A.M.C.

CHAPTER 1.

The wind was howling round the rugged spires of the Cloth Hall, and the moon shone down on the carriage bringing the elite of the old town to the festivities arranged to celebrate the 73rd term of office of Jacques Hallaert, the venerable mayor of Typers. Also the same moon shone down on the stalwart form of Intha Pink, the pioneer. He sighed as he passed the brilliantly lighted scene of festivity, thinking of days gone by and all that he had lost. As he plodded his way, clad in gum-boots, thigh, pairs one, he soliloquised aloud thus:—" What a blooming gime! They gives me a blooming nail, they gives me a blooming 'ammer, and then they tells me to go and build a blooming dug-out." At that moment Intha fell into a crump-hole, and then continued his soliloquies thus:

(To be Continued.)

PAGES FROM THE LIVES OF GREAT MEN.

Our NEW COMPETITION

Can YOU read character ?

Are YOU a judge of human nature !

YES ! ! Then YOU take the prize

Send 5s. to Fritz opposite the Dueks when a handsome nosecap will be sent post free.

TAXIS ! TAXIS ! TAXIS !

OUR new consigment of highly decorated cars are now placed at the convenience of the public, These are handsomly appointed throughout and can be easily known by the Red Cross painted on each side. Whistle three times or ring up,

TELEGRAPHIC ADDRESS: „Ripped, Wipers.. TELEPHONE, 1. Cenral.

WHY PUT UP WITH THE OLD HAT ?

A new consignment of HATS just arrived from England Buy one now and be the perfect little gentleman. Rod or Brass bound at proportionately higher prices.

Apply S. TAFF & Co., RUE DE LILLE.

NOW THE WINTER NIGHTS ARE WITH US NO BETTER TONIC CAN BE HAD THAN

RHUMATOGEN

Cures FLATUANCE. COLD FEET. ETC., ETC.

CAN BE TAKEN WITH TEA OR SIMILAR BEVERAGE. OBTAINABLE FROM ALL Q, M. STORES.

BUILDING LAND FOR SALE.

— —

BUILD THAT HOUSE ON

HILL 60.

BRIGHT—BREEZY—
&
INVIGORATING

COMMANDS AN EXCELLENT VIEW OF HISTORIC TOWN OF YPRES.

FOR PARTICLARS OF SALE APPLY:—

BOSCH & CO MENIN.

On February 30th,

Sale

Sale

Sale

A Large Quantity of SECOND-HAND FURNITURE SLIGHTLY DAMAGED. HARDWARE.

Tell your friends about it.

9, RUE D'MENIN.

Telephone : 14, RUINS.

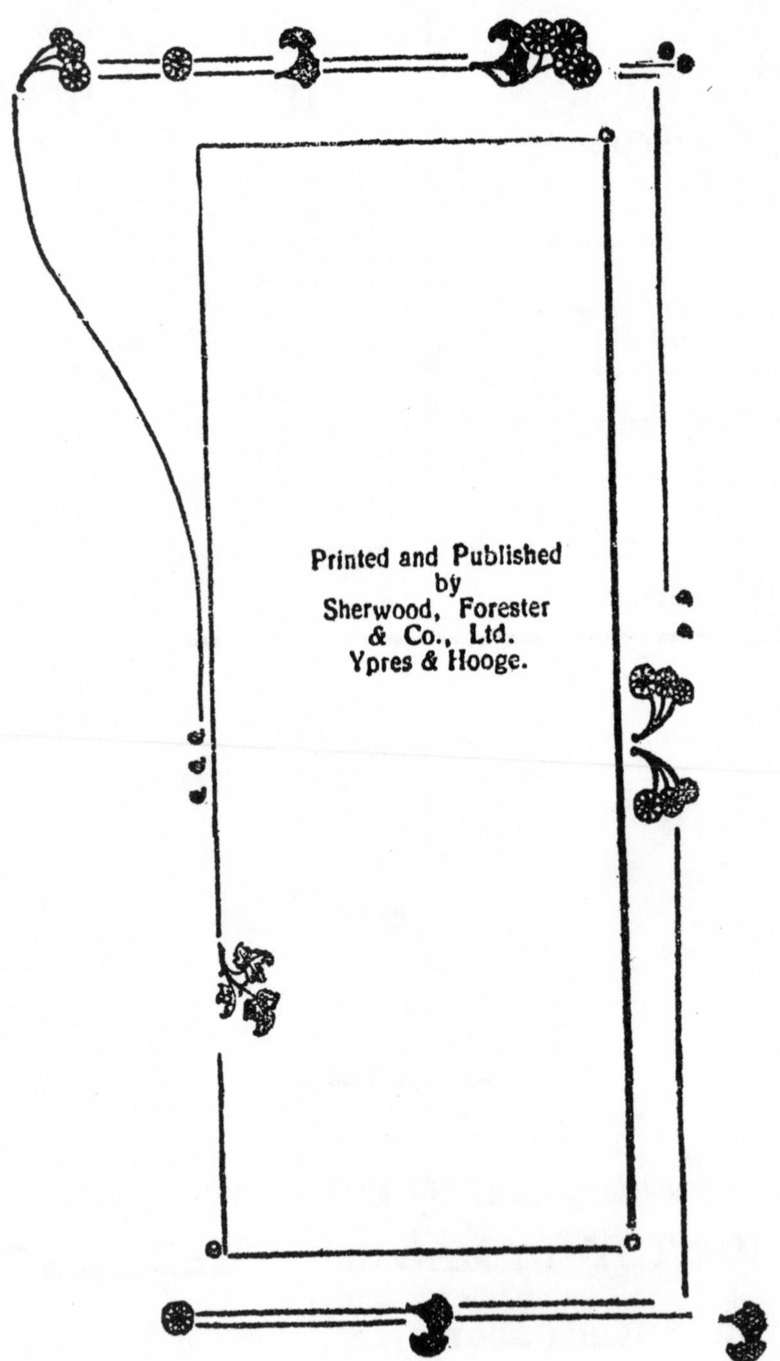

Printed and Published
by
Sherwood, Forester
& Co., Ltd.
Ypres & Hooge.

THE
WIPERS TIMES.
OR
SALIENT NEWS.

No 2. Vol 1. Saturday, 26th February, 1916. Price 100 Francs

NO CHILDRENS PARTY COMPLETE WITHOUT IT.

ARCHIE

THE NEW MECHANICAL INVENTION.

NOT A TOY.

NOT A COMPLICATED MACHINE.

A Child Can Use It.

—o—o—o—o—

With Belt and Five Cartridges. In Highly Polished Box, 4s. 6d. Extra.

Sole Agents for Ypres and District: Messrs. ANTI, AIRCRAFT and CO.

Cloth Hall.

YPRES.

THIS WEEK

THE GREAT

Silent PERCY

BRINGS THE HOUSE DOWN.

—o—o—o—

THE

THREE SISTERS

HUN-Y

IN THEIR LITTLE SONG SCENA
Entitled:

STAR SHELLS SOFTLY FALLING.

—o—o—o—

THE BROS.

WHIZZ-BANG

These merry little fellows get there every time.

ETC., ETC.

—o—o—o—

Entire change of Programme Weekly.

—o—o—o—

BEST VENTILATED HALL IN THE TOWN.

PRICES: 1fr. to 20frcs.

MENIN GATE.

CINEMA.

Nightly,

THE GREAT

Spectacular Picture

INFERNO

50,000 Artistes have been engaged to produce this colossal work, at enormous expense. Music and effects of this great picture by the International Orchestra.

OTHER ITEMS

—o—o—o—

MARLEY TAPLIN.

—o—o—o—

Piggles goes a Sniping.

ETC., ETC.

—o—o—o—

POPULAR PRICES.

THE
WIPERS TIMES.
OR
SALIENT NEWS.

No 2. Vol 1. Saturday, 26th February, 1916. Price 100 Francs.

Editorial.

As our previous issue was so well received by the public, we hasten to produce our second number. At the last moment (by the payment of an enormous sum of money) we were able to secure the services of Winifred Honey-Saxwell, the well-known serial writer. Also we propose to make an effort to secure articles from other well-known writers. Of course the production of a high-class journal of this nature means enormous expense, but we do not mind that if our efforts meet with success. We are hopeful of getting articles from Bellary Helloc, and Cockles Tumley, but may not receive them in time for this number. Also Major Taude has promised to send us his views on the situation. These will be useful. We hear that Messrs. Hun and Co. are claiming a larger circulation than ourselves. This is false, and we are prepared to place our figures before any chosen tribunal. For the benefit of the public we now state that our figures are :—

Copies printed — 100
Disposed of — 100
Returned — NIL

and we now challenge any other paper in Wipers to beat our circulation.

We also wish to draw the attention of the public to our "insurance scheme." Full particulars will be found on Page 4 of the present issue. This scheme entails vast expense for us, but we do not mind that, as the one object of our existence is to help the public. Who drew your attention to the disgraceful state of the roads, and the crack in the Cathedral spire and many other evils? Buy the paper that tells you the truth! All others are rotten, and the truth is not in them. We have raised the nominal price of the paper to 100 francs for appearance sake only. However, we are very grateful for the subscriptions to hand, and "The Padre's" Charity will benefit accordingly.

THE EDITOR.

To Grafton Street.

Now Hope lies buried, all that once could give
A satisfaction, or could soothe the eye,
With signs of work, which, being done, would help
Those others who with jar of rum did hasten
About their nightly duty in the line;
And who with ease could lightly scuttle on
By duckboard or by traverse; now undone
And by a cruel and unseemly fate
Are made to nightly journey on a road
Well set with pitfalls, crump holes, and their feet
Must hasten to their journey's end, or else
Some quick and hasty whizz-bang meet them full
Upon the jar and break it; awful thought;
For Grafton Street our fond and cherished child,
No mother ever saw with fonder eyes
Her offspring than did we our traverses,
Our fire-bays, height and end of our desires,
Our dug-outs roomy, gaze upon them now
And say with me our nightly hymn of hate;
Oh! Grafton Street in vision I have seen
A newer better namesake of thine own.
It's duckboard walk resounds with nightly tread
Of hosts which shelter in their dug-outs sound
A dressing station which shall be replete
With every comfort human can devise.
Poor Hun in folly set, on folly bent,
To kick the pricks, of better knowing naught
Think ye that Grafton Street can signify
A ruin so complete as that to which
Your own must be; the day now hastens on
And e'er the evening falls on men at peace
Your cries for mercy shall in truth arise,
And mercy thou shalt have when all is done
And Justice truth and peace shall reign alone.

OUR NEW SERIAL.

Herlock Shomes at it Again.

CHARACTERS :—Same as last week.

SYNOPSIS :—

Intha Pink, a pioneer, while passing the Cloth Hall, Typers, the scene of a dinner given to commemorate the 73rd year of office of the mayor of that town, falls into a crump-hole. Here we left him.

CHAPTER 2.

SHOMES AND HIS METHODS.

We now leave to the imagination of our gentle reader the nature of Intha's soliloquies in the crump-hole, and turn to a series of tragic events which were occuring in the Denin Road. It being feast night in Typers, the road was surging with a merry crowd pushing and jostling their way, eager to taste the delights the town had to offer, but there were, amongst that motley throng, two people who were destined to play principal parts in the most profound and murky mystery, that had ever baffled the aged and doddering constabnlary of Typers —One was Honoria, the fair but ænemic daughter of the shell-fish merchant of Hooge, and the other was—Shomes!—

That night the shell-fish merchant, having run out of vinegar, had despatched his fair daughter to Typers to procure a fresh supply, and all had gone well with her until reaching the Culvert, she, catching sight of the lifeless form of Bill Banks, gasing placidly at the sky, had given three heart-rending shrieks and fallen in the dark and silent waters of the Bellewarde Bec—the waters flowed on—but this was not to pass unnoticed —Holmes was in the district, and whipping out his vermoral sprayer with his right hand, he gave three rounds rapid into his forearm, while with his left he proceeded to tune up his violin. Dr. Flotsam, who had been walking in his shadow, hearing the haunting strains of the violin, rushed forward to his side, exclaiming "What is it, Sholmes?"—Sholmes with that grandiloquent gesture for which he is justly famed, said "You know my methods, Flotsam!" and fell into the Bec—Flotsam not to outdone, seized the vermoral sprayer, and fell in also—the water of the Bec flowed on.—

(To be Continued.)

N.B. Next week:—A fresh supply of characters, and another thrilling instalment.

People We Take Our Hats off To.

—:0:—

9th Royal Sussex.

Things We Want to Know.

—:0:—

1.—Who discovered the salient.

—0—

2—Why.

—0—

3.—Whether the "Christmas tree" expert mentioned last week is not likely to have a rival shortly.

—0—

4.—And if a pretty competition is likely to be seen.

Answers

to Correspondents.

—0—0—0—

ETHEL.—No, we have none of Kirsenner's pictures in our editorial sanctum This austere chamber still retains it's scheme of simplicity. (But if you have any we have a friend whose views are not our own, who might like them.)

—:0:—

S. LACKER.—We read your letter with much interest. We fully appreciate the many difficulties which beset your path, and thus deprive the country of your services. We know how hard it is to decide between two obvious duties, and must commend your fortitude in having chosen the harder part.

—:0:—

OVIUM.—We have found that hens lay better if their exertions remain undisturbed. The ideal place you mention to encourage industry on the part of your poultry would be difficult to find. The best we can suggest is that you establish a poultry farm at Hooge or neighbourhood. Here at least your hens would have a counter excitement which we have aways found is a great Inducement.

—:0:—

WORRIED.—In affairs of the heart we should advise you to write direct to Sylvia, who will deal with all these knotty problems in our next issue.

OUR GREAT INSURANCE SCHEME.

INSURE AT ONCE BY PLACING AN ORDER FOR THIS PAPER WITH YOUR NEWSAGENT

Why face the awful danger of submarine

Without being Insured. 10,000,000 (ten million), has been subscribed at the local bank to carry out the largest Insurance Scheme instituted by any paper.

In the event of death caused by a submarine, anywhere in the Wipers district, your next of kin will be entitled to claim 11s. 7d., if you had at the time of death, one of our coupons fully-signed, and bearing name of Newsagent.

PLACE YOUR ORDER AT ONCE TO AVOID DISAPPOINTMENT !!!

By Belary Helloc.

In this article I wish to show plainly that under existing conditions, everything points to a speedy dis integration of the enemy We will take first of all the effect of war on the male population of Germany. Firstly, let us take as our figures, 12,000,000 as the total fighting population of Germany Of these 8,000,000 are killed or being killed hence we have 4,000,000 remaining. Of these 1,000,000 are non-combatants, being in the Navy. Of the 3,000,000 remaining, we can write off 2,500,000 as tempermentally unsuitable for fighting, owing to obesity and other ailments engendered by a gross mode of living This leaves us 500 000 as the full strength. Of these 497,250 are known to be suffering from incurable diseases, this leaves us 2,750 Of these 2 150 are on the Eastern Front, and of the remaining 600, 584 are Generals and Staff. Thus we find that there are 16 men on the Western Front. This number I maintain is not enough to give them even a fair chance of resisting four more big pushes, and hence the collapse of the Western Campaign. I will tell you next week about the others, and how to settle them

Stop-gap.

Little stacks of sandbags,
Little lumps of clay ;
Make our blooming trenches,
In which we work and play.

Merry little whizz-bang,
Jolly little crump ;
Made our trench a picture,
Wiggle, woggle, wump.

An Ode to Q.

—o—o—o—

Listen reader, while I tell you
Stirrings deeds both old and new
Tales of battles during which we
—Chits received from Batt. H. Q

—:o:—

Fought we had a losing battle
All the day and all the night.
All communications broken,
Never was there such a plight.
Now the Hun comes o'er the sandbags
In one long unbroken mass—
Just in time—the welcome message
"Indent now for helmets gas

—:o:—

Shelled they'd been for three days solid
In a trench just two feet high.
Couldn't get retaliation
Matter not how they might try.
Binks's men had held the trenches
(Binks is NOT his proper name),
Savagely he sent the message
"Carn't you stop their purple game ?"
Anxiously they wait the answer,
What a brave but serried band.
Here it comes—Binks grabs the paper
"Deficiences not yet to hand !"

—:o:—

Have you ever heard the tale, lad,
How we took the trench at A ?
Said the good old 92nd,
Here we are, and here we'll stay
What a tale of awful trial,
Cut off was our food supply.
If we do not get some bully
—Bread or biscuits—we shall die.
The foe comes on in countless thousands
Bearing down with savage cry.
Jones receives a frantic message
"Indent now for gum boots thigh."

—:o:—

Thus you see, O gentle reader,
Why the O. C. Coys are grey.
These and other kindred worries
Are their portion day by day.

QUIT THIS TOMFOOLING !

—o—o—o—

A Business Trench Wanted.

—o—o—o—

By COCKLES TUMLEY.

—o—

This week I am going to tell you a few home truths—it will not be pleasant reading—I shall not spare you my business is to tell you the truth Now listen to me :—Quit this tomfooling and let us have a business trench.

Months ago I told you what would happen to unrevetted trenches when the rain came, months ago I told you of the futility of batterless, bermless trenches —What have you done ?—I ask you what HAVE you done ? The answer shame upon you wretched people, is NOTHING—NOTHING Can you hear the voice of babes yet unborn to you crying down the ages—NOTHING ? Can you see yourselves, aged and toothless, still shrinking from the withering, unrelenting finger of scorn ?—I tell you stop—stop it now—at once ! Stop this purile babbling about not knowing—stop these imbecilical mumblings about not thinking—above all—STOP THIS DAMM'D NONSENSE !

An awful thought has come to me
Of sad disaster that might be ;
Just suppose a 12 inch shell
Fell right on this dug-out—well ;
This train of thought I'll not pursue.
(That fills the gap, and so will do !)

Correspondence.

—:o:—

To the Editor,
"Wipers Times."

Sir,

May I draw your attention to the fact that the gas mains of the town seriously need attention. I was returning from the Cloth Hall Cinema the other night, when a big leak broke out in the Rue de Lille; and it was only by promptly donning my helmet-gas, that I was able to proceed on my way.

I am, etc.,
A LOVER OF FRESH AIR

—:o:—

To the Editor.

Sir,

As a lifelong reader of your excellent paper, I hereby claim the privilege of a few lines of space to contradict "A Lover of Nature's" letter in your last issue. Firstly, I heard the cuckoo myself two days previously; secondly, he doesn't know enough about birds to differentiate between species; and thirdly, in order to provent his again wasting your valuable space, I suggest that what he really heard was a sniper calling to it's mate.

Yours etc.,
ONE WHO KNOWS.

—:o:—

To the Editor.

Sir,

On taking my usual morning walk this morning, I noticed that a portion of the road is still up. To my knowledge the road has been in this state of repair for at least six months. Surely the employees of the Ypres Corporation can do better than this.

I am,
EARLY RISER.

—:o:—

To the Editor,
The "Wipers Times."

Sir,

As a student of the winged world of many years standing, and also the proud possessor of a not invaluable collection of practically all of the varied species of birds, both large and small, which are to be found in these parts, I cannot rest until I have put pen to paper to contradict most emphatically the utterly ridiculous statement contained in the letter published in your last week's issue over the signature of "Lover of Nature," to the effect that he is prepared to swear that he heard the cuckoo in the neighbourhood of the Menin Road recently. The call which he claims to have heard was, as anyone with only a slight knowledge of the subject must know, undoubtedly issued by that quite common bird known as the BURRD, which had possibly escaped from some local orderly room.

Yours truly,
A BURRD FANCIER.

War.

—:o:—

Take a wilderness of ruin,
Spread with mud quite six feet deep;
In this mud now cut some channels,
Then you have the line we keep.

Now you get some wire that's spiky,
Throw it round outside your line,
Get some pickets, drive in tightly,
And round these your wire entwine.

Get a lot of Huns and plant them,
In a ditch across the way;
Now you have war in the making,
As waged here from day to day.

Early morn the same old "stand to"
Daylight, sniping in full swing;
Forenoon, just the merry whizz-bang.
Mid-day oft a truce doth bring.

Afternoon repeats the morning,
Evening falls then work begins;
Each works in his muddy furrow,
Set with boards to catch your shins.

Choc a block with working parties,
Or with rations coming up;
Four hours scramble, then to dug-out,
Mud-encased, yet keen to sup.

Oft we're told "Remember Belgium,"
In the years that are to be;
Crosses set by all her ditches,
Are our pledge of memory.

By a Visitor.

—o—o—o—

If you happen to be a fortunate visitor to Ypres in these energetic times, there is much to see and learn for those who move about with their eyes open. By a fortunate visitor I mean when you chance to arrive on one of the quiet days —days when the number of shells sent in by the Hun does not exceed 100 per hour (meal times excepted)—you are then able to move about in comparative safety. As a visitor one tries naturally to imagine something of what the historic old town looked like before modern artillery began to destroy the work of hundreds of years, and although one can see all these ruins of buildings, note the terrific effect of shell fire on walls many feet thick, one somehow feels how impossible it is to describe what Ypres looks like; one has to see it to understand the awful dead, forsaken appearance of the place. Then if your visit has brought you up at a time when the old town is lighted up by a full moon, and you happen to be of a somewhat sentimental turn of mind, you will find yourself marvelling at the wondrous beauty of the ruined city, somehow the odd spires, broken towers, fragments of massive walls, fronts of demolished houses all have their rough jagged edges softened by the moonlight, and from these thoughts it is but a step to go on and try to reason out the why and wherefore of these things. One is almost tempted to doubt if there is an over-ruling Power for Good in this world in which we live, and to attempt to reason that no possible good can come out of such appalling misery and desolation; but surely this is another case of the finite mind coming into contact with the Infinite? Then listen! away to the east a faint whistle through the air, then another, coming this way—an explosion, and the guide says—"They're shelling Hell-Fire Corner again,"then quiet again, and later on as you wonder across the Square, you see the motor ambulances wending their way back to Pop. with their loads of mauled humanity, somebody's loved ones, to be looked after and tended by skilled hands—with no effort spared to alleviate pain and repair the damage—and as you travel home you will have many things to remember and think about—after your visit to Ypres,

One Who is NOT "A Padre,"

Sporting Notes

The Spring Handicap, was run for on the Hooge Course last Wednesday, and the sport was all that one could desire. The course being in rare condition—as stated in our last number—and the candidates trained to an ounce. The locally-trained animal "East Wind" just managed to catch the judge's eye first, but the much fancied "Chlorine" fell at the Culvert. The greatly advertised continental candidate "Fritz" took fright at the "gate," and so figures amongst the "also ran." "Whizz-bang" who was intended to make the running for "Fritz" started off at a great pace, but soon shot his bolt. "H.E." then took the lead but was audibly broken before the distance was reached. "Tommy" and "East Wind" soon had "Frost" cold, and they went on to finish an exciting race, "East Wind" winning, as previously stated, by a nosecap.

Stop Press News.

3.30 HOOGE.

Whizz-bang 1
H.E. 2
Others fell. 8 runners.

The crack is widening in the cathedral spire. Steps must be taken.

Mr. Krump has arrived in town.

4 p.m. Question asked in the House, by Mr. Toothwaite, as to what measures had been taken to stop the war. Mr. Pennant answered "Tape Measures." (Loud Cheering.)

THE EXHIBITI ON OF 1916.

SCENIC EFFECTS BY "FRITZ."

—o—o—o—o—

FULL OF VARIETY and FUN

—o—o—o—o—

GONDOLAS ON THE MOAT NIGHTLY.

—o—o—o—o—

POMPEII A BACK NUMBER.

—o—o—o—o—

FIREWORKS BY DAY AND NIGHT.

—o—o—o—o—

MANY SIDE SHOWS.

—o—o—o—o—

ANY 'BUS Motor Lorry, or Ambulance, will drop you there. Also the Ration-waggon passes your door. Come early! Band on Ramparts, 3-5.

NEW AND MAGNIFICENT WINTER GARDENS.

—o—o—o—o—

At The Hotel Des Ramparts.

BUILT ON THE ROOF.

THIS is a splendid Glass Edifice, the View is not interfered with the surrounding Country is full of Interest, embracing as it does

THE LARGE SOLDIERS' TRAINING GROUND

Hotel Prices as usual. Ring up or wire.

TELEGRAM: , PIONEERS WIPERS TELEPHONE: 102 SEE'UM

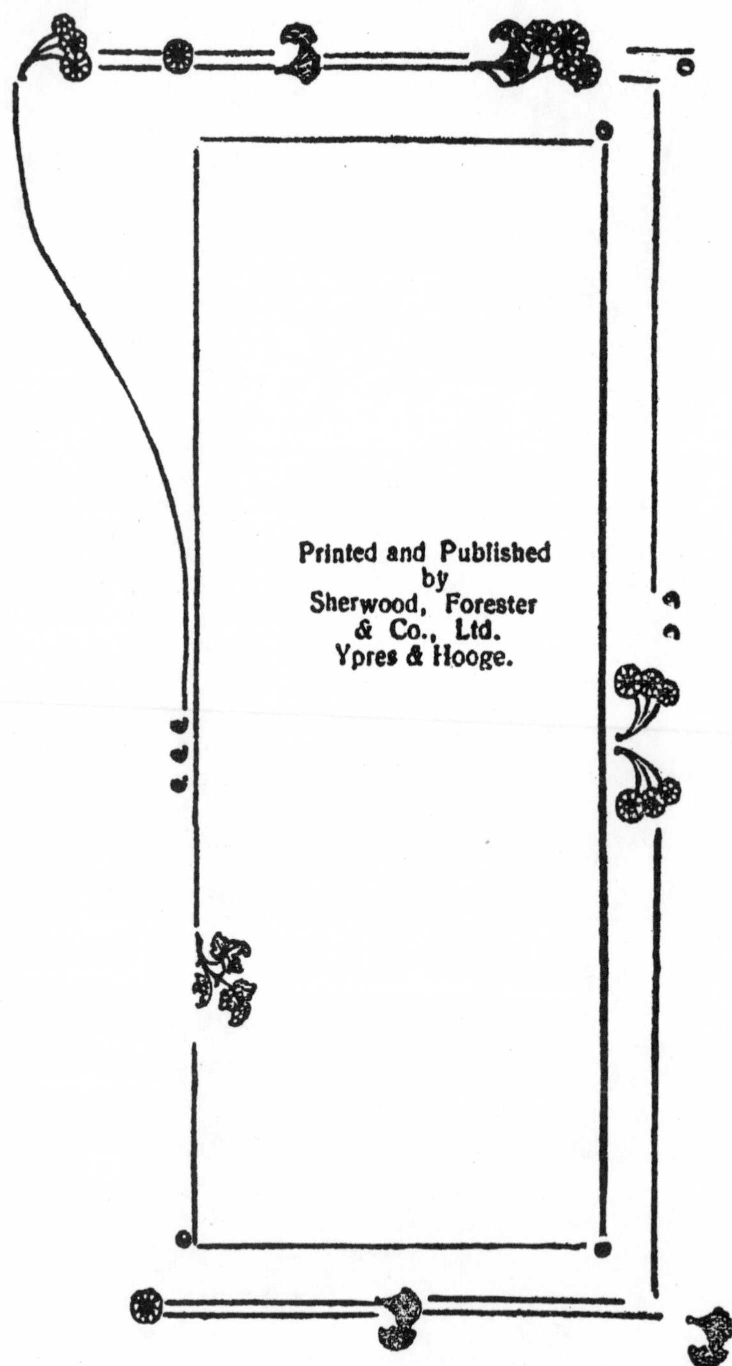
Printed and Published
by
Sherwood, Forester
& Co., Ltd.
Ypres & Hooge.

THE

WIPERS TIMES.

OR

SALIENT NEWS.

No 3 Vol I. Monday 6th March, 1916. Price 200 Francs.

Are you tired of that hum-drum Existence

—The Existence that Kills—

IF SO

JOIN THE NEW AND GORGEOUSLY APPOINTED

NIGHT CLUB

(NEXT DOOR TO HOTEL DES RAMPARTS.)

And Lead a Gay aud Fast Life.

—o—o—o—o—

MANY DARING INNOVATIONS.

—o—o—o—o—

All The Best People Go There.

CLOTH HALL.
YPRES.

Great Attraction This Week

Messrs. INFANTRY, ARTILLERY & Co.

Present their Screamingly Funny Farce,

ENTITLED:

BLUFF

THIS FARCE PROMISES TO BE A GREAT SUCCESS AND A LONG RUN IS EXPECTED.

—o—o—o—o—

QUARTERMASTER & COMPANY

The World's Famous Back Chat Comedians

(A GREAT SHOW.)

—o—o—o—o—

A STIRRING DRAMA,

ENTITLED:

MINED

A MOST UPLIFTING PERFORMANCE.

—o—o—o—o—

ALL THE LATEST PICTURES.

ENTIRE CHANGE OF PROGRAMME WEEKLY·

—o—o—o—o—

Best Ventilated Hall in the Town.

PRICES AS USUAL.

THE WIPERS TIMES. OR SALIENT NEWS.

No 3. Vol. 1. Monday. 6th March, 1916. Price 200 Francs.

Editorial.

Firstly, we must apologise to our numerous subscribers for the delay in bringing out our third number. Owing to the inclemency of the weather our rollers became completely demoralised, also the jealousy of our local competitors, Messrs. Hun and Co, reached an acute stage, and brought some of the wall down on our machine. But we have surmounted all these difficulties by obtaining, on the hire-purchase system, a beautiful Cropper? (I think that's the name) machine. This machine is jewelled in every hole, and has only been obtained at fabulous expense. So that we are once more able to resume our efforts towards peace, and by still telling the truth to onr subscribers we hope to retain their confidence, which may have been shaken by pernicious utterings of the Yellow Press during our silence. Our great insurance scheme met with instant success, and we have already paid out three sums of 11/7 owing to an unfortunate accident on the Zillebeke Bund, where a celebrated firm of commission agents took the knock. At the urgent request of the printing staff we have just inspected our new machine. It is certainly a ghastly looking arrangement, and we hesitate to trust our ewe lamb in it's rapacious maw, but as it is either that or no ewe lamb we'll risk it. We hear that the war (to which we alluded guardedly in our first number), is proceeding satisfactorily, and we hope shortly to be able to announce that it is a going concern. So for the time being there we will leave it, and turn to graver subjects. We regret that there is still reason to deplore the inability, inefficiency, ineptitude and inertia of our City Fathers with regard to the condition of the roads (these are mostly up still).

and the lighting of the town. We should like to see these matters taken in hand at once. There are many more justifiable reasons for dissatisfaction on the part of our fellow townsmen, notably the new liquor laws. We hear that the new night club, which has recently been opened near the Hotel des Ramparts, prepares a beautiful "cup" for it's patrons. This is a step in the right direction, and long may it flourish. All the stars can be seen there nightly, and consequently all visitors will have reason for satisfaction. This being our grand summer number, we have doubled the price, as is usual on these occasions. Before closing we must thank our numerous subscribers for the kindness we have received, both congratulatory and financial.—A happy Xmas to you all!

THE EDITOR.

People We Take Our Hats off To.

—o—o—o—

76th I.B.

—:o:—

The French of Verdun.

The corp'rl and the privit they
Was standing in the road.
Do you suppose, the corp'rl said,
That rum is "a la mode?"
I doubt it! said the privit as
He shouldered up his load.

Correspondence.

—o—o—o—

To the Editor,
"Wipers Times." 3/2/16

Sir,—I read, with feelings of disgust, a letter in your last week's issue over the nom-de-plume of "One Who Knows." Know's what?—I ask! Nothing!—I reply. One who has not the courage to even sign his own name. I am surprised that the editor of a paper with the circulation that you boast should have found room for such a scurrilous, lying effusion. The ignorance of the person is visible in every sentence. Will you please find room for this letter, as otherwise my reputation may suffer in the eyes of those who do not know the true facts.

I am, Sir, yours faithfully,
"A LOVER OF NATURE."

P.S.—I re iterate that I am the first to hear the cuckoo this season.

—:o:—

To the Editor.

Sir,—May I encroach on your valuable space to a small extent. We had a somewhat heated argument at Unity Villa the other night, and wish you to give us a ruling on the point. The question raised was, "Are the engineers better pioneers than the pioneers are engineers." The argument was continued at the neighbouring estaminet, but no definite conclusion was arrived at.—Thanking you in anticipation,

I am, yours faithfully,
ONE WHO HAS TRIPPED AND FALLEN.

—:o:—

To the Editor.

Sir,—Whilst walking along the Rue de Lille the other night, a gentleman (sic) coming in the opposite direction accosted me quite abruptly with the words "Who are you?" When I told him not to be inquisitive he became quite offensive, and assumed a threatening attitude. This incident was repeated several times before I had reached the Square. I endeavoured to find a constable, but could not. Where are our police, and what are they doing? Have any more readers had the similar unpleasant experience?

Yours, etc.,
TIMIDITY.

OUR NEW SERIAL.

Herlock Shomes at it Again.

CHARACTERS :—Same as last week.

SYNOPSIS :—

INTHA PINK, a pioneer, while passing the Cloth Hall, Typers, the scene of a dinner given to commemorate the 73rd year of office of the mayor of that town, falls into a crump hole, where he is left solloquising. In the meantime, whilst a merry throng is making it's way along the Denin Road towards Typers, HONORIA, the fair but ænemic daughter of the shell-fish merchant of Hooge, whilst passing by the Culvert, catches sight of the lifeless form of BILL BANKS, and forthwith falls into the Bellewarde Bec, the waters of which flow on. This incident is notic d by SHOLMES and DR. FLOTSAM, who were passing by the Culvert at the time, they both thereupon fall into the Bec, the waters of which continue to flow on.

CHAPTER 3.

THE MYSTERY OF THE CLOSED GATE.

We now return to our friend Intha Pink, who, having soliloquised for exactly 13 minutes without once pausing to take breath or repeating himself, decides to extricate himself from the crump-hole into which he had so inadvertently fallen. While thus engaged, the silvery chimes of the clock on the Cathedral spire burst forth into song announcing the magic hour of zero p.m. "Bother!" ejaculated Pink in true Pioneer fashion, "At a quarter past zero I promised to meet Lizzie at Fell Hire Corner. I must indeed get a move on, otherwise she will be wroth." With that he picked up his hammer and his nail from out of the crump-hole, and proceeded at a rapid pace to the corner of the Square, where, after having his boots polished and some of the mud brushed from off his clothes by Bertie, the boss-eyed boot boy, he went off at the double along the road leading to the Denin Gate. He had not proceeded very far when perforce his pace had to slacken on account of the density of the merry crowd advancing in the opposite direction in close column of humps, all bent on spending a merry evening at the Cloth Hall. But Pink's mission was not a gay one, neither was he in a merry mood ; a deep plot was hatching in the Pioneer's fertile brain, in which, let it be whispered, lovely Lizzie was to play a not unimportant part. On reaching Trueside Corner he entered the little shop kept by Sandy Sam, the suspected spy and sand-bag merchant. "Evening, Sam," said Pink. "What, you, Intha!"—replied the old man—"What's in the air?" "Whizzbangs and air-crumps mostly, to-night,"—answered the other—"but I'm in a hurry, I want a good sand-bag." This article having been produced, and approved of, Intha paid the bill with a worthless cheque on Fox's, and placing his hammer and nail in the sand bag and slinging the latter over his shoulder again, took to the road ; such was his hurry that, generally observant as he was, he did not notice the shadowy figure of old Sam following in his wake. When within fifty yards of the Denin Gate the suspected spy took his S.O.S. signal from out of his pocket, unwrapped same, and hurled it into the air, this being almost immediately answered by three piteous howls from the direction of the gatekeeper's dug-out, where Tim Squealer, the sand-bag merchant's foster-son resided. Intha, still intent on his night's work, hurried on until he reached the Gate, where he fell over a cunningly concealed trip wire, at the same instant a soft, buzzing sound was heard, increasing in volume and ending in a loud crash!—The Pioneer was trapped!!—THE DENIN GATE HAD CLOSED!!!

(To be Continued.)

Next Week :—An entirely new set of characters, and another thrilling instalment.

Things We Want to Know.

—o—o—o—

The name of the Brig. Major, who, in relief orders, mentioned that one battalion of a famous regiment would find billets in three houses in Street Verbod te Wateren.

* * *

The name of the red trimmed officer who has a penchant for 5A.

* * *

The name of the Major who capitulated to the dark-eyed Belgique at the "Chateau."

* * *

Whether the bridges at a certain place are to entice the Bosche to the wire, or the wire to prevent us using the bridges.

* * *

What is Zero.

* * *

Why no steps are taken to stop the enemy, seen by a sapper officer, working behind our lines.

* * *

Whether the strong point at C2 should not have another letter in front of it.

* * *

The name of the M G.O. who has come to the conclusion that the only reason the Hun planes visit Pop. is to bomb his camp. (The personelle of which, we believe, is three N.C.O.'s and one private.)

* * *

Are we as OFFENSIVE as we might be.

"Now this 'ere" war, the corp'rl said,
Has lasted long enuff'"
"Gorblime," said the private with
His voice exceeding gruff,
"Not 'arf it aint!" and drew his nose
Across his sheepskin cuff.

Urgent or Ordinary.

—o—o—o—

There was a time when first I donned the Khaki—
Oh, martial days in Brighton-by-the-Sea!—
When not the deepest draught of Omar's Saki
Could fire my ardent soul like dixie tea.
I dreamed of bloody spurs and bloodier sabre,
Of mentions—not too modest—in despatches;
I threw my foes, as Scotchmen toss the caber,
And sent my prisoners home in wholesale batches;
Led my platoons to storm the Prussian trenches,
Galloped my guns to enfilade his flank;
Was it H.M.'s own royal hand, or French's,
That pinned the V.C. on my tunic? SWANK!
Those dreams are dead: now in my Wiper's dug-out,
I only dream of Kirchner's naughtiest chromo;
The brasier smokes; no window lets the fug out;
And the Bosche shells; and 'Q' still issues bromo.
"For information"—"Urgent"—
"Confidential"—
"Secret"—"For necessary action, please"—
"The G.O.C. considers it essential"—
My soldier-soul must steel itself to these;
Must face, by dawn's dim light, by night's dull taper,
Disciplined, dour, gas-helmeted, and stern,
Brigades, battalions, batteries, of paper,—
The loud 'report,' the treacherous 'return,'
Division orders, billeting epistles,
Barbed 'Zeppelin' wires that baffle G.H.Q.,
And the dread 'Summary' whose blurred page bristles
With 'facts' no German general ever knew.
Let the Hun hate! WE need no beer-roused passions
To keep our sword-blade bright, our powder dry,

The while we chase October's o'erdrawn rations
And hunt that missing pair of 'Gum-boots, thigh.'

GILBERT FRANKAU.

2/3/16.

Answers

to Correspondents.

—o—o—o—

COMMERCE, YPRES.—We are very much afraid that the County Council will refuse you a street hawking licence—still there is no harm in applying for one.

—:0:—

GRATEFUL READER.—Bravo!—Glad you like the paper. Yours is one of the countless homes we have brought a little sunshine into.

—:0:—

X.Y.Z., ZERO, AUNTY and others will be answered in due course.

The privit to the sergeant said
"I wants my blooming rum."
"Na poo," the sergeant curtly said,
And sucked his jammy thumb.
"There's 'soup in loo' for you to-night."
The privit said, "By gum!"

LOVE AND WAR.

—o—o—o—

In the line a soldiers's fancy
Oft may turn to thoughts of love.
But too hard to dream of Nancy
When the whizz-bangs sing above.

—§ † §—

In the midst of some sweet picture
Vision of a love swept mind,
Bang! "A whizz-bang almost nicked yer!"
"Duck, yer blighter, are yer blind?"

—§ † §—

Take the case of poor Bill 'Arris
Deep in love with Rosy Greet,
So forgot to grease his tootsies,
Stayed outside and got "trench feet."

—§ † §—

Then remember old Tom Stoner,
Ponder on his awful fate.
Always writing to his Donah,
Lost his rum 'cos 'e was late.

—§ † §—

Then again there's 'Arry 'Awkins,
Stopped to dream at Gordon Farm.
Got a "blightie" found his Polly
Walking out on Johnson's arm.

—§ † §—

Plenty more of such examples
I could give, had I but time.
War on tender feelings tramples,
H.E. breaks up thoughts sublime.

—§ † §—

"Don't dream when you're near machine guns!"
Is a thing to bear in mind.
Think of love when not between Huns,
A sniper's quick, and love is blind.

By Belary Helloc.

—:0:—

Last week I outlined the collapse of the Western Campaign. This collapse, as is obvious, has already begun. This week I will deal with the Eastern theatre. Here we have a field full of conflicting interests, and it will take me a little longer to arrange things satisfactorily here. However, I will begin on the logical basis of counting Bulgaria out, as she has already been on the same side six months which is as much as could be expected. This leaves us Austria, Germany, and Turkey. Take the united numbers of these belligerents as 16,000,000. The front we will cut into three, namely North, Central and South. On each section we will say there are 5,000,000, Germans on the North, Austrians Central, and Turks South. Firstly, the North Section. The Germans could not possibly have these numbers, as last week I proved conclusively that they had only 2,150 on the Eastern front, so that disposes of 4,999,850. Of the remainder (2,150) 2,000 are suffering from cold feet due to the extremely rough weather. This leaves us 150, and one may, without undue optimism, claim that this number will not suffice to stop our Allies. This then disposes of the Northern Section. To come to the Central. Here there are many other factors to take into consideration. The Isonzo must play a considerable part, and here we can estimate losses at 3,475,691. This leaves 1,524,309. Of these, 524,309 are suffer- from Alpites (a fell disease contracted through perpetually climbing mountains.) This leaves us a million. Take it that the line runs thus—(if we could reproduce I'd draw a sketch)—it thus becomes obvious that of the million, 900,000 are non-effectives, and of the 100,000 remaining, of these 90,711 are busy watching what the Germans are doing. This leaves us 9,289, which number I maintain is completely inadequate for the purpose required. Now to come to the Southern Section. Here the difficulties are multiplied and the five million Turks are confronted with an impossible enterprise. Of this number fully 3,705,812 are suffering from chronic coryza due to fighting in the fez. This leaves us 1,394,188. We must deduct 897,432 as losses sustained at Kut, Erzerum and elsewhere, so that the line running thus:—(once again the impossibility of reproduction prevents me from making the whole thing clear) we see that there are but 496,756, but we have yet to deduct the vast number required to make Turkish Delight. This number on the latest census was 456,521, so that we have left 40,235. Deduct from this the non-effectives, and we find that the Southern Section is held by 1,419 men only, so that by logical deduction we can prophecy that the Eastern Campaign must end disastrously to the Central Powers. Should there be any other theatres that need to be settled I will touch on them next week.

Stop Press News.

Birdcage Plate, 4 p.m. :—

Surprise	......	1
Saps	......	2
Racket	......	3

Also ran—Flying Hun.

S.P.—Evens, 6-4, 5-1, 100-1 Flying Hun.

———

Further rise in property.

———

5 p.m.—Mr. Tingle asked why all leave for soldiers at the front should not be stopped for ever.—Mr. Pennant replied that many of those who have been ornamenting England's popular seaside resorts for a year or more have volunteered to relieve some of those in France, so that leave could still go on in modified form. (Loud cheers.)

A DWELLER IN WIPERS' ELEGY TO THAT TOWN.

—o—o—o—

(With apologies to Grey.)

A six-inch tolls the knell of parting day.
The transport cart winds slowly o'er the lea.
A sapper homeward plods his weary way,
And leaves the world to Wipers and to me.

—§ † §—

Now fades the glimmering star shell from the sight,
And all the air a solemn stillness holds;
Save where a whizz-bang howls it's rapid flight,
And "five rounds rapid" fill the distant folds.

—§ † §—

Beneath the Ramparts old and grim and grey,
In earthy sap, and casement cool and deep;
Each in his canvas cubicle and bay,
The men condemned to Wipers soundly sleep.

—§ † §—

Full many a man will venture out by day,
Deceived by what he thinks a quiet spell;
Till to a crump he nearly falls a prey,
And into neighbouring cellar bolts like hell.

—§ † §—

A burning mountain belching forth it's fire,
A sandstorm in the desert in full fling;
Or Hades with it's lid prised off entire,
Is naught to dear old Wipers in the Spring.

Sporting Notes.

Owing to the frightful state of the ground during the last fortnight, practically all types of sport have had to be suspended. This is the long arm of coincidence as we have no more space in this number.

Our Hero's Troubles

Sketch by "Peter"   Engraver, Sapper E. J. Couzens, R.E.

Pioneer (soliliquizes):—"They gives us a —— nail, they gives us a —— hammer, and they tells us to go and build a —— dug-out."

ALL ROADS LEAD TO
STAPLES
THE UNIVERSAL PROVIDER!

PRIVATE TELEPHONE: — — — — — — — — — Two Lines
TELEGRAPHIC ADDRESS: — — — — — — — — — "Dump"

—0—0—0—0—

Models of latest fashions in Trench Trimmings exhibited on the premises.

—0—0—0—0—

WE HAVE WATER JUST LIKE YOU!

—0—0—0—0—

Unsolicited Testimonial from "Mother," a regular customer:—"The Sandbags I obtained from you have helped me more than anything to realise what stuff Belgium is made of."

—0—0—0—0—

Obstacle Courses Arranged For Sports.

—0—0—0—0—

ANYTHING YOU WANT FROM A TINTACK TO A RAILWAY (INCLUDING SEVERAL WHITE ELEPHANTS.)

YOU WANT IT! WE HAVE IT (PERHAPS)!!!

AND LIKE TO SEE YOU GET IT!!!

—0—0—0—0—

Dug-out Furniture a Speciality.

—0—0—0—0—

ALL THE LATEST IN BARBED WIRE, ETC.

—0—0—0—0—

SUMMER SALE NOW ON.

STOP! STOP!! STOP!!!

NOW THAT SPRING IS COMING

YOU REQUIRE SHADE.

WE ARE IN A POSITION TO OFFER THE PUBLIC

250,000,000 SAPLINGS

OF THAT FULSOME, PROLIFIC AND UMBRAGEOUS PLANT,

THE POPLAR

—0—0—0—0—

WHAT ARE YOU GOING TO HANG THAT HAMMMOCK ON?

—SURELY NOT THE FISH HOOK—

Therefore Buy While Opportunity Offers.

—0—0—0—0—

OLD WORLD AVENUES A SPECIALITY.

—0—0—0—0—

ADDRESS: FILL, POTS & Co. RENINGHELST.

MENIN GATE CINEMA.

—0—0—0—0—

This Week Nightly,

ATTILA. The Hun

IN THREE PARTS, FEATURING

INTHA PINK.

SOME FILM. BOOK EARLY.

—0—0—0—0—

OTHER PIECES

CHARLEY GOES GUNNING.

—0—0—0—0—

THE MISSING NOSECAP. ETC., ETC.

—0—0—0—0—

PRICES AS USUAL

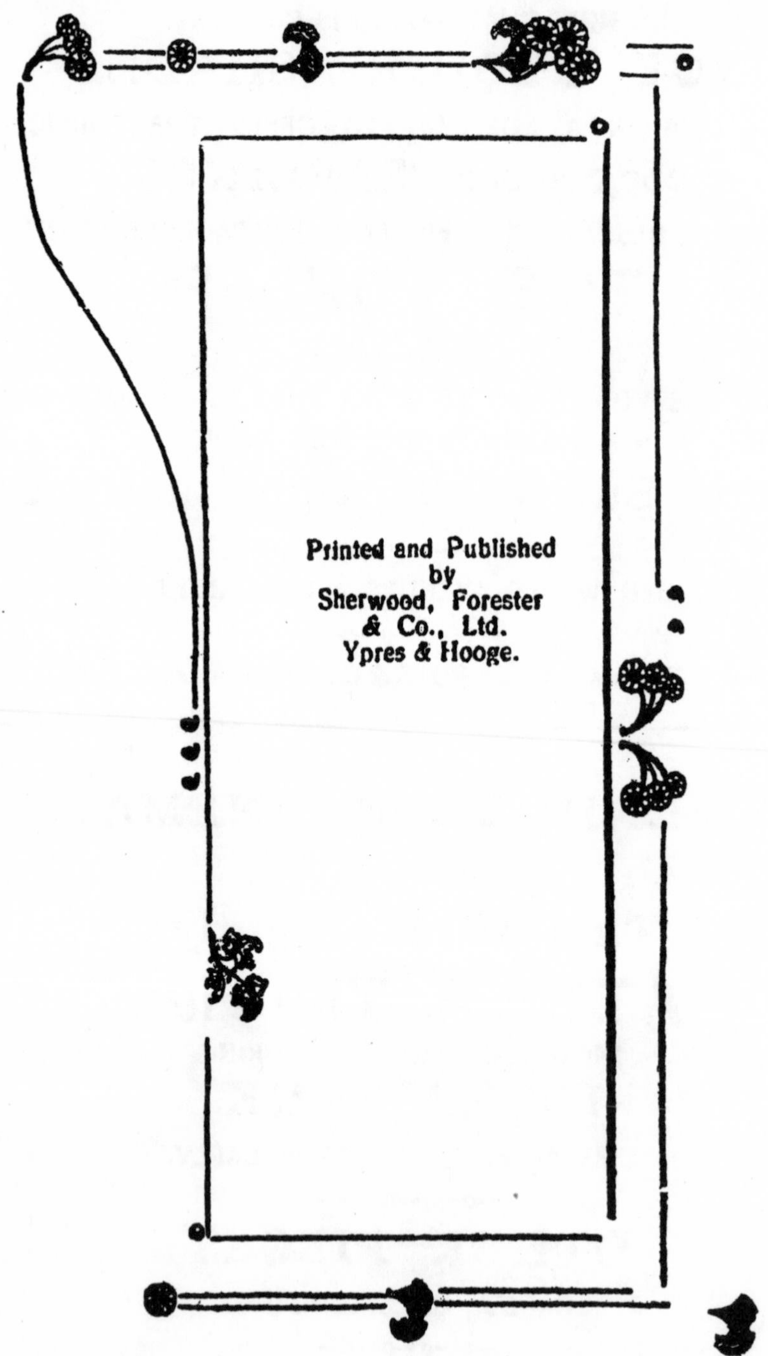
Printed and Published
by
Sherwood, Forester
& Co., Ltd.
Ypres & Hooge.

THE WIPERS TIMES.

OR

SALIENT NEWS.

No 4. Vol 2. Monday. 20th March, 1916. Price 50 Centimes.

HAS YOUR BOY A MECHANICAL TURN OF MIND? YES!

—o—o—o—o—

THEN BUY HIM A

FLAMMENWERFER

INSTRUCTIVE—AMUSING.

—o—o—o—o—

Both young and old enjoy,
This natty little toy.

—o—o—o—o—

GUARANTEED ABSOLUTELY HARMLESS

—o—o—o—o—

Thousands Have Been Sold.

—o—o—o—o—

Drop a postcard to Messrs. ARMY, RESEARCH and CO., when a handsome illustrated catalogue will be sent you.

CLOTH HALL, YPRES.

THIS WEEK

GROSSE FRITZ

The World's Greatest Mimic and Impersonator
In His World Famed One Man Show.

INTRODUCING THE FOLLOWING CHARACTERS:

WILHELM — — — — — — THE BOCHE
FERDY — — — — — — THE VULGAR
SULTANA — — — — — THE MORMON
FRITZ — — — — — — THE ANTIQUE

A REALLY REMARKABLE SHOW—VIDE PRESS.

ENGAGED AT ENORMOUS COST.

—0—0—0—0—

SAPPER AND PARTY.

IN THEIR SCREAMING FARCE, ENTITLED:

"STUCK IN A GUM-BOOT."

—0—0—0—0—

JOCK McGREE

IN HIS FAMOUS SONG

"Trenches Ain't the Proper Place for Kilts."

—0—0—0—0—

POPULAR PRICES.

—0—0—0—0—

Ventilated throughout by Bosch and Co.

THE WIPERS TIMES. OR SALIENT NEWS.

No 4. Vol 2. Monday. 20th March, 1916. Price 50 Centimes.

EDITORIAL.

This week we have the pleasure to place before our readers the first number of Volume 2. Also we publish herewith a balance sheet:—

	Francs.
Subscriptions received ...	395
Already given to the Padre's Charity ...	225
Balance in hand ...	170
	395

Our subscription list has grown to an alarming extent, and we much regret that we have been unable to supply all who have sent for copies. Our new machine has given the greatest satisfaction in every way, and has fully warranted the enormous amount outlaid. Mr. Belary Helloc has unfortunately caught a cold while attending an outdoor meeting of his constituents at Hooge, and is consequently confined to bed in his luxurious suite of apartments at the Hotel des Ramparts. Our reporter interviewed him with a request for an article, but he was only well enough to reply "Getterlongoutervit." However, Mr. Cockles Tumley was run to ground in Oxford Street, and promised to weigh in with an article after he had attended a meeting of his creditors at the Cloth Hall. Still the City Fathers neglect our repeated warnings, and in the election next week Mr. Shembertons Willing, who is fighting the constituency on the "Better Lighting" platform, will pvt up a winning fight against the absurd addle-pated policy of those effete wrecks who sit in the Corporation of the City. Must we again mention that there is a crack visible in the Cathedral spire? Surely it should be obvious to anyone who has the interests of the City at heart. Is it necessary that we again draw the attention of those concerned to the fact that the buildings are encroaching on the fairway? Let us turn from this sickening spectacle of fatheaded complacency to a fairer scene. Owing to the enterprise of one who prefers anonymity, we shall be able to sit in the shade during the summer nights that are coming. Kew Gardens within a few minutes' walk of the Hotel des Ramparts! What a magnificent dream! And as we sit telling the old sweet tale in the shade of some mighty poplar, let us not forget that, but for the magnificent generosity of one who prefers to remain unknown, we might still have had to sit on the shadeless banks of the Moat. Remembering that, let us vote for SHEMBERTONS WILLING. This week we have reduced the price to 50 centimes on account of the paper famine. Many happy returns of the day!

THE EDITOR.

People We Take Our Hats off To.

—:o:—

The French.

"It's you for guard again to-night,
Outside the Q.M.'s store!"
"Oh, strike me lucky!"—then replied
The private very sore—
"If that is so, well then I 'ope
You lose the ruddy war."

For Exchange.

FOR EXCHANGE.—A SALIENT, in good condition. Will exchange for a. PAIR of PIGEONS, or a CANARY. —Apply Lonely Soldier, Hooge.

Cockles Tumley.

—o—o—o—

HALT! STOP RIGHT NOW!!

—:o:—

Twenty years ago I told you what was going to happen. If I didn't I meant to. Now I'm going to ask you all to back me, I'm appealing to you, you! the independent electors of Britain. Are we going to stand it any longer? Are your women nothing to you? Brrrr!!! Are we going to put up with the business methods of Q. Why should we have business in the Army? Business must go. There! now I've said it,— BUSINESS MUST GO. Let us have no more paltry pandering to business methods. Why should we put up with the tyranny of writing pencils, carpenter, one? Let us call a spade a spade, and a "can, oil, lubricating, armourer's" an armourer's lubricating oil can. I shall be addressing meetings at Hooge, Zillebeke, and Hell Fire Corner. Roll up in your thousands, and give the lie to everybody. Who pointed out the crying need for a business trench? Brrrrrrr! Let us grasp this growing evil fearlessly and scotch it. Business in the Army! Heavens!! And we might have been caught unawares had I not warned you. How much you all owe me! Still we'll say no more of that. But now that I've warned you it's up to you. Remember that, all of you. Stop it! STOP IT!! STOP IT!!! Brrrrrrrr.

COCKLES TUMLEY.

LOST.

LOST, on Thursday night last, DIAMOND BRACELET, about 11 p.m., between the Menin Gate and Hooge. Thought to have been lost when owner was returning from the second house at the Cloth Hall. Finder will be suitably rewarded.—Mrs. I. Pink, Stables Avenue, Hooge.

SOME KNOWLEDGE.

Way back from home
Across the foam
For Hunnish blood a-thirsting,
Came Captain Bass
(As green as grass)
With knowledge simply bursting.

—§ † §—

In training days
His studious ways
Caused all to gaze in wonder,
On field days long
When all went wrong
He never seemed to blunder.

—§ † §—

Now strange to say
The very day
That Bass arrived in Flanders,
Another too
Arrived at "Q"
His name was Percy Sanders.

—§ † §—

How different he
Appeared to be
In contrast to our hero,
He did not roar
For Hunnish gore
His spirits seemed at zero.

—§ † §—

With buttons bright
And Sam Brown tight
This twain went into battle,
How happy they
Upon that day
How sweet their childish prattle.

—§ † §—

My simple lay
I grieve to say
To ghoulish taste now panders,
For you will see
That Captain "B"
Is killed and so is Sanders.

—§ † §—

Upon the ground
A dud they'd found
(It caused them stupefaction).
In para. 3
Said Captain "B"
We'll find our course of action.

—§ † §—

It says, I see
Said Captain "B"
In fact it gives quite clearly,
With primers dry
You blow it high
Said Captain Sanders "really ! !"

—§ † §—

It seems to me
That para. 3
Is merely futile raving,
The trouble's less
Continued "S"
To drop it on the paving.

—§ † §—

And Captain "B"
Agreed with "P"
His method seemed so clear,
They'll never more
See England's shore
They've left this mortal sphere.

Things We Want to Know.

—o—o—o—

The most pop'lar tree in Belgium.

—:o:—

The price of second-hand Flammen-werfer.

—:o:—

Who leads in Kirschner collections.

—:o:—

The name of the gallant Major who has shares in 5 A.

—:o:—

Is this a sample of telegram usually sent by a Staff Officer on taking over the command of a battalion.—"Please send two bottles of whiskey by car to LILLE GATE AAA Urgent AAA"

—:o:—

The name of the officer who originated the idea.

OUR NEW SERIAL.

Herlock Shomes at it Again.

CHARACTERS :—Same as last week.

CHAPTER 4.

Returning to our friend Shomes who has, for some little time, been cooling his ardour in the Bec, during which period he has contrived to make the acquaintance of Honoria his fair companion in distress. Breathing undying love and vowing to save her, he hoists her on one shoulder, his vermoral sprayer on the other, and commences his itinerary towards Messrs. Crump, Hole and Co's circular scoop warehouse abutting on Hordon Goose Farm. Bending low with his precious burden, Shomes' mind begins to wander and so does his foot as he comes a terrific "purler" over a loose duck-board. Buzzing Bill, the Breezy Butcher of Bellewarde, witnessing the disaster, and being especially solicitous for the safety of his customers, shouts in stentorian terms " beat it for the tall timbers."

Meanwhile Intha Pink having extricated himself from the disaster which overtook him at the Denin Gate, reappeared safely with his sandbag, hammer and nail intent on reaching the trysting place where Lizzie is awaiting him.

" What of the night ? " is his kindly remark to Vera, one of the " Cinema " girls, who has surreptitiously, tentatively, and furtively, dodged the managerial eye, and had slipped out for a breath of fresh air.

" How you startled me, Intha ! " she said, " Are you going to meet THAT woman again ? "

" Ah ! Vera, to what lengths will your jealousy lead you ?" said Intha chidingly.

At that moment Silent Percy arrived unheralded on the scene. " Poor Vera," said Intha, as he crawled out of the ditch and once more gathered up his hammer and nail, " she never would have been happy anyhow."

While this tender scene is being enacted Chumley Marchbanks, the knut of Bond Street, having strolled down Grafton Street to pay a visit to the new night club " des Ramparts," which had sprung into fame very recently, inadvertently, and owing to the inadequate lighting took the yellow 'bus at Fell Hire Corner, and found himself in Bellewarde. All might yet have gone well with him had he not fallen over Crook, the Cambridge Cracksman, who after emptying his pockets pushed him into the Bec. —The waters flowed on.

(To be Continued.)

Next week :—A new set of characters, and another thrilling instalment.

Little Jack Horner at Hell Fire Corner,
Sat down a biscuit to chew,
He didn't care for the shells that flew there,
He knew what his biscuit could do.
There came a twelve-incher, but Jack didn't flinch, sir,
He grasped at his biscuit, and waited,
And then true and well, with biscuit met shell,
And the crump with a sigh detonated.

SOME DREAM.

In Wipers, where the whizz-bangs dance,
I mused upon the Great Advance.
I read (though most by heart I knew)
Ream upon ream from G and Q.
Which fearsome reading nearly done,
I slept—and dreamed we smashed the Hun:
Dreamed we had left our sodden trenches—
The well-known holes, the well-known stenches—
And forward stormed for wealth and wenches.
(Even in dreams, my eagle mind
Perpended Prussia's womenkind—
Deciding, if it came to shooting,
I'd rather I were shot for looting)
Rifle nor mortar, gun nor lance
Had wrought—at last—our Great Advance:
Our freshest troops, our A.S.C.
It was that gave us victory!
Yea! 'Twas the Army Safety Corps
Drowned Belgium's swamps in German gore.
Wagon on wagon, team on team,
I watched their quarter-locks agleam,
Mad squadrons of my whiskied dream.
'Whips over' on each 'heavy draught'
They leaped the wire; and, leaping, laughed;
Then furious with uplifted crops
Hacked their red path through Clonmel Copse;
The while their deadly Fifty-fives'
Took countless toll of limbs and lives.
Black columns down the Menin Road.
In endless streams their motors flowed . . . .
Vainly, the flower of William's flock
Strove to withstand this awful shock.
No human force could hope to dam
Those waves of Plum and Apple jam;
Bavaria's stoutest infantry
Paled at the sugar, black with tea;
Proud Prussia, trained to meatless days,
Reeled and fled back in sheer amaze
As, joint to joint and knee to knee,
Charged home Fred Karno's Cavalry . . .
And now, alone, in Glencorse Wood,
Undaunted, little Willie stood,
And eyed the foe, and eyed the food:
Too long he tarried! F—sch—r smote
Full on that gorged and greedy throat
With a faked requisition note . . . .
'Twas Mine! Chill terror at my breast,
My traitor soul. in dreams, confessed;
And woke to find—not Army Scandals
But shortage in our ration candles.

GILBERT FRANKAU.

13/3/16

LONELY PRESIDENT wishes correspond with anyone. Can write a charming note. Has corresponded with most of the crowned heads of Europe.—Write "Dignitas," Washington, U.S.A.

(Advt.)

TO MY CHUM.

No more we'll share the same old barn,
The same old dug-out, same old yarn,
No more a tin of bully share,
Nor split our rum by a star-shell's flare,
So long old lad.

—:0:—

What times we've had, both good and bad,
We've shared what shelter could be had,
The same crump-hole when the whizz-bangs shrieked,
The same old billet that always leaked,
And now—you've "stopped one."

—:0:—

We'd weathered the storm two winters long,
We'd managed to grin when all went wrong,
Because together we fought and fed,
Our hearts were light; but now—you're dead
And I am Mateless.

—:0:—

Well, old lad, here's peace to you,
And for me, well, there's my job to do,
For you and the others who lie at rest,
Assured may be that we'll do our best
In vengeance.

—:0:—

Just one more cross by a strafed road-side,
With it's G.R.C., and a name for guide,
But it's only myself who has lost a friend,
And though I may fight through to the end,
No dug-out or billet will be the same,
All pals can only be pals in name,
But we'll all carry on till the end of the game
Because you lie there.

Military Definitions.

HOOGE .... See Hell.

QUARTER MASTER or MASTER QUARTER, ONE or Q.M. — A bird of strange habits:—when attacked covers itself with indents and talks backwards.

RUM .... See Warrant Officers.

DUMP .... A collection of odds and ends, sometimes known as the Divisional Toyshop.

HELL .... See Hooge.

FOKKER .... The name given by all infantry officers and men to any aeroplane that flies at a great height.

ADJUTANT ... See grenades or birds.

INFANTRYMAN .. An animal of weird habits, whose peculiarities have only just been discovered. It displays a strange aversion to light, and lives in holes in the earth during the day, coming out at night seeking whom it may devour.
In colour it assimilates itself to the ground in which it lives.

GRENADES ... These are used to cause annoyance to any luckless person who happens to be near them.

BIRDS .... Are of two kinds only.—The Carrier Pigeon (a delicacy for front line trenches), and the nameless, untamed variety usually collected by junior officers.

ADIEU TO THE SALIENT.

—o—o—o—

The news is confidential! At least, as yet, it is not known to everybody. Nevertheless it is true. Had I the vocabulary I could tell you what I think of this charming spot. Words having failed me, I bid it "Good-bye" with a silence more eloquent than words. For we are leaving the Salient and going into "rest"!!—

Whatever trials "rest"? may hold, whatever the future may have for us, I think that always I shall be glad to have seen the Salient. A month there holds more than a year elsewhere. "Wipers"! He's a strange man who can gaze on that unmoved. Who, that has known it, will forget the high-strung tension of the Menin Road, who, unmoved, can pass those fields of crosses? The Menin Road and all it means. To know all the by-paths and alternative ways so as to dodge when shelling starts! To know all its holes and ditches when machine guns loose! Can there be any emotion to equal that of lying prone in a crump-hole with a machine gun ripping across your back. Hell Fire Corner! aptly named. The span from there to Hooge, who that has slithered along it in gum boots thigh will ever forget. And now I no more to ponder as to which route to use. No longer the old question "where are they putting 'em to-night? For we're going back to "rest"!!

But not all—some of us remain. Poor lads: There they stay in the Salient and crosses mark the PRICE they paid. Always, when the strain of the Salient may have left us, the memory of those crosses will remain, and those true hearts who sleep there may rest assured that we, who worked with them, fought with them and hoped with them, will exact the price. Ypres, and all you mean farewell! To those who come after us good luck! We are going back to "rest"!!!

Correspondence.

—:o:—

To the Editor,
The "Wipers Times."

Sir,

In perusing your excellent journal I was particularly impressed with the interest yonr two correspondents take in "bird life in the trenches." Whether the cuckoo who sang, or the cuckoo who heard the aforesaid cuckoo sing are either in existence, is to my mind absolutely immaterial. I can emphatically state that I heard the nightingale, and challenge the whole of your clientile to deny the fact.

I am,
Yours faithfully,
A NOCTURNAL PROWLER.

—:o:—

To Editor, ",Wipers Times"

Sir,

A great deal of valuable space has been recently taken up in your paper by absurd correspondents re the cuckoo. All I have to say is: Damn the cuckoo!

Yours, etc.,
FED UP.

NOTICE.

We regret to announce that an insidious disease is affecting the Division, and the result is a hurricane of poetry. Subalterns have been seen with a note-book in one hand, and bombs in the other absently walking near the wire in deep communion with the muse. Even Quartermasters with books, note, one, and pencil, copying, break into song while arguing the point re boots. gum, thigh. The Editor would be obliged if a few of the poets would break into prose as a paper cannot live by "poems" alone.

FOR SALE.
THE SALIENT ESTATE.
COMPLETE IN EVERY DETAIL.

INTENDING PURCHASERS WILL BE SHOWN ROUND ANYTIME DAY OR NIGHT
UNDERGROUND RESIDENCES READY FOR HABITATION.

—o—o—o—o—

Splendid Motoring Estate! Shooting Perfect!!
Fishing Good!!!

—o—o—o—o—

NOW'S THE TIME. HAVE A STAKE IN THE COUNTRY.
NO REASONABLE OFFER REFUSED.
DO FOR HOME FOR INEBRIATES OR OTHER CHARITABLE INSTITUTION.

Delay is dangerous! You might miss it!!

—o—o—o—o—

Apply for particulars, etc., to

Thomas, Atkins, Sapper & Co., Zillebeke and Hooge.

HOUSEBREAKERS: WOOLEY, BEAR, CRUMP & CO. TELEGRAMS: "ADSUM, WIPERS."

HOLIDAYS.
Stop! Stop!! Stop!!!

Where are you going to stop during your Summer holidays.

—o—o—o—o—

WHY NOT STOP AT

HOTEL DES RAMPARTS, WIPERS

EXCELLENT VIEW. CLOSE TO RAILWAY STATION.
LIT THROUGHOUT BY ELECTRICITY.
M. AND V. DIET.

—o—o—o—o—

TAKE THE "MOAT WATER" CURE.

—o—o—o—o—

TERMS VARY.

TELEPHONE: 102, SEEUM. TELEGRAMS: PIONEERS, WIPERS.

MENIN GATE CINEMA.

THIS WEEK NIGHTLY.

"TRANSPORT BILL"

Goes With A Rattle! One Huge Row!

Don't Miss It On Any Account!

IN TWO PARTS: FEATURING,

TOMMY—THE MULE.

THIS HIGHLY TRAINED ANIMAL IS SOME GOER.

—o—o—o—o—

OTHER ITEMS:

Tommy Takes An Holiday.

—o—o—o—o—

Leave Train.

—o—o—o=o—

Latest War Pictures.

—o—o—o—o—

PRICES AS USUAL.

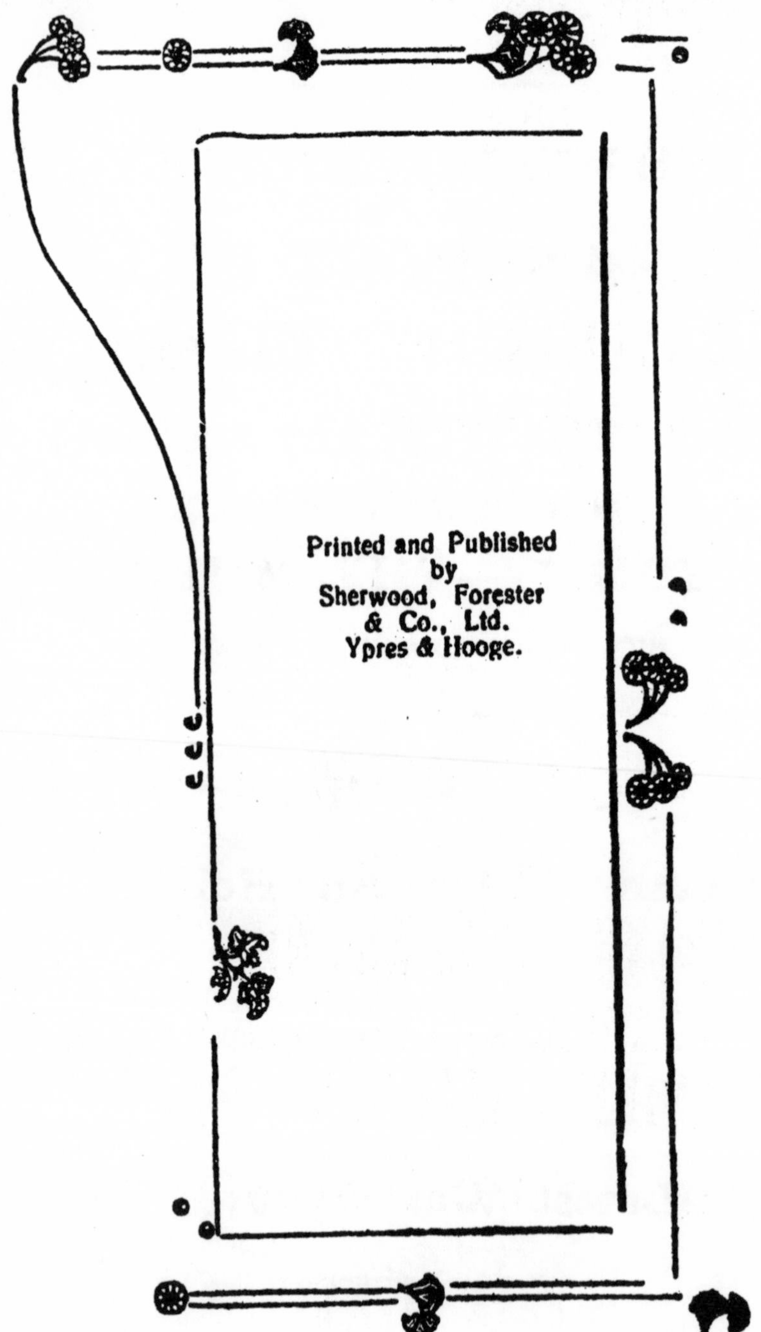
Printed and Published
by
Sherwood, Forester
& Co., Ltd.
Ypres & Hooge.

THE "NEW CHURCH" TIMES.

WITH WHICH IS INCORPOPATED

THE WIPERS TIMES

No 1. Vol 1. Mondav. 17th April, 1916. Price 5 Francs.

"DEAD COW FARM" CINEMA.

THIS WEEK

GRAND OPENING NIGHT.

THIS MARVELLOUS PALACE ERECTED AT FABULOUS EXPENSE WILL OPEN ON THURSDAY NEXT WITH THE WONDERFUL FILM

HE DIDN'T WANT TO DO IT.

FEATURING:

"Wata Funk" The Conscientious Objector.

—o—o—o—o—

OTHER ITEMS.

—o—o—o—o—

PEEPS THROUGH A SNIPERS COPE.

—o—o—o—o—

FLOUNDERS IN FLANDERS.

—o—o—o—o—

PRICES: 5fr.; 2fr.; 1fr.

THE "NEW CHURCH" HIPPODROME.

THIS MAGNIFICENTLY EQUIPPED MUSIC HALL WILL RE OPEN ON

MONDAY NEXT.

RE-DECORATED THROUGHOUT NO EXPENSE HAVING BEEN SPARED.
COME IN YOUR HUNDREDS. STANDING ROOM FOR THOUSANDS.

GRAND CENTENARY PERFORMANCE AT WHICH

All The World-famed Artistes

WILL POSITIVELY APPEAR, INCLUDING:

WILLIAM O. N. ZOLLERN

IN HIS SCREAMINGLY FUNNY FARCE, ENTITLED

'THE BIG PUSH' 'OR OVER-DUN'

This is evidently in for a long run, and the celebrated William jun., shows all his old irrepressability.

ETC., ETC.

Doors open always. **Book early.** **Prices as usual.**

TO COLONELS AND COMPANY COMMANDERS.

Are you interested in your young? Yes!
Then send them to

Pro. Coster's Academy

Bring them up hardy and train them for a military career.

—o—o—o—

THOROUGHLY COMPETENT TUTORS ONLY EMPLOYED.

—o—o—o—

Tuition given on Deportment, etc.

—o—o—o—

Next Term Commences, Wed. 19th Inst.

—o—o—o—

Write for Prospectus and Syllabus of Training. Hundreds of Testimonials from grateful Commanding Officers.

—o—o—o—

TERMS MODERATE.

—o—o—o—

Telephones: 999, "Wall."
Telegrams: "Technique."

IS YOUR FRIEND A SOLDIER?
DO YOU KNOW WHAT HE WANTS?
NO!! WE DO!!!

—o—o—o—

Send Him One of Our Latest
IMPROVED PATTERN COMBINATION
UMBRELLA & WIRE CUTTER

—o—o—o—

These useful appliances can be used simultaneously. No more colds caught cutting the wire. He will be delighted with it and will find a use for it

—o—o—o—

PRICES:
- Gold Plated 500fr.
- Silver Plated 39fr.
- Ordinary 15fr.

With a Shooting Stick Attachment 5fr. extra.

—o—o—o—

SEND HIM ONE AT ONCE.

—o—o—o—

THE NOUVEAU ART CO., SPITALFIELDS.

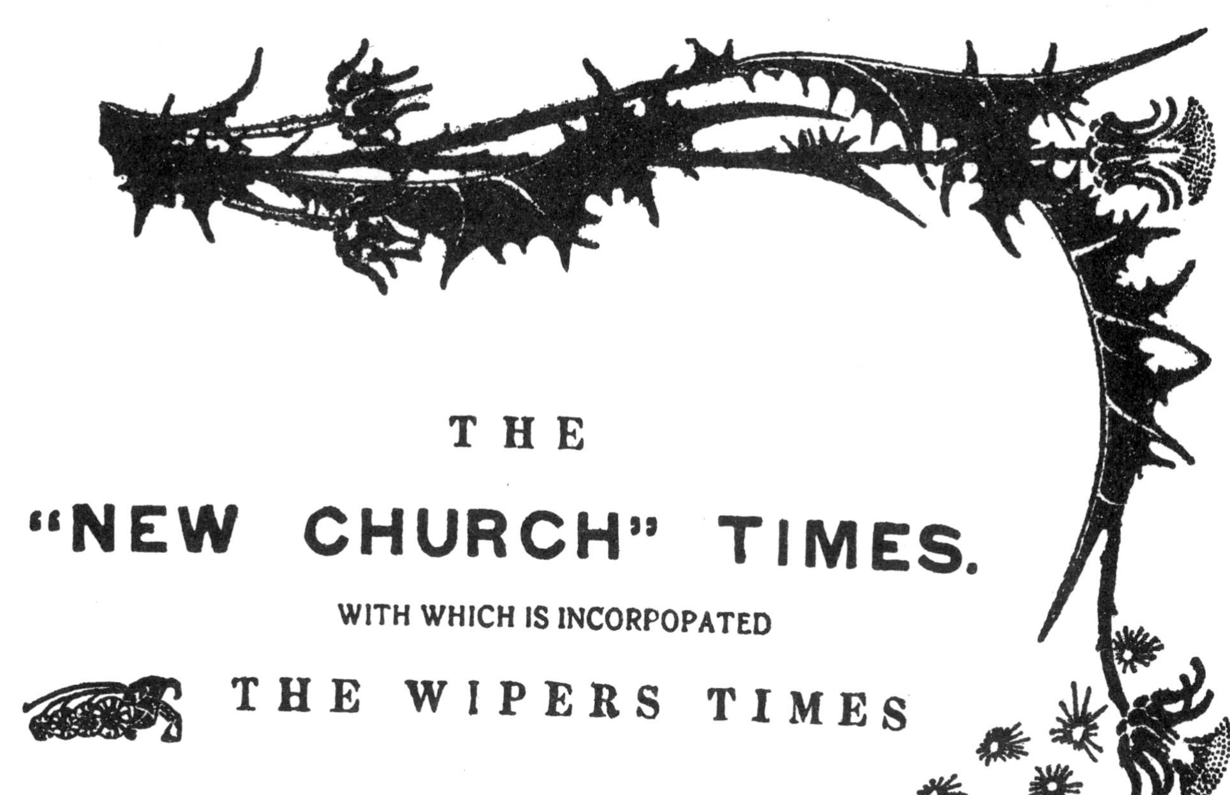

THE "NEW CHURCH" TIMES.

WITH WHICH IS INCORPOPATED

THE WIPERS TIMES

No 1. Vol 1. Monday, 17th April, 1916. Price 5 Francs.

EDITORIAL.

Owing to reasons over which we had no control, we regret to announce that the Wipers Times is now defunct. But through the enterprise of a wealthy syndicate all rights, plant, etc., belonging to that earnest periodical have been acquired at a fabulous figure, and are now incorporated in the new venture. Also the highly salaried staff has elected to follow the fortunes of their Editor, so that we may still hope to retain the confidence of our readers. We hope to introduce many new features shortly, including a new competition which will be open to all above the rank of Colonel. We are having a most luxurious set of offices erected, but fully believe that the incredible sums to be expended will be warranted by an increased circulation. As we have left the scene of our serial before the writer had managed to extricate most of the characters from the Bellewarde Bee, we shall have to trespass on the readers' credulity to bring some of them back, otherwise it it will spoil the continuity of this enthralling tale. We have just returned from leave which is becoming a greater trial than ever. To leave this land of brightness and, by spending two hours on a Channel boat, to be placed right into an atmosphere of gloom and indefinitness. Oh! ye of little faith, wake up and smile for the summer is upon ye. Let your step be brisk and your hearts light for "even as ye have sown so shall ye not reap," and for that thank your lucky stars, for though ye have tried for eighteen months to lose the war yet have ye not succeeded and victory is at hand. So go ye unto the uttermost ends of darkness, yea, even unto Piccadilly and Westminster, and preach the gospel of cheeriness and hope. We notice with deep concern that the fell disease poetitis is on the increase. This may be accounted for by the arrival of Spring, and though the picture of little lambs gambolling among the whizz-bangs may be beautiful and romantic, yet our paper hungers for prose and will not be satisfied. Now we place ourselves with the utmost confidence in the hands of our readers, relying on the support so readily given to the defunct "Wipers Times."

THE EDITOR.

Farewell *Yperen! Yperen farewell!
Long have I known thee, and known thee well!
Thy stoney streets, thy shell-pitted square,
Looted thy houses for dug-out ware,
Looking for cellar cool and deep,
With a shell-proof roof where I could sleep.

—§ † §—

No longer need thy ways to prowl,
With ears attuned for crump's shrill howl,
'Twixt doubtful joys to hesitate,
The Menin Road, or old Lille Gate?

—§ † §—

But in my sleep I'll dream of thee,
And always in my thoughts thou'llt be,
Perchance my fate may be to see
Another place resembling thee,
But that foretells a future warm,
Where other little devils swarm,
Thy prototype can but be—well
Why should we mince the matter—HELL.

*Yperen—The Belgian name for Wipers, used here to baffle the enemy.

THE MYSTERY OF 999.

—o—o—o—

By COCKLES TUMLEY.

—o—

Tanked up in the North and having a little spare time I went into the local hostelry, where mine host and myself were soon in deep discussion. "What ho!" said he, "I think the German Crown Prince is the animal referred to in the Bible as "Balaam's ass." This gave me furiously to think. Ten toes, ten fingers. That gave me the clue. Here it is. Think of a number. 3?—right. Add now ten fingers ten toes—23!—add 979. Take away the number you first thought of, and there you are—999. By Jove, this is weird. Try again, ten fingers, ten toes, and it's the tenth of the month. Let us multiply—1,000. Take away 1, and there you are again—999. This begins to be creepy. We'll be having the Crown Prince turned into a pillar of salt in a minute. Once more ten fingers, ten toes, two eyes and one nose, and eleven letters in his title. Multiply—2,200. Take away 1,201, and there you are again—999. There seems to be no loophole. Here again, "Jonah was in the whale three days and three nights." For the whale take the German Army, an animal of voracious appetite, but with a very small swallow, and there you are. As we all know, the whale couldn't digest Jonah, and the German Army is having the job of it's life to keep the Crown Prince down. One could continue indefinitely and point out parallels, but space forbids. But isn't it phenomenal? Brrrrrr, I must never get tanked up in the North again.

COCKLES TUMLEY.
10/4/16.

A FEW WORDS.

I read in last month's WIPERS TIMES, the Editor was sick of rhymes; the best of reasons, I suppose, that I should henceforth stick to prose. No more I'll sing how transports wait, bi-nightly, at the Menin Gate, while some unthinking driver sits, well in effective range of Fritz—and galls his mules and smokes and spits: no more I'll turn the mordant line till 'Q' clerks blush incarnadine; or strafe our deadly A.S.C., in tuneful stanzas twenty three. No, never more I'll twang the lute—my Pegasus, that rope-galled brute, I'll treat as Balaam did his ass; groom, turn the hairy out to grass!

Verse was alright when we were pent in that unkindly Salient; but here, where April's early breeze wafts perfume over Neuve Eglise (if this takes place, I'll bet my shirt Division Signals "Gas Alert") an easier part is mine to play for Editors who never pay.

Is it not good, dear friends, to hop away from Reninghelst and Pop; only on others' maps to see the walls that once were Potije; to leave the sinful whiskied throng that filled the Ramparts all night long, the snares that wait for youthful feet in City Square and Regent Street, the pit that yawns for wicked ways where Hell Fire Corner's Shell-fires blaze; is it not good, my friends, to perch in safety by this dear new church? For here the frisky April lamb lies down, nor cares one tinker's damn, for these our unprotected guns pointing dumb muzzles to dumb Huns: and here each happy trench is made to help the open enfilade; and here we sleep beneath a roof which isn't even Pip-squeak proof—and e'en the WIPERS TIMES I ween, becomes a Parish Magazine.

Oh my dear friends, how sweet. how strange, this restful quiet, this peaceful change. Here let us rest while spies release with loving hands the dove of peace, that carries under wing (not beak) all knowledge our opponenls seek: here let us stretch our airy wires, (remembering 'he who digs, perspires') and hope that never hostile shell shall cut the lines we love so well.

Oh, my beloved parishoners, hark how the happy Hunlet purrs: see what a little kindliness has done to ease his frightfulness, turned into love his ravening lust and to caress his bayonet thrust.

Better is charity benign than Vickers gun and deadly mine; better the brother love of Heaven than nine-point-two or four-point-seven!

Dear friends, with this sweet thought I close my this week's task of parish prose: may Heaven be pleased my flock to bless: . . . . yet, when in doubt, call S.O.S.!

GILBERT FRANKAU.
10/4/16.

THE EDITOR'S LAMENT.

—:o:—

Oh pity! pity! ill wind blows
My one tame poet's flown to prose,
And he on whom our hopes were based,
Whose tuneful efforts weekly graced
Our columns, has the awful taste
To "prose it."

—:o:—

Oh! graceless churl, with scathing line
Your Editor t'incarnadine
To make his pale cheek flush with shame,
To hint at pay in lieu of fame,
And make him in despair exclaim
I'll "Franc out."

—:o:—

And yet perchance his kindly soul
Knows not he's put me "up the pole,"
His next week's effort well may be
A gem of thought and poetry,
Which we will class eternally
Gilbertian.

THE EDITOR.

OUR NEW SERIAL.

—o—o—o—

HERLOCK SHOLMES AT IT AGAIN.

—o—o—o—

Characters :—Same as before.

—o—o—o—

CHAPTER 5.

—o—

Snowflakes were falling heavily around Hordon Goose Farm, where we left Herlock with the fair Honoria. Breezy Bill, the Bouncing Butcher of Bellewarde, had just been hit in the neck by a whizz-bang when the chug-chug of a motor cycle was heard. "Can it be Intha?" cried Honoria, while Sholmes proceeded to tune his violin. "No!"—roared he, as a motor despatch rider came round Fell Hire Corner—"News at last from my Baker Street Squad." Hurriedly tearing open and reading the despatch, the true Sholmes stood revealed in all his strength and method. Seizing his vermoral sprayer, he rapidly squirted an enormous dose into his forearm. Just then the voice of the faithful Hotsam was heard calling "Where are you. Sholmes?" "Here" replied the great detective, rapidly emptying his revolver at the approaching figure. "Thank goodness I've found you at last, but you nearly got me that time," said Hotsam admiringly. "Never mind, better luck next time" said Sholmes, sotto voce, to Honoria. Aloud, "To work, there's mischief afoot. Thank heaven I attended that two days course at the Technical School, I shall now be up to all their dodges." Drawing a searchlight from his pocket, he read the fateful message :—

> "Division moves to-morrow at dawn AAA You will assemble all characters at zero fifteen outside Cloth Hall, Typers, P 13 D 1-1 in time to catch the underground for *——— at zero twenty AAA On arrival there steal any rations you can find, and carry on with serial AAA—Editor."

(* Censored—ED)

"At last!" shouted the great sleuth. "At last!" shouted the others, as they busily collected the usual paraphernalia of the great man. "Hotsam," cried Sholmes, "send off the orderly sergeant at once to warn all Characters. Then meet me at the Denin Gate." With these words he disappeared into the gloom and a crump-hole. All these arrangements having been made, Hotsam and Honoria continued their journey down the Denin Road, arriving in Typers just in time to meet Intha Pink before he left for his nightly work. Having rapidly given him a summary of all that had happened, they went into a neighbouring estaminet to await the fateful hour of zero.

(Another long and thrilling instalment next week.)

In dug-out cool I sit and sneeze,
Safe from a whizz-bang's mauling ;
Dreams come my appetite to tease,
Fond visions which my fancy please
Of maids divine, enthralling,
And glorious times when our job's done,
My thoughts you'll echo—"Damn the Hun!"

Correspondence.

To the Editor,
"New Church" Times.

Sir,

On looking at some of the pictures published by the daily pictorial papers in England I am affected by a peculiar feeling of nauseau. This is especially noticeable when the subject happens to be peace meetings in Trafalgar Square, etc. Surely, if at home they must have peace meetings, and must tolerate conscientious objectors, then these might be hidden from the public eye. The only way to heal open sores is to bind them up and the ventilation of full page photos is not likely to be benefical to our best interests, besides making rather a disgusting exhibition,

I am, Sir,
Yours faithfully,
A LOVER OF DECENCY.

—§†§—

To the Editor,
"New Church" Times.

Sir,

May I encroach upon your valuable space to draw your attention to the fact that for some days now, the clock in the tower of the church at Wulverghem, has not received the amount of attention necessary to its good running.

This fact has caused many of the workers in our little village to miss their early morning trains to Messines.

I am, etc.,
"TEMPUS FUGIT"

—§†§—

To the Editor,
"New Church" Times.

Sir,

In reference to a letter in your columns may I quote Call Haine on the subject, viz:—

God made the bee,
The bee made honey;
Pioneers do all the work,
R. E.'s get the money.

Yours faithfully,
JUSTITIA.

RUBAIYAT OF A "LINE" SUBALTERN.

The passing whizz-bang shrieks and bullets hum
Yet, gentle stranger, to my dug-out come;
To you I'll unfold knowledge which may help,
But first methinks will ope a jar of rum.

—§†§—

This is a cheery place you will allow,
A tin of beef, a jar of rum, and Thou
Beside me, squatting in a pool of mud,
And dug-out is not Paradise enow.

—§†§—

Alas! Alas! When M.G.'s spat I swore,
I swore and swore—and then again I swore!—
While on my tummy lay in dank pool deep,
And bullets through my fav'rit breeches tore.

—§†§—

And then! And then with five-nine crump you bet,
The wily Hun bust up our parapet,
Blew off my roof, and made that blooming hole,
Through which you're now so quickly getting wet.

—§†§—

The surly blighter shoots, and having shot
Moves on, while you are cursing quite a lot,
And on your tummy crawl through feet of mud,
Nor pause till you've retaliation got.

—§†§—

But hist! 'Tis secret known to only few,
We're going "o'er the top," and going through,
And then! And then! Old Fritz will pay in kind
The debt he owes the likes of me and you.

DUG-OUT MUSINGS.

Idly toying with a paper, something caught
My passing eye—
Just a picture, and the subject, can you guess?
A man both hale and fit,
With a touch of MOTHER WIT!
Puts his fingers to his nose and saunters
On into his stye,
And this record left to grace the daily press.

Having gazed at this in wonder, then
I sat me down to think,
And to ponder how such things had come to be,
Had old England changed so much
Since the years when I lost touch?
That a cur can claim attention
While we hover on the brink,
And with effort are in sight of victory

England! What a strange digestion!
Strain at gnats
And swallow kine,
May we pray that you will soon shake off the dope,
And a cur with fingers spread
Follows where he may be led
Knowing well, that, though his conscience is
Unable to define
The only way of duty, yet there's but one given line,
And to take it is his last remaining hope.

Answers

to Correspondents.

LOVER OF NATURE.—Nothing doing, that bird's dead.

PRO BONO.—Noise you complain of is our new metre gun. Certainly, will have it removed if it disturbs your sleep.

SUBALTERN.—No, the death penalty is not enforced in the case of murdering an adjutant, as you can always be able to prove extenuating circumstances.

YOUNG OFFICER.—It is not "the thing" to wear turned up slacks and shoes when "going over the top," in fact, you run the risk of being sent back to your unit if discovered.

TROUBLED.—Certainly think you have just complaint against people in next dug-out, and if you care to take the matter further there is no doubt that you will get damager. It certainly was scandal if, as you affirm, the picture was one of Kirschner's.

Spring is coming, watch the whizz-bang
As it shrieks with mad delight,
All the how'zers howl the message
As they break the still of night,
Through the winter, long and weary,
Cold and dreary, we have passed,
Lived and slept in Hell's own muddle,
Fed and worked in filth and puddle.
But here's end to all our worries,
Spring and sun have come at last.

Things We Want to Know.

—o—o—o—

When the sale of whisky will be introduced in Bailleul?

—:o:—

Whether the pop'lar Poplar tree's as pop'lar as it used to be?

—:o:—

Whether certain officers have taken shares in the Hôtel Faucon, and what's the attraction?

—:o:—

Whether a well-known firm of commission agents isn't getting rather fed up with hurriedly changing it's quarters? (N.B.—We think this frequent sudden "flitting" might have a bad effect on this firm's custom, as the public are rather apt to fight shy of these "Here-to-day-and-gone-to-morrow" firms—verb. sap.)

—:o:—

Whether the urgent wires of a well-known C.O. (already referred to in these columns) have been more frequent during the recent hot weather?

—:o:—

Whether one of the leaders in Kirchner collections has not got his nose in front rather by innuendo than superiority in numbers, and if the others concerned are not straining every nerve to make up leeway?

The Editor would welcome articles from anyone in the Division, and would esteem it a favour if anyone knowing of buried talent would see that this is brought to light and exercised. Payment is made on the same generous lines as during the run of the "Wipers Times." So will everyone with a little spare time please dash off something and send it along.

SECRET NO. 99.

—o—o—o—

(To be eaten as soon as read.)

—o—o—o—

Corps Cuttings.

—o—

(a) ARTILLERY.—The enemy put 35 shells into N. 502, z. 10 1/2, 6 3/4 at 7'35 a.m. this morning. Considerable damage done to the "Toughs" Rum Ration. A gas shell of the XYZ variety fell near the sentry at A.1.b.1.1. In common with many of his kind he had no helmet gas. His language was awful.

(b) SNIPING.—Inactive—more expected when we get our new issue of silver-plated tin hats.

(c) TRENCHES & WORKS.—One man was seen shovelling at T. 10.9, 5 1/2, 2 7/8 at 10'49 a.m. He wore a light green cap with a blue peak—he had no tunic on, and his trousers were torn by the left knee.

A new trench is being dug from X 2. b. 10.10. Sandbagging also is evident here—the enemy is probably using the same earth to fill them.

(d) GENERAL.—At X. 2. C 9 1/2. 9 1/2 a man climbed a tree, put his left leg over a branch, pulled out a bright blue handkerchief with red spots on it, and waved it three times. This was evidently a signal.

A puffing noise was heard at 9'30 p.m. coming from the direction of the railway at N.2.C. Probably an engine.

A train left O.3. a.2.0. at 7'35 p.m., giving three short and two long whistles before it started.

Transport, loud cries, whistling and general movement was noticed at Crump Farm. Evidently a new dump. Our artillery have been advised of this fact.

Two green lights went up at 11'30 a.m. opposite Trench 132. They broke into three red and finally four green on coming down.

Stop Press News.

LATEST PEACE RUMOUR.—"The Crown Prince is willing to dispose of his famous collection of valuable antiques from France and Flanders if suitable price can be obtained." The American President is writing a note about it.

RACING.

—:o:—

VERDUN STAKES

—:o:—

Piou-Piou 1

w.o.

Fritz, who was advertised to appear, had to give up the engagement, as he has turned out a roarer.

OUR SHORT STORY.

Two soldiers were carrying feather mattresses up to the front line trenches when one stumbled. "Strike me pink, Bill," said one, "what's this?" "A dud," said, Harry. "Ho, is it?" said Bill, "let's see!" Picking up a maul which lay handy they saw . . . . The war went on.

LOST.

LOST, STOLEN, or STRAYED.—Two HUNS. Appearance, fed up and miserable. Peculiarities, hunger and a dislike of sudden noises. Mislaid somewhere in trenches at ———. Will finder please communicate with THE UMPTIETH DIVISION, Muddy Brook Alley, and he will be suitably rewarded.

OUR NEW COMPETITION.

—o—o—o—o—

PRIZES { First Prize, 5,000,000fr.
Second Prize, 2,500,000fr.
Third Prize, 1,250,000fr.

MANY OTHER PRIZES.

Open to all above the rank of Colonel. Simple—Easy. All you have to do is to fill in the last line of the following verse.

There was a young General of forty,
A year at the front made him sporty;
To say it I grieve,
When he went on leave,
— — — — — —

Send your solution and a 1fr. Postal Order to the Editor, who reserves the right to give the prizes as he deems fit. A Postal Order must accompany each solution.

ARE YOU GOING OVER THE TOP?

IF SO BE SURE TO FIRST INSPECT OUR NEW LINE OF VELVETEEN CORDUROY PLUSH BREECHES.

BE IN THE FASHION AND LOOK LIKE A SOLDIER.

ALL ONE PRICE, 9s. 11d.

THOUSANDS OF TESTIMONIALS FROM ALL FRONTS.

SEND FOR THESE AND ILLUSTRATED BROCHURE ENTITLED:

"Breeches And Their Wearers" Or "Legs Make The Officer."

Address: POND & CO., WULVERGHEM. Agents all along the line

ARE YOU TIRED, HOT & THIRSTY AFTER A LONG WALK? YES! THEN DROP IN AT BUS FARM THE NEW TEA SHOP.

—0—0—0—

Tastefully Fitted.
General Attractions.
Walloon Waitresses.

—0—0—0—

FAMOUS CRUMPET HOUSE.
AIRY TEA ROOMS.
SPECIAL ACCOMODATION FOR MOTORISTS.
SWITCHBACK NEAR BY.
TAKE THE TUBE OR GREEN 'BUS.
PARTIES CATERED FOR AND WEDDING BREAKFAST'S ARRANGED.

—0—0—0—

TELEPHONE: 102, HOP.
TELEGRAMS: "MOVING."

TRY OUR NEW CIRCULAR TOUR. EMBRACING ALL THE HEALTH RESORTS OF

LOVELY BELGIUM.

—0—0—0—

Books Of Coupons Obtainable From

R. E. Cruting & Co.,

London. Agents Everywhere.

—0—0—0—

Our expert Guides meet all trains, and our excellent system of G. S. coaches will make you realize what travelling is.

—0—0—0—

BEAUTIFUL SCENERY ON ALL CIRCUITS.

—0—0—0—

NO SALIENT FEATURE OMITTED.

—0—0—0—

BOOK AT ONCE TO AVOID DISAPPOINTMENT.

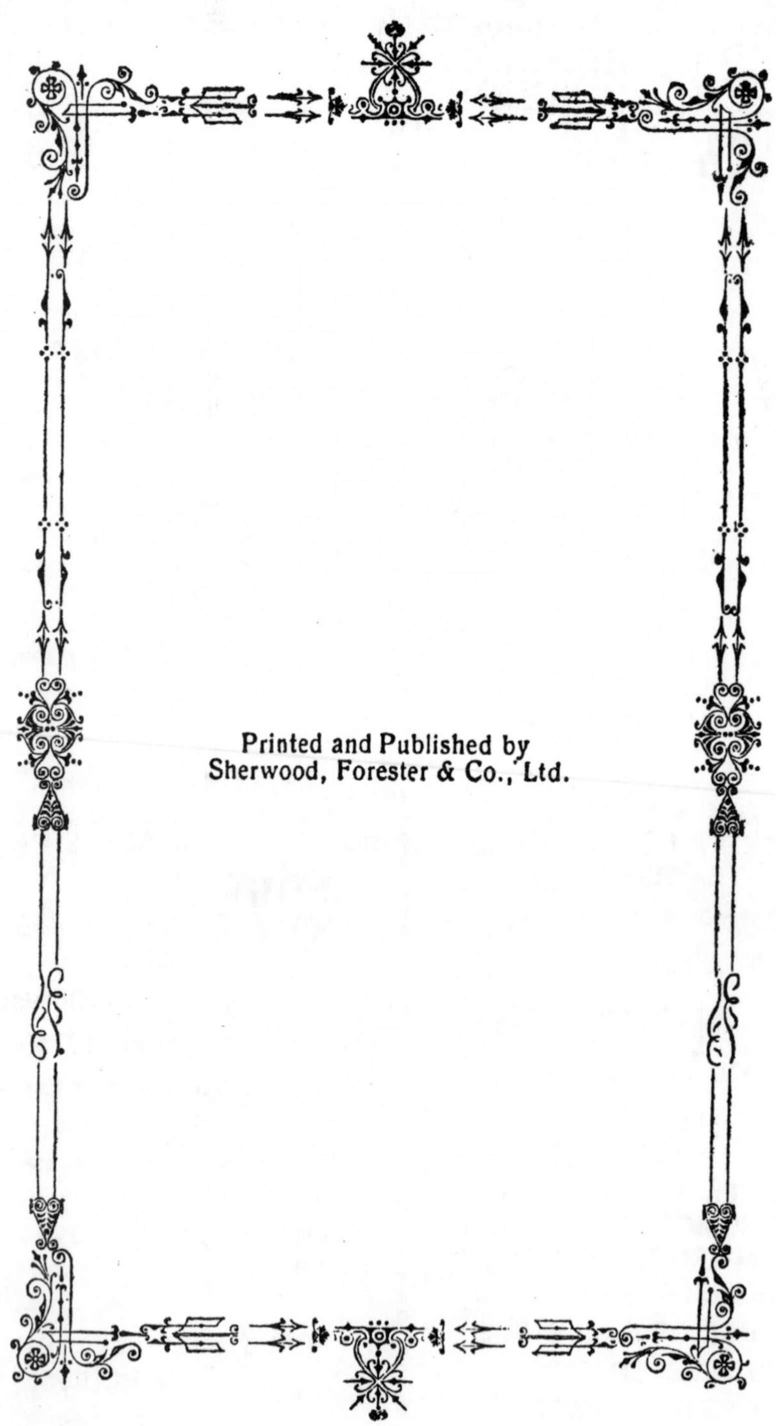

Printed and Published by
Sherwood, Forester & Co., Ltd.

THE

"NEW CHURCH" TIMES.

WITH WHICH IS INCORPOPATED

 THE WIPERS TIMES

No 2. Vol 1. Mondav. 8th May, 1916. Price 10 Francs.

"DEAD COW FARM" CINEMA

THIS WEEK—SPECIAL PROGRAMME.

"PIPPED ON THE PARAPET."

THIS EXCITING TALE HAS BEEN FILMED AT ENORMOUS EXPENSE, FEATURING THE CELEBRATED SCOTCH COMEDIAN,

MAC KENSEN.

—o—o—o—o—

 OTHER ITEMS. 

—o—o—o—o—

"OVER THE TOP."

A SCREAMING FARCE.

—o—o—o—o—

"THE EMPTY JAR."

A RUM TRAGEDY

—o—o—o—o—

PRICES AS USUAL. OPEN ALWAYS.

THE NEUVE EGLISE HIPPODROME

GRAND NEW REVIEW, ENTITLED:

"SHELL IN"

POSITIVELY THE GREATEST SPECTACULAR PERFORMANCE EVER STAGED.

BRINGING BEFORE THE PUBLIC AT ONE AND THE SAME TIME THE FOLLOWING HIGHLY-PAID STARS:

THE CRUMPS.
LITTLE PIP-SQUEAK
DUDDY WHIZZ-BANG.
HURLA SHELLOG, etc., etc.

THRILLING OPENING CHORUS ARRANGED BY LEWIS VICKERS.

Exciting! Hair-raising!! Awe-inspiring!!!

SEE WHAT THE PAPERS SAY. BOOK EARLY. PRICES DOUBLE THIS WEEK.

TO HARASSED SUBALTERNS.

—o—o—o—o—

IS YOUR LIFE MISERABLE? ARE YOU UNHAPPY?

DO YOU HATE YOUR COMPANY COMMANDER?

—o—o—o—o—

YES! THEN BUY HIM ONE OF

OUR NEW PATENT TIP DUCK BOARDS

YOU GET HIM ON THE END—THE DUCK BOARD DOES THE REST

—o—o—o—o—

Made in three sizes, and every time a "Blighty."

—o—o—o—o—

"If once he steps on to the end,
'Twill take a month his face to mend"

—o—o—o—o—

WRITE AT ONCE & ENSURE HAPPINESS

THE NOVELTY SYNDICATE, R.E. HOUSE Tel.: "DUMP"

THE "NEW CHURCH" TIMES.

WITH WHICH IS INCORPOPATED

THE WIPERS TIMES

No 2. Vol 1. Monday, 1st May, 1916. Price 10 Francs.

EDITORIAL.

Oh, Belgium ! Here in the last number we spread ourselves on themes of lovely Spring, and you, with the basest ingratitude, have turned the whole thing into a wash-out. Well ! A trench without three feet of mud wouldn't seem homely anyway so perhaps you are right. This is our grand double Easter number (although the baker forgot to leave the hot-cross buns at the door) and the price is consequently doubled. We hope shortly to be able to announce the result of our "last line" Competition, but as our judging staff is at present in bed with a bad cold, caught while swimming back from the trenches the other night, all the correspondence is accumulating and the heterogeneous mass is awaiting his perusal. The sad and touching picture of a General awaiting the arrival of a D.R L S. announcing that he has won one of our mammoth prizes haunts us. However, there need be no anxiety, every effort will receive consideration in due time, and the prizes will go to the proper quarter. We are very glad to see that street noises are not so prevalent in our new neighbourhood, but even here there is room for improvement. We regret to state that we have been involved in a libel action over a little controversy in our columns re the premature appearance of an infernal member of the feathered tribe. This has caused us much inconvenience, but in order to exonerate ourselves in the matter we publish a resumé of the proceedings showing clearly the doubtful character of the petitioner and his associates. From the resume it can clearly be gathered that he is actuated by purely sordid financial motives, and undoubtedly, that he gained 500fr. will far outweigh the fact, that in so doing, he ventilated a mode of living which is as questionable as it is precarious. However, these petty nuisances happen to all papers sometime or other. We have hopes of obtaining an article from the pen of Mr. Belary Helloc on "How to win the war," but this may not arrive in time for this issue. We should welcome correspondence from readers with reference to the promotion of inter-divisional sports, etc., especially with regard to cricket. We are looking forward with pleasurable anticipation to a fine Bank Holiday, and expect to see a big throng of pleasure seekers. The rush to the sea should beat all records, and big crowds are prepared for at the international show at Verdun. Wishing you all a pleasant holiday.

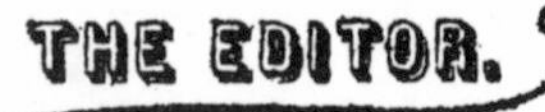

MINOR WORRIES.

If the Hun lets off some gas—
Never mind.
If the Hun attacks in mass—
Never mind.
If your dug-out's blown to bits,
Or the C.O.'s throwing fits,
Or a crump your rum jar hits—
Never mind.

—:o:—

If your trench is mud knee-high—
Never mind.
You can't find a spot that's dry—
Never mind.
If a sniper has you set,
Through dents in your parapet,
And your troubles fiercer get—
Never mind.

If you're whizzbanged day and night—
Never mind.
Bully all you get to bite—
Never mind.
If you're on a working party,
Let your grin be wide and hearty,
Though the sappers may be tarty—
Never mind.

—:o:—

If machine guns join the muddle—
Never mind.
Though you're lying in a puddle—
Never mind.
If a duckboard barks your shin,
And the barbed wire rips your skin,
'Tis reward for all your sin—
So never mind.

—:o:—

But this warning I'd attest—
Have a care.
When your Div. is back at rest—
Then beware.
When that long three months is over,
And you've lost your canteen cover,
Shoot yourself or find another—
Have it there!

—:o:—

Have you all your drill forgotten?—
Luckless wight.
Through those months so rain besotten—
Day and night.
On the left you'll form platoon,
Willy nilly, six till noon,
Front line trench will seem a boon—
Drill's a rite.

—:o:—

Oh! you poor unhappy thing—
Be not sad.
Just remember when all's wrong—
And you're mad.
Though your worries may be great,
They're but part, at any rate,
Of old Fritz's awful fate—
Buck up, lad!

HOW TO WIN THE WAR.

By BELARY HELLOC.

HAVING very little time at my disposal this week I only intend to roughly outline my plan for ending the war satisfactorily and quickly. Briefly then to do this we must reduce the war to a man to man encounter. Take things like this. The line held on all fronts is 1,500 miles (circa). That is 2,640,000 yards. Now we must get that number of our troops and allot one yard per man. Give each man a bomb, and at a given signal let them all go over and each to account for his own particular opponent. This would account for 2,000,000 of the enemy (that is giving the generous allowance of 640,000 failures), besides putting him to much inconvenience. Each time the enemy brings up reinforcements and re-establishes his line then repeat the performance. I think I may safely say that, after the tenth or eleventh attack, the enemy would be ready to consider the advisability of making terms rather than continue the war. This is merely a rough outline of my plans, and superficially it may seem that there are objections. However, I think these may well be dealt with as they arise.

BELARY HELLOC.

People We Take Our Hats off To.

—:o:—

Mr. Asquith, for at last making up his mind.

Answers

to Correspondents.

—:o:—

COLONEL.—We are surprised that you should have sent such a story to an earnest periodical like this.

LOVER OF NATURE.—We've had just about enough of you and your birds. The mere fact that you've found a cuckoo's nest with three eggs leaves us cold. If it costs us 500 francs just because you heard a gas-horn and mistook it for the cuckoo, we shudder to think what might happen if we don't nip your natural history nosings in the bud.

SUBALTERN.—Yes, every junior officer may carry a F.M.'s baton in his knapsack, but we think you'll discard that to make room for an extra pair of socks before very long.

KNOWLEDGE.—No, Ypres is not pronounced "Wipers" because it was once the centre of the handkerchief industry.

STAFF-OFFICER.—We sympathise with you in your little trouble, and advise you to write to "Cynthia," our 'love-expert, about it.

ANXIOUS ONE.—No, its no good worrying us. The judge will go through all answers in good time, and the prizes will go to their proper destination. We also regret to say you put ten answers on one coupon, and it's either another nine francs or nothing doing.

THE EDITOR much regrets the delay in the production of this number, but the cognocenti will excuse the tardiness on account of disturbed nights, etc.

OUR NEW SERIAL.

—o—o—o—

HERLOCK SHOLMES AT IT AGAIN.

—o—o—o—

SHOT IN THE CULVERT.

—o—o—o—

FINAL INSTALMENT.

—o—o—o—

Characters :—Same as before.

—o—o—o—

CHAPTER 6.

—o—

Sholmes and Co having arrived at their new sphere of action speedily got going again. Intha Pink seized his hammer and nail and fell off the bus when near Hyde Park Corner. Meanwhile Hotsam had disappeared into the darkness, on a mysterious errand, taking the fair Honoria with him. Lizzie, as she saw his stalwart form disappearing from her sight, cried "Do not leave me Herbert," but a curse was her only answer. In despair she threw herself in the way of a passing whizz-bang and disappeared from our tale. Intha crept rapidly towards his objective, and had almost succeeded in attaining his end, when a machine gun spat in his direction. Completely perforated; yet he smiled happily, and murmured "It's a blightie." Here we leave him, and turn to a series of eventful happenings on the banks of the Douve Hotsam, still dragging Honoria and perspiring freely, had managed to reach the lifeless form of Bill Banks, when a 17in. shell detonated between them. Hissing out "We are discovered" he hurriedly grabbed Honoria and made off. But not far. Alas! His foot slipped, and with his burden he fell into the turbid waters below. The waters flowed on. Sholmes, appearing on the scene some hours after, rapidly began looking for clues. Having found some, the great detective started off, but too late, the gas was on him, and he had left his vermoral sprayer in the bus. And so ends this remarkable history of persistence and sagacity. The great enemy of the criminal is now only a name, but his methods must always remain one of the marvels of the criminal history of our nation.

THE END.

[N.B.—Should there be a few characters not dealt with in this Chapter the reader must understand that they all met their deaths in the liquid fire attack.—THE AUTHOR.]

Hoof Beats.

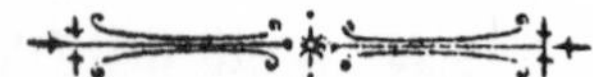

Maconochie! Maconochie!
Bully beef and biscuits!
Hullo, damn it! that's a crump,
How those bangs give me the hump;
Here's another! Where's she dropping?
Duck! or pieces you'll be stopping!
Plum and apple! beef and biscuit,
Well, here goes, I'd better risk it;
Just round here, there is no telling
When the Hun begins his shelling
How good my dug-out seems to me
Maconochie! Maconochie!

A BRACE OF GROUSE.

Two papers on a single day
Have roused my spirit to the fray.
Muse mine, my double-barrelled gun!
And let us strafe them, either one.

THE LEFT BARREL.

[Reference :- New Church Times.
No. 1, Vol 1.]

—0—0—0—

When I was yet a long-haired child,
I always wanted to be wild;
And when I came to man's estate
Assidously did cultivate,
With every effort I could make
The reputation of a rake.
With that in view, I drank, I swore,
I hung about the darkling door
Whence issued to their waiting lords
The beauties of the British boards;
I gambled maximums on Zero,
Was blackballed at the Trocadero;
I wore the greenest Trilby hats,
And hushed loud socks with louder spats:—
Till girls from Camberwell to Kut
Declared me a most wicked nut . . .
Alas! my pride is brought to shame,
My Editor decrees me "tame."
"Tame poet"? ? I! who was by far
The fastest at the Empire Bar,
Who drank my whisky and my Schweppe
From Monte Carlo to Dieppe;
And did most passionately squeeze
Flappers I met at Tango-teas;
And treated Connie Ediss twice
To wafers and vanilla ice!
Thou! editor who loathest rhymes,
Thou! printer of the "New Church Times,"
Take back your words that bite like flame!
"Poet"—perhaps: but never "tame"!

THE RIGHT BARREL.

[Reference, Tatler, April 26th,
P. 110,.]

—0—0—0—

Where pictured beauties fan desire,
And "Eve"'s' a weekly prattler
One draws us "Pictures in the Fire"
Well paid-for by "The Tatler":
But with a club We fain would bash
Your well-groomed head, my "Sabretache."

—:0:—

For you have given—and survive!—
And I who write have read it,
In number Seven, Seven, Five,
To other men the credit
For all the ads, the prose, the rhymes
We printed in "The Wipers Times."

—:0:—

We do not mind your words of praise,
We'll let you call us witty;
(Reviews are scarce these warlike days,
As paper in your City)
But what, to us, is praise you give
To soldiers of another "Div."?

—:0:—

Learn please—and for the future steer
Your course with more precision—
That we who write these words of cheer
Are not the "6th Division."
We would not hitch Apollo's Car
To anything so regular!

—:0:—

We are—but no, We may not state
For any linotypers,
Whose presses held the Menin Gate
Against the Bosche at Wipers.
Yet, "Sabretache," if you are wise,
Quadruply you'll apologize.

GILBERT FRANKAU.
6/5/16.

"ONE WHO KNOWS" v. WIPERS TIMES."

Proceedings in this case were opened at the Courts of Justice, Wipers, on April 20th in the hearing of Mr. Justice Starling. A large crowd was present in court as the case had aroused considerable interest, the Press and naturalists were notably represented.

Counsel for plaintiff—Mr. Cockles Tumley—opened proceedings with a stirring address roundly denouncing the "Wipers Times" for the letter published in their number of March 6th over the nom-de-plume of "A Lover of Nature." This letter he affirmed was untrue and libellous in the extreme, and he thought that this paper exceeded journalistic freedom to an almost criminal extent, and that it ought to be stopped. He finished his address thus:—"The passage chiefly taken exception to reads as follows: 'I am surprised that the editor of a paper with the circulation you boast should have found room for such a scurrilous, lying effusion The ignorance of the person is visible in every sentence.' This extract undoubtedly throws extreme doubt in the public mind as to the general veracity and knowledge of one of our foremost citizens, and I think I am extremely moderate in asking damages to be assessed at only one million francs.

Mr. Tumley then called various witnesses to prove his client's good standing and social position, and finally the plaintiff himself walked boldly into the box, and took the oath with the utmost assurance and "sang froid."

After putting a few minor qnestions Mr Tumley sat down, and Mr. Maurice Aviary—counsel for the defence—rose and hurled a bombshell into the court by asking the plaintiff if he wasn't a leader of one of the bloodthirsty gangs of desperadoes who nightly render Hooge and district "unsafe."

Plaintiff:—It is true that I've been seen in the district in company with other good citizens, though I can't admit of anything but a law-abiding behaviour on my part.

Counsel:—Have you ever entered those well-known dens of vice "The Culvert Dug-out," "Half Way House" or "Railway Wood Dug-out"?

Plaintiff:—I have, but I disagree with you as to the real nature of these places.

Counsel:—Are you a member of the New Night Club adjoining the "Hotel des Ramparts"?

Plaintiff:—I am, but you are again entirely wrong in your insinuations.

Counsel:—Is it not true that you are in great financial difficulties at present? Now be careful how you answer.

Plaintiff.—I am.

Counsel.—Are you not only bringing this case to see what you can get out of the "Wipers Times"?

Plaintiff:—I am bringing this case to try and clear my good name.

The plaintiff then stood down looking rather less confident of the issue than previously, and Mr Maurice Aviary addressed the jury in his well-known style and love for dramatic effect, concluding with the following words, "I have clearly proved that plaintiff lives by his wits, and consorts with the most doubtful characters, I appeal to you to exonerate my clients, and bring your verdict in accordingly.

After some deliberation, however, the judge eventually said that, although plaintiff was not a man of any great virtues, he thought the paper was wrong in printing the letter, and damages were assessed at 500 francs with costs.

WHAT A HOPE!

The Editor has ordered me
To write a batch of rhymes
To finish off this number of
His bally "New Church Times."

—:o:—

The Editor's a mighty man
His will it must be done,
I'd like to know if he can make
The clock strike less than one

Some Poet.

SPRING-TIME 

 THOUGHTS.

Thank Heaven we are running out of winter and into spring. "Oh, to be in Flanders now that April's there!" Now that summer has begun to arrive naturally everyone is asking "What is going to happen?" and the air is full of rumours. Is it as impossible for us to go through as it was for the Germans at Verdun? The differences are distinct contrasts. On the one hand—perfect organisation, but indifferent fighting material. On the other—indifferent organisation, with perfect fighting material. The German is temperamentally a poor uphill fighter, and once his organisation is upset he will crumble. Obviously then the thing is to upset his organisation. The easiest way to do this is to suddenly make him reverse his plan of campaign, and attack him where his organisation is prepared only for attack. The point lying ready to hand for this is obviously Verdun, and, by sudden concentration there, one might achieve an overwhelming success at much less cost than will an organised and obvious push at a place prepared and ready for defence. Neuve Chapelle and Loos show us the cost of breaking through prepared ground, and the result is infinitesmal gain. Possibly the loss would be as large at Verdun, though a well calculated attack there could not easily be more unsuccessful than the two already mentioned. Also it would have the advantages of surprise and of forcing a sudden complete reversal of positions, a state of affairs which might easily prove too difficult for even the German organisation. True, the German artillery is there ready, but so it will be at any front elsewhere. Already the seeds of failure are sown in the German troops there, and it would be easier to turn this into an absolute demoralisation than to butt up against a new army on a new ground.

AMATEUR.

Things We Want to Know.

—:o:—

Who it is that makes an infernal din on a horn at 2 a.m.

? ? ?

Whether it is a fact that the amorous incarnadined major has again succumbed.

? ? ?

Whether the popular Artillery C O. helped the Belgian priest in his little trouble

? ? ?

Whether it is a fact that a noticeboard at the foot of Kemmel Hill reads.—' Anyone proceeding up the Hill will please go by main road, as a patrol is established there to enforce the stringent regulations re passes, etc. Persons going by other routes might miss patrol."

? ? ?

The name of the firm of estate agents which is trying to let Red Lodge.

? ? ?

How the poplars are coming up.

Ne'er be peaceful, quiet, or pensive,
"Do your best to be offensive,"
His success shall greatest be,
Who regards this homily.
In the future day and night be
"As offensive as you might be."

Correspondence.

To the Editor,
"New Church" Times.

Sir,

A correspondent in your last issue made a quotation from the writings of Call Haine The following quotation from the works of that famous author Carle Morelli seems to bear on the subject, viz:—

God made the horse.
The mule and eke the ass;
R.E.'s do all the work
And Pioneers the gas.

Yours, etc.,
JUSTISSIMUS.

—§ ‡ §—

To the Editor,
"New Church" Times.

Sir,

There have been several references lately regarding a certain C.O.'s whisky. I recall the last words of the correspondence re the cuckoo, and all I wish to say is:—Dam(n) not the C O's whisky.

A LOVER OF SPIRIT.

Situations Vacant.

WANTED, few WIRE-CUTTERS, good openings for sharp young men.—Apply Box 203, No Man's Land.

WANTED at once, PLATOON COMMANDER. Applicant must be offensive, and preference will be given to originality of ideas in this direction —Apply c/o this paper

WANTED, CHAUFFEURS for the Base. Must be young and active, and able to endure all the hardships attendant on base life. Good salaries given to the right men.—Apply "Adventure," Boulogne.

WANTED, good strong man as DOOR-KEEPER, Neuve Eglise Hippodrome. Ex-pugilist preferred.—Apply Stoss and Mohl, c/o this paper.

IF YOU want ANYTHING, advertise in these Columns. You're sure to get it.

"ESPRIT DE CORPS."

WE HAVE been asked by several members of the Division to mention in our columns the great advantages which would accrue if the integral units of the Division came in frequent contact with each other. Naturally one's thoughts immediately turn to inter-unit sport of various kinds. Though the Division may be separately all that can be desired, yet perhaps it would be of immense advantage if units knew each other better. There are, and will be, many opportunities for units to meet in friendly rivalry, and we all know by this time that this would meet with the approval of our G.O.C. Not only will it give us greater confidence in each other in circumstances which will most certainly arrive one day, but it would make the work much smoother if one were doing a job with cricket friends rather than chance acquaintances. The whole thing only needs such a small effort of organisation that surely it is worth while, and the friendly rivalry of a cricket field will be found to react in a thousand little ways some other day.

If you're waking call me early, call me early, sergeant dear.
For I'm very, very weary, and my warrant's come, I hear;
Oh! it's "blightie" for a spell, and all my troubles are behind,
And I've seven days before me
(Hope the sea will not be stormy)
Keep the war a'going, sergeant,
Train's at six, just bear in mind!

POILE & TROTTER,

STATIONERS AND POULTRY DEALERS,

—o—o—o—

ALL GOODS SUPPLIED HALF-PRICE TO THE TRADE.

—o—o—o—

CIRCULARS PRINTED

SEND FOR OUR ILLUSTRATED BOOKLET.

—o—o—o—

ARE YOU INTENDING TO TRAVEL?

If so send for one of our Yellow Coupons which will take you anywhere.

—o—o—o—

"If you're tired and need a rest,
Buy our ticket 'tis the best."

—o—o—o—

TELEGRAMS: "KEW."

THE ABSOLUTE INVENTORS OF THE LATEST ODDS TELEGRAM.

—o—o—o—

THE OLD FIRM.
THE OLD FIRM.
THE OLD FIRM.

NUNTHORPE, COX & CO.

—o—o—o—

This Eminent Firm of Commission Agents has once more moved into better and more

COMMODIOUS PREMISES.

And are still doing BUSINESS on their old lines.

—o—o—o—

"In one place we seldom stay."
But you'll find we always pay."

HOWFIELD & CAULETT

The Up-to-date Tailors.

AGENTS FOR POND & CO.

—o—o—o—

Come and see our

SUMMER SUITINGS.

—o—o—o—

"Be as like us as you can,
Clothes do make the gentleman."

—o—o—o—

Prices Moderate.

—o—o—o—

TELEGRAMS: "KNUTTS"

THE "MUNQUE" ART GALLERY.

—o—o—o—

ANY TUBE OR TRAIN TO HYDE PARK CORNER. THENCE BY BUS TO RED LODGE.

—o—o—o—

SPRING EXHIBITION.

—o—o—o—

Open Dayand Night.

—o—o—o—

"Crumps may come and crumps may go,
But do not miss this wondrous show."

—o—o—o—

TELEGRAMS: "R. O. JERUM"

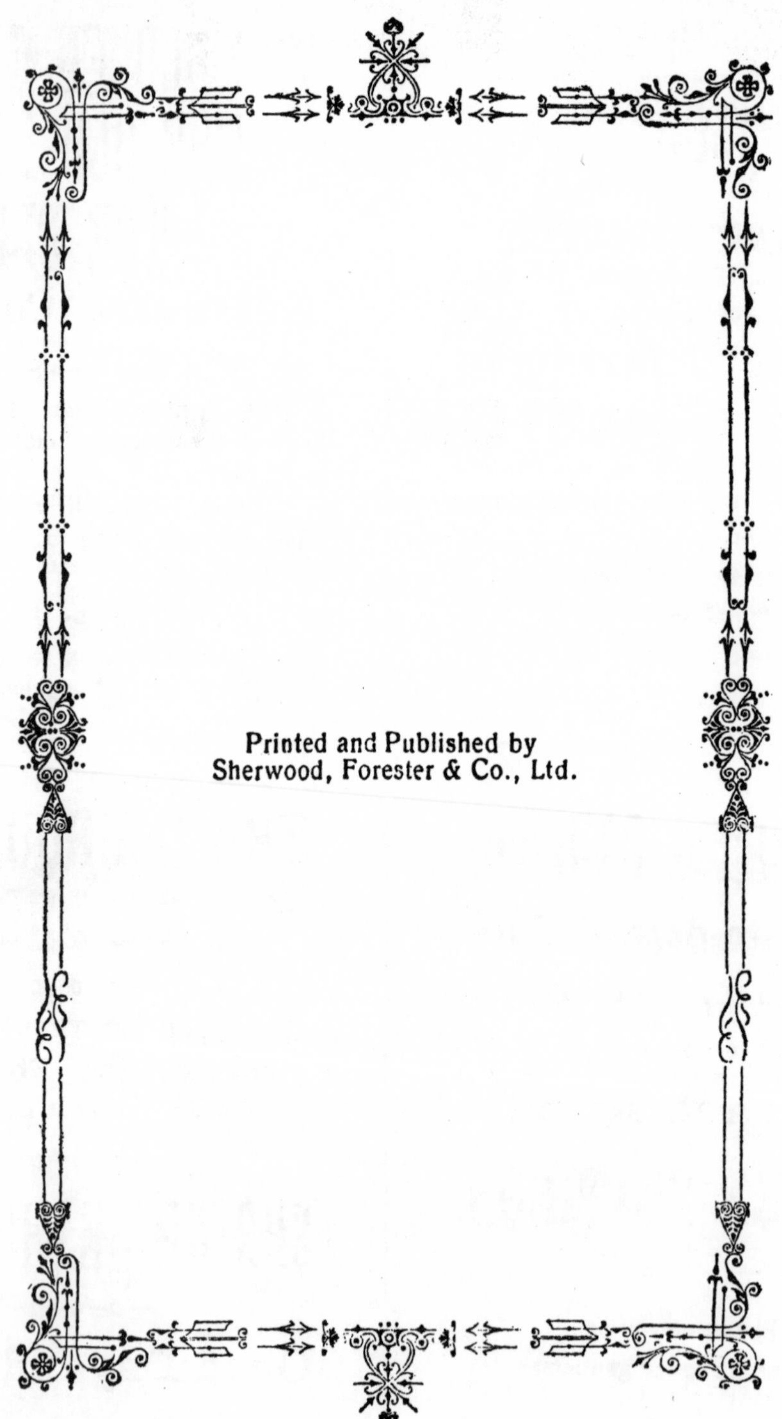

Printed and Published by
Sherwood, Forester & Co., Ltd.

THE "NEW CHURCH" TIMES.

WITH WHICH IS INCORPORATED

THE WIPERS TIMES

No 3. Vol 1. Monday 22nd May, 1916. Price 1 Franc.

Professor Dodgits Academy.

YOU SURELY CANNOT PUT UP WITH THE OLD FASHIONED SLEEPY DANCES?
NO! THEN

MOVE WITH THE TIMES AND JOIN OUR CLASS.

WE GUARANTEE TO TEACH YOU ALL THE NEWEST STEPS IN SIX LESSONS. THESE INCLUDE:

"THE DUCK-BOARD DANGLE,"
"MACHINE GUN SLITHER,"
"WHIZZ-BANG HOP" AND THE
"CRUMP CRAWL," ETC., ETC.

—o—o—o—o—

COURSES ARE CONTINUOUS DAY AND NIGHT.

PARTIES OF 100 OR MORE SPECIALLY CATERED FOR.

—o—o—o—o—

FINEST ORCHESTRA ENGAGED, PERSONALLY CONDUCTED BY

O. B. SERVER.

—o—o—o—o—

"Come and learn to skip and hop,
Ere you venture o'er the top."

—o—o—o—o—

NEUVE EGLISE HIPPODROME

THIS WEEK—AT 6.3o & 8,

CHARLIE TAPLIN

In That Stirring Drama, Entitled:

THE RUSTY DUD

OR

ALL IS NOT DEAD THAT'S DIRTY.

THE GREAT ADVANCE

Featuring Hinden Berg The Bowery Boy.

THIS FILM IS 1,000,000 FEET LONG.

—o—o—o—o—

Harvesting At Hooge.

A PICTURE OF LOCAL INTEREST.

ETC., ETC., ETC. PRICES AS USUAL.

DON'T FORGET WEDNESDAY, MAY 24th.

IS THE

THE "NEW CHURCH" TIMES FLAG DAY:

—o—o—o—o—

PROCEEDS OF SAME TO BE DEVOTED TO THE FUND FOR PROVIDING

WARM WOOLLENS FOR WAR-WORN WALLOONS.

NO ONE SHOULD BE SEEN ON WEDNESDAY, NEXT NOT WFARING A FLAG, AS THIS IS A MOST DESERVING CAUSE. THE FOLLOWING WELL-KNOWN LOCAL LADIES HAVE CONSENTED TO ACT AS STREETVENDORS;

Lady ETHEL FIVEAYE. Countess of Poperinghe; Baroness BERTHA, of Berloo; Mrs. Wm. WIGGINS, of Wulverghem; Lady WALTER WHIZZ-BANGE, of Whytchate, and many others too numerous and costly to mention.

—o—o—o—o—

WE ARE ALSO SELLING

MEDALS AS A SUBSIDIARY LINE

—o—o—o—o—

FOR FURTHER INFORMATION SEE SMALL BILLS.

THE

"NEW CHURCH" TIMES.

WITH WHICH IS INCORPOPATED

THE WIPERS TIMES

No 3. Vol 1. Monday, 22nd May, 1916. Price 1 Franc.

EDITORIAL.

AS OUR journal seems to have met with some measure of success, we have pleasure in announcing that the circulation will be increased to 250 copies, commencing with this number. The price will be standard at 1 Fr., which will go towards the purchase of paper, etc., as we are now coming to the end of the supply so kindly left us by some citizen of Wipers who stood not on the order of his going, but got. Any balance over after incidental expenses will go as usual to charity. We regret to say that the district is waning in popularity as a health resort, and several noted citizens have lately been seen "legging it" for pastures new, with a few goods and chattels and some family in tow. We are glad to see that the City Fathers of Wulverghem are going to introduce the Day-light Saving Bill, as this will mean that some soldiers, who are in the district, will be able to go to bed earlier. It really is a great blessing, and will enable all of us who are lovers of nature to take our early morning ramble an hour earlier, thus catching the lark at its best. We are pleased to be able to give the resuit of our "Last Line" Competition on Page 8. The regrettable efforts made by the competitors have again prostrated the judge, who, I regret to state, is suffering from nervous breakdown as a consequence. Can nothing be done to break the painful monotony of our gas-horns? Surely they might be fitted with some musical apparatus, and so play say "Excelsior" while arousing the slumbering inmates of Batt. H.Q. Now that summer is coming, we are considering the matter of our Annual Fly Competition. There will be the usual mammoth prizes, but no fly papers will be allowed. Each animal must be fairly shot or bayonetted. Bombing will be allowed, but any gunner found sniping flies with anything larger than an 18-pounder will be disqualified. We will announce in a later issue when the competition will commence, and trust to the honour of all not to start before the flag falls. We hear that the "Douve" mixed bathing season has commenced, and that popular little sea-side resort "Le Rossignol" ought to be crowded during the summer months. We must express the hope that we still have the support of the Division in our more ambitious scheme re circulation, and must thank one and all for the apprecia-tion shown to our previous efforts.

—:o:—

We have pleasure in announcing that the special warrants issued to the party proceeding to London to assassinate "Sabretache" of the "Tatler" have been cancelled. The individual members of the party are very disappointed as it meant an extra spell of leave, but that cannot be helped. "Sabretache" apologises most handsomely for his mistake, and explains it in a reasonable manner. So we must ask readers to send no more letters containing suggestions as to the surest and quickest way of killing him.

Thanks "Sabretache" you are forgiven,
And should we ever get a-
Nother effort from your pen,
We pray you TYPE YOUR LETTER.

There's a line that runs from Nieuport down into Alsace Lorraine,
Its twists and turns are many, and each means a loss or gain;
Every yard can tell a story, every foot can claim its fee,
There the line will stay for ever from Lorraine up to the sea.

Places memorised by symbol, little things that caught the mind,
As at Loos 'twas but a lone tree which in mem'ry is enshrined;
Perhaps at Wipers 'twas a corner, shell bespattered, held our sight,
Or a nightingale at Plug Street, sending music through the night.

Little things, yet each implanted when the nerves are tension high,
And in years to come remembered how, while gazing, death passed by;
So the line for all has sign posts, and a dug-out oft can hold
Little memories to haunt one as the future years unfold.

Though this line will be behind us as we push on to the Spree,
Yet to all it will be sacred, mud-encased though it may be;
In the future dim and distant they will tell the tale again—
The ghosts of those who held the line from Nieuport to Lorraine.

QUESTIONS A PLATOON COMMANDER SHOULD ASK HIMSELF.

ENGRAVED BY SAPPER COUZENS R.E.

1: Am I as offensive as I might be.

Hauptmann Van Horner,
In trench traverse corner,
Once heard what he thought
was a "goer";
But he was mistaken
Said Fritz Carl Von Haken,
"I'll write to his widow, I know
her."

CUPID'S CORNER.
By "CYNTHIA."

AS THE Editor has been so troubled with correspondence from lovelorn members of the Division, and feels that he is not qualified to deal with this section of his readers, he has deputed me to deal with them, and I shall be pleased to give advice in all little difficulties relating to "affaires de cœur."

—o—o—o—

ANSWERS TO CORRESPONDENTS.

—:o:—

TROUBLED.—Your letter is rather obscure. Am I to understand that you have actually proposed, or that you are merely waiting an opportunity. As you appear to be in a position to marry, I think it is your clear duty to do so at once. Remember no girl of spirit likes to be played with.

RED TAB.—Thanks for the enclosed photo. You appear to be a very nice-looking boy. I am sorry to disappoint you, but if the young lady whom you call Tina has already refused the attentions of two generals, then do you not think it would be better to dismiss her from your thoughts. It may hurt now, but will soon be over.

CLARA.—Yes, I think the major treated you very badly indeed. But do not worry, forget him, and anyway he is only a major.

GINGER.—I am surprised that you should address such a letter to a lady! You ought to write and beg her forgiveness at once. But please let me know what she answers.

CYNTHIA,
THE "LOVE EXPERT."

OUR SPLENDID NEW SERIAL.

—o—o—o—

FROM BUGLER BOY TO BRIGADIER.

OR

How Willie Pritchard Rose from the Ranks

—o—o—o—

A STORY OF THE GREAT WAR.

—o—o—o—

BY RUBY N. DARES.

—o—o—o—

CHAPTER 1.

—o—

WAR! The sleepy old town of Hampton was ringing with' the raucous cries of "special-! special!!" for it was a mild summer's evening in the fateful August of 1914. Tradesmen, workmen, artizans were all hurriedly purchasing papers—eagerly scanning the stop press news—the stop press news that sent England reeling under the shattering blow of Germany's perfidy. Groups of men eagerly discussing the news, stood at the street corners of the old town—children ran wildly about, for the moment forgotten by their parents too busily listening to the opinions of their menfolk, and now and then chipping shrilly into the conversation—then came the days of tragic silence—the retreat from Mons, and the urgent appeal for recruits . . . . .

Such were the early days of the great war in Hampton when Willie Pritchard, the son of honest parents, passed out of the Council School to take his place as salesman in the extensive and well-appointed grocery stores of Sir Jasper Jephcott, the squire of Hampton. When the appeal for King and Country went forth Willie Pritchard's heart was as lead, for had he not an aged mother depending on him for sustenance? How could he go?—how?—ah! that was the question. So Willie stayed on in the grocery store, and hid his aching heart beneath his linen apron. In this manner things went on until one day Sir Jasper suddenly coming from behind a Tate's cube box beheld our hero weeping piteously. "Come, come, William! what is the matter?"—said the kindly old squire, his own voice shaking with emotion—"Are you in any trouble, my lad. Speak! speak!! my little fellow, speak!!!" Dry sobs shook Willie's frame, and for a moment grief poignant and tempestuous held him in her terrible sway, then raising his tear-stained face from his hands he burst forth:—"SIR! SIR!!—I WOULD SERVE MY KING!!!"

(What did Sir Jasper say?—See our next instalment.)

TO MY UNTAMED POET.

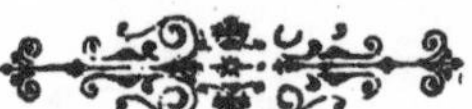

Oh, woe is me. Now, by desire
My head right in the dust I humble;
Bring sackcloth. ashes, coals of fire,
Pardon I crave that I did stumble.

—§ † §—

My pride has crumbled into naught,
Like any puff of wind it went,
(I still am half a column short,
Hence this apology's extent.)

—§ † §—

So pardon that I called thee "tame"
Who boasts a past so truly blue,
In next week's issue you may claim
The same old page—'tis kept for you.

[For explanation ask any "Intelligence" Officer.]

I had a vision yesternight;
The Great Advance was finished,
Right was triumphant over Might—
But both were much diminished:
Whence, after seven weary years
Of high forensic jaw,
Our House of Commons passed (with cheers),
"Marital Martial Law!"
Each man to have a minimum
Of five and twenty wives,
With power of adding to that sum,
And power o'er purse and lives;
Each paid and clothed, as soldiers are
By our ungrateful state . . . . . .
With penal clause of prison bar
For every celibate.

—§ † §—

Twas at St. Margaret's Westminster,
The witching hour of noon,
By warrant from Lord K—t—n—r
I married my platoon.
Willing recruits, though quite untrained,
They were—save twenty-three;
A widowette; and none complained
Of serving under me:
For though I played the martinet
In all things strictly martial,
None had MARITAL cause to fret
That I was not impartial.

—§ † §—

Lord, how we trained. By night and day
I spouted from the drill books;
Inspected kit, and doled out pay,
And entered up their bill-books.
For I had spent both time and tin
In days before "The War"
When I was but a private in
The "Husband's Training Corps";
And knew that neither love nor lust
Nor lucre's anodyne,
Saves breakage of the marriage-crust . . .
But only discipline.

—§ † §—

And then, my orders! "I shall dine
"At 8·15 pip emma
"With private Number Twenty-nine—
"Mess-butler, Sergeant Gemma.
"Glad-eye detachment will patrol
"The Empire, Tiv, and Palace—
"Full evening dress, with camisole,
"Under Lance Corporal Alice.
"Reveillé—half past ten o'clock.
"Flappers report at three,
"Lecture on tactics, 'frock and shock,'
"And 'Early morning tea.'"

—§ † §—

Twas some platoon: in form and fire,
Accoutrements or spendings,
Not even Generals could aspire
To more superb week-endings
Than I: not e'en the brassiest hat
That ever strafed in trenches,
Could find a pin to cavil at
On my efficient wenches:
For every wish that I expressed
To Number Nine Platoon,
Was law: each passed her standard test
As "fit for honeymoon"
Ere we had been two months at drill:
I was a happy wight,
And served my country with a will
By day and eke by night,
Until . . . . .
my Colonel's furious tones
Upon my dreaming broke,
And, terror in my marrow bones,
To duty, I awoke!

GILBERT FRANKAU.

12/5/16.

THE DAILY ROUND, THE TRIVIAL TASK.

SCENE I.

—:o:—

COMPANY H.Q. IN FRONT LINE TRENCH.

—:o:—

. Company Commander and Lieutenant sipping rum and smoking: Enter Corporal announcing a General in the offing. "What General?" "Brigadier, sir!" "Which way is he coming?" "From Top end, sir!" "Most of the sentries awake?" "Yes, sir, word's been passed down." Captain gets us and makes his way up trench. Meets dapper Brigadier accompanied by C.O. and Brigade Major "Evening, Blearson, how are you?" "Top-hole sir, thanks!" "Your boys fit?" "Never been stronger, sir!". General to his Major aside "Is'nt that splendid, Bobbie." C.O. to Brigadier "Blearson's Coy. has done a lot of work here sir, three dug-outs and two traverses built, and the whole trench drained." Brig.-General to his Major "Is'nt that priceless Bobbie?" "It is, sir." Brig. gets into fire bay next to sentry and peers over no man's land. To sentry: "Seen anything my boy?" Sentry (knowing its the Brigadier but pretending not to recognise him in the dark) "'Oo the 'ell are you?" Brig. coughs slightly. Sentry, "Sorry sir didn't know it was you. C 4 trench number 6 post, wind safe all correct." "Capital"—Brig. gets down and goes along trench till he arrives at another sentry post. Sentry (promptly). "C 4 number 7 pos, wind safe all correct." "Splendid. Seen anything?" "Well, sir! I thought I saw sumthink move about 40 yards 'arf right, so I gives it two rounds, and as I thought I 'eard it groan I asks the sergeant to send up a light, and it was only a tree stump." Brig to his Major, "Isn't that priceless, Bobbie?" "It is, sir." C.O. aside to Capt., "Ask him into your dug-out, I think he'd like a drink." Capt. does so. "Oh thanks very much old man, but we mustn't stay long, must we, Bobbie?" "No, sir!". They all crowd into Coy. H.Q. and drink whisky and water out of mugs, and have a chin. Brig. about ten minutes later, "Well, come on Bobbie, we must go. Thanks very much Blearson, I'm awfully pleased with the work done, and also to find your stations so alert. Isn't it perfectly splendid, Bobbie?" It is, sir." Exeunt Brig., his Major, and the C.O.

—:o:—

SCENE II.

—:o:—

A MUDDY PARADE GROUND IN DIV. RESERVE.

—:o:—

Company formed up. Enter Capt. Coy. Serg.-Major "Company, Company 'shun." Turns and salutes. Capt. "All right Sergt.-Major stand 'em at ease!" "Stannat ease." Capt. produces copy of Batt. orders and reads as follows:—"The Commanding Officer has pleasure in publishing the following letter for information of all ranks—"To O.C. Umpshires. The Brig. General Commanding desires me to say that he is very pleased with the work done by the Batt. during their last turn of duty. He also wishes me to say that he was much struck by the alertness of the sentries,"—Signed,

Robert Commentlouer, Major,
Umpieth I.B.

Companys' chests swell two inches "The C.O. has informed me that most o that letter may be specially taken to refer to the Company" (Companys' jackets feeling the strain) "I'll pay the Company at 2.30 p.m. Company! Company, 'shun! Slope hup! Dis-miss!" Turns to Senior Sub. "They can be smart when they like, can't they, it's wonderful what a little praise can do when it comes from the right people." Exeunt omnes.—The war goes on.

ONE OF THE "P.B.I"

Bang away ye 18 pounders,
Shriek ye hows in joyful strain,
Till the air with din astounders,
Leave is once more on again.

Correspondence.

To the Editor,
"New Church" Times.

Sir,

Again I must complain through your columns of the irritating increase in street cries. Now that the Daylight Saving Bill is in force surely these petty nuisances might be curtailed, and if we MUST have the morning paper and milk surely these might be left in silence at the dug-out door. Can nothing be done?

I am, Sir, Yours, etc.,
NEUROTIC.

—§ † §—

To the Editor,
"New Church" Times.

Sir,

Several noted farmers have complained of wanton injury done to their fields. They cannot catch the offenders, and the irritating frequency with which they find neat round holes dug in their fields has led them to prepare a strongly worded protest. They are supported by the Mayor of Wulverghem, and wish me to ask you if they may also rely on you.

Yours, etc.,
RIGHT IS MIGHT

—§ † §—

To the Editor,
"New Church" Times.

Sir,

As an ardent admirer of our ancient churches, I feel constrained to draw your attention to the terrible state of the church tower of "Neuve Eglise." The tower has—as any of our eminent archælogists will know—leant 3° 4' 16" to the west for many years. Taking my Theodilite (Mark I., No. 5/64) up the other day, I was astonished to find that this divergence has increased by 1° 6' 18". Can nothing be done?

I am, Sir, etc.,
CHOIR-BOY.

—§ † §—

To the Editor.
"New Church" Times.

Sir,

I notice that the "NEW CHURCH" TIMES Flag Day falls on Wed., May 24th. This is most inconvenient, clashing as it does with a meat tea and social, given on that date by the Society to which I have the honour of being Secretary. Surely we can come to a mutual agreement in this matter.

I am most respectfully yours,
JOHN TARBOTTOM,
Sec. of Society for Providing
Blue Body Belts for
Bucolic Belgians,
Le Rossignol.

—§ † §—

To the Editor,
"New Church" Times.

Sir,

I shall be much obliged if your legal adviser can give me some advice in the following difficulty. On the 29th of last month I wished to have a small bet on "Chlorine" in the 12.45 race at Wulverghem the following day. I accordingly rang up Messrs. Nunthorpe, Cox and Co., whose advertisements I had seen in your excellent periodical. I asked to speak to one of the partners, and shortly after a tremendous bellow was emitted from the telephone receiver which rendered me completely deaf in my left ear. However, I stated clearly that I wished to have one franc on "Chlorine" for a place. In my anxiety to hear if my message had been correctly received, I asked Messrs. Nunthorpe, Cox and Co. to repeat the message, at the same time putting the receiver to my right ear. Immediately the same sound as before came from the instrument, breaking the drum of my ear. As you know "Chlorine" was an easy winner in the race, but when I asked Messrs. Nunthorpe, Cox and Co. to pay up they maintained that I had backed "Bosche," who was a non-starter. Now, Sir, have I any legal claim on the firm for payment of my bet, and can I claim damages against them for the complete loss of my hearing? In any case I think that your readers should be warned against the specious advertisements of this rather shady firm.

Yours, etc.,
ROOKED.

F

RESULT OF OUR GREAT COMPETITION.

We have great pleasure this week in announcing the result of our "Last Line" Competition, which our readers will remember was started in the 1st number of the "NEW CHURCH" TIMES. The work of selection has been an arduous one, and we can hardly congratulate the various competitors on their efforts; however we have pleasure in announcing that the First Mammoth Prize of 5,000,000 Francs has been won by the Editor of this periodical with the following poetical effort, and in case you forget the first four lines we reprint the whole :—

There was a young general of forty
A year at the front made him sporty,
To say it I grieve
When he went on leave
THEY WOULDN'T BELIEVE HE WAS FORTY.

The Second Prize of 2,500,000 Francs goes to the Sub-editor for the following clever line. —

A DRINK FOR HIMSELF OFTEN BOUGHT HE.

The Third and other prizes have been returned to our Prize Fund, as we are afraid that not one of the other efforts sent in is worthy of consideration, and some of them are not even of the type that a paper of this description could print. We hope to announce another and larger competition in due course.

Now tell me Major if they're true
These cheerful things I hear of you,
Of how a maiden coyly wrote
And with this question closed her note :—
" If you're lonely and despond
Let us often correspond.
Shall we ? "

Things We Want to Know.

—:o:—

How much money changed hands when it was known that he didn't get married on leave.

? ? ?

What the anxious scarlet one answered to the little French charmer who wrote " Let us write to each other often. Shall we ?"

? ? ?

Whether any division has been offered to the " great ones " to retake Lille, Brussels, or Antwerp,

? ? ?

Who is the genius who worked out the scale of issue in A 1861/1 of 30-4-16, and how long he took to experiment before finding out exact numbers.

? ? ?

Whether the air in a certain Brig. H.Q is not becoming a bit too sultry, and if this is because of the patterns on the wall paper.

? ? ?

If Red Lodge is the health resort it looks.

WANTED

GOOD GARDENER, must be able to drive motor car, clean boots, look after baby (male), tune piano and extract teeth. Trade Union men need not apply. —Ref. Box 111, N.C. TIMES.

YOUNG MEN for giving out Hand Bills in the Messines district Must know the country well. Chance of a rise.—Write Box 80, Advt. Dept.

AGENTS for " Morning Hate " Toilet Soap. Good commision. Excellent opening for an industrious young man.— Write Box 505, c/o this paper.

WE ARE THE PEOPLE.

YOU WANT IT!! WE'VE GOT IT!!!

THEN COME TO US

DOPE AND CURRIE

Livery and Bait Stables. Registry Offices.

—o—o—o—o—

LESSONS IN DEPORTMENT, Etc., Etc.

—o—o—o—o—

Did I hear you say you wanted a Domestic Servant?

SPLENDID! THEN STEP THIS WAY.

And what for you, Sir—A Charger?

YOU'RE IN LUCK'S WAY---WE'VE THE VERY THING.

—o—o—o—o—

ROLL UP! ROLL UP!! ROLL UP!!!

TELEGRAMS: "VATICAN," BAILLEUL.

TOWN HALL, PLUG ST.

—o—o—o—

Special Visit Of The

WELL KNOWN LADY LECTURER,

MRS. INTHA PINK

(OF HOOGE). SUBJECT:

"Playing the Game In the West."

—o—o—o—

A Precis of the Lecture can be had at the door for the small charge of 2d.

—o—o—o—

ADMISSION BY PROGRAMME.

HALT! WHO GOES THERE?

WINDOW CLEANER!

Pass Window Cleaner—All's Well if you belong to the Wulverhgem & Messines Window Cleaning Company.

—o—o—o—

Now that the DAYLIGHT SAVING BILL has been passed you must make the most of your Windows! Comoris?

THEN GO TO THE WULVERGHEM AND MESSINES

WINDOW CLEANING CO.

o—o—o—

Ring up Wulverghem and Messines Window Cleaning Co., Messines, when an interesting little Booklet, entitled:

"Windows, Their Uses and Abuses."

—o—o—o—

TELEPHONE: 123.

TELEGRAMS: "SHATTERED," Messines.

Printed and Published by
Sherwood, Forester & Co., Ltd.

THE

"NEW CHURCH" TIMES.

WITH WHICH IS INCORPOPATED

THE WIPERS TIMES

No 4 Vol. 1. Monday. 29th May, 1916. PRICE 1 FRANC.

NEUVE EGLISE HIPPODROME.

This Week—Daily at 8.3o.

—o—o—o—o—

SPECIAL ENGAGEMENT FOR ONE WEEK ONLY OF

Willie Hozenzollerns No. 1 Company

In the New, Great and Stirring Drama—Entitled :

"BIG GUNS."

The entire original caste—Including that versatile and popular Artiste :

"HARRY HOWITSER AS THE HOUSEBREAKER."

" A thundering good show." ' A very moving little sketch."—Vide Press.

—o—o—o—o—

OTHER ITEMS.

TEWLIES TROUPE OF TRICK TRICYCLISTS.
MEALES MUSICAL MULES.
BEERSONS BEWILDERING BIRDS and

Prof. Windup the "Mystery Monger"

IN HIS FAMOUS SÉANCE

"WHERE DID THAT ONE GO?"

—o—o—o—o—

Moving Pictures Popular Prices

EXCURSIONS DAILY.

—o—o—o—o—

THE DRANOUTRE, WULVERGHEM AND DEAD COW HOTEL CHAR-A-BANC SYNDICATE.

—o—o—o—o—

THIS SYNDICATE HAS ACQUIRED A LARGE AND SPLENDIDLY EQUIPPED SERVICE
OF MOTOR AND G.S. CHAR-A-BANCS
AND WISH TO ANNOUNCE THAT THEIR TOURING SEASON IS IN FULL SWING.

—o—o—o—o—

Special trips will be arranged weekly to MESSINES, COMMINES and other places of local interest. The old church of Wulverghem is well worth a visit.

—o—o—o—o—

We also have a special Car running to PLUG STREET WOOD. This sylvan retreat is full of interest.

—o—o—o—o—

PRIVATE 'BUSES FOR HIRE.

—o—o—o—o—

TELEGRAMS: "CHAR A-BANC." ADDRESS: KEW.

SAPPER BROS LTD.

CONSULTING ENGINEERS.
LAND DECORATORS.
EXCAVATING CONTRACTORS.

Contracts Accepted In
France, Flanders and Gallipoli.

Buy One of our Up-to-date 17in Proof Funk-holes.

NOBODY SHOULD BE WITHOUT ONE.

—o—o—o—o—

TELEGRAMS: "UBIQUE." TELEPHONE: "102, VISITUS."

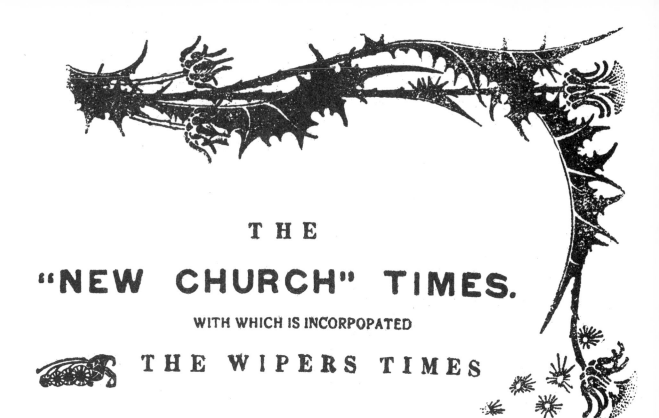

THE

"NEW CHURCH" TIMES.

WITH WHICH IS INCORPOPATED

THE WIPERS TIMES

No 4. Vol 1. Monday. 29th May, 1916. Price 1 Franc.

EDITORIAL.

SUMMER is really with us at last, and those dreary winter months now only a memory quickly melting in the sun. We are glad to be able to announce that the Division has responded splendidly to our appeal for copy, and in consequence we shall be able to publish much more regularly, provided, of course, that the supply continues. It is gratifying to see the whole hearted support given to this paper, and we should like to take this opportunity of thanking one and all. Also, it is good to see the spirit of cheeriness, unity and understanding which is pervading the whole Division, and which emanates from our G.O.C. and Brigadiers. Our mammoth Competitions are so popular that we must have some more of them as we still have some odd millions to give away. We hope our readers will like the splendid new serial. Each chapter is more enthralling than the last, and when Willie—but there we must keep quiet or we shall be forestalling the author. Our flag day was an enormous success, and our fair staff succeeded in forcing an entrance everywhere. Some of the well-known ladies who assisted are so enthusiastic that they want us to have a flag day regularly. We are considering the idea. Countess Fiveaye made as much as 500 francs for the fund, and the pretty picture presented by the Belle of Berloo getting five francs out of the elegant Staff Captain charmed all beholders. However, the fund for providing "Warm Woollens for War-worn Walloons" has benefited accordingly. We have received several complaints about the "Here to-day and gone to-morrow" methods of a certain firm of Commission Agents who have been advertising in our columns, and our Special Commissioner is investigating same. We must say, however, on our own behalf, that we accepted the advertisement in all good faith, and cannot be held responsible for breach of contract on the part of any of our advertisers. We hear that an eminent firm of financiers is inaugerating a char-a-banc motor service for the summer months, to work in co-operation with the syndicate which has taken over the "Dead Cow" Hotel, so that residents in this delightful district will have the opportunity of moonlight motor trips, pulling up at the famous old hostelry en route. The country is looking particularly well just now, and farmers report things coming up everywhere. As our correspondence has increased to such an alarming extent, we have had to increase our already enormous salary list, and may have to approach the authorities with a view to importing a female staff, and are ready to receive applications for appointments now—publishing side only—as the editorial sanctum must remain quiet. Further Competitions will probably be announced next week. As we have a lot of copy we want to use up, this is our Grand Double Summer Number. The price remains the same as the cover was printed before we struck this brilliant idea. Having originated the idea, however, we intend having a summer number yearly, and the "Empire Day" issue (approx.) will be chosen for the purpose.

Poile and Trotter, Poile and Trotter,
May I ask you if you've got a
  Season ticket you can issue
  To the press if so, we wish you
Would endorse and send it here,
Will you Poile and Trotter dear?

AUNT ANNIE'S CORNER.

TENDER TALKS TO TINY TOTS.

—:o:—

My dear little Tot-ties,—

Thank you so much for the nice let-ters you have sent me tell-ing me all a-bout your lit-tle games. Your Auntie al-ways likes to know what her Tots have been doing, and that they have been good chil-dren.

—:o:—

Bertram has wrote to me a long let-ter tell-ing me all a-bout his tin soldiers that a kind friend gave him some time ago. I hope some day some one will give him some more of them.

—:o:—

Roger has a col-lec-tion of pretty pic-tures which he looks at every day. All his lit-tle friends like to look at them too.

—:o:—

Johnnie has a friend named Reggie they go long walks to-geth-er. Isn't that splendid, Tots? Johnnie has a nice lit-tle girl friend that he writes let-ters to some-times.

—:o:—

I want all ot you to write to me please, and I will al-ways answer your let-ters if you have been good chil-dren.

Isn't this pretty:—

There was a little man,
  He had a little gun,
He shoots it when he can,
  But has never hit a Hun.

—:o:—

It was sent to me by a lit-tle friend named Gilbert. He of-ten writes love-ly poet-ry like this. Isn't he clev-er.

Good-bye until next week, Tots.

Your loving,
AUNTIE ANNIE.

A DAY FROM THE LIFE OF A "SUB" IN DIVISIONAL RESERVE.

BY HIMSELF.

—o—o—o—

12·40 a.m.—Sleeping peacefully.

12·45 a.m.—Not sleeping peacefully.

12·50 a.m.—Awakened by a noise like a fog-horn gone quite mad.

12.55 a.m.—Realise someone has smelt gas, cannot find gas-helmet or shirt.

1 a.m.—Grope about for matches and candle—find out to my discomfort several extra articles of furniture in the hut—curse volubly.

1·5 a.m.—People rush in to remind me that I am orderly "bloke." Have heated altercation with "next for duty" as to when term of office ends. Matter settled by the entrance of C.O.—AM orderly officer.

1·15 a.m.—Stumble round camp—rumour of "Stand-to"—curse abominably.

1·30 a.m.—Rumour squashed—gas alarm false—somebody's clockwork motor-bike horn came unstuck—curse again—retire to bed.

3·30 a.m.—Sleeping peacefully.

3·35 a.m.—Alarming noise. Somebody with bigger feet than sense of decency, enters the hut; and knocks over a bully-beef box doing excellent work as a chair, collides with everybody's field-boots, mistakes my bed for his, and sits down on same— . . . .

3·59 a.m.—Order restored by Company Commander.

6·0 a.m.—Reveillé.

6·30 a.m.—Get up, and wearily put on one or two garments, including somebody else's tie. Spend pleasant moments searching for my wandering collar stud.

7 a.m.—Go out and wave my limbs about for 45 minutes to the tune of "Head backward be e-e-nd."

7·45 a.m.—Try to shave—we have one mirror amongst six.

8 a.m.—Breakfast. The cook has plentifully peppered the sausage, put salt in my tea by mistake.

9 a.m.—Take party to and from the baths—one man has no cap badge—collect a bird from Adjutant. Have a bath myself, when nicely soaped the water gives out, becoming mud—curse offensively.

10 a.m.—Orderly room—attend with Company conduct sheets, collect another bird. Make arrangements for a cage and a supply of seed for same.

11 a.m.—Retire to hut and quaff a stoop of ale.

11·5 a.m.—Two in-command arrives inopportunely, speaks his mind and retires.

11·10 a.m.—Inspect my huts and men, their clothes, rifles, gas-helmets, feet, etc.

12 noon.—Realise I am not being as offensive as I might be, so go and annoy the next Company (who were working last night); by creeping in, starting their gramaphone with the loudest, longest and most loathed record, and creeping out again.

12·10 p.m.—Angry "sub" in pyjamas enters; am busy writing letters. After a few choice remarks about people in general and myself in particular, he goes away.

1 p.m.—Lunch.

2 p.m.—Sleeping peacefully.

4·30 p.m.—Tea.

5 p.m.—Fall in working party, astonishing number in my platoon suffer from bad feet at this hour. Discuss their ailment with them, and inspect members affected.

6·30 p.m.—Reach lorries and pack men in. No. 9999 Pte Jones X falls off and sprains his ankle, and proceeds to camp.

7·30 p.m.—Arrive at rendez-vous and await R.E.

8 p.m.—Await R.E.

9 p.m.—Await R.E.

9·15 p.m.—R.E. arrive in the shape of one most intelligent sapper.

9·30 p.m.—Loaded with material, proceed to job.

9·45 p.m.—My sergeant rushes up. Pte McNoodle, a sheet of corrugated iron, a duckboard, and a crump-hole full of water have got rather mixed. Leave a lance-corporal to straighten matters.

10 p.m.—German machine-gun annoying. Grateful for tin-hat.

1 a.m.—Return to lorries.

2 a.m.—Reach camp and retire to bed.

Messrs. NUNTHORPE, COX and Co.

—:o: –

INVESTIGATION BY "NEW CHURCH" TIMES COMMISSION.

—:o:—

An enquiry has been held by this paper into the method of business and general standing of the firm of com mission agents doing business under the name of Messrs. Nunthorpe, Cox and Co.; a commission was accordinglv selected from our staff and visited this firm in their new premises. Our representatives met with every sort of attention and hospitality, but being experienced men of the world they did not let this influence their minds, rather did they look on these tokens of goodwill with some suspicion The representative of the firm when questioned with regard to the allegatons made about their repeated movements, said that they had serious drainage difficulties in their recent offices, and their landlords had refused to put the matter right As one of these offices was in the vicinity our representative visited it, and certainly found cause for complaint about a very distinct odour though they were unable to finally decide against any drains, as the sanitary arrangements seemed to be altogether of rather a primitive order. The case of one of our readers was then discussed he stated that he had backed "Chlorine" for the "May-day Stakes" at the "Bull Ring Course" last month, the wire was produced and inspected, and cer tainly bore a time after that at which the race was advertised to start, though on close examination it seemed that this mark had been tampered with, and as no record could be found at the post office we could produce no evidence that the bet was in order. The general appear ance of the offices and staff seemed to be satisfactory, as did their accounts and bank balance, though this latter may have been fictitious. On summing up all the evidence gleaned we would rather advise caution when dealing with this firm though we think their stability is such that they could hardly refuse to pay on any properly acknowledged transaction.

ANSWERS TO

CORRESPONDENTS.

999.—YOUR little effort, though both terse and amusing, is hardly of the "timbre" to appeal to the staid and pious readers of this journal. Why not try the "Winning Post"?

B. G.M.—Above paragraph for your attention and future guidance, please.

MURIEL.—No, up to the present officers on the Staff do NOT wear red gas helmets; but your suggestion is a good one, and will be forwarded to the right quarter.

SADIE.—He did not really marry his platoon, so there is still hope for you.

FOR SALE.

HOUSE-BOAT complete with sides and bottom, now moored in the lower reaches of that idyllic river "La Douve." Owner having gone on a long journey has no further use for same, and will accept almost any offer.—Write "Boating" c/o "New Church" Times.

(Married men of the latest armies will receive 104 pounds per annum in addition to the usual separation allowance.)

Northcliffe, my Northcliffe,
  In days that are dead
The bard was a scoffer
  At much that you said,
A fervid opponent
  Of "Daily Mail" Bread.

The bard never dreamed
  That it mattered a jot
If you trusted in soap
  Or put peas in your pot,
Or how many aeroplanes
  England had not.

And when you backed Blatchford
  To bark at the Bosche,
Or when you puffed Willett
  As wiser than Josh—
Northcliffe, my Northcliffe,
  I own I said "Tosh."

Northcliffe, my Northcliffe,
  Now here at thy feet
The poet craves pardon
  Tho vengeance be sweet
As the peas that thou prizest
  In Carmelite Street.

Forgive me past trespasses,
  Hark to my trope,
To my words that are softer
  Than Lever's Soft Soap,
For only through thee,
  Has a suppliant hope!

Northcliffe, my Northcliffe,
  Ah! greater than Mars
Or double-faced Janus
  Whose portal unbars
The flood-tide of battle
  Napoleon of "Pars."

Whose words are uncensored,
  Whose leader compels
Greys, Asquiths, McKennas,
  And eke double L's,
With contraband cotton
  And scandal of shells,

Who rulest the Seas,
  And the Earth and the Air
And the manifold medals
  "Base" Officers wear,
Northcliffe, my Northcliffe,
  Now hark to my prayer!

When the "Hide-the-Truth Press"
  And the "Slack 23"
Have yielded sword, money,
  And trident to thee
And K.J. and Boosey
  And Pemberton B.

Remember, while paying
  The Derby man's rent,
His rates, his insurance,
  And more than he spent,
That others SAID NOTHING,
  GOT NOTHING, but WENT.

They were somewhere in France,
  While the Derby man bucked
To his wife, and in sheets
  Was connubially tucked . . .
But no one pays them
  For the homes that they chucked.

They were crouching to crumps
  While he cried at a Zepp,
He was dancing what time
  They were taught to "Keep step,"
And he gets a hundred
  Per an. PLUS the Sep-

aration allowance!
  By Carmelite House,
If a Man be worth anything
  More than a Mouse,
Northcliffe, my Northcliffe,
  THESE CHAPS HAVE A GROUSE.

GILBERT FRANKAU.

22/5/16.

"COMIC CUTS."

A CRITICAL ESSAY.

[Communicated.]

—o—o—o—

Para 1. The inner facts of how Intelligence is worked has always appealed to the lay mind, that is the mind which deals in mystery, the secret sign, the four fingers behind either ear before you sit at meat, or the striking of a match on the seat of someone else's trousers instead of your own.

Para 2. (a) Are you merely a Dr. Watson prostrate before the omniscient schoolmaster ; (b) an 1849 Family Herald or a pal of Eve, Evelyn, and Evelinda ; (c) a Peri at the New Church Gate or right in it with Dead Cow ?

Para 3. Personally I am so soaked in the knowledge of the cult that I never go round the line without regarding everything from the point of view of the most doubting Thomas that ever lived. (a) I see a rotten booby with one sheet of corrugated and one layer of sandbags, and recognise at once the Frenchiest of dug-outs, which would make an ordinary 17'' obus hesitate considerably and then give up the unequal contest and retire hurt. (b) I hear a bullet, quite a solitary one too, cheerfully sizzing along anywhere from Pilkem to Isonzo, and I will locate it with all the hunting thoroughness employed by your last year's girl's solicitors to serve her writ for breach. I will tell you where, how, why, and when the dammed thing was made, the type of rifle and the maker's mark (whether for Casement shipment, or home consumption only)—and I don't stop at little things like that —I find you a tree it left, the man who sighted the rifle, the colour of his (a) hair and (b) socks and when (a) and (b) were last washed ; what he had for lunch and where he made so much smoke basting his Schnitzel, and tell you exactly what he thinks about "wait and see."

Para 4. The obvious is always the incorrect. Assumption is as bad as a breach of the commandment or in your front line parapet : and in the case of the former about as common as sub-section 7.

Para 5. Even a harmless, fool thing like a hedge must never, never be accepted as a hedge and nothing more, like the something violet by the stream : I can tell you different from that, by Jove ! It's a very naughty false hedge, something man made with hands, not nature with the aid of fertilisers : and, if you go anywhere near it, it will get up and run at you and bark, and then become at will either an (a) O.K. or D.R.L.S. multiplane, (b) a mine shaft or (c) an Aaron's rod a thousand times reproduced, or some rotten thing. (i). Don't think the Douve uses the usual official channels : it doesn't. We know to our cost it over-runs banks that don't belong to it just as much as Sinn Feinism tries to.

Para 6. Things to me are not what they seem to the lay eye : opposition to the accepted theory is the proof of brains of a high order, the key to promotion. I never agree with my enemy while I am in the way with him, I get him out of my way, particularly if questions of seniority crop up. sub. (i). If I meet an optimist, I pessimize right down to the bed of the Styx [H. 3. L. 7 1/2. 2.] and even press him well down in the mud of it to remind him of its Belgian confrére. sub. (2). If a pessimist, gently remind him of the horrors we used to suffer :—Ascot, the River, Billie Carleton at a tête à tête lunch at the Berkeley, et après . . . , the National, a shooting trip, or a sole colbert at the Marigny after the Grand Prix in those dire days before we became Masters of our Fate and Servants of the King ; those days when S.P. was as removed from a Sniper's Post as your chosen gee from the judge, when the numbers went up.

Para 7. After all we are teaching something. Most people now know a cross is nine times out of ten an O.P., an ambulance with the Red Cross is a transport for M.G., and the Hun word for hospital is Wittenberg. It shews the type of enemy that prostitutes anything connected with about the only sign average humanity always holds sacred.

Para 8. Opposition to me is galling where merit is so éclatant, whatever the Higher Command think about it—anyhow next week I am going to put up the ribbon of the "Order of the Impenitent Sapphira, with crown." To avoid unnessary correspondence, I may say the first chapter of the Order, the most ancient in the world, was held on the banks of the Petite Kishon on 1st April, 3762, B.C.: the ribbon is purple as the news in the 17 I.B. Summary: and finally that the decoration is now long overdue and payment is requested herewith, or forthwith [See Rules for Guidance of Officers in Distress.].

Para 9. Don't think I am grousing: I would a sight sooner watch one man walk along the Messines-Gapaard Road at 7·39 p.m., in his trousers relined with his old pale passionate puce pyjamas, and his Hunny bosom swathed in last year's soiled pattern blouse from some Unter den Linden fashion shop, followed by three (3) cyclists sons of shame testing wire by cutting it, and after a decent interval of 9 hours a caterpillar running a difficult and tortuous race with a homing pigeon, than I would sit in the Row and watch neuters. They seem out of place anywhere near that very robust gentleman represented by the Statue of Achilles, and the mere comparison is odious.

Para 10. I like the way the O.P.'s are named too: (sub i) Doesn't Thatched Cottage remind me or you of one up River with topping little girlies who loved the Brighton Métropole for occasional week-ends? (sub ii) Doesn't Heath Trench in name if not in smell remind one of Dartmoor? (sub iii) And then surely one must be happy at Rossingnol with name and bird both with us contra punting a machine gun playing from Ash Road. (sub iv) Even to be in Winter Trench is like a breath of Adelboden, ski and snow shoes: doesn't that keep one cool this hot weather even if you are suddenly found by G.O.C. ignorant of the quantity of grenades Mills Mark V. stored there.

Para 11. I could tell you a lot more good news like, how to get Petite Munque beer on Sundays, the exact date when leave is next stopped, and where Glycerine is and why: but time presses for the Summary, and I must try and increase my news sheet somehow. I pump for this with all the ardour of a mining major for water, and he has me cold every time. Everything is always "normal." I can't give you many columns, but I always give veritas even in vino. (Advt.)

Para 12. Duty calls: a study of all text books recalls the importance of personal relations among officers. I must go and see Topperton and find out the result of his mating Tschschtoff with fuse marked

N.B.G. 999. With z
7 black and
1916. I. green rings
ZZ: Grrr. and yellow cap.

picked up at point 37°. W of 4. Huns' Farm. Such a triple alliance should produce peace. Will it? Please.

Para 13. I suppose the little blue eyed boys still sing "I O. triumphe stet domus" at school just as in prehistoric days: but do they put the dot between the I and O thus—I.O., in the modern manuer, or are they backward as the silly old Caius Ludicrous who wrote the song B.C. and call it IO? Which? I wonder.

GRANDPA.

SEMI-DETACHED.

At a lofty elevation
Floating lazy in the sun,
What an ideal occupation
Keeping watch on brother Hun!

—:o:—

Though a "sausage" is my villa
Far from angry whizz-bangs' scream,
I can watch the caterpillar,
And all things are what they seem.

—:o:—

In a contemplative manner
When the "big push" is begun,
'Tis from here I'd love to see it
From my place up in the sun.

OUR SPLENDID NEW SERIAL.

—0—0—0—

FROM BUGLER BOY TO BRIGADIER.

OR

How Willie Pritchard Rose from the Ranks.

—0—0—0—

A STORY OF THE GREAT WAR.

—0—0—0—

BY RUBY N. PARBS.

—0—0—0—

CHAPTER 2.

—:0:—

BACKWARD BEND! Backward b-e-e-nd! Willie was now in the Army, No. 12345, William Pritchard, Blankshire L. I. With what energy he threw himself into early morning physical drill! Standing near was Willie's platoon officer, none other than Clarence Algernon St. John Jephcote. As Jephcote's eye landed on Willie his face took on an expression of malignant and deadly hatred, muttering "Curse you! and again curse you!" For Willie loved and loved successfully. For months Clarence had pestered Maggie, the mill lass of Millward with his unwelcome attentions, but with a haughty look Maggie now bade him begone. And so:—here we find them, and things looking very murky for poor Willie. Muttering again "Curse you!" Clarence strode off the parade ground.

—0—0—0—

CHAPTER 3.

—:0:—

(SIX MONTHS LATER.)

"CHARGE!" The word rang out in the clear morning air, and the men of the Blankshires sprang to the order. Leaping eight lines of German trenches Willie Pritchard, now Sergeant of No. 1 Platoon, quickly got in some deadly work. Having lost his sword early in the engagement, Willie picked up a German 18 pounder which was lying handy and using it as a flail, was soon in a circle of dead and wounded. Hacking his way through, and shouting "Follow me!" Willie very quickly had turned the German retreat into a rout. But where was Clarence? Muttering "Curse you!" he had followed Willie out of the trench, and they had become separated during the melee. Surrounded by twenty-nine Germans, Clarence was putting up a magnificent fight, but at the critical moment his sword broke, and there seemed nothing for it but surrender when a flying figure appeared on the scene. It was Willie. Plying his awful weapon with deadly accuracy, Willie had soon hacked his way to Clarence, and shouting "Follow me!" dashed after the flying enemy. Muttering "Curse you!" Clarence went after him. Towards evening Willie began to feel tired, and rallying the Blankshires made preparations for passing the night. Clarence had meanwhile caught up with them and trouble was looming in the near future, when the General appeared on the scene, asking for Sergeant Pritchard. Wonderingly Willie went forward and saluted. "Sergeant Pritchard," said the General, "henceforth you are no longer Sergeant but Captain Pritchard, V.C., D.S.O." Overcome by emotion, Willie was led from the scene. Muttering "Curse you!" Clarence followed him, and handed over the acquittance rolls.

—0—0—0—

CHAPTER 4.

—:0:—

THE MORNING broke on the battlefield. Willie awoke refreshed, and having stretched himself, aroused his men, and told them to prepare to continue the battle. Willie was now weaponless, but nothing daunted on they went, and soon caught up with the flying foe. Yesterday's performance was repeated, and utterly demoralised the Germans were driven back to the Rhine, there to make a stand on the further bank. But how had it fared with our hero? Clarence's heart was full of bitterness and hatred, and muttering "Curse you! curse you!!" had taken a shot at Willie's flying figure. Narrowly missing Willie's head by two or three yards, the bullet had perforated Von Blinkenberg, the German Generalissimo. But Willie by this time was bleeding from eighteen wounds, and sat down on the nearest parapet to staunch them. Clarence, creeping up behind him, this time made certain and hit Willie on the head with a revetting maul which he had found. Muttering "Curse you!" as Willie fell he stole away into the darkness.

(WHAT DID WILLIE DO?—See next week's instalment.)

THE LECTURE.

If at any time you happen to be at all depressed—though of course this is extremely unlikely out here where there is so much to interest and delight one—find out whether there is a lecture on anywhere, given by the G.S.O. first or second of a Division about to be relieved, to the officers of the relieving Division, and go to it at once. It will make you realise that war is worth while. Roughly speaking, the show will be as follows:—The room is packed with an expectant but nervous conglomeration of officers, of whom certainly not more than the first two rows will hear a word of the glad tidings. That doesn't matter, however there is a screen and a magic lantern which you may be deluded into thinking is going to show you a reasonably clear picture of the trenches—don't be had by it—it's only a trap. Well, eventually a Staff Officer mounts the platform, and you gather from his opening remarks that he has been deputed to give the lecture, that he is not much of a hand at the job, and that you must forgive him. This is greeted with sympathetic noises—the audience apparently attempting to ingratiate themselves into his good offices thereby, and hoping that if they are successful in this he'll let 'em down with a minimum of forgetfulness. The Staff Officer is not moved in the least. He proceeds as follows:—"As a matter of fact I haven't been up to the front line for—er—some time (the audience appear incredible) but when I was last up, A 1 had fallen in, and of course most of the communication trenches had been—er—crumped in." The audience seem to appreciate the fact that there are still a few trenches extant "I will now show you some photographs of the craters." The operator having woken up, the lantern is lit, and a beautiful bright light, accompanied by a very realistic imitation of the odours encountered at Hooge is given. Unfortunately the lighting effects are poor, but anyway you have a quiet ten minutes in which to give your pal instructions what to do with your corpse. Eventually a picture is shown, which may remind you of your late Uncle Bill, who used to suffer severely from warts. As the lecturer invariably holds his pointer at least one foot from the screen, you will naturally look at the wart indicated by the shadow, but that always adds to the amusement, and you can run a book as to which smudge is the crater. The grand finale is always worth paying attention to. "The enemy shoot at you from three and a half sides, some officers make it three and three quarters, though personally I incline to the latter view." The Staff Officer then tells you that he doesn't think he has anything more to say, and though everyone seems grieved to hear it, he subsides into a chair next to the G O C. The best part of the lecture is, of course, that it leaves you with a magnificent thirst.

P.B.I.

No doubt you know the great ones, and if here but lightly drawn,
In this my lay divisional you'll find them I'll be sworn;
But should you fail then blame the scribe whose pen had little skill
To draw the man his mind's eye saw, although he had the will

—:0:—

1

Who scans you o'er with piercing eye with monocle attached
And makes you wonder how he knows some folly you have hatched?
Those countless things you should have done, but didn't, haunt you while
You're answering politely, then he leaves you with a smile

—:0:—

2

Who, by his gracious ways and help in time of toil and stress,
Has smoothed full oft a weary path (and lent aid to the Press)
Who'll spin a yarn of countries far—and one thing I must mention—
Has earned the love (!) of Frightful Fritz, who pays him much attention?

—:0:—

3.

Who is't can make a job of work a pleasure all the while,
And "priceless" though his words may be, more priceless is his smile,
Who makes you think by word and look your job is his pet hobby?
The picture would not be complete without attendant "Bobbie."

4

Then he, the latest to the fold, by manner bright and breezy
Can make what seems the hardest job both quickly done and easy
Whose speech the shamrock doth disclose, whose walls are decorated
With visions lovely where one finds both art and beauty mated

—.0:—

5.

At once to Kew my thoughts are drawn, and there are stationary
Lost in an admiration of such virtues which can vary
To any point the wind may blow, and in this our division
The quotient you will find in Kew Politeness and Precision.

—:0:—

6.

This one you'll find but lightly touched, although 'twould take a ream
His various virtues to extol, whose merit is extreme,
Without his presence there's a Batt. would very, very rum be,
Yet here I may not name him or the Editor would glum be.

—:0:—

7

Back to H.Q. There dear old—no! 'tis here I must not name him
Lest he should roll an eye at me, and few there are who'd blame him
Who always seeks a "field of fire," though careful of a wetting,
Is always full of anecdote, the Vatican his setting.

—:0:—

The Editor impatient roams, my ardour is diminished
His eye agleam for copy is, he's asking if I've finished.
Another time if fate is kind my ditty I'll renew,
This week the Editor decrees that one full page will do.

LANCELOT'S LETTERS TO LONELY LADIES.

FLANDERS

May, 1916

YOU poor little Dears :—

How we pity you, how we sob for you, and how often we think of you with great big tender thoughts. I wish we could invite you all to come out here and look round, even in Flanders you would find the country quite charming, in parts, just now, but—on second though s—much as we should love to have you with us, the responsibility of your presence would be too great, but leave being about due we will come home and see you instead.

Tell me, though, do you REALLY all wear those short skirts and things we see such pretty pictures of in the Illustrated Papers from Home?

This is a nice time to come home for a swift, short week is not it? I have visions of little runs to Skindles, lunches at Prince's, "Mr. Manhatten" in the evening and so on, in a land where gas-gongs, whizz-bangs and stand-to's are not allowed.

Are you very much afflicted with "rumourists" at Home? They exist in droves out here, and this is just their busy season. They may be divided into two distinct classes, opti-rumourists and pessi-rumourists. The first named are, at heart, good fellows but save me from the latter. I met one the other night; said he'd been lunching with some gents of the Corps who "knew things," and that he'd "heard" that the Division was not going out to rest for another five months, that the Huns were massing in prodigious numbers just opposite our own pet bit of line, and that all leave was on the point of being stopped indefinitely. No, if I've got to mix with rumourists give me the opti type, the sort who has a brother high up in the diplomatic service whom he knows is taking 100 to 8 on the war coming to a satisfactory conclusion by next Thursday week.

I heard such a funny one about one of our majors the other day. He lost his way in a bit of the country he was ill acquainted with. The day was hot and dusty, the major was hot and thirsty when—lo and behold—he saw, leaning in a somewhat negligent attitude against a gate a private soldier.

"Which way to the Officers' Mess of the Umpshires?" shouted our tired and weary major

"Along the road about half a-mile on the left, sir, answered the Tommy, nodding his head in that direction, but otherwise motionless

"Why the — — don't you spring to attention when an officer addresses you?" roared our friend now thoroughly roused

"Because sir" said the man very meekly, "I'm doing F P No 1, and am tied up to this 'ere gate"

And he's a nice little major man too.

Good-bye and God bless you all,

LANCELOT.

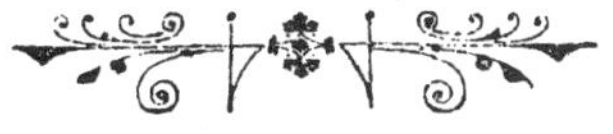

Oh! To be in Flanders in a gas alert,
How I love a "stand to" in a little shirt
When the wind's erratic, and you're dining in Berloo,
Don't forget your P.H.G. and take it in with you.

Correspondence.

To the Editor,
"New Church" Times.

Sir,

May I use the columns of your periodical to ventilate a grievance. On many occasions lately when proceeding to and from my work (I am a window cleaner at Wulverghem) I have been pestered by thousands of women selling flags for some charitable (sic) cause. Only yesterday a forward female had the audacity to ask me to buy a flag to assist in the purchase of a blue body-belt for a bucolic Belgian. This, sir! I maintain is monstrous, and the sooner something is done the better. Only last Sunday I gave a franc to provide Warm Woollens for War-worn Walloons and now, what with the Daylight Saving Bill and other things which deserve your attention life is becoming too much of a trial. Surely you will move in this matter.

I am, Sir,
Yours, etc.,
WALTER WIGGINS.

To the Editor,
"New Church" Times.

Sir,

As a dabbler in the arts, and that of painting in particular, it has been my habit recently to visit the famous Petite Munque Galleries from time to time in search of some new gem. A few days ago I made one of these calls, and was surprised to find this home of art overrun with excursionists; these latter, though probably very worthy citizens, had evidently not come to study the paintings; I therefore would most respectfully suggest that some reasonable steps might be taken to stop a repetition of this—in my opinion—most undesirable state of affairs. Possibly "Cooks" could be induced not to include this place in their list of attractions, as all true lovers of art would, I imagine, be able to nose *it out* for themselves.

Yours, etc.,
"ART FOR ART'S SAKE."

Things We Want to Know.

—:o:—

If it takes one adjutant one hour to purchase one hundred francs worth of lace; how long will it take all the adjutants in the B.E.F. to buy up all the lace in Belgium.

? ? ?

Whether it is a fact that the Editor of this paper has cabled an offer to the "Berliner Tageblatt" with a view to incorporating that enterprise with the "New Church Times" at an early date.

? ? ?

Whether a certain big man with attendant grandparent enjoyed his (pub?) crawl a short time ago, and were the cellars full.

? ? ?

The name of the Intelligence Officer who sternly rebuked his opposite number for not keeping his eyes on his own boat.

? ? ?

How Grandpa enjoyed his trip to Messines.

WANTED.

STRONG YOUTH as LAMPLIGHTER for Wytschaete—good wage paid if work satisfactory.—Apply Wytschaete Urban District Council.

AGENTS for ART. HILLERY'S HOT CRUMPETS—Good opening for a forceful young man.—Write Box 110, "New Church" Times.

MEN of GOOD EDUCATION to join the Army—good pay—no worry—brilliant prospects.—Apply R. E. Cruting and Co.

Are You Ambitious? Does Anyone Stand in Your Way?

IF SO, COME AND TAKE A COURSE OF INSTRUCTION AT OUR FAMOUS

PYROTECHNIC INSTITUTE.

WHEN YOU HAVE QUALIFIED IN OUR COURSE

THE WORLD WILL BE BEFORE YOU.

A Brass Hat will be within your reach.

TERMS VARY, with rank of person to be removed, from 1 centime (Huns all ranks) to 500 francs for Generals.

OWING TO NEW TELEGRAPHIC REGULATIONS OUR CORRESPONDENCE COURSE HAS HAD TO BE DISCONTINUED.

—o—o—o—o—

Anarchist Societies Specially Catered For.

—o—o—o—o—

ALL KINDS OF BOMBS PROVIDED AT SHORT NOTICE.

—o—o—o—o—

ILLUSTRATED CATALOGUE FREE.

—o—o—o—o—

KEITH, HINDERSLEY AND CO

TELEPHONE: "102, BANG." TELEGRAMS: "BUST UP."

SHORTS! SHORTS!! SHORTS!!!

—o—o—o—

HAVE YOU GOT NICE KNEES?
DO YOU WANT TO SHOW 'EM?

—o—o—o—

Call and see our new Summer Stock of

SHORTS

All Colours, all Sizes, but one Quality only.

—o—o—o—

We guarantee to show more leg than any firm in the trade at lower prices.

—o—o—o—

RED BUTTONS FOR THE STAFF A SPECIALITY.

—o—o—o—

FANCY TRIMMINGS AND HEM-STITCHED EDGES EXTRA.

—o—o—o—

JERUM AND CO.,

SPORTS OUTFITTERS.
Sole Agents to Boy Scouts Association.

THIS SPACE TO LET.

Printed and Published by
Sherwood, Forester & Co., Ltd.

THE

KEMMEL TIMES.

WITH WHICH ARE INCORPORATED

The Wipers Times & The "New Church" Times.

No 1. Vol 1. Monday. 3rd July, 1916. Price 1 Franc.

THE "SPANBROEKMOLEN" OPERA HOUSE.

—o—o—o—o—

THIS WEEK—FOR ONE WEEK ONLY.

—o—o—o—o—

PROFESSOR SCRAPPER'S

PERFORMING TROUPE OF HIGHLY-TRAINED ANIMALS.

—o—o—o—o—

Screaming Farce Entitled:

"Who Pinched Our Entanglement."

—o—o—o—o—

THOMAS ATKINS

WITH HIS FAMOUS SONG:

YES, SIR! YES, SIR!! THREE BAGS FULL.

—o—o—o—o—

Book Early to Avoid Disappointment

—o—o—o—o—

PRICES: 10fr.; 5fr.; 1fr. Boxes from 20fr.

THE KEMMEL TIMES.

WITH WHICH ARE INCORPORATED

The Wipers Times & The "New Church" Times.

No 1. Vol 1. Monday. 3rd July, 1916. Price 1 Franc.

EDITORIAL.

MANY startling things have happened since our last number. Firstly there is the death of Lord KITCHENER. True he was known to most of us by name only, yet it was a name that meant a lot to us, and although nothing can make any difference to the result of the war, one would have liked him to have seen that end which he will have done so much to bring about. Then there is the naval victory, which has probably had a great bearing on the duration of the war. Had Fritz been content with saying that, having found more trouble, than he had anticipated, he hit out and ran away, one might have passed it all over, and said that for a Hun he did as well as could be expected. However, the pitiful spectacle of William, Tirpitz and Co. shedding tears of blood in their anxiety to prove to a pack of poor deluded sausage eaters, that they had blown the British Navy off the map, ceases to be amusing and becomes a disgusting spectacle of monomaniacal absurdity. Meanwhile here everything has been merry and bright. The meat tea and social in aid of the fund for providing blue body belts for bucolic Belgians was an enormous success. Also a very successful sports-meeting was held, which is reported on more fully elsewhere. We are pleased to be able to congratulate many members of the Division on the new and well-earned ribbons which adorn their manly breasts. Also we should like to express the regret felt throughout the whole Division at the temporary disablement of Colonel CUNNINGHAM. and the hopes of all that he will soon be with us again. We have lately heard from several people "in the know" in England that peace is to be declared this month. Should it take place before this issue is before the public, then will all subscribers please call at our offices, when they will be presented with a copy and a gold watch, as a slight remuneration for their kindly support. We are glad to be able to announce another of our mammoth competitions, particulars of which will be found on page 8. The interest which these arouse is very flattering, and we almost feel tempted to increase the prize-money. We must thank the senders of all kindly letters of appreciation of the new serial, and feel that the enormous amount outlaid to secure the rights of this thrilling tale is more than repaid by the satisfaction we have been able to give our readers. It is unfortunate that the weather is so unsettled, as this may detract from the success of the forthcoming regatta on the "Douve." However, we may still hope to see a large and fashionably dressed crowd, as there are many counter-attractions should the weather prove unkind. We must thank those members of the Division who have sent us copy, and express the hope that they will continue, and that many others will also send along something when the spirit moves them. We have lately taken up another and more luxurious suite of offices in a very prosperous neighbour hood, and are consequently compelled once again to change the name of our periodical. We confidently hope to receive the same support from the public as was accorded to the previous journals which are incorporated with the "Kemmel Times."

THE EDITOR.

A Major once polite, urbane,
Did cook espy in smock of blue,
And Tommy heard amazed "Bon jour,
Bon jour. comment vous portez-vous?"

SPORTS.

On Thursday, the 8th ult., the Royal Fusiliers held a very successful little meeting at Bulford Camp, and Col. Hancock and the officers were at home all the afternoon. The meeting was favoured by very fine weather and was a great success from the word go. There were certain events open to the 24th Division which drew fairly representative entries, notably the tug-of-war, in which some very interesting heats were decided, to be won finally by an excellent team of the Leinsters who well deserved their victory. Perhaps one of the most interesting events from a spectacular point of view was the Officers V.C. Race which drew about 11 entries, some of the efforts at remounting with the dummy caused a certain amount of good-natured laughter, but the winner showed excellent judgment and skill both in his heat and final. The meeting struck a note that we have more than once advocated in our columns; a more frequent occurrence of this type of friendly rivalry brings the members of the various units into closer contact with each other, and promotes a greater "Esprit de corps" in the division as a whole, not to mention the relaxation from things more serious which such occasions afford.

As a final word Col. Hancock and his officers were truly excellent hosts, and we thank them one and all for a very enjoyable day, as well as congratulating the executive on the able manner in which everything was carried out.

HOW THE PEASANTS LEFT HOOGE.

VIDE A SPECIAL-CORRESPONDENT.

MR. TEECH BOMAS, WRITING ON LAST SCRAP AT HOOGE, IN SEVERAL LEADING LONDON DAILIES.

—.o:—

Of course, as Teech says, it was a thrilling sight to see the peasants of Hooge trekking back to Wipers in the merry month of June. There was Lizzie of the corner estaminet well to the fore, and all the other local celebrities in close attendance. Have you ever seen the peasants of Hooge frolicking in "No Man's Land" and picking gooseberries in Railway Wood? No! Well, you surprise me. I really must tell Teech. Bye-the-way, I wonder he did'nt tell us what happened to all the gee-gees in training at the stables. Can't you see those dear peasants calling at the Culvert for a spot before legging it down Menin Road en route to the Hotel des Ramparts where friend Boniface is always on hand to deal out hospitality. That must be SOME glass that Teech uses if, by its aid, he saw the church at Hooge get knocked out of the perpendicular. Poor old church! What happy hours we can remember in the shadow of its ivy-covered walls (I don't think.) However, on the strength of Teech's observations, the Editor has cut this special reporters salary down to a minimum for missing all these thrilling sights. Well, Tina, it only runs to a bottle of bass to-day, so pour it out clear and I'll tell you all about the British Army.

P.B.I.

WHO IS IT?

See him standing in his "'plus twos,"
Winking at the girls who pass.;
Note the polish on his brogue shoes,
Always looking in the glass.

See him sitting in his office,
Writing orders for his chief;
See him dashing to his billet,
Keen to see the next releif.

See him writing to the Chateau,
Love has filled his face with glee,
Life no more is dull and flat, oh!
" We will write, love, oft, shall we?"

STRAFE KAPTING.

Things We Want to Know.

——:o:——

The name of the subaltern who told the Major that to take his wife to Nottingham Goose Fair was like taking a sandwich to the Lord Mayor's Banquet.

? ? ?

Whether the London papers are aware there are a few BRITISH troops on the western front.

? ? ?

What Fritz said when he hurriedly left his sausages the other day.

? ? ?

Whether Tina's knowledge of troop movements is more profitable than her canteen.

Jack and Jill on top of a Hill
Had built an O Pip Station,
But Frightful Fritz blew it to bits
To their great consternation.

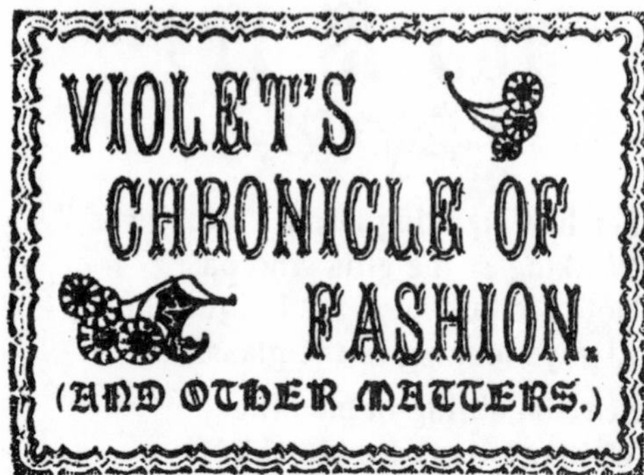
VIOLET'S
CHRONICLE OF
FASHION.
(AND OTHER MATTERS.)

HOW do you do, everybody? I enter your pages introduced by no less a person than our mutual friend "Sabretâche" of "The Tatler." He vows that henceforth your motto will be "Quo fas(hion) et gloria ducunt." A man guilty of perverting Latin in that manner would be capable of anything, and I leave it to the Gunners themselves to avenge the outrage and devise a suitable punishment. If their imagination fails, they might call in the aid of any member of the "'New Church' Times" staff who has ever had to decipher "Sabretâche's" handwriting. They would be sure to receive some happy suggestions!

* * *

WELL, here I am, ready to lead you gaily along the avenue of Fashion, also down all sorts of fascinating by paths on the way. To expound Fashion's whims to an audience of mere males is no light task, their ignorance of the technicalities of dress creates difficulties. I was recently describing to an interested pal the glories of an evening gown of taffeta. "Sure you know what that is?" "Oh, rather," he answered, "I used to have shirts and pyjamas made of it—stripey stuff!" Imagine an evening frock of striped shirting!

* * *

SO I shall not risk creating weird pictures in your minds; but I'll tell you of some of my purchases this week, or rather ours, for sister Nancy and I have been together on a shopping expedition. Mighty good time we had too; spent a couple of days helping two of the boys on leave to enjoy themselves, and that means, as everybody knows, not a single minute wasted.

CHOOSING frocks for Nancy is a delightful task. She is PETITE, with a slim dainty figure lots of auburn hair, REAL auburn, the rich, deep, coppery sort—and a lovely complexion. She wanted a frock for Alexandra Rose Day, and she chose a filmy white muslin, very simple, with lots of dear little frills from hem to waist, where a wide azure-blue ribbon gave the necessary touch of colour. The waist-ribbon is important nowadays, our skirts are so full and our bodices so loose that we need a trim and taut waist-line to secure an attractive silhouette. The hat to complete Nancy's outfit is a big shady white one, azure-blue ribbon round the crown; and when she gazes up from under the becoming brim at her defenceless victims on Rose Day, I'm thinking they'll succumb without a struggle, so the harvest should be a rich one.

* * *

MY own pet extravagences are shoes and stockings. I wish you could see my new BOTTINES, black toes and white uppers, of course, a la "Eve," and so high; for not a scrap of a gap must there be between boot tops and skirt-edge, and the latter is still at a deliciously high level. A windy day witnesses many revelations, some more fearful than beautiful, and only those of us who are conscious of our—ahem!—"stockings" being faultless dare face a real gale.

* * *

MY latest effort is a poultry farm to supply eggs for the wounded. I wanted the special hens whose eggs go to the hospital to wear a Red Cross badge round their necks, to show they were real war-workers. Failing that, I tried making a cross in red ink on a dozen eggs, hoping the chicks would hatch out branded for life as Red Cross layers. But they weren't even layers, much less Red Cross-ites, for every blessed one of the dozen hatched out a cockerel!

Au revoir,

VIOLET

"THE NUTS OF THE OLD BRIGADE."

In New Church yard, on a smashed tombstone,
A Gunner Adjutant sits alone.
His breeks are patched and his tunic torn;
His cap is floppy and battle-worn;
His hair is long and his eyes are wet
With the unstaunched tears of a vain regret.
And he doesn't care how the gas-winds blow,
If the crumps burst high or the crumps burst low,
Or whether the notes are flat or sharp
That he twangs from the strings of his minstrel-harp,
As he sings in the mournful cypress-shade
"The Lay of the Nuts of the Old Brigade."

—0—0—0—

Oh where are the Nuts of the old Brigade,
The Nuts that used to be here?
They have left their Gunners and motored away,
Shall I find them at Kemmel or at Fleurbaix
Or in Tock Twenty-seven Beer?

—0—0—0—

Oh where is Johnnie the Brigadier
The joy of his glittering Staff?
In the hottest hour of the bloodiest fight,
He was never flurried or impolite,
When he asked for a COUNTERSTRAFE.

Oh where is Bob o' the big moustache?
An alien Adjutant shoots
For the Major-man that I used to know,
With his Kirchner ladies all in a row,
And his seventeen pairs of boots.

—0—0—0—

Oh where is Caw-Caw the Captain bold,
The pride of the tailor shop?
Is he writing chits for his G.O.C.?
Or writing to fairies he never showed me
When we used to billet in Pop.?

—0—0—0—

Oh where and oh where is Nick-it-and-run,
And whom does he call 'my dear,'
At dead of night on the telephone,
When he tells you secrets the Boche has known
For the better part of a year?

—0—0—0—

And where is my boy of the Signal Corps
With the white and blue on his arm?
In what O.P. do his gig lamps shine?
Who damns his buzzing and curses his line
When the horns shriek Gas-alarm?

—0—0—0—

Oh where are my lost interpreters,
And what the deuce do they do?
Are they buying port by the wagon-load,
Or galloping hard on the hard high road
To draw their pay in Baloo?

—0—0—0—

Oh give me the Nuts of the old Brigade
The Nuts of the right good cheer!
I wish I were with them, wherever they went,
Though I'd rather it wasn't The Salient . . . .
And so would the old I. Beer.

GILBERT FRANKAU

19/6/16.

OUR SPLENDID NEW SERIAL.

—0—0—0—

FROM BUGLER BOY TO BRIGADIER.

OR

How Willie Pritchard Rose from the Ranks

—0—0—0—

A STORY OF THE GREAT WAR.

—0—0—0—

By RUBY N. DARES.

—0—0—0—

CHAPTER 5.

—:0:—

NIGHT ON THE BATTLEFIELD.

POOR little Willie's was indeed an unenviable plight. Staggering to his feet, he hastily pulled a roast duck from his haversack, and with the remains of a bottle of whisky proceeded to relieve the pangs of hunger which assailed him. His head was aching badly from Clarence's felt blow, but after having eaten he felt better, and began to look about him for his men. On the way Willie met the General who greeted him thus "Hello Willie how's your father?" "I have no father, sir" replied our hero, "But auntie is very well except for a slight touch of the jaundice." At that moment a 17 inch shell fell behind them. Before it could explode Willie had whipped off his coat and thrown it over the deadly missile which immediately exploded harmlessly. "Thank you, Major Pritchard" said the General. "Major, sir" said Willie hesitatingly, "Yes, you will be gazetted to-day" said the General and passed on. Willie, coatless but undaunted, soon caught up with his men who were now rounding up Germans in all directions, and here for the moment we will leave him. Meanwhile what had happened to Clarence? After hitting Willie on the head with a maul (G.S. head) he strode off into the darkness muttering "Curse you." Passing the night in a neighbouring estaminet Clarence, next morning, fell in with a roving band of the Stumpshires and took command of them. Word having come down that the British left was in danger Clarence hurried to the rescue, and by a timely movement averted the danger, and the Germans hurriedly retreated. Clarence pursued them all the afternoon, and had almost caught them, when another party of Germans helped them to rally. Things looked awkward for Clarence, when all of a sudden a party of English emerged from the local estaminet and fell on the rear of the Germans who immediately capitulated. To his dismay Clarence recognised in their leader none other Willie Pritchard. Muttering "Curse you" he went to meet him. A General who happened to have been watching the fight now came up to Willie, and seeing him coatless said "What is your rank" "Major, sir" said Willie "Well" said the General "You are promoted Colonel here and now." "Thank you, sir" said Colonel Pritchard feelingly. Muttering "Curse you" Clarence strode off.

(WHERE WAS MAGGIE?)

Another exciting instalment next week.

People We Take Our Hats off To.

—:0:—

The British Navy.

—:0:—

The Russians.

—:0:—

The French.

—:0:—

The Canadians.

HOW TIRPITZ WON THE BATTLE OFF JUTLAND.

Von Tirpitz was an admiral, his beard flew bold and free,
He called up all his captains and " My gallant lads," quoth he,
" The day has come, ten thousand ' Hochs ' and though I stay at home
My spirit will be with you. Now prepare to brave the foam ! "

—§ † §—

The captains tried with one accord to raise a pleasant grin,
Yet each one wondered when and how the trouble would begin ;
Their ships they put in dry dock, had the barnacles removed,
While by the aid of countless " steins " the outlook they improved.

—§ † §—

" What ho, my merry mariners ! " said Tirp. one day in May,
" Art ready now to sweep the sea and end Britannia's day ?
Has each of you his Iron Cross, and flannel next his skin ? "
With one accord they answered " Ja ! " " Gut ! now we can begin ! "

—§ † §—

So Tirpitz crept unto the gate, and peered out o'er the sea,
While gravely muttering in his beard " I'd rather you than me ! "
" The coast is clear," he shouted back, " make haste ' The Day ' is here ! "
Then shut the gate behind them, and consoled himself with beer.

—§ † §—

When on his homeward way he paused, this master of the gales,
And drove into his statue half a ton of six inch nails ;
" Hoch ! hoch ! " quoth he, " now I must go and write up my report
Of this, our greatest victory, and lessons it has taught."

—§ † §—

So he and Wolff sat down to think, and soon one came to see
The mighty German fleet had won a glorious victory,
So " wire the news around at once, the time is getting short,
The world must have our story ere our ships get back to port."

—§ † §—

Then back went Tirp. to Kiel again, and peeping through the gate
He saw some ships returning in a mighty flurried state,
" What's this ? " he cried, behind his beard his face was turning pale,
And straightway to his statue went and drove another nail.

—§ † §—

" Ho ! ho ! my gallant lads," quoth he, " why make such frantic haste ?
You come as though by devils chased, and little time to waste."
The pale and shaky captains muttered through their chattering teeth
" We've won a great big vict'ry, all the foe is underneath."

—§ † §—

" If that is so " quoth Tirpitz, " why this frantic need for haste,
Why not remain and glut on joys of which you've had a taste,
Why leave the field of victory whose laurels wreath your hair ? "
" Well, to be honest 'twas because the British fleet was there."

—§ † §—

" Oh well ! " said Tirp., " the glorious news is speeding on its way,
And 'twill be known the whole world 'oer ere breaks another day ;
If we can't win by ships and guns we can at least by tales."
And then into his statue drove another ton of nails.

Correspondence.

To the Editor,
"Kemmel Times."

Sir,

I feel it my duty to bring to your notice the disgraceful manner in which the Metropolitan Board is carrying out their duties. The countryside is obscured by clouds of dust, and I have yet to see the first water cart operating. Now that the motoring season is in full swing the evil is very apparent, and something should be done at once.

I am, Sir,
Yours Faithfully,
PRO BONO PUBLICO.

—:o:—

To the Editor,
"Kemmel Times."

Sir,

It would appear that a certain amount of uneasiness still prevails among a certain section of your public, as to the bona-fide nature of this Firm. (The enclosed note, value 5 francs, was found shortly after the call of your representative at these Offices, and we have great pleasure in returning same to you.) Doubtless you will see your way to re-assure that section of your public already referred to as to the scrupulous honesty of the firm. The report of your representative which appears in the last issue of your paper, though not unfavourable, does not appear sufficiently definite to remove the feeling of uneasiness in the public mind, which has unfortunately made itself felt lately and caused a considerable decrease in our business.

Yours faithfully,
NUNTHORPE, COX & CO.

June 8th, 1916.

[Our representative asserts that he lost 50 francs. Verb sap.—ED.]

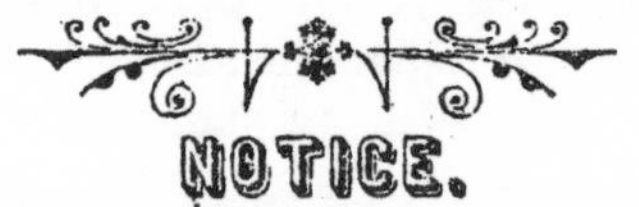

NOTICE.

—:o:—

Owing to pressure on our space, also the many calls on our time by hostile demonstrations in our neighbourhood, we are compelled to hold over numerous answers to correspondents.

OUR MAMMOTH COMPETITION.

—o—o—o—o—

FIRST PRIZE: 10,000,000 Francs.
SECOND PRIZE: 5,000,000 Francs.
THIRD PRIZE: 2,500,000 Francs.

THOUSANDS OF OTHER PRIZES!

ALL YOU HAVE TO DO:

SUPPLY THE LAST LINE OF THE FOLLOWING LIMERICK:—

"There was a fair Belgian of Locre
Who smothered herself in red ochre,
When people asked "Why?"
She exclaimed with a sigh"

— — — — — — —

Every Attempt to be accompanied by a FIVE-FRANC NOTE.

—o—o—o—o—

The Editor's decision is ABSOLUTELY FINAL, and in the event of TWO ANSWERS BEING CORRECT, he will award the Prize AS HE THINKS FIT.

ADDRESS ENVELOPES:—"Competition," Editor, "Kemmel Times."

OUR NEW INSURANCE SCHEME.

—o—o—o—

IS YOUR DUG-OUT IN A DANGEROUS POSITION?
WE WILL INSURE IT FOR YOU AT A VERY SMALL CHARGE.

—o—o—o—

Send for our Booklet

OR DROP US A CARD WHEN OUR AGENT WILL CALL ON YOU.

—o—o—o—

If your dug-out's insecure,
Against the crump we will insure.

—o—o—o—

THE

COOKER INSURANCE CO.

POILE & TROTTER.

—o—o—o—

This Eminent Firm

HAS LATELY ADDED A

House Agency

TO ITS OTHER ACTIVITIES.

—o—o—o—

DO YOU WANT A HOUSE?

—o—o—o—

WE WILL GET YOU ANYTHING YOU LIKE.

—o—o—o—

ALL UP-TO DATE VENTILATION AND SANITARY ARRANGEMENTS.

—o—o—o—

All Business under the personal supervision of our

MR. TROTTER

—o—o—o—

Ring up or Wire.

MUNQUE ART GALLERY.

—o—o—o—o—

This Magnificent Collection Of

OLD MASTERS

Has moved into a more Central Position.

—o—o—o—o—

ANY 'BUS WILL TAKE YOU IF IT'S GOING THAT WAY.

—o—o—o—o—

SOME VERY VALUABLE ADDITIONS

HAVE LATELY BEEN MADE, AND PATRONS WILL FIND THE GALLERY WELL WORTH A VISIT NEW ADDRESS:

CENTRAL GALLERIES DRANOUTRE.

—o—o—o—o—

TELEPHONE: "102, KNEWD."

Printed and Published by
Sherwood, Forester & Co., Ltd.

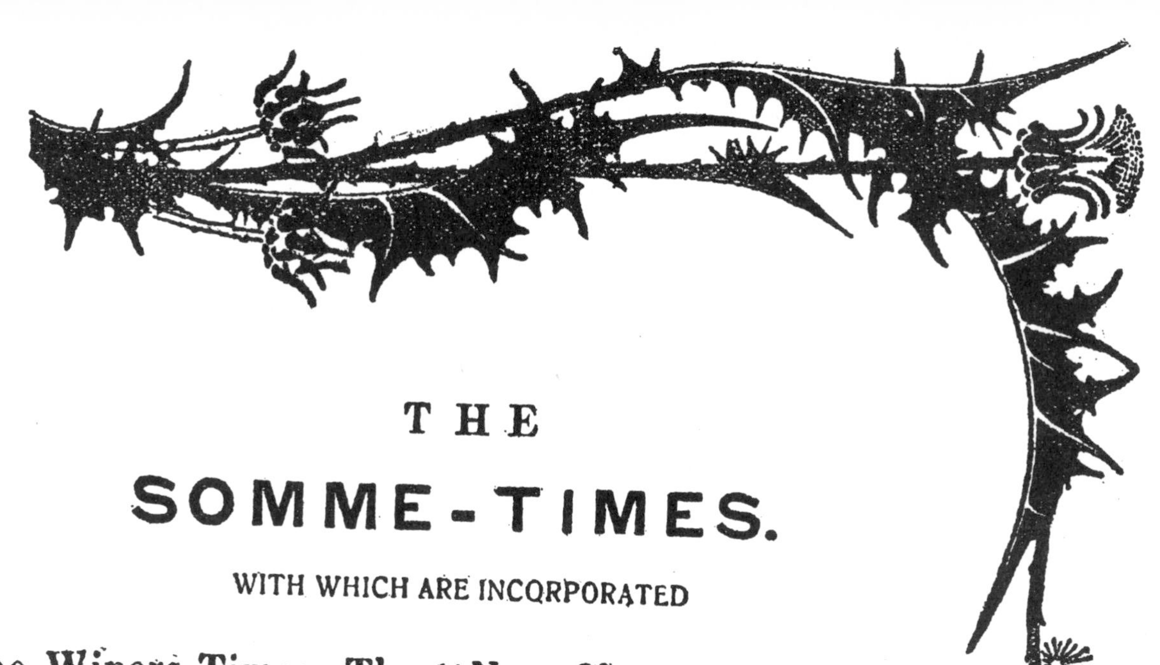

THE

SOMME-TIMES.

WITH WHICH ARE INCORPORATED

The Wipers Times, The "New Church" Times & The Kemmel Times.

No 1. Vol 1. Monday. 31st July, 1916. Price 1 Franc.

THE CONTALMAISON OPERA HOUSE.

—o—o—o—o—

THIS WEEK.

The Great Spectacular Drama, Entitled:

"THERE'S ONE MORE RIVER TO CROSS."

INTRODUCING THE CELEBRATED MALE IMPERSONATOR,

LITTLE WILLIE.

—o—o—o—o—

THE THREE LORELEI

IN THEIR SONG SCENA, ENTITLED:

"OH WILLIE COME HOME BEFORE YOU GET HURT."

—o—o—o—o—

The Original Bottle-nosed Comedian,

FRITZ

IN HIS NEW SKETCH

"I'VE HAD SOMME."

—o—o—o—o—

ALBERT - POZIERES - BAPAUME CIRCUIT.

—o—o—o—o—

Grand Touring Concert Party.

BY SPECIAL ARRANGEMENT WITH

PROFESSOR SCRAPPER.

—o—o—o—o—

THE FOLLOWING WILL BE THE PROGRAMME (W.P.)

—o—o—o—o—

TROUPE OPENING CHORUS.

1. Song—"When the midnight choo-choo leaves for Pozieres."

2. Solo—"Up I came with my little lot."
Enrico WALTHALLO.

3. Concerted item—"Come along over the garden wall."
BY THE TROUPE.

4. Grand chorus and glee—"I'm much more happy than when I was free."
Sung by Messrs. BOSCH.

5 Song and Chorus—"Pray tell me gentle Hunlet are there any more at home like you."

6 Grand concerted number---"Another little drink would'nt do us any harm."
BY THE TROUPE.

—o—o—o—o—

BOOK EARLY. PRICES DOUBLE.

THE

SOMME-TIMES.

WITH WHICH ARE INCORPORATED

The Wipers Times, The "New Church" Times & The Kemmel Times.

No 1. Vol 1. Monday, 31st July, 1916. Price 1 Franc.

EDITORIAL.

WELL! Here we are in July with the thermometer still hanging round in the fifties. The war seems to be drawing nearer to its only conclusion, and two or three friends of ours in the Division are thinking of buying a farm at Hooge and settling down immediately they get back from Hunland, although we personally think they would have a much better chance of decent profits if they mined there instead of farmed. The name of the present issue is not yet decided for good and sufficient reasons. By the time these lines appear the 24th Division will be very near its second birthday and, should it be possible at the time, we think it would be a good idea to hold an open ghymkana to celebrate the occasion. On another page is the report of a cricket match held at Locrehof Farm. This was a most interesting event, and the sight of some of our cheery Brigadiers. (the war forgetting, by the war forgot from 2-7 p.m) gambolling on the village green was most inspiring. Our special reporter was there and has done the match in his best style. Also, we have attached to our staff at an enormous salary Mr. Teech Bomas the well-known war correspondent. His thrilling articles will be read with great interest by everyone, especially as he sees incidents overlooked by all others. Our mammoth competition met with the success which has attended its predecessors, and the judge has retired to his dug-out with a case of whisky, 10 sacks of mail and a headache. The result will be published in due course. Our thrilling serial is drawing to its conclusion, and we are making arrangements for another Herlock Shomes story. We also hope to introduce several new features shortly, including another mammoth competition. Should this issue be very much delayed we hope our readers will understand and excuse it on account of the many calls on our time. Since the above was written certain things have happened which have decided the name of the present issue. Whether we shall have time or not to fill all the pages is another thing, and our readers will understand if the number is produced with a blank page or two. We think it better to take this course than wait till after the show to produce a full number. And now there is one thing we would wish to do, that is, to wish God-speed to all our pals in the Division. We've all had many weary and many good times together. Who that has known it can forget the joy of a spot in the Culvert dug-out, and the many other haunts known to most of us? Whatever comes we can rely on the old Division to give a good account of itself. So here's to you all, lads, the game is started, keep the ball rolling and remember that the only good Hun is a dead Hun. Good luck be with you all, and when we pull out—well—call in at the editorial sanctum for a spot and a chin.

THE EDITOR.

There was a young girl of the Somme,
Who sat on a number five bomb,
She thought 'twas a dud 'un,
But it went off sudden—
Her exit she made with aplomb!

TO MINNIE.

(Dedicated to the P.B.I.)

In days gone by some aeons ago
That name my youthful pulses stirred,
I thrilled whene'er she whispered low
Ran to her when her voice I heard.

—:o:—

Ah Minnie! how our feelings change,
For now I hear your voice with dread,
And hasten to get out of range
Ere you me on the landscape spread.

—:o:—

Your lightest whisper makes me thrill,
Your presence makes me hide my head,
Your voice can make me hasten still—
But 'tis away from you instead.

—:o:—

You fickle jade! you traitrous minx!
We once exchanged love's old sweet tales
Now where effulgent star-shell winks
Your raucous screech my ear assails:

—:o:—

No place is sacred, I declare,
Your manners most immodest are,
You force your blatant presence where
Maidens should be particular.

—:o:—

You uninvited do intrude,
You force an entrance to my couch,
Though if I've warning you're about
I'll not be there, for that I'll vouch.

—:o:—

Name once most loved of all your sex,
Now hated with a loathing great,
When next my harassed soul you vex
You'll get some back at any rate,

CRICKET.

—o—

WITH APOLOGIES TO CAPT. F. B WILSON (Late of the Daily Mirror.)

—o—

X. I. B. v, LOCREHOF.

—o—

It was a great game, we won of course, and Roger Rum got a blob, bless him. Anyway I won ten bob, and how Johnny did love it. Small wonder too, as he had actually registered more'n forty on the tins before he had his middle ash rather badly bent, watching 'em like the meanest private watches dear Minnie at Spanbroekmolen and connecting every time too he was. What an innings, in other words the real bons. As for the Editor he revelled in it—he is rather roguish with the crimson rambler. Was I there? Search me as they say in Horace, AND I may tell you that the day before when the Editor was batting I removed all three pegs with the second ball (the only reason it was'nt the first was because I'd previously arranged to let him get a couple by serving up a full toss well outside the crux peg providing he did the same to me when I staggered into the centre) well, as I've said, the Editor got a couple and then went out—quick—and during the remainder of the innings proceeded to prop up the bar at the regimental canteen during closed hours too—the horrid florid Forester! By the time, therefore, I took my stand he'd forgotten all about our little do, and hanged if the very first time he swung the spheroid at me it was'nt accompanied by a fearful crash of ash. He's no sportsman as you may or may not know, but I'm getting a trifle off the rails so I'll continue. The Professor turned up for a moment, and we assured him we weren't playing too much cricket but merely combining same with a little bombing practice. And what about our sometime Rugger international? I don't care to tell you how many he got as he's my C.O. so ask the Editor if you want the news. The wicket was as beautiful as Tina, and we had a priceless day although Bobbie was'nt playing.

P.B.I.

GOD-SPEED.

For a year we've taken what came along,
We've fought or worked and we've held our line,
Till August finds us "going strong,"
The game's afoot and the goal's the Rhine.

—:o:—

Through summer's heat and the winter's gloom
We've tasted the joys that the Salient holds,
A filthy dug-out our only room,
Where our only comfort a jar enfolds.

—:o:—

We've learnt the game in a grim hard school,
Where mistakes had a price that 'twas hard to pay,
With Death sitting by and holding the rule,
And conducting our studies by night and day.

—:o:—

But we've also learnt, and 'tis good to know,
That the pal of a dug-out's a friend worth while,
For friendship made 'neath the star-shell's glow
Means "Help every lame dog over a stile."

—:o: -

Now we have arrived in pastures new,
Where the Hun's taking lessons that once he gave.
Here's the best of good luck to all of you
In the teaching of blackguards how to behave.

EVE, BLANCHE,
AND
PHRYNETTE.

(WITH APOLOGIES TO THE SPIRIT OF JAMES ELROY FLECKER.)

Three picture-papers Smith and Sons send weekly,
And three dear ladies write therein from Blighty;
Write every week to tease us in our exile,
Of Maude s latest hat and Edith's newest nighty.

—§ † §—

THIS IS THE SONG OF THE PRETTY PRATTLER;
WHO SIGNS HERSELF "EVE" IN EACH THURSDAYS "TATLER."

—§ † §—

Mistress of fash.—a little rash but awf'ly smart, and awf'ly CHIC—
I gad about in Belgrave Square and write you what I've done each week.
Phrynette may wield a Gallic pen, and Blanche make love to her R.N.,
But I and Tou-tou still shall sway our darling Khaki Soldier-men.
Look on my pics. O B.E.F.—Fish drew them all. Do you suppose
A man could love a girl who'd got no whiskers and a pukka nose?
Look on my frocks 'cos they're the rage, dear Phyllis wears them on the stage;
(And I puff 'Tina' in MY page—and so we're quits O Soldier-man!)
Am I not simply just too sweet, the fluffy dream you'd like to meet
And take for walks down Regent Street, when you're on leave, O Soldier-man?
But you may only dream, and scan my funny face, dear Soldier-man,
And wonder if you can't or can, FOR LEAVE IS CANCELLED Soldier-man!

—§ † §—

TRES MOUTARDE, IF YOU UNDERSTAND HER,
IS COUSIN BLANCHE, OF "THE BYSTANDER."

—§ † §—

I am the girl who loves the sea. O Sailors take me out to tea!
With anything in blue and gold, the Carlton's good enough for me.
The Tête-à-tête, the palm-embowered, the half-a-crown, the Khushi tea,
The hold-my-hand the lets-discuss-where-we-will-go-this-evening tea.
Then, after tea, you'll drive me home; and you shall smoke, and Blanche shall comb
Her .... is it gold or brown or black this hair of mine? And then will roam,
Down dear old Bond Street to the Ritz: and you shall say "Those fluffy bits
Of lace upon your pink CHARMEUSE, you darling Blanche, just give me fits."
Thereafter we will go and see—unless of course you're bored with me—
The very nicest show in town—I think, don't you?, the Gaiety.
Then on to Ciro's where we'll dance some rather dinky fox-trot steps—
And in the car you'll hold me rather close because I'm scared of Zepps.
Bad boy to ask if I'll allow one kiss upon my marble brow;
And what a silly place to kiss .... we're very hot in England now!

—§ † §—

LAST AND NOT LEAST (HER, I HAVE MET)
A LITTLE SKETCH OF FRIEND PHRYNETTE.

—§ † §—

Mine is the PIQUANT Gallic touch; a word, a word and I had said
The little more, the overmuch that makes the printer-man blush red.
Just like my LINGERIE I choose the phrases which you's read out there;

And Gladys never draws QUITE bare—
because we think its bad for you's.
Poor lonely you's who write to me, I tell
you's stories, frilly ones—
Half French, half English, double-paged,
my pretty-pretty pattern runs.
I write about my woman friends as
PETITES AMIES—you's, confess
How much that MOT-A-PROPOS lends to
your Phrynette of naughtiness!
Did I tell you's of Dolly, who's fiancée
to a brace of you's;
And how that MECHANTE Margot lost a
pair of ROSE DU BARRY shoes?)
What would you's do, poor lonely you's,
without my letters to peruse,
I seem to hear you's voices shout a
hundred thousand loud NA POO's!

GILBERT FRANKAU.

31/7/16.

A MESSAGE FROM MR. TEECH BOMAS.

BY OUR SPECIAL CORRESPONDENT MR TEECH BOMAS.

—:0:—

MR TEECH BOMAS SPEAKS.

—:0:—

No Man's Land, 20/7/16.

I write from the middle of the battlefield. There are a lot of bullets but I don't mind that. Also the air is thick with shells. That also I don't mind. Let me tell you all about it while I can think clearly. Before the battle commenced I took up a favourable position in No Man's Land, the little larks were larking and the morning was fine. Then Hell broke loose and as things got really hot I climbed up the rope of a sausage and joined two A.S.C.'s who were also watching the proceedings. Let me tell you of the gallant dash of the Umpshires: Into the pick of the Prussian Guard they dashed. The few of the Guard who remained cried "Kamerad" and surrended. That rush was epic. I then walked over the German lines to have a look at them. There were a lot more bullets but what would you? Now I thrill with an ecstacy. Here they come, the wood is ours. Strange associations, here we see the submarine co-operating with the cavalry and shells falling thickly. Then—the peasants—I witnessed the thrilling scenes of the last peasants leaving their happy farms in No Man's Land, harnessing their mongrel dogs into their little carts and driving off when the battle got a bit hot. It was epic. Taking a place is one thing but putting it back is another. Profound but true, and so the wood was won. A correspondent must always see to write. This may appear unnecessary to the cognoscenti, but it is so. To-morrow I will tell you more. I return now to the battle.

H. TEECH BOMAS.

TRENCH CONVERSATIONS.

—o—o—o—

NO II.

—:0:—

SUB. (To man wearing cardigan over shirt on blazing hot day)—"What the deuce are you wearing your cardigan for on a day like this?"

MAN.—To keep my shirt clean, sir!

The Kaiser once said at Peronne
That the Army we'd got was "no bon,"
But between you and me
He didn't "compris"
The size of the job he had on

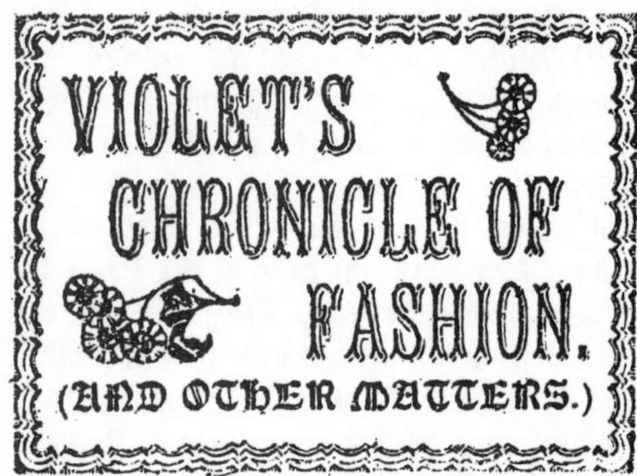
VIOLET'S
CHRONICLE OF
FASHION.
(AND OTHER MATTERS.)

PITY the poor Fashion Chronicler! An account of what we've been wearing this month would read more like November than July, for furs have been more in evidence than muslins. But we still contrive to look charming, so what does it matter? Even when a Burberry is the only sensible wear by day, we can always enjoy our glad rags in the evening. Such a jolly little dance we had here last night. Where is here? Well, not so very many miles from that well-known Camp of Little Muddy Huts, whence came most of our guests. All leave being stopped—of course—and a whole army of P.M.'s being on the alert along the three miles to the station, our gallant partners had to follow the time-honoured custom and depart from camp by motor in the opposite and unguarded direction. After a big detour and an hour's run they arrived here in excellent spirits. The orchestra was fine, the floor was A 1, the sitting-out rooms were "de luxe." So the whole affair was voted a huge success when the party set off on the return journey at three o'clock this morning in their motley collection of cars and Fords. Extraordinary how much more you men enjoy anything if it is "out of bounds."

I WAS up in town this week—so glad I'm not a Londoner, who can never know the joys of that unfailing tonic, a visit to town. Shopping, did you say? No, thank you, not for me, while "Sales" are on. I saw two of the new revues, and if anyone has leave shortly due, he should not miss "Some" at the Vaudeville, the brightest show I've seen for a long time. Lee White scores a huge success, so does little Betty Bolton, while pretty Billie Carleton is more charming than ever. (Do I notice Grandpa showing signs of interest?) "We're all in it," at the Empire, is likely to be a big success; you can imagine the very pretty effect of the rose scene, where dainty maidens climb ladders of roses to the tune of a haunting refrain,—it delighted the first night audience immensely.

I TOLD you, did'nt I, that high winds meant adventures while our skirts are so short? Well, last week I saw a pretty girl's skirts blown right over her head by a lively gale. I was reminded of the ad. in one of our recent numbers "Have you got nice Knees? Do you want to show'em?" Fortunately, the lady's lingerie and limbs were alike irreproachable, and I was not the only spectator who hugely enjoyed her confusion as she vainly battled with the surging billows—I mean the billowing serge. But an outraged Mrs. Grundy rushed at her—This is actual fact—and hustled her into the nearest shop; so our vision of ankles, etc., was cut short.

OFFERS of assistance with this column continue to reach me from all quarters. One well known perverter of mottoes even offers illustrations; but though his copy must have spoilt the eyesight of many good printers, I don't see why his drawings should be allowed to spoil their morals. I doubt whether the samples he submits would ever reach the printing department, they would be probably confisticated by our staid Editor. Another correspondent thinks the terms of colloboration could be settled over a little lunch at Prince's, and will I please fix an early date? He's evidently a man of ideas. But I resist all blandisnments; this is my column and mine only. You know, some day in the long distant future your Vi will be a gentle, silvery-haired old lady—oh, still dainty and very charming I promise you—and when the children gather round and say "What did you do in the Great War Granny?" she'll proudly answer with a reminiscent smile, "I was on the Staff, dears—the Staff of the 24th Division Times."

TRENCH CONVERSATIONS.

—o—o—o—

NO I.

—:o:—

KIND COMPANY COMMANDER (To Man in Trench)—"That aeroplane's a bit low?" MAN IN TRENCH—"Yes, sir." K.C.C.—"It's a Boche, isn't it?" M.I.T.—"Yes, sir." K.C.C.—"I don't seem to know your face, are you one of the latest drafts?" M.I.T.—"No sir, I'm a gunner." K.C.C.(musing)—"That's the worst of these Batt. Lewis Gunners, one never gets to know them." (Aloud) "I suppose you often fire at Boche aeroplanes when they fly low?" M.I.T.—"No, sir." K.C.C.—"Haven't you got any A.A. mountings for your gun?" M.I.T.—"No, sir." K.C.C.—"Well, of course, even if you haven't its really quite simple for you to fire your gun from the shoulder, isn't it? M.I.T.—"No sir, it 'ud be 'ard to get the right amount of elevation, it would." K.C.C.—"Why, my man?" M.I.T.—"'Cos I'm the signalling corporal for the 4·5 Howitzer Battery coverin' yer, and it 'ud give yer a bit of an 'eadache firing the ruddy gun from the shoulder, it would!"—(COLLAPSE OF K.C.C.)—The war proceeds. [P.B.I.

OUR SPLENDID NEW SERIAL.

—o—o—o—

FROM BUGLER BOY TO BRIGADIER.

OR

How Willie Pritchard Rose from the Ranks.

—o—o—o—

A STORY OF THE GREAT WAR.

—o—o—o—

BY RUBY N. DARES.

—o—o—o—

CHAPTER 6.

—:o:—

WILLIE now found himself Colonel in command of one of the finest infantry battalions in the British Army. Having seen that all his men had had enough to eat, and had cleaned their horses, he sent round to see that all the cannons had been swabbed down. Clarence had followed him muttering dark threats, the while casting malignant glances at his stalwart back. This did not disturb Willie, whose thoughts had turned to home and Maggie the Mill-lass of Millwarde. Where was she, and what was she doing? Heaving a bitter sigh Willie turned, and to his horror saw that he was surrounded. The enemy had completely enveloped him in the dark, and Willie saw that it would be a fight to the death. Seizing a bugle he aroused his slumbering troops, and made ready Who shall tell of the horrors of that time? For four days Willie and his gallant band held out. No food—all the water gone—what could he do? An honourable surrender was the only course open to him. He was just on the point of hoisting the white flag when—Hark! What is that? Can it be? It is! It isn't! It sir! Hurrah, the Band of the Royal Tiddley Umpshires. The enemy fled at their approach. Willie hastened forward to meet his rescuers. As they came nearer Willie saw the Commander-in-Chief at their head. Saluting, Willie reported to him that all was well. The Commander in Chief promoted him Brigadier on the spot, and told him to go to the ambulance to get a drink. As he was pouring himself out a spot he happened to glance at the comely figure of a Red Cross nurse who was in the van. "Maggie!!!" "Willie!!!" In a moment they were in each others' arms Muttering "Curse you!" Clarence strode off.

OUR MAMMOTH COMPETITION.

We have great pleasure in announcing that the 1st and 2nd prizes of the above Competition have again been won by the Editor and Sub Editor respectively with the following praiseworthy efforts We reprint the verse *in toto* for the edification of those who were not fortunate enough to see it,

There was a fair Belgian of Loere,
Who smothered herself with red ochre,
When people asked why
She exclaimed with a sigh,

The following line was successful in gaining the 1st prize:—

I'M SUCH AN INVETERATE JOKER.

The 2nd prize was awarded for the following line:

I'VE FALLEN IN LOVE WITH A STOKER

As usual no other efforts were worthy of consideration, so we were compelled to return the balance of the prize money to our bank.

Correspondence.

To the Editor,
"Somme-Times."

Sir,

I should like to draw your attention to a recent discovery of ours which we have made by judicious inter-breeding. It is the "Parrotidgin" and it is the result of crossing the parrot and the pigeon. It should be of immense use to the War Office as the bird can deliver its message by word of month. It requires careful feeding and judicious handling. Our efforts in this direction are still proceeding and we will advise you of any further results.

We are, sir
Yours faithfully,
GRANDPA and NICKETT,
Ornithologists.

Things We Want to Know.

—o—

The name of our most recent encarnadine acquisition who has a pretty taste in visiting cards and where he got them.

? ? ?

The name of the brunette infantry officer who succumbed to measles of the Hun variety and where he caught them.

? ? ?

Whether most of the Division goes to the BIG Town to see the CATHEDRAL.

? ? ?

Whether we still have the Munque collection of Old Masters with us and if there have been any recent additions.

On account of the many calls on our time and space we are compelled this week to curtail the space alloted to our Correspondence and Answers to Correspondents.

ARE YOU A VICTIM TO
OPTIMISM?

—0—0—0—0—

YOU DON'T KNOW?

—0—0—0—0—

THEN ASK YOURSELF THE FOLLOWING QUESTIONS.

—0—0—0—0—

1.—DO YOU SUFFER FROM CHEERFULNESS?
2.—DO YOU WAKE UP IN A MORNING FEELING THAT ALL IS GOING WELL FOR THE ALLIES?
3.—DO YOU SOMETIMES THINK THAT THE WAR WILL END WITHIN THE NEXT TWELVE MONTHS?
4.—DO YOU BELIEVE GOOD NEWS IN PREFERENCE TO BAD?
5.—DO YOU CONSIDER OUR LEADERS ARE COMPETENT TO CONDUCT THE WAR TO A SUCCESSFUL ISSUE?

IF YOUR ANSWER IS "YES" TO ANYONE OF THESE QUESTIONS THEN YOU ARE IN THE CLUTCHES OF THAT DREAD DISEASE.

WE CAN CURE YOU.

TWO DAYS SPENT AT OUR ESTABLISHMENT WILL EFFECTUALLY ERADICATE ALL TRACES OF IT FROM YOUR SYSTEM.
DO NOT HESITATE—APPLY FOR TERMS AT ONCE TO:—

Messrs. Walthorpe, Foxley, Nelmes and Co.

TELEPHONE 72, "GRUMBLESTONES." TELEGRAMS: "GROUSE."

STOP! & THINK!!!

—0—0—0—

Messrs. NUNTHORPE, COX & CO.
Are now opening their book on the

Summer Meeting.

—0—0—0—

THE OLD LIBERAL PRICES ARE ON OFFER.

5 1 the field for the BAPAUME STAKES
All in, Run or not.

We Always Pay!!!

—0—0—0—

Midsummer Handicap.

1-3 ATKINS and ANZAC.
100 1 THE FLYING HUN.

—0—0—0—

Do not trust financial crocks,
Put it on with Nunthorpe, Cox.

—0—0—0—

Telegrams: ' REDTABS."
Telephone: Six Lines, "102 Back'um."

Mr. HOWFIELD

Begs to notify his many kind Patrons that he and Mr. CAULETT have DISSOLVED PARTNERSHIP owing to a little difference of opirion and he is carrying on business in NEW and COMMODIOUS PREMISES with

Mr. NORLETT.

—0—0—0—

COME & INSPECT OUR

New styles in tine Tiles
Great cops in gorgeous props

AND REMEMBER THAT

If you're going o'er the bags,
Come and see our new glad rags.

—0—0—0—

THE SAME FINANCIAL LATITUDE ALLOWED OUR CUSTOMERS AS HITHERTO.

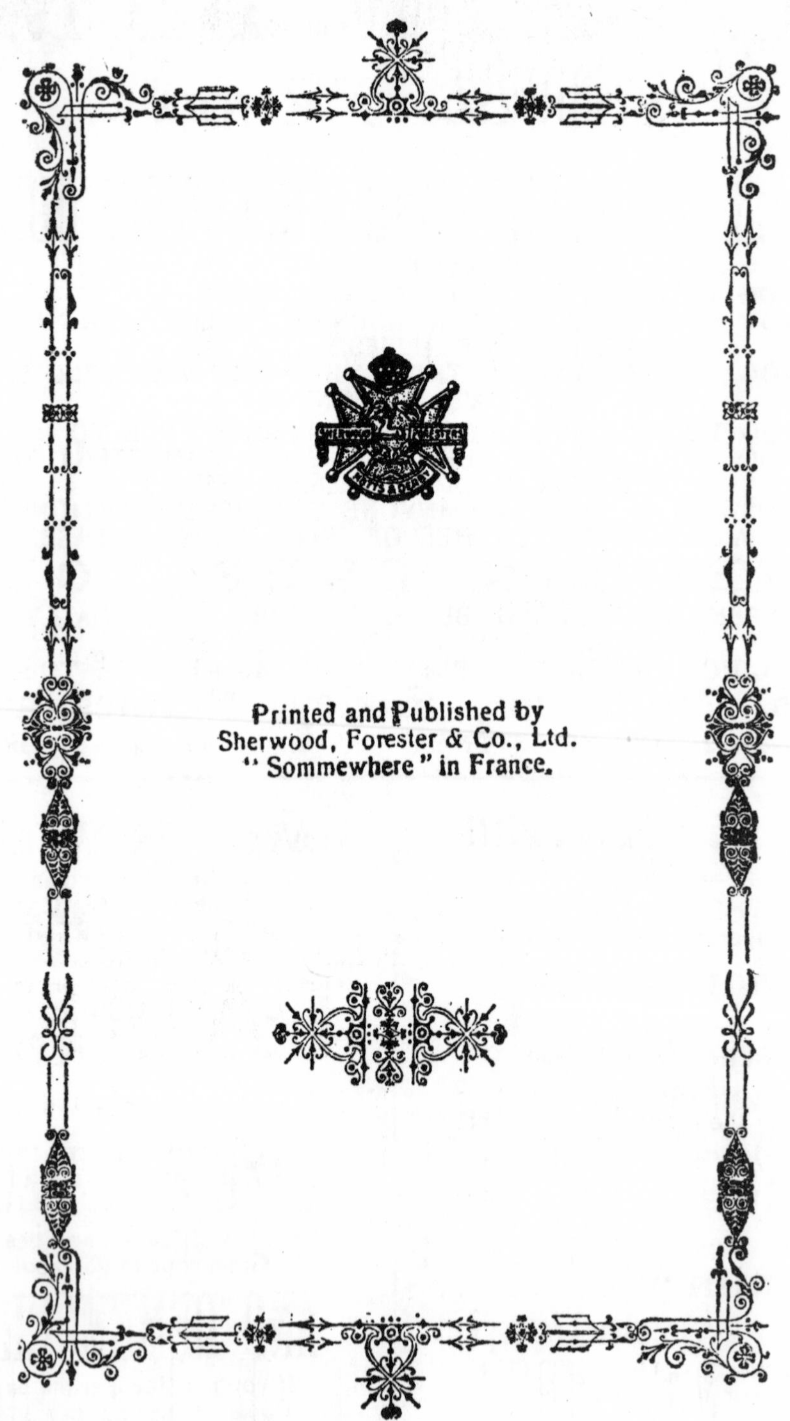

Printed and Published by
Sherwood, Forester & Co., Ltd.
"Sommewhere" in France.

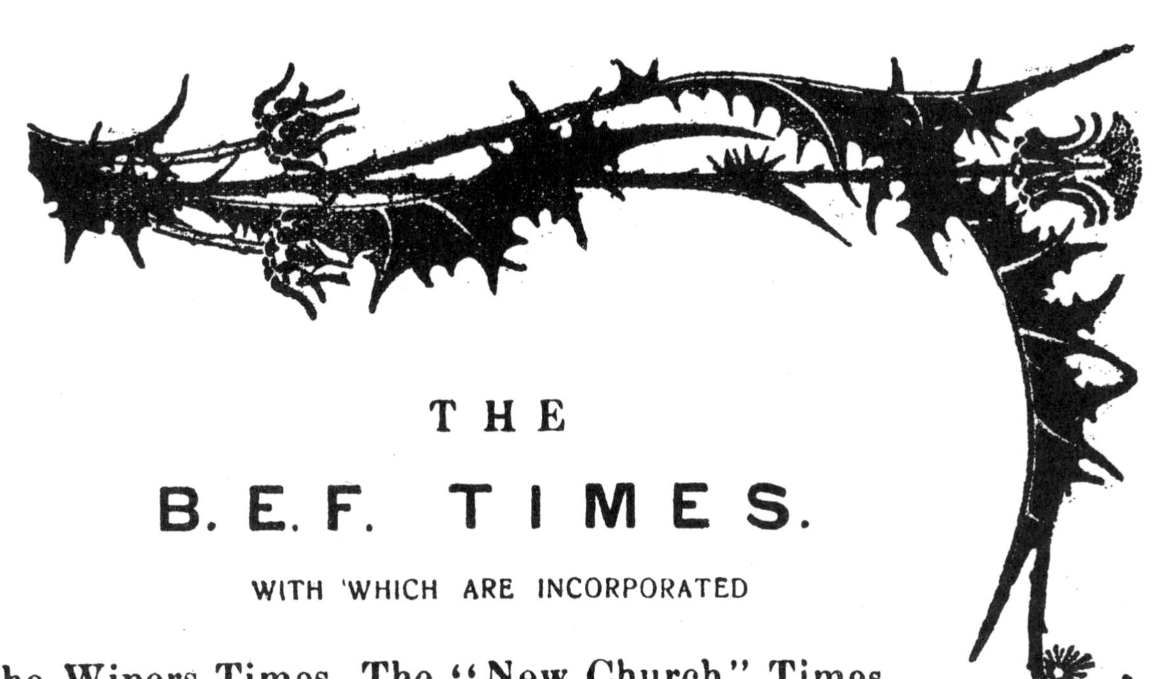

THE

B. E. F. TIMES.

WITH WHICH ARE INCORPORATED

The Wipers Times, The "New Church" Times,
The Kemmel Times & The Somme-Times.

No 1 Vol 1. Friday: 1st December, 1916. Price 1 Franc.

GUILLEMONT HIPPODROME.

—o—o—o—o—

THIS WEEK—GREAT REVUE.

HULLO TANKO

FAMOUS "ALL STAR" CASTE,
BOSCH BEAUTY CHORUS

—o—o—o—o—

PRECEDED BY A LIVELY CURTAIN RAISER, ENTITLED
ZERO PLUS 5.

—o—o—o—o—

Screaming Farce, Entitled

IT'S A WAY THEY HAVE IN THE ARMY.

—o—o—o—o—

"No Treating" Order Absolutely Ignored, and
We still have a Promenade.

BOOK EARLY. PRICES AS USUAL.

USE THE L.B.M.L. RAILWAY AND

TRAVEL IN COMFORT

—o—o—o—o—

Our new Branch Lines are now Open. We can take you over the Battlefields of Europe. TOURISTS SPECIALLY CATERED FOR. Regular Passengers can obtain Books of Tickets at Greatly Reduced Prices.

—o—o—o—o—

We are now running TWO EXPRESSES DAILY and Business Men will seize this opportunity of saving time.

—o—o—o—o—

FOR TIMETABLES, ETC., WRITE :—

S. APPER,
General Manager,
L.B.M.L. Railway.

ARE YOU READY FOR WINTER?
HAVE YOU GOT YOUR WINTER'S KIT?

We can supply you from the

"Dernier Cri" in Macintoshes To Gum Boots.

—o—o—o—o—

The very latest things in Trench Coats with a flounced "Moire" lining and dainty motifs.

Send at once or you'll be late,
A soldier must be up-to-date.

HOWRIE and NORLETT,
Seventy-third Street.

THE

B. E. F. TIMES.

WITH WHICH ARE INCORPORATED

The Wipers Times, The "New Church" Times, The Kemmel Times & The Somme-Times.

No 1. Vol 1. Friday, 1st December, 1916. Price 1 Franc.

EDITORIAL.

A LONG time has elapsed since our last number. This was unavoidable, in fact at one time it seemed that our tenth number would also be our last, as the press was marooned in the midst of a disturbance which is taking place down South. However the outfit is once more safely housed, and our new premises, although draughty, are at least in a quieter situation where the street calls and other noises are not so persistent. Many cheery faces are missing from the Division; and it seems we must get a new lot of contributors. For reasons over which we have no control we are compelled to alter the title of our journal, and so we now appear under the all-embracing name of "The B. E. F. Times." May we here and now beg everybody to send along every incident which might be adapted, humorous or otherwise. We have great pleasure in announcing that, for an enormous fee, we have secured another effort from the pen of the author of "Herlock Shomes." Owing to the popular demand some characters of the story have been resuscitated, we will leave to the reader's imagination how they got over the little difficulties in which the end of the last serial saw them. The first instalment appears in this number. We are fortunate in having another graphic article from our special correspondent Mr. Teech Bomas. Also we have opened a new branch in "Our Matrimonial Column," and any candidates for a suitable partner can probably be accommodated from the splendid selection of charming young ladies we have on our books. For this branch we have secured the services of "the brunette infantry officer" whose graceful figure and bronzed complexion were such a feature at Prince's and the Piccadilly Grill Room in the dear dead days when we fondly imagined war to be other than wallowing in a dirty ditch. It was all very well for NAPOLEON to shout about every soldier carrying a Field Marshal's baton in his knapsack, after all he knew very little of war. The nearest approach nowadays is a tin of bully in a sandbag, and anyway even if you had a "Field Marshal's baton," then you'd have to dump it to make room for another pair of socks or you'd be over 35 lbs. We have an article from our special correspondent, who has just spent two years in a German front line trench disguised as a Hun. He had breakfast with the Crown Prince, and relates his experiences in a thrilling article. We have pleasure also in announcing a new competition. We should like to extend a welcome to all those who have recently joined the Division, and to express the hope that they will try to assist us by sending along copy. This also applies to all other units of the B. E. F., and we hope to receive enough copy to enlarge our numbers to 12 pages.

THE EDITOR.

TOMMY IN FRANCE.

—o—o—o—

"Oh! madamerselle, chery madamerselle,
You come for a nice promenay?
Yes, its always the same with your 'apres la guerre,'
And your 'me no compris' what I say,
Come along Bill to the old 'staminet,'
Though the beer may be rotten it still is a 'wet,'
A hunk off a loaf and a glass, me and you,
What's that old lady? Oh! damn it, 'Napoo.'"

"O.C. Companies will render a return,"
'Tis imperative that Q. should quickly learn,
If you're short a tin of bully
Please investigate it fully,
"O.C. Companies will render a return."

—:o:—

By the 16th inst. the O.C. Coys will state
If they've got an engine driver or a mate,
Or if some benighted private
Ever managed to arrive at
Excellence in sticking coal into a grate.

—:o:—

Are your men nonconformistic'ly inclined,
When you've had your cheese what happens to the rind?
Why was plum and apple jam
Substituted for the ham?
And your "eskimo" return is much behind.

—:o:—

Is your Company addicted to trench feet?
Do you save the bones from out your daily meat?
Have you men who can hew lumber
If so kindly send the number,
Is your S.A.A. affected by the heat?

—:o:—

Do you wonder at the awful careworn smile
On the face of every O.C. Coy, the while
In his sleep you'll hear him murmur
"Have I got a man from Burma,
Or a sergeant who can go and dam the Nile?"

FRAGMENTS FROM FRANCE.

—:o:—

And it came to pass in the early forenoon, having partaken of a frugal meal of clorinated tea and Tickler, I sallied forth and gained the chalky fastnesses of WHISKY CRATER, completely oblivious of the dangers I encountered from our own artillery and Tock Emmas! Scorning the periscope, I slowly elevated my bust above the parapet.

"Jee-rusalem—surely this is not the result of excessive thorassic lubrication? No, no, a thousand times NO! It cannot be since last night the Quartermaster once more failed us, and the Army Service Corps had registered another hit."

There, before my startled gaze appeared the familiar form of Ginger Fritz of Doodles!

Alas! What memories that name conjures up! Fritz of Doodles!

But, what a change!

Quantum mutatus ab illo as we used to say in our schooldays!

Gone was the greasy evening dress, and in its place the field grey uniform.

Gone too his happy smile, and in its place a look of concentrated hate.

He stopped! He looked! He listened!

Then he saw me.

With true Prussian instinct he levelled his musket and pointed it in my direction.

Like a flash an inspiration seized me! "Waiter" I cried at the top of my voice. "Waiter! A brandy and soda! A bun for the lady friend!"

At the sound of the well-known voice he started; his lethal weapon clattered to the ground, and with leaps and bounds he answered the call.

In two of the proverbial shakes he was beside me in the trench.

As I led my now smiling prisoner down the C.T. I had visions of how I would spend my week's leave. Doodles of course would be one of my first calls!

I was about to thank Fritz for the good turn he had done me, when I suddenly thought of A.O. 1965/3 . . . damm it all! I forget the rest of it—but I do remember that I can't go on leave for at least another four months,

VIRTUE.

Now you subs of tender years
For your morals, it appears,
(You must admit they're open much to question)
There is shortly going to be
A morality O.C.,
Who will see that vice does not spoil your digestion.

His H.Q. is going to be
Close by Leicester Square, and he
Will parade his Batt. for duty every night,
In his ranks we'll shortly see
P'raps a Bishop or M.P.,
Who will see that virtue's path you tread aright.

If on leave and pleasure bent
At Victoria, a gent
Will grab you as you're dodging off alone,
Will escort you to H.Q.,
When you'll quickly find that you
Are provided with an aged chaperone.

Your amusement will depend
On how much she'll let you spend,
And you'll dine at Lyons or an A.B.C.,
Should you dare to want a drink,
With a look she'll make you think
What an awful well of sin a sub can be.

You may smoke one cigarette,
Ere retiring you will get
All your orders for the morrow's pleasure feast,
Hand your cash in charge, and then
Off to bed as clock strikes ten,
Feeling that in former days you were a beast.

You will come to learn and love
Programmes as described above
For you must admit that you were most immoral,
You will find when leave's expired
That your fancies will have tired
For the glass that sparkles, and for lips of coral.

MY IMPRESSIONS.

—:0:—

BY THE MAN WHO HAD BREAKFAST WITH THE CROWN PRINCE.

—:0:—

AFTER a lot of manœuvring, I had managed to obtain an interview with the Staff Officer who was in charge of the Prince's valuable collection of "Objets de vertu." As I was perfectly disguised as a Bond Street Art Dealer my task was made much easier. By way of opening up the conversation I commented on a beautiful painting which I was told the Prince had bought from a poor Belgian woman After several hours conversation, during which I extolled the virtues of all the Prince's purchases, I was invited to take breakfast with the Prince himself What a heavensent opportunity. Of course I accepted with alacrity, and was shortly ushered into his own apartments "Hullo" said the Prince with his usual jocularity "How's your father" "My parent is enjoying his usual health I thank your Highness" I replied "May I venture to ask, how you are progressing at Verdun?"

"Verdun be damned" howled this spoilt favourite of fortune. "I never want to hear of the place again I was there, or at least near there some days ago, and made a speech to my soldiers —jolly good speech it was too—all the fancy bits about father and myself and 'places in the sun,' and that even if they were all killed I'd remember 'em in my prayers before turning in and the damned ungrateful fellows didn't even give me a 'hoch.' Father was cross"!

"And may I ask your Highness" I ventured, "How is his Imperial Majesty, your father." "Rotten" candidly replied the Prince, "He's really fed up with old Tirpy and Falky. You see, Tirpy told him either to go away, or come and run the damned fleet himself, and when papa told Tirpy that, as far as he could see, the fleet ran itself, Tirpy got cross and shot a poor old woman who was just going to knock a nail in his statue. So between the lot of them, life is becoming unbearable. Papa is so hasty."

"And may I ask your Highness's opinion of the military situation?" I ventured.

"Tophole" the Prince replied with enthusiasm. "If it lasts five or six years longer I shall have one of the best collections in the world."

"And the new English Army" I slyly remarked.

"Pah" snapped the Prince, as he savagely spat at his orderly "You wait till I've finished with Verdun, I'll attend to them."

Seeing that the interview was over, I took my leave and went, feeling confident that my disguise was unpenetrated.

Stop Press News.

—:0:—

GREAT ROBBERY AT THE MUNQUE ART GALLERIES.

—'0'—

We regret to announce that a burglary has taken place at the Munque Art Galleries. This valuable collection of old masters has been stolen and evidence points to an old hand at the game. Suspicion has fastened on William, jun., the Potsdam pincher. No further details yet to hand.

Generals von Sauerkraut and Hauptmann von Götzer wish to pair for the winter. Any acceptances should be addressed to O.C. Huns, Bapaume.

We hear that a traverse has been sunk at P 42 C 1·3. It is feared that this is likely to be a total loss. Submarines are suspected.

Miss Minnie Werfer arrived at the front, but went off suddenly.

TO THE P.B.I.

AN APPRECIATION.

Gone is the Summer, and gone are the flies,
Gone the green hedges that gladdened our eyes;
Around us the landscape is reeking with rain,
Gone is all comfort—'tis Winter again.

—§ † §—

So here's to the lads of the P.B.I.,
Who live in a ditch that never is dry;
Who grin through discomfort and danger alike,
Go "over the top" when a chance comes to strike;
Though they're living in Hell they are cheery and gay,
And draw as their stipend just one bob per day.

—§ † §—

Back once more to the boots, gum, thigh,
In a pulverised trench where the mud's knee-high;
To the duck-board slide on a cold wet night,
When you pray for a star-shell to give you light;
When your clothes are wet, and the rum jar's dry,
Then you want all your cheeriness, P.B.I.

—§ † §—

They take what may come with a grouse just skin-deep,
In a rat-worried dug-out on mud try to sleep;
Do you wonder they make all the atmosphere hum,
When some arm-chair old lunatic grudges them rum;
And they read in the papers that "James So-and-Such
Thinks that our soldiers are drinking too much."

Leave the Tommy alone Mr. James So-and-Such.
There are vices much nearer home waiting your touch;
Take yourself now for instance, examine and see
If your own priggish virtue is all it should be;
Give those of a larger life chance to enjoy
A charity wider than that you employ.

—§ † §—

Don't let Tommy's vices shatter your sleep,
When you write to the "Times" stick to "Little Bo-Peep,"
As a subject she's really much more in your line
Than licentious soldiery, women, and wine,
So here's to the lads who can live and can die,
Backbone of the Empire, the old P.B.I.

PIONEER.

Who Invented The Tanks?

—o—o—o—

We notice much discussion going on in our English contemporaries re the inventorship of the tanks. We could settle the matter here and now, but modesty compels us to keep the matter secret. If they have been helpful in winning the war we are content.

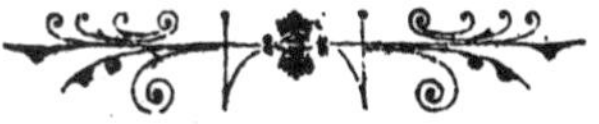

The prisoner with mournful look just sadly murmured "Who'd
Have thought that Prussia's best should thus so quickly have been looed?"
"Ho yus," said Tommy with a grin, "and bloomin' well napooed."

OUR SPLENDID NEW SERIAL.

—o—o—o—

"NARPOO RUM."

-o—o—o—

BY THE AUTHOR OF "SHOT IN THE CULVERT."

—o—o-o—

DRAMATIS PERSONAE:

—o—

Cloridy Lyme — A Sanitary Inspector.
Madeline Carot — A French Girl.
Intha Pink — A Pioneer.
General Bertram Rudolph de Rogerum—The Earl of Loose.
Lord Reginald de Kheathorpe — His Son.
Q. Wemm — A Storekeeper.
L. Plumernapple — A Soldier.
Herlock Shomes —The Great Detective.
Dr Hotsam — His Admirer.

—o—o—o—

CHAPTER 1.

—o—o—o—

"MY DEAR Hotsam, nothing of the kind I assure you," said Shomes, in his comfortable dug out in Quality Street. "My methods are based on deduction For instance, you hear someone coming up the stairs. Well, that is all the untrained ear can hear, but I know it's a soldier with many ribbons, an Irish accent and a friend named Reggie How do I know? My dear fellow— At that moment the door opened, and General Bertram Rudolph de Rogerum entered. Casting himself in a chair he demanded a cocktail. "Well, my dear general," said Shomes, placing his finger tips together, "how can I help you?" "What! you know me?" gasped the general "Oh yes!" said Shomes, as he tilted his vermoral sprayer and squirted a quart into his left arm

"Well," said the general, "I have come about a very mysterious affair Three nights running the Brigade rum ration has disappeared"

"Good heavens!" ejaculated Hotsam

"Aha!" said Shomes, "this promises to be a most interesting case." With that he picked up his violin, and proceeded to play dreamily. "Now I am ready, general, tell me all about it."

"Well," said the general, "as you know, my men mostly dislike rum, so that when it comes up I have it put in one of the outhouses, Three mornings ago, when my son, a priceless lad, if I may say so and above suspicion, went to look at it, he found it had disappeared. This has happened on both the following nights, and so I thought you might be able to help us."

"Have you no clue at all?" snapped the great detective.

"Only that Wemm's store seems to be more popular with the soldiers than formerly," said the general.

"Leave the matter in my hands, general, I will find your rum," said the detective, With that the general went off jauntily, whistling "Another Little Drink Wouldn't do us Any Harm."

Immediately he had gone Shomes sprang up. "Now Hotsam, we must to work!" Hastily throwing off his smoking jacket, he donned a tin-hat, mackintosh and gum boots, and disappeared into the night.

Meanwhile in the lovely French evening, Plumernapple was paying court to Madeline Carot, the pretty daughter at the local estaminet. "Well, it's only 'arf past eight," he murmured, "and there ain't no perlice corprel about." "No compris," she gurgled, as she made to shut the door. Picking up his A frame, he sadly made his way along the road.

At Wemm's store a very merry party was in progress, and Hotsam, taking the air, strolled across there. Pushing open the door, he saw Q. Wemm entertaining many friends from among the neighbouring troops. He was immediately made welcome, and a mug of hot liquid was thrust into his hand Casting his eyes round, they fell on a heap of jars in the corner "The Rum!" he gasped—

(WAS IT?)

(Read next thrilling instalment.)

(To be Continued.)

Owing to shortage of paper we have been obliged to restrict this number to 8 pages, so that many things are unavoidably held over. However, we hope that our Grand Xmas Double Number will follow close on the heels of this, and will contain our New Competition and many popular features.—(ED)

HOW THE TANKS WENT OVER.

—:o:—

BY OUR SPECIAL CORRESPONDENT,

Mr. TEECH BOMAS.

—:o:—

In the grey and purple light of a September morn they went over. Like great prehistoric monsters they leapt and skipped with joy when the signal came. It was my great good fortune to be a passenger on one of them How can I clearly relate what happened? All is one chaotic mingling of joy and noise No fear! How could one fear anything in the belly of a perambulating peripatetic progolódymythorus. Wonderful, epic, on we went, whilst twice a minute the 17in. gun on the roof barked out its message of defiance. At last we were fairly in amongst the Huns. They were round us in millions and in millions they died. Every wag of our creatures tail threw a bomb with deadly precision, and the mad, muddled, murderers melted. How describe the joy with which our men joined the procession until at last we had a train ten miles long. Our creature then became in festive mood and, jumping two villages, came to rest in a crump-hole. After surveying the surrounding country from there we started rounding up the prisoners. Then with a wag of our tail (which accounted for 20 Huns) and some flaps with our fins on we went. With a triumphant snort we went through Bapaume pushing over the church in a playful moment and then steering a course for home, feeling that our perspiring panting proglodomyte had thoroughly enjoyed its run over the disgruntled, discomfited, disembowelled earth. And so to rest in its lair ready for the morrow and what that morrow might hold. I must get back to the battle TEECH BOMAS.

OUR MATRIMONIAL COLUMN.

—:o:—

Everything in this department receives the greatest discretion and secrecy, and correspondents may be assured that all correspondence is treated with the utmost delicacy.

—:o:—

CAPTAIN.—35, handsome and dashing appearance. Thoroughly domesticated and capable of looking after the home. Feels lost in his present position of Camp Commandant. Fond of dogs. Would welcome correspondence with a view to matrimony. Money no object as he has his pay.—Write Vatican, c/o this paper.

—:o:—

BRIG GENERAL.—Young — charming personality—feels lonely Bashfulness has made him take this way of settling his future happiness, and he would like to correspond with some priceless young lady matrimonially inclined.—Write Rudolph, c/o this paper.

—:o:—

BRIG. GENERAL. — Companiable—jocose—domesticated—loving. Is feeling his unattached condition very much, and seizes this opportunity of making overtures to some sympathetic young lady. —Write Jock, c/o this paper.

—:o:—

LIEUT.-COLONEL. — Gone grey through loneliness. Feels that his life could be brightened by the introduction of a female element. Romantic dispositon, and has had many "affaires," but would entertain an opportunity of settling down Widow preferred. Money no object, but would like one with small public house—Write Buffs, c/o this paper.

—:o:—

LIEUT.-COLONEL.—Tall and striking appearance. Just recovered from wound, feels lost now without feminine attentions, and would welcome correspondence that might ultimately end in providing him with congenial society for life.—Write Rugger, c/o this paper.

—:o:—

(Many thousand advertisements are held over for lack of space.)

THE WAR LORD AND THE CHANCELLOR.

(With apologies to the late LEWIS CARROL.)

The War Lord and the Chancellor,
Were walking hand in hand;
They laughed like anything to see
The devastated land;
"If this belonged to us," they said,
"It really would be grand."

—0—0—0—

"If fifty Huns with fifty guns,
Swept it for half a year;
Do you suppose," the War Lord said,
"That vict'ry would be near?"
"I doubt it," said the Chancellor,
And shed a bitter tear.

—0—0—0—

"You always were a pessimist,"
The frowning War Lord said;
"Oh! Highest One it is because
I always look ahead;
Before this War is finished you
And I will both be dead."

—0—0—0—

"Don't talk like that I do beseech,"
The War Lord wailed aloud;
"To win this War by any means,
You know that I have vowed;
With Zeppelins and submarines,
And waves of poison cloud."

—0—0—0—

"Oh! chuck it Bill," the Chancellor
Said with a rueful air,
"You know quite well with 'frightfulness'
We've tried them everywhere,
And got it back with interest,"
Bill glared and tore his hair.

He danced with rage, he howled and swore,
And vowed that he would see
That Army so contemptible
Would very quickly be
By every kind of "frightfulness"
Sent to eternity.

—0—0—0—

The Chancellor spoke loud and long,
With rhetoric inspired;
He spoke of love, and peace, and food,
He spoke till he was tired;
And when he paused he turned around—
The War Lord had expired!

Extracts From Contemporaries.

—0—0—0—

1.—(From "Corps Intelligence Summary," Nov. 1/14.)—"ALARMS.—Dogs have been HEARD BARKING in the trenches and ALSO GEESE. Confirmation is required as to whether the geese are in the trenches or wild geese flighting."

2.—(From "John Bull," Nov. 18/16.)—"The case of a certain BATTALION of the Duke of Wellington's Regiment is instanced to us. FIFTEEN THOUSAND STRONG, they have been at Skipton, Derby, etc. . . "

We have been asked by Lt.-Colonel Cunningham and Major Twiss to say "Good bye" for them to the many friends they have in the Division, to express their regret at having to leave them, and to wish them all the best of luck. We should like to say here, that in losing Lt.-Colonel Cunningham and Major Twiss, the whole Division feels it has lost two good pals, and that wherever they may go the wishes of the Division will be with them.

WHY WEAR THAT CHARLIE CHAPLIN?

—o—o—o—

WOULD YOU LIKE A LONG FLOWING CAVALRY MOUSTACHE?

—o—o—o—

WE CAN HELP YOU.

—o—o—o—

SEND AT ONCE FOR THE NEW MOUSTACHE TRAINER:

"THE DOPELET"

Made in Three Sizes and Materials:—

SILK — — 10 Fr.
CANVAS — — 5 Fr.
EXPANDED METAL — 2 Fr.

—o—o—o—

DOPE & CURRIE,

BROKEN HILL,
FRANCE.

POILE & TROTTER.

Mr. POILE wishes to announce to his many clients that, although he has severed his connection with Mr. Trotter, he is still doing business on the old lines. His Tourist Coupons have become more popular than ever. Send for one at once. They are still printed on the favourite yellow paper. Irish and Scotch clients specially catered for.

POILE,

Kew.

OUR DIVISIONAL STORES.

UNDER ENTIRELY NEW MANAGEMENT.

JARRIE AND CAMES, LTD

You want it! We've got it!! If we havn't try something else, it's just as good. Drop a P.C. and our Mr. Jarrie will call on you. (Perhaps Ed.)

—o—o—o—o—

One teaspoonful Cames's Curry and you'll never notice the cloridylime in your tea.

—o—o—o—o—

Follow the duck-boards! All lead to our well stocked branches, where you will be treated with civility and promises

NO TICK

Head Office: CONDY'S LANE, BRAKESMOUNT

Telephone: 5, "INAROW." Telegrams: "SCOTCHMAN."

Printed and Published by
Sherwood, Forester & Co., Ltd.
B. E. F.

GRAND XMAS DOUBLE NUMBER.

THE

B. E. F. TIMES.

WITH WHICH ARE INCORPORATED

The Wipers Times, The "New Church" Times, The Kemmel Times & The Somme-Times.

No 2. Vol 1. Monday 25th December, 1916. Price 1 Franc.

PALACE OF VARIETIES, L---- (CENSORED ED)

—o—o—o—o—

POSITIVELY THE GREATEST COLLECTION OF ENTERTAINERS WHICH HAS EVER BEEN GOT TOGETHER AT ONE PLACE AND TIME.

FOR ONE WEEK ONLY.

—o—o—o—o—

Miss MINNIE WERFER.

ALWAYS MEETS WITH A THUNDEROUS RECEPTION.

—o—o—o—o—

THE ALLIMAN FAMILY—Glee Singers.

COMPLETELY NEW NUMBERS, INCLUDING:—

"La Paloma," "They Didn't Believe Me."

—o—o—o—o—

The Irish Troupe Of Quick Change Artists.

IN THEIR AMUSING SKETCH,

"Won't You Come and Play in Our Yard."

—o—o—o—o—

GRAND OPERETTE, ENTITLED:—

WILLIAM, TELL!

GRAND MALE CHORUS.

AS PERFORMED BEFORE MOST OF THE CROWNED HEADS OF EUROPE.

DURING WHICH BETHMANIANO WILL SING

"I Would Row Wilson if Wilson Would Row Me."

—o—o—o—o—

PRICES DOUBLE. BOOK EARLY.

ANTI-ZEPPELIN CURTAIN LOWERED TWICE NIGHTLY.

LILLIES LECTURE HALL.

—o—o—o—o—

THE COMMITTEE has shown great enterprise in securing the services of all the CELEBRATED LECTURERS, and hopes to make this a popular feature during the coming winter.

All Buses Stop At The Door.

Don't be disappointed if you can't get in, come again.

Patrons from the front specially catered for in a large and commodious Market Square.

NEXT WEEK'S PROGRAMME.

MR. HITEOF BLISS

WILL GIVE A LECTURE ON

"PERMUTATIONS & COMBINATIONS."

If for knowledge you should thirst,
Take good care to get here first.

Admission Free. Come Early and Often.

Applications for Reserved Seats must be made to :—

FURS, TARMEY and Co.

GRAND CHRISTMAS BAZAAR.

HAVE YOU A FRIEND AT THE FRONT.

IF SO WHAT NICER PRESENT COULD YOU SEND HIM THAN OUR NEW

"VERMORLET."

This can be used either as a Soda-water Syphon or Anti-Gas Sprayer. Complete with 12 Bulus for each purpose, 50 Francs.

—o—o—o—o—

ALSO OUR NEW

"Combination Respirator and Mouth Organ."

The dulcet tones of the Mouth Organ will brighten even the worst Gas Attack.

—o—o—o—o—

WE SPECIALISE IN NOVELTIES.

—o—o—o—o—

Come and View. You will not be urged to buy. Or drop a Field Post Card, and we will send you our Illustrated Catalogue Printed in Seven Languages.

—o—o—o—o—

See our new Waterproof Suits. They are made to resist the damp of the Trenches. and only the best Metal is used in their construction.

—o—o—o—o—

HEROD'S, UNIVERSAL PROVIDER.

THE

B. E. F. TIMES.

WITH WHICH ARE INCORPORATED

The Wipers Times, The "New Church" Times, The Kemmel Times & The Somme-Times.

No 2. Vol' 1. Monday. 25th December, 1916. Price 1 Franc.

EDITORIAL.

NOW we have arrived at our "Grand Double Xmas Number" (this by-the way is provided the paper arrives in time) and the first thing any good Editor does, is to wish all his readers the very best of good wishes. Between ourselves I think the least said about "Peace on earth, goodwill to man" the better, when most of the inhabitants of this planet are trying to "put it across" someone or other in the most unpleasant way that lies handy. We have received many of the Xmas Nos. of our English contemporaries, and we must say that it is about time England had a war, if the popular taste runs in the direction indicated by most of the coloured plates. It is good to see that England has at last realised that we are at war, and has fixed the price of officers meals, although we fully endorse the views expressed by the Brigadier who wanted an extra pat of butter at an A.B.C. and was told he had already spent ninepence, and so was up to his limit. But it is undoubtedly a step in the right direction, and by the time the war is in full swing it will not surprise us to see many innovations of this sort, in fact, one might venture to prophecy that a few more years of war, will see officers restricted to a three shilling taxi fare. If we are to win the war then officers will really have to make every sacrifice. But it is pleasing to see that England has shaken herself and means business. Also we think that our contemporary the "Daily Mail" should be suppressed. It is always urging some drastic step, and calling attention to the war. In fact, so strong and persistent at times became its hysterical shouting, that some decisions were actually reached. All this is very unnerving, and we really think that the total suppression of the Northcliffe Press is the only way of ensuring the preservation of a respectable and dignified "festina lente" policy. Should the war be hurried we, the Editor, would lose our job, and so would many others, a fate horrible to contemplate. Out of work, and thrown on the mercy of a hard and cruel world, good heavens! Put more coal on the fire! My dug-out has suddenly become chilled. A bas Northcliffe a bas "Daily Mail". Taisez vous! Mefiez vous! Les oreilles ennemies vous ecoutent! During our nocturnal rambles the other night, when the country was bathed in a soft light, the joint production of moon and star shell, we met a PESSIMIST. He was a strange elfish creature, and seemed in the depths of despair. A broken rum jar at his side, and the mute evidence of his appearance testified to the utter abandonment of all hope. He opened up the conversation with the remark "We've lost this 'ere war." "Come cheer up old chap all is not yet over" we remarked in a futile endeavour to throw a little light into the darkness "Hover" he exclaimed as he took off a gum boot and emptied a stream of liquid mud into a dixie full of tea belonging to the next dug-out. "Ho, then yer don't read the papers. 'Ere's Ilarious Belloc says all's lost in the East, 'ere's Bottomley says we're sitting on a volcano, and a lump of pineapple gone through the rum jar. I'm going over the top to kill a 'un. I'm that fed up." Seeing the impossibility of disputing his point we passed on, deep in thought. "Surely, surely," we thought "they must realise everything possible is being done. Here we have officers meals limited to five shillings, and they're not to wear evening clothes any longer. Good heavens! Can the fellow not realise what an effort we are making. And so we returned home, saddened by our experience, and killed three rats on the way in the irritation of the moment. But this, by-the-way, is our Xmas Number and we have rather side-tracked:

"Good King Wenceslas looked out
On a frosty morning."

Can you imagine a picture of "Good King Wenceslas" sticking his nose out of a dug out and saying what he thought of war in general, and Huns in particular? Try and imagine the dear old lad as a platoon commander at "stand to" on a Xmas morning! He'd have carolled some We have great pleasure in announcing that our new Mammoth Competition will be found on the last page. We are awaiting news of several new and interesting features which we hope to include in this number which we expect to be able to increase to twelve pages. Violet returns to the fold in this number, and we will have to forgive her for her temporary desertion which she has explained prettily to us. We should now like to wish you one and all the best of luck at Xmas and during the coming year.

THE EDITOR.

SHATTERED ILLUSIONS.

—o—o—o—

It may be love that makes the world go round,
Yet with the statement oft I disagree;
It was not love (on that I'll bet a pound)
That, last night, made the world revolve round me.

—o—o—o—

I cannot bring my mind to realise
That love inspired friend Fritz, when he propelled
A Minnie of a most terrific size
In my direction, so, I had him shelled.

Intelligence Summary.

—o—o—o—

X REGIMENT.

—o—o—

For the 24 hours ending in the Early Morning. (?)

7 a.m.—Bosche seen at K.42.b.9.7, wearing a pair of boots. (Normal.)

8·45 a.m.—Hun aeroplane pursued one of our carrier pigeons over our lines. After a burst of M.G fire, our pigeon was seen to crumple up and crash to the ground.

9·30 a.m.—One of our machines in retaliation dropped a 200 ton bomb on a German at H.69.b.2 3. Good results were observed. Our machine returned safely.

11·5 a.m.—Enemy fired 10 Pomegranates and one Pumpkin into our sap at H.62.c.7.8.

Noon—.A bombardment by our Stokes's guns was followed by shrieks and groans from the enemy trenches.

12·50 p.m.—Enemy fired 80 Minnies. Seventy of these exploded in our front line. No damage was done. Our heavy artillery at once replied by bombarding our own support line for two hours. At the finish of the bombardment our support line was completely obliterated. This proves the superiority of our ammunition.

3 p.m.—Sniper located at H.Z.0.5, dispersed by the fire of our heavy artillery.

4.10 p.m.—Four sandbags in our front line damaged by T.M. fire. A Court of Inquiry will be held to fix the responsibility for placing them there.

6.50 p.m.—A Very light fired by a Bosche burst into puce and yellow stars. These were thought to be crescent shaped. Nothing unusual followed.

9.50 p.m.—Strange noise heard near, sounded like an ostritch in the Bosche trenches munching glass. or a train.

12 m.n.—Flight of 20 Zeppelins seen by officer on duty, who failed to report on the proper form, and no action was taken.

2.50 a.m.—One of our patrols brought in a pink garter, whereby an important identification has been established.

4·10 a.m.—Bosche heard playing a barrel-organ in No Man's Land. Organ located at H 22 c.3.4. After a heavy concentration of fire the music ceased. The organ had disappeared by daylight.

Christmastide, Christmastide, mistletoe and holly,
Lovely girls and ingle nook
Gaiety where'er you look
In each magazine or book
Banish melancholy.

—:o:—

In my brazier as I gaze
Pictures come and pictures go,
Dimly seen across the haze—
Christmases we used to know.

—:o:—

Now the coals burn clear and bright
There I see a merry throng
Round the fire, one Xmas night,
Laughter ringing loud and long.

—:o:—

Now the glow has disappeared,
And my dug-out's overcast,
Just outside the night is seared
With a shell, or Minnie's blast,

—:o:—

Now again she's burning clear,
Visions come of better days,
Gone discomforts that are near,
Hope around my dug-out plays.

—:o:—

Pictures come and pictures go,
Yet one truth alone remains,
He who strikes the best last blow,
He it is the prize who gains.,

—:o:—

So what matter mud or snow ?
Spring and Summer come in turn,
Better days will come, and so
Burn, my good old brazier, burn.

THE WAR IN THE EAST.

—:o:—

Major Taude, B.C.

—:o:—

Of course all the tactics employed in this campaign are wrong. I have studied the whole affair carefully (from maps and the histories of previous wars) and I find them absolutely contrary to all the rules laid down by Julius Caesar and Hannibal. I well remember the excellent results obtained by my adoption of the tactics used by Bruce at Bannockburn, and I consider that it was due to these that I obtained the splendid moral victory over the Church Lads' Brigade, at Shepherd's Bush, in 1870. I have proved time and again in my articles that the opposing force can only hope for success so long as it beats the defending force, and that, once the positions are reversed, then the defending force will become the attacking force. War and tactics have been my constant study, and I feel sure that a more careful scrutiny of my works would lead to an earlier successful termination of the war. There was that successful little affair of mine at Clapham Common which might be emulated with advantage by Sir Douglas Haig in his Western campaign. Verb. sap.

OUR SHORT STORY.

—:o:—

It was Xmas morning in the trenches! M-m-m-m-m-m.

THE END.

Peace, peace, let us have peace,
Quoth Bill with a face grave and long;
You can see we have won
Ere you've really begun,
So let's chuck it while I'm going strong.

Gone are the days of the Seventythird,
When never a quail or a grouse was heard,
Gone are our smiles—each eye has a tear
For gone is our priceless Brigadier;
We ne'er shall forget his cheery face,
Tho' we've got another to take his place.

—§ † §—

Gone is the Transport Officer too
"Dear old Charles" whom all ranks knew,
Knocked out by a shell for a Bosch who flew,
They say that the air for miles went blue;
We ne'er shall forget his cheery face,
Tho' we've got another to take his place.

—§ † §—

Gone half of the firm who advertise,
He never again will dazzle our eyes
With the wonderful cap, with its band so red,
He wore on the back of his curly head;
We ne'er shall forget his cheery face,
Tho' we've got another to take his place.

—§ † §—

But there's still one left of the old Brigade,
Who always pretends he's old and staid,
He teaches the new ones how to go
In the ways of the others we used to know;
We ne'er shall forget his cheery face,
And want no other to take his place.

—§ † §—

They've not gone far, and we hope some day
To meet 'em again when we're all at play,
When the Huns have gone where all Huns should be,
And we're playing at soldiers near Camberley;
To chin of the things we have seen and heard
And the things we did in the Seventy-third.

T. G.

RATS.

I want to write a poem, yet I find I have no theme,
"Rats" are no subject for an elegy,
Yet they fill my waking moments, and when star-shells softly gleam,
'Tis the rats who spend the midnight hours with me.

—o—o—o—

On my table in the evening they will form "Battalion mass,"
They will open tins of bully with their teeth,
And should a cake be sent me by some friend at home, alas!
They will extricate it from its cardboard sheath.

—o—o—o—

They are bloated, fat and cunning, and they're marvels as to size,
And their teeth can penetrate a sniping plate,
I could tell you tales unnumbered, but you'd think I'm telling lies,
Of one old, grey whiskered buck-rat and his mate.

—o—o—o—

Just to show you, on my table lay a tin of sardines—sealed—
With the implement to open hanging near,
The old buck-rat espied them, to his missis loudly squealed,
"Bring quickly that tin-opener, Stinky dear!"

—o—o—o—

She fondly trotted up the pole, and brought him his desire,
He proceeded then with all his might and main,
He opened up that tin, and then—'tis here you'll dub me "Liar!"—
He closed it down, and sealed it up again.

—o—o—o—

Have you seen one, should a rival chance to spoil his love affair,
Bring a bomb, Mills, hand, and place it underneath
The portion of the trench where that said rival had his lair,
And then he'll pull the pin out with his teeth.

BY ORDER.

—o—o—

Oh dear! Nearly a column to be written, and the Editor has detailed me for the job. He won't have anything about the War, as he says he's "fed up" with that subject, so what on earth shall I yarn about? I wonder if he's heard the tale of the Transport Officer and the rum. Of course there are many tales of T.O.'s and rum. The oldest one of all is the one of the T.O. who didn't like rum. But this tale I'm going to tell you is true. There was once a T.O. who was coming up with the rations. The said rations included "rum for weary soldiers." Also the cargo had a consignment of tear-gas in a rum-jar for the M.O. to try a few experiments with. That is all the tale—but I may as well add that the T.O. recovered. Did you ever hear the tale of the General, the Tommy, and the letter. Oh! I mustn't tell that tale, what a pity! (I wonder how many tales it takes to fill a column.) Did you ever hear the tale of the five officers in a dug out? One I am afraid had too great a fancy for alcoholic stimulant. A great big fat rat appeared. Silently they all looked at one another. "I didn't see it!" blurted out our alcoholic friend. That ought to about do it, so, having obeyed orders, I'm off to bed. Adios!

INTELLIGENCE.
SUMMARY MEASURES.

"O" the Observer who stood at his post,
And at 3 on the 10th saw a small German host
Going East with a cart, so he had a good look,
And proceeded to make—a note in his book.

—:0:—

"D" the Division who read the next day
The report "O" had rendered, and sent it away
To Corps, where it rested, until bye-and bye
The Army decided that those Huns should die.

—:0:—

So a mandate was issued to Corps as a start,
To slaughter those Huns going East with a cart,
Which mandate was then with decision and ease
Pushed on to Division, "for action please.

—:0:—

Division post-haste, or as near as could be,
Sent word to the gunners of what "O" could see,
The gunners prepared with shot and with shell,
To blow those said Germans from here into Hell.

—:0:—

With lanyard in hand, and with cool flashing eye,
They scanned all the landscape, they scanned all the sky—
And here we will leave them, gazing apart
For the Huns who—A WEEK AGO—passed with a cart.

CURSE THEM!

—0—0—0—

By HORATORIO COCKLES TUMLEY.

—0—0—

CURSE them all! There—I've said it, that's straight from the shoulder. CURSE them all! And in years to come motherless babes and babyless mothers will echo my cry. Damn their procrastinating habits and their futile compromises. Why cannot the People be told the whole truth? Why hide it from them? I can hear the cry echoing down the ages, "Why?" But I will give them a word of advice:—Be careful! Be very careful!! Or the curses of millions of babyless mothers to be will descend on your addlepated heads. Be careful how far you try the temper of the people, lest they turn and rend you. Shall the people know nothing? No! I tell you and the voice of the indignant multitude thunders with me "No!" Vox populi! Vox Dei! and in years to come myriads of motherless babes will rise and cry "Vox populi! Vox Dei!" Take heed then before you have gone too far, for the mandate of the People is too great a thing to trifle with. So be warned in time. We will not brook interference. Shall the People's Rum be tampered with? No! A thousand times No! When you took away their sandbags I told you what would happen. And now you contemplate an even greater crime. Let us have a Business Rum-Jar. About the same size as the tanks. But do not interfere with the People. Give us a Business Q.M.G.! Good heavens, what have I said? Well there! Let it stand. But don't keep the People in the dark. Think of those poor babyless mothers and remember, IT'S UP TO YOU. CURSE THEM! Br-r-r-r-r.

HORATORIO COCKLES TUMLEY.

TEMPORA MUTANTUR.

In childhood's days my wayward fancy ran
On battle, and a soldier brave was I,
I led my men to action with elan,
We dashed ahead resolved to do or die.

—0—0—0—

Yet in my pictures scarce can I recall
What means we used to circumvent the wire,
Nor how we fought the direst foe of all,
If we had mud then mem'ry is a liar.

—0—0—0—

Green fields and sunlight, swords and prancing steeds,
And pistols with some score yards range at most,
In pleasant lands which furnished all my needs,
In fancy fought my foe from post to post.

—0—0—0—

Ah, childhood's days! No prancing steed have I
Who, day and night, must wade through seas of mud
Attired in tin hat, mac, and boots, gum, thigh,
I almost think my childish dreams were dud.

—0—0—0—

No flight of fancy ever found me glad
A filthy dug-out, full of rats, to see;
I cannot e'er remember being mad
Chloride of lime to sample in my tea.

—0—0—0—

No flying-pigs, or Minnies, had a place
In battles which my fancy freely waged,
No shrieking cans of death came out of space,
No stinking gas the air of war outraged.

—0—0—0—.

Will future battles fought in childhood's dreams
Still hold romance and chivalry entire?
Or will the coming child draw war which teems
With Hun barbarities and Kultur's fire.

AUNT ANNIE'S CORNER.

—:0:—

TINY TALKS TO TINY TOTS.

—:0:—

MY Dear Lit-tle Tot-ties,

It is a long time since I have been able to an swer your nice lit-tle let-ters, for your Aunt'ie has been bus-y. Clev-er Tot-ties will know what bus y means. It means your poor Aunt-ie has had to WORK. Work is a hor-rid thing, and I am sure my Tot-ties never have anything to do with it, do they? Some of my Tot-ties have writ-ten me lit-tle let-ters all about Christ-mas. Here are the ans-wers to them.

—:0:—

DEAR Buf-fy,

It was so nice of your friends to lend you all their sol-diers to play with. Per-haps one day Santa Claus will put a lot in your stock-ing of your very own. That will be nice, won't it? And you must be careful not to break them. I hear you have been to school too. I hope you were a good boy.

—:0:—

DEAR little Mor-ice,

I am sorry Santa Claus made such a silly mistake, and put some curl-ing tongs in your stock-ing. Never mind, you will be able to give them to your lit-tle friend Ken-neth. He will be pleased. I am glad you have a nice new red hat. Also you tell me you are fond of dogs. That is kind of you..

—:0:—

DEAR Rog-er,

I am sorry you have been ra-ther un-well late-ly, but I hope you are bet-ter now. You did not tell me what Santa Claus put in your stock-ing, but I hope it was some thing nice. Have you been for any long walks late-ly? I am glad you are going to have a par-ty. That will be nice, and all your lit-tle friends will en-joy it very much. You must be pol-ite to them, and show them your new pic tures.

—:0:—

Good-bye, Tot-ties,
Your Ev-er Dov-ing
AUNT ANNIE.

OUR SPLENDID NEW SERIAL.

—o—o—o—

"NARPOO RUM."

—o—o—o—

BY THE AUTHOR OF "SHOT IN THE CULVERT."

—o—o—o—

DRAMATIS PERSONAE:

—o—

Cloridy Lyme	— A Sanitary Inspector.
Madeline Carot	— A French Girl.
Intha Pink	— A Pioneer.
General Bertram Rudolph de Rogerum	—The Earl of Loose.
Lord Reginald de Knellthorpe	— His Son.
Q. Wemm	— A Storekeeper.
L. Plumernapple	— A Soldier.
Herlock Shomes	—The Great Detective.
Dr. Hotsam	— His Admirer.

—o—o—o—

CHAPTER 2.

—o—o—o—

IT was Xmas. The sturdy figure of General Bertram Rudolph de Rogerum was plodding along the snow-covered road jauntily whistling a Xmas carol. Every now and then a frown crossed his handsome face as he thought of the missing rum ration, and how the evidence seemed to point to none other than his son, Lord Reginald de Knellthorpe, Had Reggie in a reckless moment stolen the rum? Heaving a deep sigh he fell into a crump hole which had been hidden under the white mantle of winter.

Meanwhile what was happening at Wemm's store? At Hotsam's exclamation "The Rum" a guilty look spread over Wemm's face, and his assistant guiltily stole through the door. Hotsam sprang in front of the jars, "Open one" he thundered. Shakingly Wemm complied, and poured out a glass of the liquid. Hotsam examined this and found it to be solution for vermoral sprayers. With a nod to Wemm he went out. On returning to his dug-out he found Lord Reginald de Knellthorpe in possession of the armchair shooting rats.

"Hullo, old boy" said Knellthorpe, "what about papa's rum."

"Look here Reggie," said Hotsam, "Do you know anything about it? Shomes is on the track and you might be able to help him." Reggie paled. "Shomes" he gasped, picking up his helmet gas, "Shomes! Good heavens, then all is lost.', Staggering to the door he disappeared into the night.

Mixing himself a drink Hotsam sat down and began to go over the evidence, Suddenly the door opened, and the Earl of Loose entered. "Good evening, General," said Hotsam. "General be dammed," snapped Shomes' voice, "Has Reginald de Knellthorpe been here?" "Just this minute gone," said Hotsam. Dashing to the door Shomes rapidly disappeared, followed by Hotsam. Suddenly two shots rang out, and Shomes dropped in the snow, crying "Follow him, follow him." Hotsam dashed madly in pursuit, and didn't stop till he fell down the shaft at the Old Fosse.

Picking himself up, Shomes returned to his dug-out and bound up his wrist where the shot had struck him. Baring his forearm he injected a gallon out of his vermoral sprayer and picked up his violin.

Down in the village Madeline Carot sat at the door of her old mother's estaminet. Her face brightened as she saw the sturdy figure of Intha Pink coming up the road. "Oh Intha," she exclaimed "I thought you were never coming to see me. Where have you been?"

Hurriedly glancing up and down the road Pink slipped into the estaminet and closed the door. "Rum!" he gasped.

Madeline got him a glass of rum which he swallowed at a gulp. "Has Shomes been here" he demanded. "Yes," she replied, "He was here this morning, and had a glass of rum."

"Then we are lost," shouted Intha, and disappeared through the door.

Hotsam, meanwhile arrived at the bottom of the shaft. Taking his flash lamp from his pocket he proceeded to examine his position. The first thing his light fell on was a pile of jars stacked in a corner. "The rum!" he gasped.

(WAS IT?)

Read next thrilling instalment.

(To be Continued.)

OUR MATRIMONIAL COLUMN.

—o—o—o—

OWING to the enormous success of this new feature, we shall have to increase our staff. Letters continue to pour in, and we have as many as 500 applicants for the Cheery Brigadier who advertised in our columns last week, and he has several of these applications under consideration at the moment. The greatest secrecy is observed in dealing with this delicate subject, so any other candidate wishing to take advantage of our columns may do so with impunity.

—o—o—o—

GUNNER LT.-COL.—Tall and striking appearance. Distinguished career. Is tired of his present lonely existence, but owing to an exaggerated sense of modesty fears to approach any likely young lady on the subject. He would welcome correspondence which might eventually secure him congenial companionship.

He loves his guns, yet these he'd miss
To taste the joys of married bliss.

—Write enclosing photo to GUNS, c/o this paper.

MAJOR.—Under 40, strong, tall and slightly war-worn, but has taken no prizes in beauty competitions, would like to meet young and lively widow (without family) with view to marriage. One who can mix cocktails and play good hand at auction preferred.—Write STUDY, THE BUFFS, c/o this paper.

BRIG.-MAJOR.—Young and good-looking, whose priceless personality and charming manners have fractured many feminine hearts, wishes to settle down. Applicants for his hand must be young, pretty, open-minded, and not of jealous disposition.—Write REGINALD, c/o this paper.

SAPPER.—In the prime of life. Hides a charming genial nature under an outward manner which has been mistakenly called gruff. Fond of walking and outdoor exercises. Keeps car. Would like to correspond with a kindred spirit. Write and send sketch in scale.—SAPPERCOL, c/o this paper.

Things We Want to Know.

——:o:——

What is the story about "Mother."

? ? ?

When is the regulation referring to hunting stocks and crops going to apply to shooting suits

? ? ?

The number of bones that have been sent to the soup kitchen up-to date, and what is being done with them

? ? ?

The name of the motorist who has a passion for collecting cows on the Boulogne Road, and what the natives think of his pet hobby.

? ? ?

Whether a certain officer is shortly publishing a little song entitled "Why was I so careless with the boots."

? ? ?

Whether a Camp Commandant we know can give us a return of the number of dogs in his district size, colour and pedigree.

? ? ?

Whether the new collection of Old Masters at the Munque Art Gallery doesn't beat the old one.

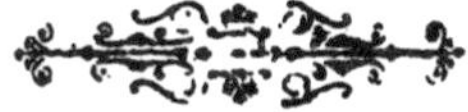

Mr. Teech Bomas.

—o—o—o—

We regret to inform our readers that as Mr. TEECH BOMAS has left for his usual winter trip to warmer climes, all proceedings will be stopped meanwhile. The battle will be resumed immediately on his return, when we hope to have further graphic articles from his pen. —ED.

People We Take Our Hats off To.

——:o:——

The French.

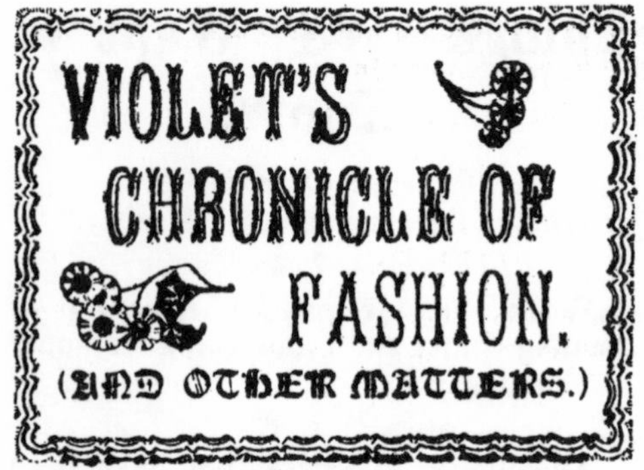
VIOLET'S
CHRONICLE OF
FASHION.
(AND OTHER MATTERS.)

(SUBS. NOT TO READ THIS—ED.)

—o—o—o—

YOU have doubtless heard of the sub. who defined a lady as one who wears stockings that are silk all the way up (Which is perhaps hardly fair to those whose misplaced ideas of economy lead them to purchase what the shops call "silk-ankles.") Well, he will have to revise his definition, anyway. For not only our stockings must be silk nowadays, but all "les dessons." Never has lingerie been more fascinating,—or more extravagant; but girls whose war-work prevents the wearing of pretty frocks may be forgiven if they indulge in frillies instead. Garments are fairy-like in their filmy beauty,—camisoles are airy fragments of chiffon, lace, and ribbon just blown together, petticoats are real poems, while as for night-wear, even the simplest designs are artistic triumphs, and the materials are so dainty and sometimes so diaphanous that the result seems a mere ghost of a nightie!

I CAN imagine our own Press Censor looking anxious as to what I'm going to say next, so I'll ease his mind by changing the subject. One of the nicest evening gowns I've seen lately is one of my own: a lovely soft fuchia red satin with little glimpses of deep pansy-purple at waist and hem; rich bead embroideries gleaming through the net of the bodice; rather daring, but effective, for I was a "little devil" twice and "a witch" three times in a single evening, and, according to George Robey, if you are called a witch you just know you've "got there." Sister Nancy—she of the auburn hair—has a sweet dance frock of layer on layer of fluffy tulle in softest shades of pink, mauve and pale blue. But I won't try to describe the effect when she's wearing that, or there will be a sudden rush for special leave And it wouldn't be any use, because we are both booked up for leave engagements till the middle of January. Applications for dates beyond that will be duly considered and dealt with in rotation.

DANCES still flourish down in "our village," much to the joy of the inhabitants of the local camps. The boys of one regiment have earned our gratitude by bringing over their own band, for it's getting difficult to find a good orchestra; think we shall have to give other regiments a hint to do likewise, the invitations might conclude "Pretty partners provided, but bring your own music." It is nice to see those same partners as the most charming butterflies imaginable at night, for nearly all are the busiest of bees by day. We appreciate our gaieties now, after hours of sewing at a depôt, serving at a canteen, making shells, or minding babies while their mothers make them!

MANY kind correspondents inquire after my poultry farm. It still flourishes finely, I can see myself with a Rolls-Royce if eggs remain at fourpence each much longer. My latest achievement is the Non Stop Hen, guaranteed to continue laying when every other bird in the kingdom has gone on strike, and admitted to be a triumph of breeding. (If

Grandpa and Nickett should need any aid in perfecting their valuable discovery the Parrotidgin, my expert advice is at their service.) Orders for pens of Non-Stops for the trenches are flowing in rapidly as their fame spreads, (what could be nicer for the C.O.'s breakfast, or more soothing for his temper, than a fresh-laid egg?) and the Khaki breed are specially trained to lay on undeterred by noisy and muddy surroundings.

CONGRATULATIONS to my consoeur —I suppose that is the correct feminine!—of "The Tatler," our beloved "EVE," on her decision to introduce herself at last to an eager world. Not by name, mais cela n'importe, we have for so long had to be content with an imaginary vision of the fair scribe. It is enough for the present to have an authorized version of the picture. EVE,—"salut!"

A CORRESPONDENT basely suggests that the removal to another sphere of action some weeks ago of one GILBERT FRANKAU is not unconnected with a poem of his in the "Somme-Times." His ode to those charming ladies, EVE, BLANCHE, and PHRYNETTE, was appreciated by no one more than by the present writer. But my correspondent's idea is that "at least a brief sonnet might have been written to VIOLET," who "must have felt a trifle piqued;" and that it was hearing that I was on his track that made our gifted contributor seek safety in distant regions! I can only reply that such trifles as poetical tributes weigh not at all with one who has such indisputable indications of favour as the Editor's approval (Ahem!), her enormous salary (double that of TEECH BOMAS), and the huge increase in the paper's circulation since she joined the staff.

A PARAGRAPH in my last chronicle concerning officers who invite me to lunch promptly brought me a letter from friend "Sabretâche." He wrote me that I "must NOT go out with any of those soldier devils—one never knows!" Well, advice from a man like "Sabretâche" is not to be ignored, and he will be pleased to know that I have obediently refused all luncheon invitations, and gone to dinner instead every time.

VIOLET.

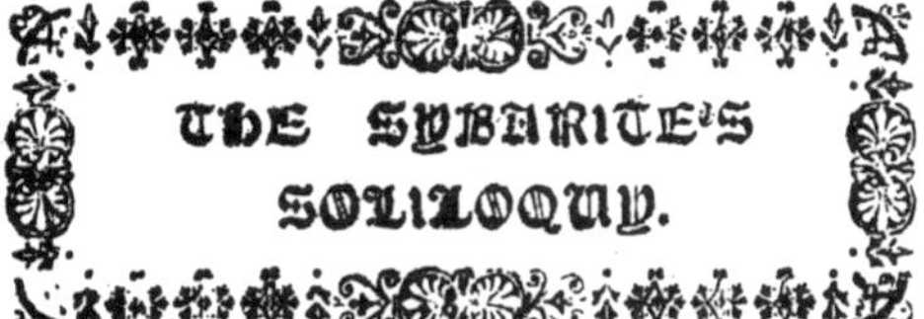

THE SYBARITE'S SOLILOQUY.

Dearest, at break of Dawn, I need you most,
And, as you, in your silver shrouded dress,
Gambol before my eyes, I daily bless
The coins that made you mine, the trifling cost,
That sold you into bondage, such as this;
To be my Slave, Enchantress of my Soul,
To pay, afresh, each morn, the levied toll,
That I extort from you—a honied kiss.
And, as, upon my cheeks, my rugged chin,
Your scented lips, you passionately press,
In muscadine abandon, I caress
Your adipose delight, and with a grin,
Each morning, half awake, for you, I grope
Oh Stick of Superfatted Shaving Soap.

C. L. P.

FAREWELL.

—:o:—

We have been asked, by many of his friends in the Division, to say good-bye to Brig.-General Jelf for them through our columns. His old Brigade feels his departure acutely. It is no reflection on our new Brigadier to say that he will have a hard job to occupy the place held by General Jelf in the hearts of all ranks, who one and all knew him for a chum. We wish him a speedy recovery, and he will know that he carries with him all our wishes for his future success, and refer him to the last verse of "Gone" in this number.

Here also we should like to extend a hearty welcome to our new Brigadier, and to express our conviction that his popularity will equal that of his predecessor. "Le roi est mort, vive le Roi."

THE EDITOR.

Correspondence.

To the Editor,
"B.E.F. Times."

Sir,

May I ask for the assistance of your widely read columns to further the interests of a much neglected charity. I refer to the fund for providing flannel pyjamas for our troops in the front line. We hear on reliable authority that these poor fellows are very short of pyjamas, and in many cases have only one pair. Surely something can be done to help them in this matter. We were so successful with our fund for providing "Umbrellas for our gallant sailors," that we have great hopes of our new appeal. All contributions must be sent to the secretary.

I am, Sir,
Yours faithfully,
ELIZA STIGGINS, Hon Sec.

OUR MAMMOTH COMPETITION.

BURIED TREASURE.

NOW IS YOUR CHANCE.

We have buried cheques for the amounts offered in the following places :—

1.—BETWEEN HOOGE CHATEAU AND THE CULVERT ARMS.
2.—IN THE GROUNDS OF DEAD COW FARM.
3.—BAPAUME.

Hidden clues as to the resting place of each cheque will be given in our great serial "NARPOO RUM." All you have to do is to closely follow the adventures of General Bertram Rudolph de Rogerum, and go and collect the money.

CHEQUES ARE VALUED AT :—

10,000,000 Francs.
5,000,000 Francs.
2,500,000 Francs.

THE EDITOR'S DECISION IS FINAL.

When found if you have any difficulty in cashing the cheques write at once enclosing a 10 franc note to :—

COMPETITION EDITOR, B.E.F. TIMES.

When another will be sent you.

THE CALLANSEEUM THEATRE OF VARIETIES.

To-day at 2-15; Every Evening at 8-30.

MR. THOMAS ATKINS PRESENTS

HIS STUPENDOUS XMAS REVUE.

THE BING BANGS ARE HERE.

By MEW NISHEN-WURKURS.

MUSIC BY R. TILLERY. LYRICS BY REDATS.

INTRODUCING:

TINO: The world-famed sleight-of-hand artist.

WILHELM: Who will sing "Peace, Peace, Glorious Peace."

HIND and BERG: Sword swallowers and nail eaters.

ALSO THE

WOTHEHELLSITMATOGRAPH

FEATURING:—THE WESTMINSTER TROUPE IN

ALL CHANGE HERE.

DOORS ALWAYS OPEN. PRICES AS USUAL

Now Open! Now Open!! Now Open!!!

—o—o—o—

BURNEY'S AMERICAN BAR

-o—o—o—

DRINKS!

DRINKS!!

DRINKS!!!

—o—o—o—

We cater for all palates, and even the most hardened will find something unique in a

NORTHANTI COCKTAIL.

—o—o—o—

THE SWIFTEST DRINK YET INVENTED GUARANTEED TO CURE: OPTIMISM, PESSIMISM, RELIGIOUS MANIA and CHRONIC THIRST.

—o—o—o—

If you can say:—" Royal Marine Light Infantry" after taking three of our specials you get your money back.

—o-o—o—

Subalterns under 14 and Generals over 90

Not Admitted.

HAVE YOU COMFORTABLE

WINTER QUARTERS?

—o—o—o—

IF NOT, THEN DROP A P.C. AT ONCE WHEN OUR MR BLEWES WILL CALL ON YOU.

—o—o—o—

TRY ONE OF OUR NEW AIRY 17in. PROOF DUG-OUTS. THESE ARE

Guaranteed Rat-proof

—o—o—o—

DON'T DELAY PLACE YOUR

CONTRACT AT ONCE.

—o—o—o—

THESE ARE NOT

Jerry-built Residences.

—o—o—o—

If you're really nice and deep,
Minnie rocks you off to sleep.

—o—o—o—

WRITE:—

SHERWOOD, FORESTER & Co.
Contractors to H.M. Government.
Telegrams: "KNOTTS."

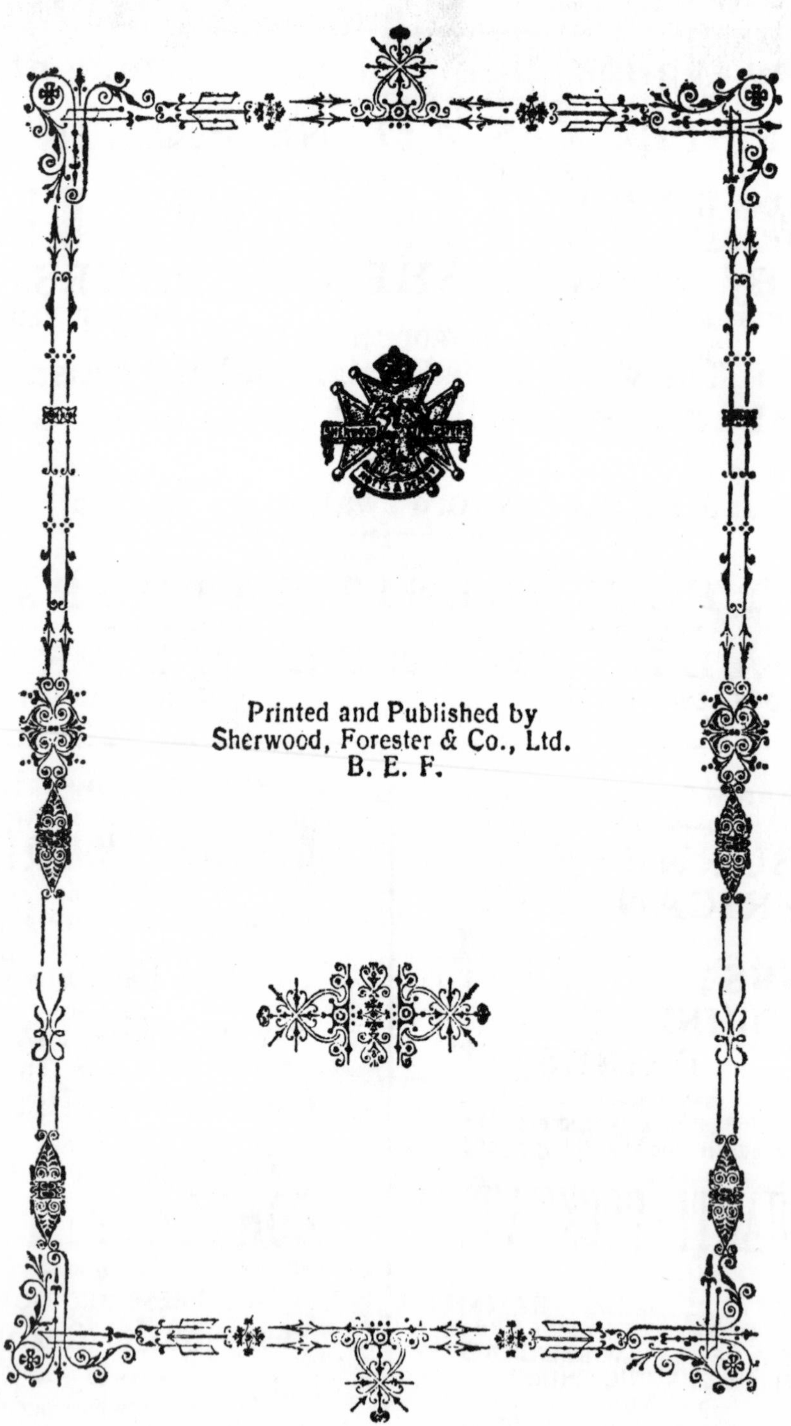

Printed and Published by
Sherwood, Forester & Co., Ltd.
B. E. F.

THE B.E.F. TIMES.

WITH WHICH ARE INCORPORATED

The Wipers Times, The "New Church" Times, The Kemmel Times & The Somme-Times.

No 3. Vol 1. Saturday January 20th, 1917. Price 1 Franc.

PALACE OF VARIETIES, L - - - - (CENSORED, ED.)

THIS WEEK,
GRAND CHRISTMAS PANTOMIME.

BABES AND THE WOOD.

SPECIAL ENGAGEMENT OF ALL THE STARS, INCLUDING:—

THE ATKINS FAMILY:
CELEBRATED "A" FRAME EQUILIBRISTS AND DUCKBOARD DODGERS.

THE SIX HOWS.
Knockabout Comedians.

MAGNIFICENT SCENIC EFFECTS
Lighting by the Very Light Company, Ltd.
Dresses by Inn Dent and Dados.

BOOK EARLY. PRICES AS USUAL.
NO TREATING ORDER ABOLISHED. BRING YOUR OWN WHISKEY.

THE CALLANSEEUM
PALACE OF VARIETIES

SPECIAL ENGAGEMENT OF THE AERIAL TROUPE

"THE FLYING PIGS."

FILM FARCE, ENTITLED:—

"TICKLING FRITZ."

By the P.B.I. Film Co., of the UNITED KINGDOM and CANADA.

SIGNOR NAYLORI,

THE "TRIP-WIRE" EXPERT.

BOOK EARLY. CHARGES MOBILE.

Magnificent Dining Rooms on the premises where you can have as many courses as you like.

WHY GO TO SWITZERLAND?

ALL THE ATTRACTIONS OF WINTER SPORTS, AND IN GREATER VARIETY CAN BE OBTAINED IN THE NEW "OBERLAND."

—o—o—o—o—

STAY AT THE

"HOTEL DE BRASSERIE,"

UNDER SAME MANAGEMENT AS THE

"HOTEL DES RAMPARTS, YPRES."

—o—o—o—o—

Wonderful Cuisine. Terms Moderate.
Climate Healthy. Good Shooting.
Ski-ing on the Crassier. Tobogganning on the Famous Mountain Way Run.

—o—o—o—o—

Telephones: PRIVATE EXCHANGE. Telegrams: "PIONEER."

THE
B. E. F. TIMES.

WITH WHICH ARE INCORPORATED

The Wipers Times, The "New Church" Times, The Kemmel Times & The Somme-Times.

No 3. Vol 1. Saturday, January 20th, 1917. Price 1 Franc.

EDITORIAL.

JANUARY 1st, 1917. Here's the best of luck for the New Year to all our readers. Whatever it may have in store for us, we can at least be thankful we are not Huns. If they were anyone else but Huns one might feel sorry for them, and send them a card of sympathy for the trouble in store. If we were Old Moore, and gifted with prophetic insight, we would go as far to make a note in our diary, "1917—Disturbances in Europe" However, we will leave prophecy to those who understand tactics, etc., and Major Taude, B.C may be induced to send us an article on "What the Germans will do in 1917." There also we could sum the matter up briefly by saying, "Get it where the bottle got the cork," but we prefer to have the matter more eloquently expressed by him. We have now completed our first year of journalism, and are feeling quite old hands at the game, talking learnedly of "dis-ing" and chases, furniture, etc. It was certainly a lucky day for us when we found the old "Jigger," otherwise we should have been hard put to it to fill in all the spare time which we have on our hands during these pleasant winter months. Talking of Winter we are of the opinion that it should change places with Autumn and be called the "Fall." Personally we think there's a lot too much fall about it. We are often glad to be able to think we are only soldiering for pleasure. It would be terrible to think that we HAD to do it. Well! We are getting through the Winter somehow, and soon shall be thinking of Spring. "In the Spring a young man's fancy lightly turns to thoughts of —" grenades, hand, Mills and any other lethal article he can lay his hands on. America seems to abound in humourists, and President Wilson is rather undermining Mark Twain's reputation ' A new edition of "The Innocents Abroad" from the pen of the gifted President would be certain of instant success. As we are writing a terrible rumour has reached us, that whiskey will shortly be "na-poo." This is the most unkindest cut of all, and as the sub-editor crudely puts it "No whiskey, no war." Can anyone imagine calling at the "Culvert Arms" and being told that whiskey was "Off." Good Heavens! It will be the ruin of many a good old-established house, and we should not be surprised if many of the most popular dug-outs in the line had to shut their gas-curtains. However, all this and more we will bear for England's sake, but it is going to be a dry summer. We must request all competitors in our new Competition not to go in massed formation to search for the buried cheques as it inconveniences the Hun. Sections of ten at 50 yards interval would be advisable, and we wish to state here that the Menin Road East of the Culvert Arms is closed to all vehicular traffic including buses. As our previous appeals have met with very little response we should like to make a fresh effort and remind all readers that copy is urgently required if we are to keep up to 12 pages, and beg one and all to send something along. Once more wishing you all the best of luck during 1917.

Let me like a soldier fall,
Upon an open plain;
For if I trip and fall in a trench,
I could never get up again

In dug-out cool I sit and freeze as on the war I ponder,
My thoughts on Huns and guns don't please, and so begin to wander,
Green fields, and peace, and lovely girls, or in my club I'm drinking,
When outside—bang—and of the war, I'm thinking, thinking, thinking.

I freely curse the blighted Hun who interrupts my fancies,
And with his frightfulness breaks in on memoried romances;
No Wilson I, nor has my pen much skill in temporisals,
So naught is left for me to do, save swift T.M. reprisals.

I hate all Huns, yet most hate I, that surly livered blighter,
Who with persistence breaks my sleep, with his ten times-a-nighter;
When fast asleep, and in the arms of Morpheus or some other,
The rotter looses off and then—oh, damn it, there's another

Yet I will wait, and patiently, to catch the blighter bending,
And constantly unto my aid will summon guns unending;
With six-inch Hows, and every kind of gun will wreck his dwelling,
And when we'll hold his requiem mass, our Stokes shall do his knelling.

OUR SPLENDID NEW SERIAL.

—o—o—o—

"NARPOO RUM."

—o—o—o—

BY THE AUTHOR OF "SHOT IN THE CULVERT."

—o—o—o—

DRAMATIS PERSONAE:

—o—

Cloridy Lyme — A Sanitary Inspector.
Madeline Carot — A French Girl.
Intha Pink — A Pioneer
General Bertram Rudolph de Rogerum—The Earl of Loose.
Lord Reginald de Knellthorpe — His Son.
Q. Wemm — A Storekeeper.
L. Plumernapple — A Soldier
Herlock Shomes — The Great Detective.
Dr. Hotsam — His Admirer.

—o—o—o—

CHAPTER 3.

—o—o—o—

IT was raining. Shomes, who had business of a pressing nature that night, shuddered as he pulled aside the gas curtain of his dug-out, and looked up and down the trench. Dropping the curtain hastily he injected a good dose from his vermoral sprayer, and disguised himself as a sergeant. He then swallowed half-a-pint of rum and went out into the night, to proceed on an urgent and secret mission to the "Culvert Arms" at Hooge. Making his way along the duckboards to the waiting aeroplane he jumped aboard and disappeared into the darkness Meanwhile, the Earl of Loose was in a very troubled state of mind about his son. In addition to the mysterious disappearance of the rum Reggie had been playing fast and loose with the pretty dark-eyed daughter at the neighbouring chateau. So much so indeed that the poor old Earl was considering the advantages of sending Master Reginald back to school, Professor Spot had just recently opened a finishing school for young gentlemen in the neighbourhood. He had just made up his mind to send Reginald for a course when his eye fell on the young scapegoat ambling along smoking a cigarette, and without his gas helmet. Choking back a expletive the General hurried after him. and was only just in time to see him disappear into the corner estaminet where Madeline dipensed beer daily. The General stealthily approached, and looking through a back window saw Reginald with the girl in his arms. On the ground was a stack of rum jars at which Reggie was pointing while saying something to the girl At this sight the General clutohed at his collar and swooned. Hotsam, who on examination, had found all the jars at the bottom of the Old Fosse to be empty and of a condemned pattern, gathered himself together and proceeding by the old workings soon found himself by the corner estaminet. Hearing laughter and voices he made his way to the back, and fell over the unconscious form of General Bertram Rudolph de Rogerum, the Earl of Loose. Picking himself up he looked in at the window.

"The Rum!" he gasped.

(WAS IT?)

Read next thrilling instalment.

(To be Continued.)

There was a little Hun, and at war he tried his hand,
And while that Hun was winning war was fine you understand,
But when the others hit him back he shouted in alarm,
A little drop of peace wouldn't do me any harm.

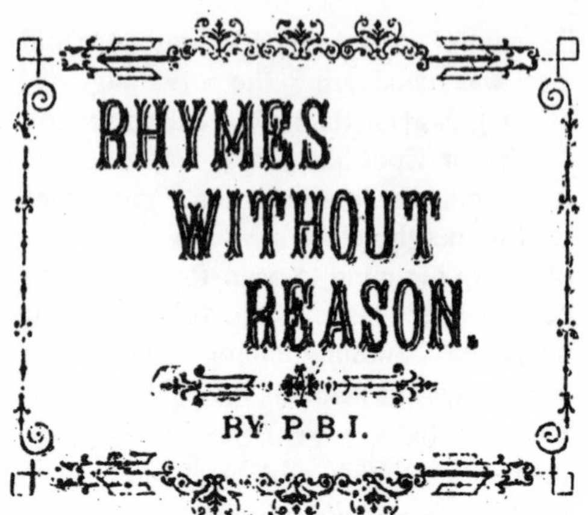

RHYMES WITHOUT REASON.

BY P.B.I.

FOREWORD.

—o—

Arise, My Muse, and from the muddied trench
Let us give utterance to malicious thought,
Shouting aloud the things we never ought
Even to dream of: come, you shameless Wench,
With tongue in cheek let us set out to strafe
Gunners and Sappers, and the Gilded Staff.

-o—o—o-

(I.)

Gunners are a race apart,
Hard of head and hard of heart.
Like the gods they sit and view
All that other people do:
Like the Sisters Three of Fate,
They do not discriminate.
Our Support Line, or the Hun's,
—What's the difference to the Guns?
Retaliation do you seek?
Ring them up, and—wait a week!
They will certainly reply
In the distant by-and-bye.
Should a shell explode amiss,
Each will swear it was not his:
For he's never, never shot
Anywhere about that spot,
And, what's more, his Guns could not.

(II.)

Sappers are wonderfully clever by birth,
And though they're not meek, they inherit the Earth.
Should your trenches prove leaky, they'll work with a will
To make all the water flow up the next hill
(And when I say "work," I should really explain
That we find the Labour, while they find the Brain).
They build nice, deep dug-outs as quick as can be,
But quicker still mark them "Reserved For R.E.":
And, strangely, this speed of theirs seems to decline
As the scene of their labours draws near the Front Line.

—o—o—o—

(III.)

Realising Men must laugh,
Some Wise Man devised the Staff:
Dressed them up in little dabs
Of rich variegated tabs:
Taught them how to win the War
On A.F.Z. 354:
Let them lead the Simple Life
Far from all our vulgar strife:
Nightly gave them downy beds
For their weary, aching heads:
Lest their relatives might grieve
Often, often, gave them leave,
Decorations, too, galore:
What on earth could man wish more?
Yet, alas, or so says Rumour,
He forgot a sense of Humour!

—o—o—o—

AFTERWORD.

—o—

And now, Old Girl, we've fairly had our whack,
Be off, before they start to strafe us back!
Come, let us plod across the weary Plain,
Until we sight Tenth Avenue again:
On, up the interminable C.T.,

Watched by the greater part of Germany:
And, as we go, mark each familiar spot.
Where fresh work has been done—or p'r'aps has not:
On, past the footboards no one seems to mend,
Till even VENDIN ALLEY finds an end,
And wading through a Minnie-hole (brand-new),
We gingerly descend to C.H.Q.,
Our journey ended in a Rabbit-hutch—
"How goes the Battle? Have they Minnied much?"

P.B.I.

Things We Want to Know.

—:o:—

The name of the Camp Commandant who bought up all the whiskey in Bethune owing to early advice of the coming drought.

? ? ?

The name or the M.O. who is not a doctor.

? ? ?

If it is true that he takes an umbrella on his walks, as "Archie" duds are so plentiful.

? ? ?

Whether two notorious red-hats were disappointed over a little question of "Who's HE taking with him."

? ? ?

Ref. G.R.O. Q.M.G.'s Branch No. 2073:—(A)—What is a BONA FIDE rum drinker. (B)—Whether whiskey cannot be supplied on the same terms to BONA FIDE whiskey drinkers.

Extracts From Contemporaries.

—:o:—

EXTRACT FROM "TIMES," 15/1/17.

—:o:—

"GERMAN GOLD CAPTURED NEAR RIGA.—PETROGRAD. Jan. 13.—Among the trophies captured during the Riga offensive and counted up to the present are 50 machine guns, 30 guns, the treasury chest of the 364th Infantry Regiment containing 335,000 marks (16,750 sovs.) in coin, 300 horses, two armoured motor-cars, 50,000 gas masks, 50,000 uniforms, 15,000 rifles, 20 field kitchens, and 10,000 bottles of brandy. —REUTER."

Some chest!

TO MY MARRAINE.

I love you for your kindliness and grace,
And wonder how it happens, that you deign
To send me sweets and gifts, my dear MARRAINE,
Across the intervening miles of space
Your portrait, in the evening mists, I trace,
While doing sentry, in the mud and rain,
The sky is dark above; but free from stain
Or blemish, is your lovely visioned face.

—o—o—o—

However long this war goes on, MARRAINE,
I'll love you, I'll adore you, to the end;
But all the Doctor's Magic cannot shake
From my inside, this unaccustomed pain,
I pray you, I implore you, not to send
Another sanguinary HOME-MADE cake.

THE M.O. (C.L.P.)

MESOPOTAMIAN ALPHABET.

[The following has been sent us from the Indian Army by one of our old Divisional friends. He suggests that someone should have a shot at the " B.E.F. Alphabet Up-to-date." Will some please try and submit efforts early ?—ED.]

A was an Apple that grew so they say,
In the garden of Eden down Kurna way,
Till Eve came along and ate it one day,
And got thrown out of Mesopotamia.

B is the Biscuit that's made in Delhi,
It breaks your teeth and bruises your belly,
And grinds your intestines into a jelly,
In the land of Mesopotamia.

C is the poor old Indian Corps,
Which went to France and fought in the war,
Now it gathers the crops and fights no more
In the land of Mesopotamia.

D is the Digging we've all of us done
Since first we started to fight the Hun,
By now we've shifted ten thousand ton
Of matter in Mesopotamia.

E was the Energy shown by the Staff
Before the much-advertised Hanna strafe,.
Yet the nett result was the Turks had a laugh
At our Staff in Mesopotamia

F stands for " Fritz " who flies in the sky,
To bring down the brute we've had many a try,
But the shells we shoot with, all pass him by
And fall in Mesopotamia.

G is the Grazing we do all the day,
We fervently hope that some day we may
Get issued again with a ration of hay,
'Though we're still in Mesopotamia.

H are the Harems, which it appears
Have flourished in Baghdad for hundreds of years,
We propose to annex all the destitute dears—
When their husbands leave Mesopotamia.

I is the Indian Government, but
About this I'm told I must keep my mouth shut,
For it's all due to them that we failed to reach Kut-
El-Amara in Mesopotamia.

J is the Jam, with the label that lies,
And states that in Paris it won the First Prize,
But out here we use it for catching the flies
That swarm in Mesopotamia.

K are the Kisses from lips sweet and fair,
Waiting for us around Leicester Square,
When we wend our way home, after wasting a year
Or two in Mesopotamia.

L is the Loot we hope we shall seize—
Wives and wine and bags of rupees,
When the Mayor of Baghdad hands over the keys
To the British in Mesopotamia.

M is the local Mosquito. whose bite
Keeps us awake all the hours of the night,
And makes all our faces a horrible sight
In the land of Mesopotamia.

N is the Navy that's tied to the shore,
They've lashings of beer, and provisions galore,
How I wish I had joined as a sailor before
I came out to Mesopotamia.

O are the Orders we get from the Corps,
Thank goodness by now we are perfectly sure
If issued at three they'll be cancelled by four—
In this land of Mesopotamia.

P are the Postal officials who fail
To deliver each week more than half of our mail,
If they had their deserts they'd all be in jail,
Instead of in Mesopotamia.

Q'S the Quinine which we take every day
To keep the Malarial fever away,
Which we're bound to get sooner or later, they say,
If we stop here in Mesopotamia.

R for the Rations they give us to eat,
For brekker there's biscuits, for dinner there's meat;
And if we've been good we get jam as a treat
For our tea in Mesopotamia.

S & T are supposed to supply
The Army with food, we all hope when they die
They will go to a spot as hot and as dry
As this rotten old Mesopotamia.

U is the Lake known as Um-el-Brahm,
Which guards our left flank from all possible harm,
And waters old G------s—barley farm
In the middle of Mesopotamia.

V is the Victory won at Dijailah,
I heard it first from a pal who's a sailor,
Who read it in Reuter on board his Mahola
On the Tigris in Mesopotamia.

W stands for Wonder and pain,
With which we regard the infirm and insane
Old *------ -------- -------- this campaign
We're waging in Mesopotamia.

(*Censored—Ed.)

X are the 'Xtras the Corps say we get,
But so far there isn't a unit I've met
That has drawn a single one of them yet
Since they landed in Mesopotamia

Y is the Yearning we feel every day
For a passage to Basrah, and so to Bombay,
If we get there we'll see that we stop right away
From this wilderness Mesopotamia.

Z I've tried very hard. and at last I had hit
On a verse which this damnable letter would fit,
But the Censor deleted it—every bit
Save the last word "Mesopotamia."

—o—o—o—

Chahels is really a horrible spot,
Where there isn't a drop of drink to be got,
Yet here we're going to be left till we rot
In the Middle of Mesopotamia.

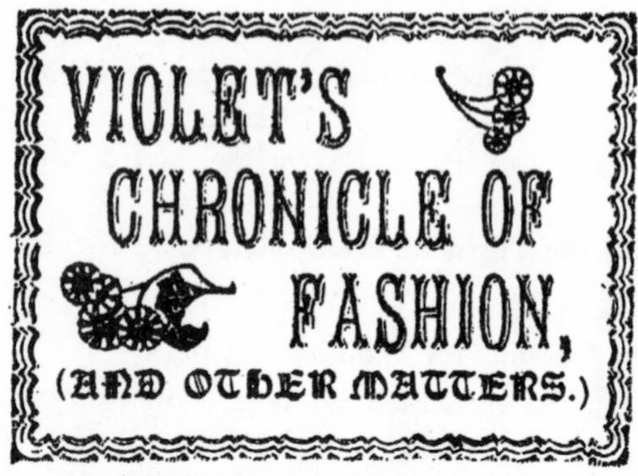
VIOLET'S
CHRONICLE OF
FASHION,
(AND OTHER MATTERS.)

THERE is little enough to record in the world of dress just now. Shops are in the throes of "January Sales," and therefore to be avoided; which makes it easier for us to keep our New Year resolutions and buy no new clothes so that by next month we shall have saved a considerable amount Then we can apply to those same resolutions that excellent motto "Let bygones be bygones," and enjoy a good spend! Yes, that's a very feminine idea of economy, I know, but you must allow us to keep a few of our dear illogical ways and inconsistancies, or, we shall grow simply too fearfully capable these strenous days; and then you won't love us any more. We know you admire Cleverness and Capability immensely, but you don't ask them to tea at the Carlton or jolly little tete'à-tete luncheons at the Berkeley unless they look charming and wear the latest frocks. And quite right too!

THIS Chronicle looks like being all "Other Matters" and no Fashion, but you shall hear all about frills and fallals next month, for a heavy mail-bag claims attention this time. I am afraid the Editor's clearly printed Instructions to Subs to leave my last Chronicle unread must have been overlooked by most of them, judging by the sudden rush of correspondence. Several cheery souls are greatly attracted by the idea of fresh eggs in the trenches, and send orders for my famous feathered egg machines to be dispatched at once.

REGINALD tells me that Dead Cow Cow Farm would be an ideal site for a poultry fancier I happen to be wanting new premises in a really salubrious neighbournood; he hasn't sufficient capital to take it up himself, but offers the suggestion for what it is worth. I should say it is worth about as much as the cheque, "In payment for one dozen hens in full lay," which he enclosed, and which the bank returned to me next morning Shame on you, Reginald,—I am wondering if you are the "Co." of that noted firm, Nunthorpe, Cox and Co.

OTHER correspondents write to fix dates with me for leave engagements; these, with the exception of one Thomas, I have answered privately. (Other applicants please note that now the earliest date that either Nancy or I can accept is March 1st.) Thomas must be a Scotchman, he's such a cautious, wary fellow. He'd love to meet Violet if only he could be sure that she is really and truly of the fair sex, but he doesn't want to risk turning up at the appointed time to find himself face to face with a brother officer with a mistaken sense of humour. This sceptical attitude of mind amuses me muchly, Thomas, (well-named!) How could you doubt me? Reflect on my dissertation on lingerie, surely you do not imagine any mere man could have given such detailed descriptions!

O course we know some men have wonderful imaginative powers,—

the way some of the advertisers in the Matrimonial Column describe themselves is enough to prove that. Whoever has heard of a Gunner of all people, with "An exaggerated sense of modesty"? Or of a "Bashful" Brigadier-General? Or of any officer of any rank in any branch of the Service who "Feared to approach a likely young lady? If there are any such, then either they have not come my way or else I must be an UNlikely young lady, for I've never noticed any difficulty about the approach.

NO Charles, the pink garter brought in by the patrol of the X Regt. on the 27th ult. (vide Intelligence Summary) was not mine. You are right in thinking that my personal assistance is frequently required at the "Times" offices, especially lately, when the stacks of replies to the marriage offers caused the staff to wire for my immediate attendance. (The Editor rightly thought that feminine intutition was needed in sorting out the letters, his susceptible subs. would have credited every applicant with the charms of Venus.) But on these occasions an extra geniality of temper amongst the staff is the only trace of my presence remaining afterwards,—certainly I never leave tangible evidence of the kind suggested by Charles.

VIOLET.

How doth the busy little Hun
These tense and nervy days?
Now daily visits have begun
He finds the loser pays!

GERMANY'S SECRET MEETING.

—:o:—

BY OUR SPECIAL CORRESPONDENT WITH THE HUNS.

—:o:—

POTSDAM, Jan. 21st, 1917,

This afternoon I was able to disguise myself as a statute in the Siegesallee, and was thus present at a meeting between the Emperors of Germany and Austria, the Sultan of Turkey and Ferdinand of Bulgaria. What a momentous moment! Shall I ever forget it? The whole plan was unfolded in front of my eyes, and every word was plainly heard by me. Let me tell you in my own words, and as succintly as if for one of our own journals. The meeting was opened by Little Willie with, "Say, Pop, its up to you, and cut out the rough stuff."

"Nix on me," said the big guy, "let Ferdy open up."

"Well," said Ferdy expectorating with skill, "Its oats for mine. And I may say right now its oats or I'm a quitter,—dollars is good, but oats sound better to me now."

"Oh" said William F. Hohenzollern, "That horse aint a starter. Dollars yer can have but nix on oats. If another slice of Yurrup helps you any its yours."

"Say, Pop," chimed in the kid, "Ferdy's a quitter and wants to beat it. What's the good of handing out the boodle?"

The coffee cooler thought his end was getting a miss so offered to swop three full harems for a good square meal but found nothing doing.

The meeting then broke up in disorder, and the various potentates hit the trail for home. This is the absolute inner history of the last meeting of the Central Powers.

KURLY KERTIN.

AN APPEAL.

There are various types of courage, there are many kinds of fear,
There are many brands of whiskey, there are ma.ıy makes of beer,
There is also rum, which sometimes in our need can help us much,
But 'tis whiskey—whiskey—whiskey I hands the courage which is "Dutch."

In moments when the front is still—no hustling whizzbangs fly—
In all the world you could not find a braver man than I!
Yet on patrol in No-Man's-Land, when I may have to stalk a
Benighted Hun, in moments tense I have recourse to "Walker."

'Tis Scotland's best which helps me rest, 'tis Mountain Dew which stays me
When Minnies rack my wearied soul, or blatant H.E. flays me,
'Twas by its aid that I endured Trones Wood and such-like places.
In times of stress my truest friend accelerates my paces.

Take what you will save only this—my evening tot of whiskey,
It gives me warmth, and helps to make a soaking much less risky,
Oh! G.O.C.'s now hear our pleas respectfully presented,
Lend us your aid in this our plight, and we will be contented.

ONE & ALL.

AUNT ANNIE'S CORNER.

—o—o—o—

TENDER TALKS TO TINY TOTS.

—o—o—

MY Dear Lit-tle Tot-ties,

Your poor Auntie has so many let-ters from her dear lit-tle Tot-ties that she can-not ans-wer them all this week, but she will talk to you about some of them. Two of my Tot-ties are very sad, and they want me to tell them what to do.

—:o:—

POOR Lit-tle Gun-ner had a love-ly pair of breech-es given to him, but a nasty boy took them and hid them. When he told the other boys about it they all laugh-ed at him and said that Mother had tak en them a-way from him. He says that the other boys laugh be-cause he likes to wear some pretty toy spurs. Ar'n't they hor-rid boys? Well, Gunner, do not be sad, the other boys only laugh be-cause they have not got such nice breech-es and spurs. They are jeal-ous.

—:o:—

THE other sad Tot-tie is lit-tle Rabs. He makes nice tren-ches, and the naught-y rain comes and wash-es them a-way. He says it is a pity, as he does not often work. Well, Rabs, don't be down-heart-ed (isn't that a big word Tot-ties?), if you keep on and work hard-er, some day you will get some-thing done. You must not take any not-ice of the big pi-on-eers who you say laugh at you, and it was not nice of you to put out your tongue at them. My Tot-ties do not do that.

—:o:—

LIT-TLE Mike Bell tells me he has gone to live fn a new place with the big boys, and has a nice new hat, a red one, and a nice coat with a red col-lar. Isn't he a luck-y boy, Tot-ties? I hope he will re-mem-ber all the nice things we taught him.

—:o:—

Good-bye Tot-ties, be good,
Your Loving
AUNT ANNIE.

A PLEA FROM THE TRENCHES.

—:o:—

EXTRACT FROM "DAILY SKETCH," JANUARY 2ND, 1917.

—:o:—

MAKING THE TRENCHES "COMFY."

—:o:—

"The mothers, sisters and sweethearts of the men in the trenches will be delighted to hear of the latest instance of the solicitude of the military chiefs for their comfort and good health. Every yard of roofing felt that can be found in the United Kingdom is being commandeered for the lining of the trenches on the Western Front. It is sound policy as well as strong sentiment which is at the back of such wise provision."

Mr. GOSSIP.

—o—o—

Dear Mr. Gossip,—

This is really splendid reading that you have given us. Now we shall be able to carry on with no fear of the future. The lack of lining in our trenches has been the one dark spot in our existence. How often we have sat on our well-aired beds and regretted the fact that we had no roofing felt to line our trenches, while only last week one of my Sergeants' asked me to indent for two or three miles, but knowing the cheese-paring policy of Q.M's I refrained. Do you think the Government will follow this up to its legitimate conclusion? You see the steps of our dug-outs are so bare, and if only it were properly represented to them, the Government might be persuaded to buy up all tne carpet and send it over. It would be so nice if our "Mothers, sisters and sweethearts" could think of us going up and down our nicely carpeted steps. Also may I bring to your notice the shameful wav we are treated in the trenches themselves. We have to walk on bare duckboards, (my pal Bill got corns on his feet through having to do this) surely we might be provided with linoleum. I put these suggestions forward in a tentative manner, and if you can do anything for us in the matter we should be so obliged. It would give such joy to our "Mothers, sisters and sweethearts." I have only mentioned essentials, such things as curtains for our dug outs, draught-preventors for the doors, and door-mats with "Welcome" on will come later. Do help us for we cannot help ourselves."

"ONE SPOT."

B.E.F. GAZETTE,

January 1st, 1917.

—:o:—

We are pleased to be able to state that a large and assorted collection of orders from foreign potentates has been received and the Division comes in for a good share. They have been allotted thus :—

To be High Sheik of the Order of the "Numero Neuf."

The A.D.M.S

—:o:—

To be Commander of the Order of the "Piebald Foal or Fatted Calf."

The A.D.V S.

—:o:—

To be Knight Commander of the Most Ancient Order of the "Magdalenes."

The A.P.M.

—:o:—

To be Companion of the Order of the "Rising Sun."

The B.M , rd I.B.

—:o:—

To be High Sheriff of the Most Noble Legion of "Kew Wemms."

The D.A.D.O.S.

—:o:—

The Expanded Medal.

The O.C., Field Coy.

Correspondence.

To the Editor,
"B.E.F. Times."

Sir,

The other evening while taking a stroll through the system of canals which festoon the district, I called at the local soup kitchen, thinking that a cup of hot refreshing soup would compensate me for having missed my evening tot of rum. I was here met with a query as to how a perspiring and angry individual could "Supply the bloomin' Harmy wi' soup, when all he could find was a couple er dead Huns, and well scraped bone, and turnip tops?" Can nothing be done?

INDIGNANS.

—o—o—o—

To the Editor,
"B.E.F. Times."

Sir,

I am a brain worker to whom peace and quiet are a necessity. After moving my quarters many times, I, at length, found a district which seemed to possess those advantages. I WAS MISTAKEN. Shortly after taking up my residence here a "lady" (of whose character the less said perhaps the better) has come to live opposite my house. I am no moralist, but I must protest against the noises in the street caused either by the "lady" herself or by persons interested in her. The "lady" I believe is known as "Minnie." Can nothing be done to move, or at least to have her kept quiet?

I am, sir,
Yours Faithfully,
"PAX."

—o—o—o—

To the Editor.
"B.E.F. Times."

Sir,

As I was going over the top last week I distinctly heard the call of the cuckoo. I claim to be the first to have heard it this spring, and should like to know if any of your readers can assert that they heard it before me.

I am, sir,
Yours Faithfully,
A "LOVER OF NATURE."

(That ought to about settle it for this year.—ED.)

To the Editor,
"B.E.F. Times."

Sir,

As one of the oldest inhabitants of our pretty little village, may I protest very strongly against the noisy behaviour of the new arrivals. So strongly have I the welfare of my fellow citizens at heart that I mean to be quite frank. The worst offender is Doctor Squiller, whose children are continually playing with the most noisy toys, the worst being a particularly blatant pop-gun. Surely the idyllic happiness of our little township should not be spoilt by such hooliganisms.

I am, etc.,
A PEACEFUL MAN.

(The question of street noises is rapidly becoming a nuisance, and the City Fathers must be brought to realise their responsibilities.—ED. "B E.F. Times.")

ANSWERS TO
CORRESPONDENTS.

ANXIOUS Your answer to "Vatican's" matrimonial advertisement will doubtless be replied to in due course. You must understand that "Vatican" is so snowed up with applications for his hand that he cannot deal with them all at once. Besides he is a red-hat, and MAY have other work to do.

ENQUIRER.—No. Two sandbags and one sheet of corrugated iron will NOT as a rule keep out a 5·9. We should advise you to consult Mr. Blewes, the well-known expert.

ARE YOU RUN DOWN!!

IF SO RUN UP TO SHAVELING'S SOUP EMPORIUM.

Doctor SHAVELING wishes to inform his numerous customers that he has recently re-decorated his commodious premises in POT STREET at enormous expense.

He has engaged a fully trained and qualified SOUP MIXER, and can GUARANTEE in future that his WONDERFUL SOUP will not contain more than 75 per cent. of coal dust, and two per cent. of flavour.

ROLL UP IN YOUR MILLIONS!!!!

Customers are respectfully requested not to use the soup cans lent to them for washing clothes in as it impairs the flavour of future supplies.

Telegrams: "STRAFED."

DO YOU LIKE WHISKEY.

—o—o—o—

IF SO

SEND AT ONCE

FOR

PRICE LIST.

—o—o—o—

We have recently cornered all the STOCK in the neighbourhood, and are now in a position to dispose of same on reasonable terms.

—o—o—o—

WRITE OR CALL, MESSRS.

Dope & Curry,

BRAKESMOUNT.

WATCH THIS SPACE

Printed and Published by
Sherwood, Forester & Co., Ltd.
B. E. F.

THE

B. E. F. TIMES.

WITH WHICH ARE INCORPORATED

The Wipers Times, The "New Church" Times, The Kemmel Times & The Somme-Times.

No 4. Vol 1 | Monday, March 5th, 1917 | Price 1 Franc.

THE FOSSE THEATRE OF VARIETIES.

This Week—Special Engagement.

THE MAUDE TROUPE

IN THEIR SCREAMING FARCE,

WHAT'S THE BAG, DAD?

FEATURING ENVER IN HIS LITTLE SONG

"I'M ALL DRESSED UP AND NOWHERE TO GO."

FILM PLAYS.

COMEDY—"WILLIE'S TURKEY."

IN THREE PARTS

Topical—"LETTING GO THE ANCHOR.",

BY HIND AND BERG FILM PLAY SYNDICATE.

PRICES AS USUAL — BOOK EARLY.

PRELIMINARY NOTICE.

MAMMOTH INTER-NATIONAL
SPORTS MEETING.

Under the Patronage of most of the
CROWNED HEADS OF EUROPE.

THIS MEETING has been organised at fabulous expense to take the place of the OLYMPIC GAMES previously billed to take place in BERLIN. In order not to disappoint the inhabitants, every effort will be made to arrange for the finish of, at least, the Marathon Race to take place in afore-mentioned city.

THE FOLLOWING EVENTS WILL BE CONTESTED:--

THROWING THE BOMBUS.
CATCH AS CATCH CAN.
OBSTACLE RACE (Open to P.B.I. only.)
TOSSING THE PIT-PROP.

AND THE

Great Inter-national Marathon Race.

To be competed for over an in and out course, all in run or not, to start at Zero and finish at Berlin (Zero will be notified later) This race must be run under the National Hun SPORTING Association Rules—all in.

Expenses of Meeting will eventually be borne by the German Government.

THE
B. E. F. TIMES.

WITH WHICH ARE INCORPORATED

The Wipers Times, The "New Church" Times, The Kemmel Times & The Somme-Times.

No 4. Vol I. Monday, March 5th, 1917. Price 1 Franc.

EDITORIAL.

SPRING is co-o-o-o-ming! Can you imagine the blithesome Hun sticking his head out of a dug-out and surveying with any pleasure the prospect of a dawning Spring? Winter's snowy mantle has gone, and in its place we have several feet of Belgium's best. The M.O. tells me that he has noticed on several occasions lately the development of web-feet in some of his clientéle. The M.O. having some slight reputation for veracity (perhaps more traditional than actual) one must accept what he says. and wonder how it is all going to end. One contributor in the last number seems to have drawn the gunners fire, but the red-hats remain still distant and aloof, ignoring the gibes of less-effulgent people. We really must congratulate the B.E.F. on the success of the War Loan, but feel sure we can beat 800,000,000 next time, and still save a bit out of our pay. Having lately been on leave we have had a good opportunity of learning how things are going on the Western Front. One cannot help feeling surprised at the obviously enormous amount of military genius allowed to run spare owing to a unobservant and decadent Government. We must express the regret that is felt generally at the departure of so many of the old crowd for newer and larger fields of activity. Of course it is nice to feel that most of the stars of the Army come from the Division yet one misses their cheery faces. It is obvious from some of the efforts submitted recently that there is plenty of talent in the Division, and so we can look confidently forward to the future, and feel assured we shall be able to keep up to twelve pages.

The lengthy instalment of the Serial in this number is attributable to the fact that we turned it over to a subaltern with ideas. SOME ideas, you will agree, and it will be interesting to see what he's going to do with the central characters taking a toss in an aeroplane Truth is stranger than fiction We have come to the conclusion that we shall either have to give up the war or the editorial chair. The sub editor has just remarked that if that's so we'd better give up the war as no one would notice it. That is only the bitterness of a disappointed man, and probably arises from a temporary severance of diplomatic relations with Messrs. Cox and Co. But, seriously! What a country! One writes nice things about the disappearance of winter's snowy mantle, and then it goes back on you and starts all over again. We must thank the few of the Division who have sent us copy, and ask the many who have Something for the paper," to jot it down in writing and send it along, as often, after a long round of visiting, all the anecdotes retailed to the Editor en route sort of get mixed up together, and much that would have been useful gets lost in transit. Greetings to all.

If I were King! Ah! Bill, if I were King,
I wouldn' touch an "A" frame or á thing,
I'd watch the sergeant split his blooming thumb,
And, when he wasn't looking, drink his rum,
I'd make the corpr'l rations to me bring,
If I were King! Ah! Bill, if I were King.

Kindly manager of Cox,
I am sadly on the rocks,
For a time my warring ceases,
My patella is in pieces;
Though in Hospital I lie,
I am not about to die;
Therefore let me overdraw
Just a very little more,
If you stick to your red tape
I must go without my grape,
And my life must sadly fret
With a cheaper cigarette,
So pray be not hard upon
A poor dejected subaltern,
This is all I have to say,

"IMPECUNIOUS," R.F.A.

ALLEGED ANSWER FROM COX'S.

—o—o—o—

Sir, the kindly heart of Cox
Cannot leave you on the rocks,
And he could not sleep in bed
Thinking you were underfed;
So if you will let us know
Just how far you want to go,
Your request will not be vain,
Written from your bed of pain,
We will make but one request—
Keep this locked within your breast,
For if others know, they'll say,
"Good old Cox is sure to pay,
Only take him the right way."

(Note.—This opens up new vistas.
—ED.)

A VOUS.

Here, in these sunny southern climes
(Its pelting in Milan this minute)
It reaches me—our "Wipers Times"
And idly I peruse what's in it:
Till, through the clanging of the trams
That thread the snow where beauty flounders,
I hear the crash of British damns,
The roar of British eighteen-pounders,
And live once more in savage North
Where life is wet, and wierd, and risky,
One of that gallant 'twenty-fourth'—
And drink once more the Sherwoods' whisky;
And meet the friends I used to meet,
Gunner and P.B.I. and Sapper,
When sweet was ration rum, and sweet
The work we did for General Capper.
Alas, those days are done, in place
Of German shells and brass-hats' strictures.
Armed to the teeth, I sternly face
Your war . . . . as shown in moving pictures!
Here Marchesine (save the mark
Strafe loudly on that grand piano!)
Divinely tall, divinely dark,
Smile on an English Capitano,
Who wears a sword, and spotless breeks,
And spurs would make a hairy tremble.
And plays the hero stunt . . . and shrieks
With laughter he can scarce dissemble
For this YOU KNOW, old comrades, tried
To breaking-point of e en YOUR humour,
That never since de Rougemont died
Was hero such a perfect 'stumer.'
You know, who tramped the Menin Road,
And visited the Culvert nightly
That I, your bard who pens this ode,
Ne'er left his crump-proof dug-out lightly,
But slaked the thirst of martial ire,
To his own utter satisfaction,
With miles of buried D.5 wire
And chits he 'passed to you for action'.
Which being so, pray you that fight
In trenches where is no steam-heating
Accept from me, your bard, to-night,
A very humble New Year's greeting.

GILBERT FRANKAU

Telegraphic address:—
Movie-King, Italy.

THE LEAVE WARRANT

Week, after weary week, I work and wait
Patiently wondering, when 'twill be my lot
To find a carpet, wond'rously wrought
On mystic looms, in some enchanted state,
Gifted with Oriental power innate
To bear me hence, to other lands, I wot
(In dreams, I sit upon it, but do not
Awake in time to ring the bell of Fate)
But willingly, indeed, I would forego
This Magic Mat, for just a little bit
Of printed, primrose parchment—and to know,
That on its face my name three times was writ.
For 'tis a genie's golden key to fit
The Gate of Leave—"Chin chin, you chaps, cheer O!"

C.L.P.

"OURS OR THEIRS."

—:o:—

SCENE: ANY BATTALION HEAD-QUARTERS IN LINE.
TIME: THE PRESENT.

—:o:—

The Adjutant is discovered doing nothing in particular.

Enter the Heavy T.M. Officer and the Medium T.M. Officer.

Both (apologetically): Good morning!
Adj. (interrogatively): Good morning!
H.T.M.O.: I'm the flying pig merchant.
M.T.M.O.: And I'm the—
Adj. (grimly): Oh! I know you all right! Sit down and have a drink!
Both: Thanks very much.
H.T.M.O.: I've come to arrange a little shoot this afternoon. (Drinks.)
M.T.M.O.: And I may as well fire at the same time.
Adj. (thoughtfully): Yes—er—what time shall we say? Have another drink?
Both: Thanks very much!
M.T.M.O: 2.30 would suit me down to the ground! I havn't had lunch yet
H.T.M.O.: Shall we say 2.30 then?
Adj.: All right! I'll have the line cleared by then. By-the-way, where's your O.P.? I should like to see the show!
Both: In Tenth Avenue.
Adj: I shouldn't have thought you could see much from there.
Both: Well you see, if you study the map, you'll find the contour gives it about three yards higher than—
Adj.: Quite so! (As they rise) Have another drink before you go?
H.T.M.O (regretfully): No, thanks very much!
M.T.M.O (hastily): Thanks very much! (gulps) 2.30 sharp then! Good morning!

—o—o—o—

SCENE 2: AN O.P.
TIME: 2.30 P.M.
TEMPERATURE: ZERO.

—:o:—

Adjutant is discovered sitting in readiness. He has a pair of binoculars slung round his neck. He has forgotten his British Warm.

Thirty minutes elapse.

Enter M.T.M.O. and H.T.M.O. with brace of telephonists.

Both (cheerily): So sorry. Afraid we're a bit late. Hope we havn't kept you waiting?
Adj. (shortly): Not at all.
H.T.M.O.: Never mind. We'll start right away. They've got their line and range. Tell 'em to report when ready.
No. 1 Tel.: Hallo, there. Hallo, hallo, hallo, No. 1 gun, hallo, hallo, HALLO, HALLO!!
No. 2 Tel.: Is that No. 3 gun? Report when ready please
No. 1 Tel.: Hallo, HALLO, HALLO!?
H.T.M.O.: Damn that wire.
M.T.M.O.: Thank Heaven, my wires all right. Fire.
M.T.M.O.: Curse. Its a dud. Tell 'em to repeat.
No. 1 Tel.: Hallo, HALLO, HALLO.
H.T.M.O.: It's no darn good. The blasted wire's gone. You'd better slip along and put it right.
M.T.M.O.: What the blazes is wrong with No. 3 gun? Tell 'em to wake up a bit.
No. 2 Tel.: Misfire, sir. Rifle mechanism blown out, sir. Just trying another, sir. Hallo No. 3, No 3 fired, sir.
M.T.M.O.: There she goes. Good. A beauty. See all that timber and corrugated iron go up? There's a duckboard and two old buckets. Excellent. Repeat.
No. 1 Tel. (returning): All right now, sir. Hallo there No. 1, can you hear? Right. No 1 ready to fire, sir.
H.T.M.O: Fire.
No. 2 Tel.: Hallo, hallo, hallo, hallo, No. 3 gun, HALLO, HALLO
H.T.M.O.: Good Lord. It's a short. Thank Heavens, it's a dud. Wait a bit though, I used a 19 fuse.
(A gigantic explosion is observed).
M.T.M.O.: Bad luck, old man.
No. 2 Tel.: Hallo, No. 3, Hallo, hallo, HALLO, HALLO. No good, sir.
M.T.M.O.: Darn these infernal wires.
(Enter battalion runner completely out of breath.)
Runner (to Adjutant): Captain Jones, sir, 'as sent me to tell you as 'ow the cook 'ouse and men's latrines 'ave been blown up, sir. A toffee apple landed right between 'em, sir.
M.T.M.O.: Oh, damn. I'm awfully sorry.
No. 1. Tel. (to H.T.M.O.): Gun out of action, sir. Bed jumped out sir.
Adj. (shivering): Thank God. A most interesting afternoon, you fellows. Let me know what time the hymn of hate comes off to morrow. Cheero!
Both: ! ! ! ! !

J. H. W.

LETTERS FROM EDIE.

—o—o—o—

Tuesday.

My very dearest Clarence,

Your long-awaited, anxiously opened, and merrily perused epistle just to hand, and here I am answering it per return. You MUST be ill, you will doubtless exclaim in your inimitably witty manner. Ah, but your hazard is a correct one, I HAVE been ill—aye and sorely so—yea verily. Two ulcers and many spots did make their abode in my throat, and did cause me to suffer much. "Yes, dear boy, the little woman nearly slipped through our fingers this time, but we've managed to pull her through."

(PHOTOGRAPHS UNREPRODUCEABLE.—ED.)

Dear Sir,

Above is a photograph, life size, of the throat of my grandmother, Femina Muggins, aged 96 years. For 60 years she could eat nothing but gin and bitters, and her throat was in a fearful state—one mass of itching sores indeed a grim sight. After one application of your hair-lotion her throat and breath were like a little child's, and notwithstanding food regulations, she consumed an entire ox for her breakfast. You are at liberty to make what use you like of this letter and photographs.—Yours truly, Jerusha Juggins (Mrs.), 595 Semolina Avenue, Tooting.

Excuse the digression. I'm up for the first time, sitting in an armchair in my bedroom, and looking charming as usual in:—(A) a mauve silk nightie, with spiders' webs embroidered on it—most seduc; (B) a black silk kimono, with almond blossoms all over it; hair done on top à la Chinois, and with large mauve bow. "The dainty dear!" I hear you and your comrades ejaculate—"How true" I can only echo.

Elsie—prepare for a shock—has just taken a post as assistant cook in a hospital at Barnet! She starts this week, and is most delightfully vague about everything. She calls it her "part" of cook, and is at present very occupied in getting a nice uniform.

England is, as you doubtless know, in a ferment at present because:—Our leading halfpenny journal is raising its price from a halfpenny to a penny—the "Daily Mail" says so, so it MUST be so.

I've been writing many decadent and Futuristic poems while in bed, they needn't rhyme, and are very simple and so effective. I'll send you some for your little paper if you like. One was called "Worm" and went something like this (you probably won't appreciate it, not having read much Futuristic poetry, but you may take it from me that its an excellent specimen of the kind of stuff that is sold in orange paper covered books with black scrolls on the covers):—

WORM.

Thou thing—
Slimy and crawling
Oozing along.
Not brown,
As men's eyes see
But reddish green,
And moist.
Death meaning nought
To thee.
Who livest
And breedest
During many ÆONS
Billions more yellow horrors
Like thyself.
Oh, Hell!

Believe me or believe me not, but I dashed that marvellous thing off in a few moments! Swonderful.

Got to have dinner now (i.e.—beef-tea and junket, ugh!) so no more. Heaps of best love to you, and "kind thoughts and remembrances" to the Major and your other little friends.

Your Loving Sister,
EDIE.

APOLOGIA PRO VITA—EJUS.

BY BEES EVEN.

Had our good champion still been in our midst, Sir,
That valiant with his motto "Write is Might,"
Thou hadst not dared to publish what thou didst, Sir,
What P.B.I. then had not dared to write.

Our FRANKAU, Sir, would soon have found an answer
To overwhelm, to pulverize, to squash
The prattlings of your poetasting prancer,
The King of Drivel, Emperor of Tosh.

Yet, while we mourn at our good GILBERT'S going,
(Or rather mourned, for he's been gone some time,)
We take this opportunity of showing
The ethics of ballistics in a rhyme.

Firstly, if you receive a daily portion
Of whizzbangs, say, or possibly H.E.,
The fault's entirely due to map distortion
Then strafe "Field Survey," Sir, but don't strafe me.

If you assume the role of "Ally Sloper,"
Don't for a moment think that we have erred,
Mistakes by METEOR explain tho faux pas;
They're sometimes very careless. so I've heard.

When not the German gets it, but the Briton,
Don't grind your teeth, and curse me for a scamp,
The obvious, only, reason I have hit on;
My predecessor left the cordite damp.

Our tears with yours fraternally we mix, Sir,
When accidents occur. We merely state
A gun's a gun, and not a life elixir,
Especially when one can't calibrate.

Again, a frantic message oft you write us;
"RACHEL is rowdy X.6.d.3.8,"
And we are well-nigh stricken by Saint Vitus—
Behind your OWN lines your co-ordinate.

If all these reasons are not deemed sufficient,
If P.B.I. has still a doubting mind;
The fault's with the "Ballistic Co-efficient,"
(In "Gunnery," Vol. 9, its all defined.

Don't think, Sir, that we try to make excuses,
A thing WE needn't do. We merely thought
We'd tell your correspondent what induces
The battery next door to shoot so short.

So, Sir, I trust that your next extra special
Shall not belittle us, nor dare to smirch
Our fair escutcheon, or I think that we shall
All things considered, leave you in the lurch.

—0—0—0—

ENVOI.

—0—

I think you'll own that, for two tyro lispers,
We've put the matter on a sounder footing.
For FRANKAU'S Pegasus—a soaring steed,
We've only got a wheeler—broken kneed,
Our poor old hairy can keep up his end,
He's only got good gunnery to defend.
But—bend your ear low down to hear our whispers—
FRANKAU WOULD NEED A KEATS IF HE WERE SHOOTING!!

BEES EVEN.

THE BACK.

—o—o—o—

As the Front is left behind, the inner meaning of the war becomes more apparent. The elusive Adjutant and the bashful R.S.M. resume their true importance in our lives, as they emerge from their hiding places: Town Majors, A.P.M.'s, Quartermasters, Mice Officers, Instructors, Lecturers, Missionaries, Experts, Staff Officers, all become like common hedgerow flowers in Springtime: and I have known a man who had seen a stray hothouse seedling from G.H.Q., but he told me the yarn in the early hours after his first bottle of O.O., when the Inland Water Transport fellow was short circuited. The further back you get the nearer you get to that spot where all the "Paper" comes from, which I will tell you about in letters of blood-red in the next number. Buy it for your unborn children: the horror of going there will keep them always good.

However, I am very happy, thank you. At the moment I live on a range where there are far more rounds per day fired in anger than in the line. Repairs prove that. Still the range is the envy of those not using it. I know that, because Lewis gunners, bombers, rifle grenadiers, and musketry recruits all like, from a flank and rear position, to get as near our targets as they can: probably from a kindly desire to increase the numbe, of hits on them. The Range Officer has a most enviable job in this little backwater of life.

It is truly a backwater with the water always backing up and defeating the working parties, and one well-read Hophni told me he always called the place Aaron's Range, because his rod had done its work so well.

A morning quickly passes in such light and refreshing work as picking up the chocolate tin-foil and paper of the previous day's firing party, helping up a refractory target constructed in the best R.E. manner, strafing about the empty cartridge cases, opening up a drain, visiting sentries and explaining to them that it really is not part of their duty to look death in the face by walking about in rear of the stop butt etc.: in fact one is quite surprised when the first party moves off hurling anathemas owing to enforced fatigues, and one is at last alone with the meagre unexpended portion of the previous day's ration in one hand and a fat flask in the right, a true horn of plenty.

And at the end of a perfect day the parties shore off happily to their billets, and shortly to the joys of the line, and I to the bosom of my —[I beg your pardon, nothing of the sort: I forgot: I AM STILL B.E.F.]

GRANDPA.

To Fill a Column.

—o—o—o—

I can't think of any good tales to tell you. Of course there's the tale of the Brigadier and the Padre, but I suppose you've all heard that. Anyway both fell ill of the flue, and were straightway tucked away into beds in the same room. The Brigadier's tales were spicy, and the Padre was very unresponsive. Both, acting independently, surreptitiously sent for their clothes. Then, in rapid succession they approached the M.O. in charge and told him that, as they felt so much better, they were off. The Editor is sitting with a towel round his head, thinking hard. He doesn't know whether, on account of the increase in the price of paper, to double the price of this journal, or reduce the size. The Northcliffe bunch, by an effort of superb patriotism has doubled the price of their efforts. Hence the Editor's dilemma Wait and see.

A is the ARMY, in which he's a veteran
Who's fought for a year from the Somme up to Meteren,
Finding in Winter each week is a wetter 'un
And passing his days in the trenches.

B for old BLIGHTY, where, so we hear,
Prices are rising, and food is so dear
That a 'sub' can't afford to even go near:
It is cheaper to stay in the trenches.

C for the CAVALRY who, (so I've heard say)
Have not seen their gee-gees for many a day,
But soon they will mount them and gallop away,
And we'll all say good-bye to the trenches.

D for the DUCKBOARDS—if placed end to end
They'd girdle the Earth, and to Heaven ascend,
But I notice they've caused a peculiar blend
Of language to thrive in the trenches.

E for the EDITOR, ruddy in hue,
He'd blue-pencil this if I said all I knew,
So I'll wish him good luck or—between me and you—
He'll send me exploring Hun trenches.

F for the FLYING CORPS—here we express
Our admiration: could we do less?
They often have helped us out of a mess,
"Cheer-oh!" from the men in the trenches.

G for the poisonous GAS that's emitted
By fighters behind the line only half-witted,
But very pugnacious, and much to be pitied
By those who live in the trenches.

H for the HUN who lives over the way:
His future is black and his present is grey:
Yet a Hun is a Hun, and as such he must pay
For making us live in the trenches.

I for the INFANTRY prefixed "P.B.,"
One bob per diem and milk in their tea:
They work day and night, after which they are free
To start on a job in the trenches.

J for the JAR—if its contents are rum
A welcome awaits it whene'er it may come:
Be it soon, be it late, there will always be some
To greet it with joy in the trenches.

K'S for the KULTUR beneficent Huns
Endeavour to force down our throats with big guns:
They send shells in packets, they send them in ones:
But Kultur's NAR-Poo in the trenches.

L is for LEAVE, our goal of desire,
Ten days in Blighty away from the mire
Hope springs eternal, and ne'er will expire
In the breast of the men in the trenches.

M stands for MINNIE, whose shriek rends the night:
They say that her bark is much worse than her bite,
And if you can dodge her you'll sure be all right:
But she isn't much loved in the trenches.

N for the NOMINAL ROLLS we send through
Daily and weekly and monthly to 'Q':
But we'd do it gladly and much worse things too,
To finish the war in the trenches,

O the OBSERVER, who sees many sights,
Such as stout German generals dancing in tights,
And performing the most inexplicable rites,
From his O-Pip in one of our trenches.

P'S for PEDICULI, horrible pests,
They make themselves happy in trousers and vests;
Though dear little fellows, they're unwelcome guests
To the P.B.I. in the trenches.

Q? Well its obvious who fills this place—
Princes of paper, the pride of our race—
Every movement and minute be sure they can trace
And send back to the man in the trenches.

R the RETURNS to be rendered by noon
Of the number of men who have seen a blue moon,
Speak Japanese, or have been to Rangoon,
Before they came out to the trenches.

S for the SAPPERS, who sin without shame,
And in spite of all efforts will go down to fame
As the men who invented the five-bob "A" frame,
To keep up the sides of our trenches.

T for the TRENCHES themselves (this is where
I must take heed what I write, or I'll swear!)
Which have blackened our souls, and have whitened our hair:
Oh! Life is a dream in the trenches.

U for the UNIVERSE, whose fate 'tis plain
Is now being settled in mud, slush and rain,
By strafing which spreads from Nieuport to Lorraine,
A line which is marked by our trenches.

V for the VICES soldiers posses,
Discovered by those who have been more or less
Claimants to fame through a line in the Press,
But never have shone in the trenches.

W for WHISKEY and WHIZZ-BANGS as well:
Of the former I've almost forgotten the smell,
Whilst the latter contribute to make it like Hell
At various times in the trenches.

X for the unknown—and twixt you and me
Fritz is now thinking (and we all agree)
That, hot as his present, his future will be
Much hotter than e'er in the trenches.

Y for the YARNS that one hears—some are true:
Others—Well! doubtless, though vivid in hue,
Are spun by those 'back,' who have never been through,
Or stood their whack of the trenches.

Z is for ZERO, the time we go over,
Most of us wish we were way back in Dover,
Making munitions and living in clover
And far, far away from the trenches.

OUR SPLENDID NEW SERIAL.

—o—o—o—

"NARPOO RUM."

—o—o—o—

BY THE AUTHOR OF "SHOT IN THE CULVERT."

—o—o—o—

DRAMATIS PERSONAE:

—o—

Cloridy Lvme — A Sanitary Inspector.
Madeline Carot — A French Girl.
Intha Pink — A Pioneer.
General Bertram
Rudolph de Rogerum — The Earl of Loose.
Lord Reginald
de Knellthorpe — His Son.
Q. Wemm — A Storekeeper.
L. Plumernapple — A Soldier.
Herlock Shomes — The Great Detective.
Dr. Hotsam — His Admirer.

—o—o—o—

CHAPTER 4.

—o—o—o—

THE CLUE OF THE TORN LETTER.

—o—o—o—

SKILFULLY landing his plane in the Square of the ancient town of Ypres, Shomes resolved to dine at the Hotel des Ramparts before proceeding up the Menin Road to the Culvert Arms. Having partaken of an excellent dinner, Shomes once more donned his tin-hat, raincoat and gum boots thigh, and proceeded by way of the Menin Gate up the Menin Road. As he walked, the fearful events of his last great adventure in that district flashed through his mind with painful distinctness. He was roused from his reverie by the weary whirr of a five-nine, and realised with a start that he had reached his destination. Looking around with a dawning sense of horror he saw that the Culvert Arms was no more. Shomes amazed, perplexed, but by no means non-plussed hastily injected a double dose from his vermoral sprayer, and sought for a clue. Down in the deep and muddy ditch where once the ancient hostelry had stood, he passed a few battered stones, and in the dark and sluggish waters found an envelope, muddy and torn, and readable as far as :—

TOR
IMES
TERS (P

Shomes spoke no word, but a close observer would have noted that his face, seen in the white glare of the Very Lights had a look of grim and purposeful satisfaction.

—o—o—o—

CHAPTER 5.

—o—o—o—

ABOUT the same time as Shomes was making his important discovery at the ruined Culvert Arms, Hotsam was endeavouring to revive the fainting Earl and at the same time to keep a vigilant watch through the estaminet window. The General at length recovered consciousness, and joined Hotsam at the window. A strange sight met their eyes. Lord Reginald de Knellthorpe stood with his back to the window supporting the fair Madeline, who appeared to be weeping bitterly. Muttering with impotent rage the old Earl thrust open the door, and followed by Hotsam, entered the room. Lord Reggie turned an amazed and tear-wet face towards them, and simultaneously the Earl and Hotsam burst into tears. Hotsam with alacrity put on his gas helmet, corked up the open rum jar, and opened the window. The General drying his tears, furiously asked his weeping son the reason of his presence there. "Well, you see, father," said Lord

Reggie "Madeline" (he tenderly wiped the eyes of the beautiful girl) "told me that she had seen some rum jars in here, and, thinking that they might contain the rum that I am suspected of stealing, I came here to examine them, they appear to contain tear gas." The Earl, with a new burst of tears, joined the hands of Reggie and Madeline, and Hotsam feeling that his presence was no longer required, strode out into the night, leaving the Earl and the young lovers smiling through their tears.

—o—o—o—

CHAPTER 6.

—o—o—o—

THE END OF SHOMES?

—o—

HOTSAM, very fatigued, at length reached the comfortable Quality Street dug-out, where he found a signaller, who handed him one of the dreaded pink forms. He resignedly took the wire and read:—

> "Meet me at YPRES at once AAA Obtain bus from GEN. BERTRAM RUDOLPH de ROGERUM AAA Urgent AAA Sick AAA"

Hotsam sighed, and after much trouble obtained the bus, and eventually reached Ypres. In the Square he found Shomes, seated in his plane. "Come, Hotsam," he cried, "Jump in, there is no time to be lost, they shall not escape us this time." Hotsam obeyed, and Shomes, having started up the motor, jumped in, and they were off. After some hours in the air, Hotsam shouted "Where are we going, Shomes?" He could not catch the answer, so was silent. Suddenly a flash! a crash! and two men and an Archied aeroplane were falling through the night.

CHAPTER 7

—o—o—o—

AT LAST?

—o—

INTHA sat in a large shell-hole in the grounds of Elvarston Castle.

He was not happy. He had been knocked down by a G.S. waggon, machine-gunned on the road, whizz-banged in the trench, and, finally, had taken his "A" frame to the wrong dump. As he rested he thought of many things. He thought of war, he thought of snow, he thought of rum. Why had he had no rum for some days now? Because some scoundrel had stolen the Brigade supply. Suddenly a great resolve grew in the soul of the Pioneer; HE would find the missing liquid! Fired by enthusiasm, he arose, and, casting away his now useless "A" frame, made his way as quickly to the Estaminet of Madeline Carot. After some protest, Madeline quietly admitted him. "I'm a bloomin' policeman now," he said, "and don't you bloomin' well forget it. I saw a staff-officer leave 'ere at eight-fifteen, wot yer goin' ter do abaht it?"

"You no tell," said Madeline, "and I give you beer."

"Narpoo!"

"I give you some rum."

"THE RUM!" thought Intha

(WAS IT?).

(Read next thrilling instalment.)

(To be Continued.)

Special News.

—o—o—o—

Our special correspondent Mr. TEECH BOMAS, having returned from his winter trip to more sunny climates, we will now carry on with the war as per schedule. "Seconds out of the Ring!"

GOOD-BYE AND GOOD-LUCK.

ONCE again we say good bye to a Brigadier, this time to our oldest friend in the Division, Gen. B. MITFORD, C.B., D.S.O., who was with us in the beginning. What an age ago it seems now since a mob of aspiring and perspiring embryo soldiers used to perform wonderful feats under his skilful guidance on the Sussex Downs. How well we came to understand the terrors of war during those final rushes on Chanctonbury Ring! In addition to the regret of losing a Divisional friend, the editorial staff has also to mourn the loss of one of the first supporters and helpers of our paper. Gen. MITFORD assisted at the inception of the "Wipers Times," and has ever since given the greatest help possible. The whole Division bids him God-speed, and our congratulations and good wishes are none the less hearty if with them are mixed the natural regrets one feels at losing a good pal. We cannot close without extending a hearty welcome to his successor.

Correspondence.

To the Editor,
"B.E.F Times."

Sir,

If you will kindly supply me with the name and address of your correspondent signing himself a "Lover of Nature," I will guarantee that he will not love Nature any more; neither will he hear any more cuckoos. No sir! not this Spring nor next or any other Spring neither. Cuckoo indeed!! I'll learn 'im.

Yours Faithfully,
"FED UP"

Agony Column.

MINNIE.—Meet me at Flying Pig 8 30.—Tock Emma.

M O.—Young, inexperienced, would like appointment with fighting battalion to gain experience.—Write M.O.

FOR SALE or EXCHANGE.—Large Country ESTATE, pleasantly situated on the banks of the Somme. Owner travelling East for the benefit of his health. No reasonable offer refused, would exchange for a couple of white rabbits, or something edible.

MESSRS. ABDUL & CO. regret that, owing to unforseen troubles, they ARE UNABLE TO SUPPLY any more Turkish Delights for the present, as there has been such a run on them.

But I'm not King! no Bill, I'm not the King,
So 'spose I've got to hump the blasted thing,
Gawd 'elp the 'un I get my 'ands upon,
One moment 'ere, and passing thence, 'e's gone,
'Tis soon we'll 'ave the blighter on a string.
"Gawd save the King, yus Bill! Gawd save the King."

There was a little Turk, and Baghdad was his home,
There was a little Hun, and he lived in Bapaume,
Each said to the other, as they shivered with alarm,
"To find another home wouldn't do us any harm."

THE PROFESSOR AGAIN PRESENTS HIS

World-famed Concert Party

IN AN ENTIRELY NEW LINE, AND WITH A BRAND-NEW SET OF STAR ARTISTS.

—o—o—o—o—o—

THE FOLLOWING ARE CERTAIN TO APPEAR:—

BILL BUGGAN,

IN A SONG SCENA:

"I NEVER COULD STAND PIMPLES."

TOM FLINT

PRESENTS HIS FAMOUS SONG:

"ANOTHER LITTLE DRINK, Etc."

TWEENY AND CO.

IN GRAND SPECTACULAR PERFORMANCE OF

"LIFE IN '72."

☛ Many other brilliant turns. A chorus of real soldiers has been obtained at fabulous cost to perform.

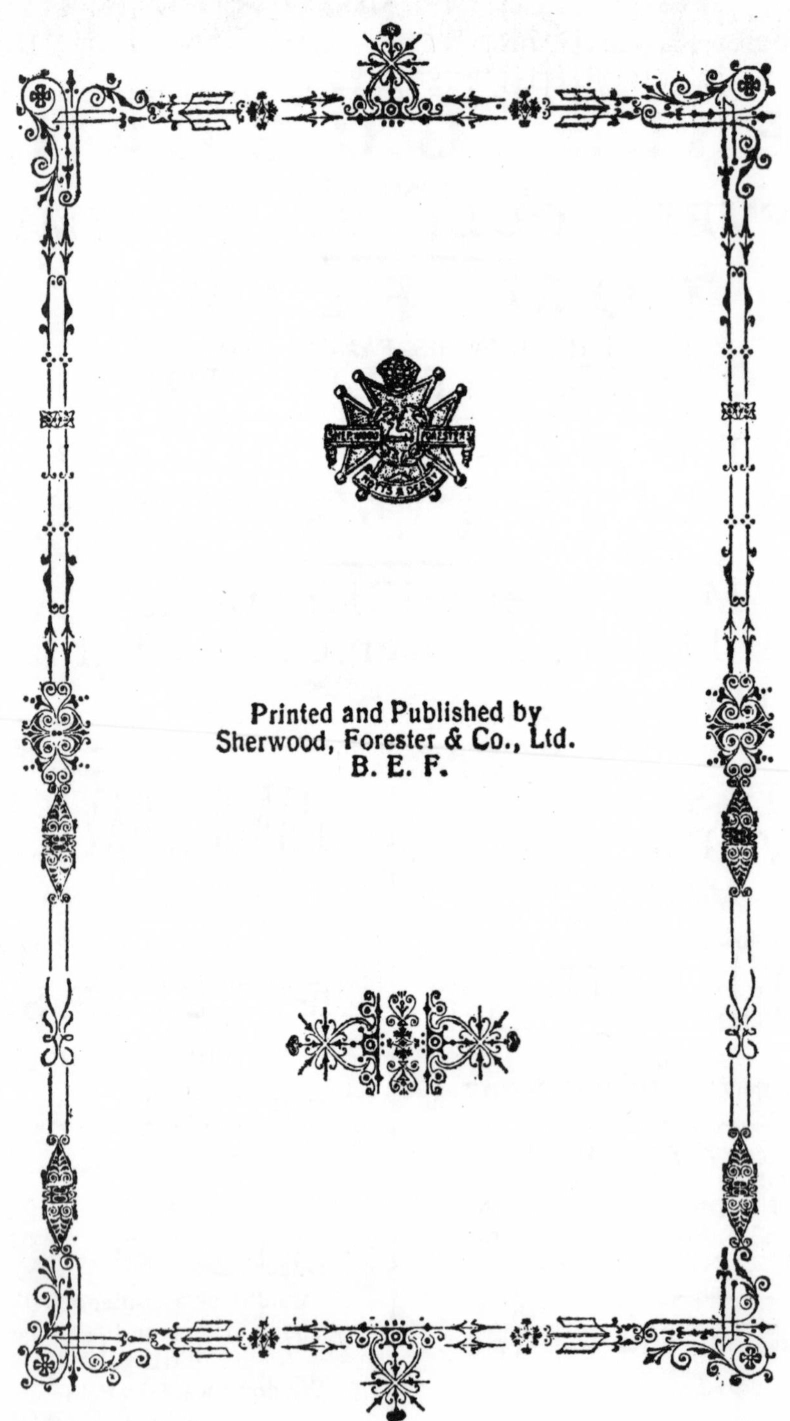

Printed and Published by
Sherwood, Forester & Co., Ltd.
B. E. F.

THE

B. E. F. TIMES.

WITH WHICH ARE INCORPORATED

The Wipers Times, The "New Church" Times, The Kemmel Times & The Somme-Times.

No 5. Vol 1 Tuesday, April 10th, 1917. Price 1 Franc.

THE FOSSILEUM

—o—o—o—o—

THE DUMA TROUPE OF QUICK CHANGE ARTISTS

STARRING :—

Rodzi & Co., in their Stirring Domestic Drama, "SPRING CLEANING."

—o—o—o—o—

Great American Film Play, Entitled :-- "TEDDY GET YOUR GUN

(SOME FILM) FEATURING THEODORE IN THE LEAD.

—o—o—o—o—

Murray's Colourmatrograph.

A TOUR THROUGH PALESTINE (Series.

NO. 3: JERUSALEM.

Publisher's Announcements.

MESSRS. STODGER AND STOUTUN.

GOD'S GOOD MAN—An Autobiography by William Hohenzollern (Author of "The Innocents' Abroad," "Misunderstood," "The Christian," etc.)

A THIEF IN THE NIGHT—By Little Willie.

THE LAST HOPE—Professor Hindenberg (Author of "Westward Ho.")

IT'S NEVER TOO LATE TO MEND—Dr. Wilson.

ERIC, OR LITTLE BY LITTLE—Dean Haig.

THE CRUISE OF THE CATCH-A-LOT—By Bill Beatty.

THE DRINK HABIT

ACQUIRED IN THREE DAYS.

If you know anyone who doesn't drink alcohol regularly, or occasionally, let me send my free book, "CONFESSIONS OF AN ALCOHOL SLAVE." It explains something important, i.e.: How to quickly become an

Expert "Bona-fide Toper."

For the first 15 years of my lite I was a rabid teetotaler, since the age of 16 I have never been to bed sober. If your trouble is with reference to a friend please state in your letter whether he is willing to be cured or not. Letters treated in a confidental manner. I can cure anyone.

Address: J. SUPITUP, Havanotha Mansions. Telegrams: "RATS."

THE

B. E. F. TIMES.

WITH WHICH ARE INCORPORATED

The Wipers Times, The "New Church" Times, The Kemmel Times & The Somme-Times

No 5. Vol 1. Tuesday, April 10th, 1917. Price 1 Franc.

EDITORIAL.

SPRING has at last really come! And with it an unusual amount of hurry and bustle all round; likewise forecasts, prophecies and conjectures, all frothy and furious We have all put our watches on one hour, and are now spending our spare time throwing away our surplus kit, sharpening our pistols and swords, and having our boots soled and heeled. We are also trying to produce this number of the paper under rather more difficult circumstances than usual, and we feel sure that our gentle readers will understand that whatever may be lacking is due to circumstances over which we have no control. We have again been fortunate in obtaining a special article from the pencil, ink, copying, one, of our old friend Mr. Teech-Bomas, which we feel sure will be read with interest. This number sees the finish of our serial "Narpoo Rum," and we wish to remind our readers of our Mammoth Competition in connection with same, particulars of which we published in our Grand Xmas Double Number last December. We still have several million francs left in our treasure chest which we should like to dispose of before the "Big Push" commences, more on account of its bulk than for any other reason. It may be a long time before we can produce another number, in which case we wish to take this opportunity of bidding all our friends "au revoir," the best of luck, and thanking them all for the kind support we have always received since the day in "Wipers" long ago when we found an old printing outfit looking for a job.

THE EDITOR.

NEWS FROM THE RATION DUMP.

—o—o—o—

The Esquimaux have broken off diplomatic relations with Germany.

—o—o—o—

The Huns are shortening their line in the West with a view to sending a number of divisions on a punitive expedition against them

—o—o—o—

Patrols of British and French cavalry swam the Rhine last night near Cologne, and are now meeting with sharp resistance in the suburbs of Berlin.

—o—o—o—

A party of A.S.C. were seen working in the reserve line.

—o—o—o—

The Czar of Russia has antiquated.

—o—o—o—

Horatio Bottomley has accepted the Turkish throne on condition they make a separate peace.

—o—o—o—

Leave is about to re-open on the Western front.

—o—o—o—

The German fleet has bombarded Wapping Old Stairs, and ruined the carpet.

—o—o—o—

40,000 Huns have surrendered. They were so thin that they walked down one of our C.T.'s in fours.

—o—o—o—

[The EDITOR takes no responsibility for the truth of the above statements.]

TEN GERMAN PIONEERS.

Ten German Pioneers went to lay a mine,
One dropped his cigarette, and then there were nine.

Nine German Pioneers singing Hymns of Hate,
One stopped a whizz-bang, and then there were eight.

Eight German Pioneers dreaming hard of Heaven,
One caught a Flying Pig, and then there were seven.

Seven German Pioneers working hard with picks,
One picked his neighbour off, and then there were six.

Six German Pioneers, glad to be alive,
One was sent to Verdun, and then there were five.

Five German Pioneers, didn't like the war,
One shouted "Kamarad," and then there were four.

Four German Pioneers tried to fell a tree,
One felled himself instead, and then there were three.

Three German Pioneers, prospects very blue,
One tried to stop a tank and then there were two.

Two German Pioneers walked into a gun,
The gunner pulled the lanyard, and then there was one.

One German Pioneer couldn't see the fun
Of being shot at any more, and so the war was done.

ON THE HEELS OF THE FLEEING FOE.

—o—o—o—

FROM TEECH BOMAS.

—o—o—

FRANCE, Sunday Afternoon.

This morning, many hours before dawn, I mounted my bicycle and rode through 174 of the 187 blasted villages liberated during the past couple of days by our troops. I am now in the 175th, 12 miles north-south-west of Peraume, seated in what remains of the bar parlour of its main Estaminet, eating a frugal meal, and talking to the oldest inhabitant. I have this moment tasted a mouthful of Hun ration bread, which the enemy was unable to destroy in his hurried departure. It is darkish blue-black in hue, and its taste is putrid, rancid, nauseating, foul and stinking.

The scenes I have personally witnessed to-day as I rapidly pedalled into village after village were thrilling, awe-inspiring, blood-curdling—in short the whole outfit was EPIC. Old men, young men, women, girls, cripples, hunchbacks, little children, large children, all in their gladdest clothes, cheered me to the echo as I flashed through the various villages, whilst the village bands played patriotic airs in the market places. Occasionally I dismounted and talked to the people. To one woman I said "What of the Hun officers?" She gave a low shrill whistle and replied with emotion "Bosch officier, no bon, plenty zig-zag." This incident, in itself trivial, sums up the situation.

On my way from the 174th to the 175th village I found myself in front of our own outposts, and amongst those of the enemy. Rapidly twisting up the ends of my moustache and turning my cap inside out, I was able to escape recognition, and observed the antics of the Hun rearguard from closer quarters than anyone has ever done before. Officers and men, Unteroffiziere, Feldwebel and Freijährige, were all gibbering with fright, and pale pink drops of sweat dripped and dropped from their mottled brows as they leapt from tree to tree.

Just before reaching this village, an exciting and almost touching incident occurred. A very tired German 17-inch shell came sizzling through the air, and burst right under my cycle. Luckily the only damage done was a slight puncture to my near off side wheel. This proves how the Bosch H E has deteriorated during the past few months.

Even now I can hear the battle raging in the near distance. I must away and leave to a later dispatch the narrative, of what I shall do and see this afternoon.

ARMA VIRUMQUE CANO.

—o—o—o—

No Prayers of Peace for me; no maiden's sigh.
Give me the Chants of War, the Viking's Song;
Battle for me; nor care I for how long
This war goes on. Tell me, where bullets fly;
Where noble men and brave may bleed and die;
Where skilful parry foils the sword-thrust strong.
Such are the tales I love. (I may be wrong—
A warrior, and no carpet knight am I.)

—o—o—o—

The D.S.O., the M.C. grace my breast;
My brow is bound with laurels and with lace;
I love this war. Perhaps you think that that
Is strange. Well I am different from the rest
Of you poor blighters. I live at the Base,
And use the Brain inside my nice, red hat.

C. L. P.

Now listen ye of mournful mien, whose bleatings rend the air,
Who spread an air of gloom where'er you go,
That though of cleverness you have p'r'aps more than your fair share,
Yet most of us just hate your wail of woe.

—o—o—o—

One day 'tis "this" and next day "that," your bogies come at will,
Of fearful ills to come you rave and rant,
You said a year ago the war was lost—we're fighting still,
The job has been no easier for your cant.

—o—o—o—

In reverse you see disaster, and a victory spurs you on
To still greater efforts in the realms of doubt,
" We'll be lured into a trap," or " we can ne'er hold what we've won,"
And " we'll all be starved to death " your constant shout.

—o—o—o—

Tis true that mostly you are those who ne'er have known the joy
Of living in ten feet of mud and slime,
Or the ecstasy which thrills one, sheer delight without alloy,
When you're dodging crumps and Minnies all the time.

—o—o—o—

So in future cut the grousing, and for God's sake wear a grin,
The time is surely coming in a while,
When in spite of all your croakings the old Huns will be " all in,"
Cut the everlasting wail and smile, man, SMILE!

" Only the Wise apologise,
Fools always must explain."
(Extract from a Great Modern Poet.)

—o—o—o—

On receipt of our verses, the Gunner grew pensive,
But quickly developed a counter-offensive;
And though the rounds mostly were duds, or fell short,
They showed themselves able to make some retort.

—o—o—o—

We all know the Sappers, of course, never shirk
From anything looking the least bit like WORK;
So pale, but determined, they swore, " He shall rue it! "
And asked for two large Working Parties to do it.

—o—o—o—

The Staff, though surprised, did not gibber or storm,
But dealt with it all on the Authorised Form;
For " G " said, " Well, I know whom THAT refers to,"
And passed the whole matter "for action " to " Q ";
While " Q " patronisingly gave it a smile,
Remarked, " Poor old 'G' Branch! "
and wrote on it " FILE."

P.B.I

Ah! P.B.I., too well we know your woes,
And why you sometimes talk in bitter strains,
Of living always tête-à-tête with foes,
Preserving us to labour on your drains.

—o—o—o—

But pause and think, before you grasp your pen,
Two sides to every argument appear;
And ere you hold us up to scorn of men,
A few poor words on our side please to hear.

—o—o—o—

Know then, O proud and turgid P.B.I.,
Our fingers to the bone are worn for THEE,
Yet still one hears thy working parties cry,
"We're working for the —— old R.E!"

—o—o—o—

Do we essay to build a modest shelter,
Just rain and windproof, to our simple taste;
Lo! yet before our backs are turned there enter
Platoons of infantry in quite indecent haste.

—o—o—o—

At times for help we ask with trepidation,
A cinquantaine of fed-up troops appears,
A few hours late, amid recrimination,
And crawls off slowly, 'spite of all our tears.

At journey's end quite half retain their tools,
And most of these are sick and tired of war,
Digging's a pastime only fit for fools,
Let the d----d R.E. go and look for more.

—o—o—o—

Dear P.B.I.! how gladly would we quit
"A" frames, and duckboards, berms, and C.G.I.,
Dream of pontoons and trestles, pathway fit
To carry our victorious P.B.I.

THE SANGUINARY R.E.

THEIR UNION OUR STRENGTH.

—o—o—o—

Gunners and Sappers, and P.B.I.,
Now each in turn has had his say,
And shown in poetical rivalry
That, though good at their jobs, they're as good in play.

—o—o—o—

At times when the nerves are a trifle taut,
And frayed at the edges, as well may be,
All tempers are—well! just a wee bit short,
Then one MUST strafe a little impatiently.

—o—o—o—

Yet their trust in each other has stood the test,
Through the depths to the heights which are drawing nigh,
Each at his job has proved "the best,"
Gunners and Sappers, and P.B.I.

A STORY WITHOUT A MORAL.

—o—o—o—

And it came to pass that upon a certain day the General Officer Commanding a Division said unto his A.A and Q.M.G. : " O A.A. and Q.M.G., render unto me by the first day of next month a Return showing the names of the number of men of this Division who have even refused to undergo the hardships of INOCULATION, in order that I may send forward this Return unto Corps., in accordance with C R.O. 758

And it came to pass that the A.A. and Q.M.G. said certain things unto his D.A.A. and Q.M.G. and unto his D.A.Q.M.G., the result of which was a Return of names to the number of fifty of men of the Division who had refused to be INOCULATED.

And it came to pass that the Return aforementioned was in due course sent forward unto Corps., in which place it became labelled with the mystic sign " P.A.," which, being interpreted, means " put aside."

And it came to pass that upon a much later date this same General Officer Commanding a Division said unto his A.A. and Q.M G.: " O A.A. and Q.M.G. render unto me by the first day of next month a Return showing the names of the number of men of this Division who have done deeds such as are worthy of reward in the form of the Medal Military, in order that I may send forward this return unto Corps., in accordance with C.R.O. 869.

And it came to pass that this Return also was duly obtained, and in due course sent forward unto Corps., in which place it became labelled with the mystic sign " P.A.," which, being interpreted, means " put aside."

And it came to pass that in due course those men who had refused to be INOCULATED were duly awarded with the MILITARY MEDAL.

Oh! great is the Corps.

Verbatim Extracts From Intelligence Summaries.

—o—o—o—

TRENCH MORTARS.

—o—

At 1·0 p.m. the " Flying Pig " dropped a round in our front line at X 9 d 5 2. The trench was completely wrecked—the crater formed being 14 feet deep and 25 feet across It is consoling to think that over 40 rounds have been fired from this gun into the enemy trenches during the last week.

(Very consoling to the P.B.I.)

—o—o—o—

OPERATIONS.

—o—

On the 21st, in W 6 b, a party of about 10 Germans entered our lines. Our bombers, however, drove them out, in addition to killing 5 of them.

(Some bombers !)

—o—o—o—

MOVEMENTS.

—o—

At Z 5 b 21 this morning about thirty men were seen doing Expended Order Drill.

(We hope it wasn't painful.)

The following is a true extract from a return of reserve rations from a certain garrison :—

Locality—Foxhall Keep.
Map Ref.—P 67 X 19-32.
Commodity—Bully Beef.
Quantity—1 Tin.
Remarks—Not Full.

(Where's Lord Devonport ?)

Rubályát of Williám Hohenzollern.

Awake, old Tirpz! Bid Hindenburg arise,
"Der Tag" has come, I long to hear the cries
Of Europe! We'll proceed to raise all Hell,
Let's use our day from dawn. Time flies! Time flies!

—0—0—0—

Dreaming, it seemed to me the World was mine,
Waking, I think that the idea is fine;
We'll wade right in to see what we can grab,
And glut ourselves with murder, rape and wine.

—0—0—0—

Come, fill the cup, and don a mask of pain
That we should have to cleanse the World again;
Consider we our cause both pure and strong,
So first we'll try our hand in old Louvain.

—0—0—0—

Should any doubt my will, or us dispute,
Man, woman, child, don't hesitate to shoot;
We'll play the policeman, and for Kultur's sake
My son, young Bill, will pick up all the loot.

—0—0—0—

How sweet is mortal sov'reignty—you see
How sov'reignty has made a God of me,
As I a God of it—play we the rolo
Thus. each one part, and that alternately.

I sometimes think that never lived so great
A monarch as myself—in fact of late
My greatness has appalled me and I bow,
I bow my humbled head upon the gate

—0—0—0—

There is no door, but that we have the key,
There is no depth debarred from you and me,
Success alone will justify our game,
So kill the land and terrorise the sea.

—0—0—0—

And if the man you burn, the child you kill,
Should even for one moment keep you still,
Think well 'tis for our sacred Kultur's sake,
And by a million murders steel your will.

—0—0—0—

Yet should success to dust and ashes fade,
And Justice rise from out the Hell we made,
We'll say that others lit the fire, and we
But fanned the flames, to mark the price they paid.

—0—0—0—

So Tirpz! with Hindenburg and me conspire,
With murder, rapine, frightfulness and fire,
Let's raise all Hell and, even should we fail,
At least we'll have "Der Tag" of our desire.

THE BULLY--BARLIN STAKES.

—o—

The Bully—Barlin Stakes took place on Friday last under the most auspicious conditions, the going being good and the average time of those who completed the course distinctly fast.

As a social event the Meeting was no less successful, a large and distinguished gathering being visible in the Paddock and on the Grand Stand, amongst whom your correspondent noticed Captain Turret and Admiral Jellicue, tastefully dressed in that inconspicuous blend of brown relieved by a soupcon of red which has become so fashionable of late. The Comptesse de Callonne looking ravishingly beautiful in a chic sandbag coat and skirt fringed with bric rubble. The Baron BYLLGEE (only capital letters can do him justice), in the Pink, many of the younger Checkes, and other notorities. Paderouski Ayetockski with his inevitable Blue and White Band played such popular items as "Buzz it and I shall hear," "You're through to Q. sir, but nobody's awake," and selections from that great tragedy "Burying Cable."

The race started punctually at 4.30 p.m., there being no false starts. Archie I and Archie II were hot favourites at the start, the betting being 4—2 on, offered freely, but with few takers. Shortly after the start, thanks to information tic-tacked back to the firm Strafit and Hate the prices and range lengthened. The Archies, however, proved as disappointing as ever to their backers, and finished a good second to Captain Tarkers "Bommy," owner up, which got off the mark like two Turkish Pashas paced by a Roumanian General. Third came the Rev. Snooker on his famous "Ironscrappes," a willing steed lacking rather in pace than pertinacity, and after that a mob of "Also rans," among whom one noticed several of the lesser lights of Bully. It is rumoured that vast sums exchanged hands over the favourite's defeat, and that the old firm of Aire, Supremacy and Suchsquish, was badly hit.

THE SUB.

He loves the Merry "Tatler," he adore the Saucy "Sketch,"
The "Bystander" also fills him with delight;
But the pages that he revels in, the evil minded wretch,
Are the adverts of those things in pink and white.

—:o:—

They are advertised in crêpe-de-chine and trimmed with silk and lace;
The pictures fairly make him long for leave;
And while he gloats upon their frills, he cannot find the grace
To read the pars of PHRYNETTE, BLANCHE and EVE.

—:o:—

Before the war, he'd hardly heard of lace and lingerie;
He didn't know the meaning of chemise
But thanks to weekly papers, this astounding mystery
Has been solved by dainty VENN and dear LABISE.

—:o:—

Before the war, he only knew of corsets and of hats,
All other vogues invoked a ribald "what ho."
But the last decree of Fashion is a dinky nightie, that's
Embroidered with his regimental motto

—:o:—

It's this war, that is responsible for teaching simple youth
All sorts of naughty Continental tricks
And already he's decided, when it's over that, in truth,
He'll buy mamma a pair of cami-knicks

R.M.O.

—th Infantry Brigade Intelligence Summary. No. 30.

—o—o—o—

From 12 noon, any date.
To 12 noon, date following.

—o—

1.—ATTITUDE OF THE ENEMY.

Aggressive, 12 whizbangs at 2 p.m. on POPE'S PIMPLE. POPE has now no pimple worthy of mention.

2.—ENEMY'S ARTILLERY.

The enemy fired a gas shell into X. The gas sentry at once sounded his jam tin; this proved most effective, no further shells were fired, and the rest of the troops in the immediate vicinity was not in the least disturbed.

NOTE.—This report should be accepted with considerable reserve, it is based entirely on the statement of the sentry who, although a worthy fellow, is not remarkable for his veracity.

3.—OUR ARTILLERY.

A bombardment was carried out by our Artillery in conjunction with Trench Mortars (Heavy, Medium and Light), Machine and Lewis Guns, and Rifle Grenades, vide operation order No. 3,000. Our casualties were slight.

4.—T.M. ACTIVITY.

There has been considerable Trench Mortar activity; our Flying Pig effectively engaged our front line trench at about M 30 6 3 9; the hostile Minnie 'SUSAN' vigorously retaliated on her adjacent Batt. H.Q. at N 15 d 6 20.

5.—SNIPING.

Our snipers claim to have hit M 14 b 4 3.

6.—PATROLS.

A patrol under 2nd Lieut. Jones was ordered to ascertain whether the sap at H 14 b 9 5 is occupied by the enemy. This patrol left our trenches at 10 p.m.; after proceeding ten yards in a N E. direction an empty tin was found, on examination it proved to be labelled 'PLUM JAM.'

NOTE.—This is considered to be a clever ruse of the enemy to convey the impression that his rations include an issue of plum jam.

The patrol returned at 10·03 p.m., having secured the above valuable identification.

NOTE.—It has been suggested that the tin had contained jam issued for the consumption of our own troops, 2nd Lieut. Jones however has reason to believe otherwise.

7.—INTELLIGENCE.

Our observers report:—

3 p.m. A man wearing a shrapnel helmet, accompanied by a dog, was observed walking along the road between S 5 a 6 8 and S 5 b 9 6.

3·2 p.m. A stout man with red face and glass eye asleep by the side of road at S 5 b 9 4.

3·5 p.m. Dog (referred to above) seen to approach stout man asleep, and remain near him several seconds.

NOTE.—It is thought that possibly a relief was taking place.

3h 5m 5sec. Stout man who had been asleep was observed to rise and throw a large stone at dog (referred to above).

3h 5m 6sec. Dog disappeared at S 5 b 9 5.

3·7 p.m. Man with shrapnel helmet observed wiping with a sandbag the head of the stout man with red face and glass eye who had been asleep, but was now evidently thoroughly awake, and showing unmistakeable signs of anger.

NOTE.—It is thought that possibly dogs have been trained to rouse sleeping sentries in case of alarm.

4 p.m. Smoke was observed at S 10 b 0 0.

NOTE.—It is considered that this is a clever ruse of the enemy to convey the idea that a fire had been ignited at this spot.

8.—REPORTS FROM OTHER SOURCES.

2 p.m. Two men wearing spectacles were seen to disappear behind a hedge at K 2 b 5 7; our 60 Pounders searched this spot with H.E., the two men, previously seen, suddenly reappeared at K 2 b 5 9. and hastily took cover in a trench at K 2 6 3. They appeared to be strangely hampered in their movements.

NOTE.—It is thought that this hedge conceals a strong point of considerable importance to the enemy.

MIDDLING OLD LIEUT.,
BDE. INTELLIGENCE OFFICER,
—th INFANTRY BRIGADE.

HOW CONGRESS DECLARED WAR.

—o—o—o—

BY

OUR SPECIAL CORRESPONDENT

Tuckis Shurtin.

—o—o—o—

MR. TUCKIS SHURTIN managed, by the wonderful enterprise and skill always shown by him on these delicate operations, to hide himself behind a life-size picture of Charlie Chaplin in the White House, and was thus present at the most momentous meeting which ever took place in the history of America.

He briefly describes, in his own picturesque language, exactly what took place.

"Wal!" said Woodrow, chewing the end of a five-cent che-root, "I'm for a show-down."

The Bull-Moose took the floor and bucked, good and plenty. "Say," he howls, "double the ante, and raise 'em sky-high for cards. I ain't in on a two-dime game. Cut it out. I'm in on a no limit, and I've got the dust. Give me half a-million boys, and I'll skin every Hun in Yurrup. Yes! sirree!!

Elihu P. showed a busted straight, and beat for the golden silence.

Big Bill threw in for the Bull-Moose, leaving Woodrow up against it.

"Wal!" said he, "write me down for a two-cent boob if I don't hand it to Willie. Say, boys, I'm in the game. Boost the ante, and sky-high for cards. I'm a bold she-wolf, and it's my night to howl."

"Rah! RAH! RAH! Woodrow. Oh! Willie, beat it! Theo's on your track, and he's hungry.

TUCKIS SHURTIN.

THEY DIDN'T BELIEVE ME!

—o—

Don't know how it happened quite,
Sure the jar came up all right?
Just as full as it should be
Wouldn't touch it, no, not me!
Sergeants very seldom touch
Rum, at least, not very much,
Must have been the A.S.C..
Anyway, it wasn't me!

Yet when I told them that I hadn't touched the jar,
They didn't believe me, they didn't believe me;
They seem to know a sergeant's thirst,
I fear they all believe the worst,
It's the rottenest luck that there could be;
And when I tell them, and I'm certainly going to tell them,
There'll be fatigues for them where'er I be,
They'll never believe me, they'll never believe that
The man who tapped the jar could not be me!

Stop Press News.

Rioting is again reported in Berlin. The Kaiser has gone to bed with whooping cough and ricketts.

—o—o—o—

The New German War Loan has reached the stupendous figure of 50,000 marks owing to the successful U Boat campaign.

—o—o—o—

Two juvenile food hogs were arrested yesterday. On examination it was found that their pockets were full of brandy balls.

OUR SPLENDID NEW SERIAL.

—o—o—o—

"NARPOO RUM."

—o—o—o—

BY THE AUTHOR OF "SHOT IN THE CULVERT."

—o—o—o—

DRAMATIS PERSONAE:

—o—

Cloridy Lyme — A Sanitary Inspector.
Madeline Carot — A French Girl.
Intha Pink — A Pioneer.
General Bertram
Rudolph de Rogerum—The Earl of Loose.
Lord Reginald
de Knellthorpe — His Son.
Q. Wemm — A Storekeeper.
L. Plumernapple — A Soldier.
Herlock Shomes — The Great Detective.
Dr. Hotsam — His Admirer.

—o—o—o—

CHAPTER 8.

—o—o—o—

WHAT CLORIDY LYME SAW.

—o—o—o—

CLORIDY LYME straightened his aching back with a groan and gazed around the stricken streets of Bapaume in the cold grey light of dawn with every appearance of profound distaste. "When I joined this 'ere mob I 'ad visions of red coats and flashin' bayonets; and now I spends my time spearin' bits o' paper and orange peel on a pointed stick," mused he. Gazing upwards at the lowering sky, he saw a strange sight. A sausage was drifting by, scarcely clearing the roofs of the ruined houses. Two men hung precariously in the rigging, and a trail rope dragged over the ground. As he watched, the rope caught in a tree stump, and the two men, hastily sliding down it, inquired of the astonished sanitary inspector their whereabouts. On hearing that they were in Bapaume, Shomes (for it was none other than he) said calmly, "Just as I thought, my dear Hotsam, my deductions are sometimes at fault but very rarely I think" Glancing sharply at the pointed stick held by Cloridy Lime, he suddenly seized it, and tore from the end a piece of paper which, after perusing, he handed to Hotsam, saying, "Just as I told you my dear fellow." Hotsam took the paper and read,

EDI
WIPERS T
SHERWOOD FORES

—o—o—o—

CHAPTER 9.

—o—

BACK AT QUALITY STREET.

—o—o—o—

"BUT my dear Hotsam, the whole thing is so absurdly simple," said Shomes curling his long wiry body up in his comfortable bunk. "What! You really have solved the problem of the missing rum?" "There never was a problem, and the rum was never stolen." "For heavens sake explain, Shomes, I really cannot follow your abstruce reasoning." "You surely remember my good fellow, that at the time the rum was supposed to have been stolen, it was almost impossible to buy whisky in this country." "Yes I remember it very well indeed, but what has that to do with the question." "My good Hotsam, cannot you follow me now" "I really cannot, Shomes" "You met the Earl and his staff many times during those trying days, did you not?" "Yes, I saw them nearly every day." "Did they strike you as men who had suddenly become total abstainers?" "No, I cannot say they did." "Well, just think a little, my dear Hotsam, whisky was unobtainable then, what did they—Pass the whisky and put on the gramophone my good fellow, I think we are entitled to a tot."

"AU REVOIR."

—:o:—

"'Tis sad but true," that with nearly every issue of the paper we have to reserve this column in order to say good-bye to some distinguished member of the Division.

This time it is our late C.R.E., Brig.-General A. Craven.

We wish to offer him our most hearty congratulations on his hard earned and well-deserved promotion, and, at the same time, say how much we shall all miss him.

He has always been a very good friend to us all, and a staunch supporter of the paper, and we should like him to know how much the whole Division appreciates his ever ready assistance, and the considerations he has always shown both in work and play.

Good luck and God speed.

Correspondence.

To the Editor,
"B.E.F. Times."

Sir,

Once again I feel constrained to draw your attention to the increasing rowdiness of the district. I am a peaceful citizen, and although somewhat behindhand with my rates, yet the injustice of the present conditions is apparent. Surely, when a quiet citizen wishes to cultivate his own small holding, it is not quite the thing to plant a 12-inch howitzer in the middle. I must protest, and if nothing is done in the matter, I announce my intention of voting against the present candidate at the forthcoming election.

I am, Sir,
FED-UP.

RESULT OF COMPETITION.

FIRST PRIZE — — 10,000,000 Francs.
SECOND PRIZE — — 5,000,000 Francs.
THIRD PRIZE — — 2,500,000 Francs.

THESE PRIZES WERE WON BY the first three contestants in our MAMMOTH COMPETITION, who reclaimed the CHEQUES. Owing to a slight misunderstanding with COX & CO.. these Cheques were returned R/D.

—o—o—o—o—

IF THE LUCKY AND SKILFUL claimants will SEND IN the old Cheques, new ones WILL BE ISSUED in lieu. We hope they will meet with a better fate, but, after all, MONEY is not everything.

THE COMPETITION EDITOR.

BUSINESS ANNOUNCEMENT

Mr. POILE

(Late POILE and TROTTER.)

BEGS TO INFORM HIS NUMEROUS CLIENTS THAT OWING TO THE SHORTAGE OF PAPER HE IS UNABLE TO SUPPLY HIS

POPULAR YELLOW COUPONS

AS HITHERTO.

THE FEW HE STILL HAS IN HAND ARE

BOOKED UP FOR THE NEXT TWO YEARS.

IN ORDER TO ENSURE SMOOTH RUNNING AFTER THIS PERIOD EXPIRES APPLICANTS SHOULD HOPE ON, AND SEND IN THEIR

NAMES AND QUALIFICATIONS.

SOMETHING MAY HAPPEN AND THEN AGAIN IT MAY NOT.

—o—o—o—o—o—

" If at first you don't succeed,
Carry on and take no heed."

CAGE HOTELS, LIMITED.

—o—o—o—

The Proprietors can strongly recommend any of these Hotels for a SUMMER HOLIDAY to all Gentlemen (?) of

GERMAN NATIONALITY

who are in need of a real rest after the noise and nerve strain attendant on life in the trenches.

—o—o—o—

These HOTELS are pleasantly and airily situated, in pretty parts of France, with excellent views

FACING THE FRONT

—o—o—o—

Electric and Barbed Wires Throughout.
Good Shooting in the Vicinity.

Attendance Free.

—o—o—o—

' You'll find our charges very light,
Compared with those you had last night."

Emo's "Fruity Ports"

—o—o—o—

C.O.'S LOOK AT YOUR SUBALTERN'S TONGUES!

DO THEY SUFFER FROM HEADACHE AND FEEL DEPRESSED IN THE MORNING?

DO THEY WANT TO GO OVER THE TOP IN THE EVENING?

—o—o—o—

What they want is :—

EMO'S "FRUITY PORTS."

—o—o—o—

GET A BOTTLE TO-DAY!

—o—o—o—

" If your Subs. are out of sorts,
Give them EMO'S FRUITY PORTS."

Printed and Published by
Sherwood, Forester & Co., Ltd.
B. E. F.

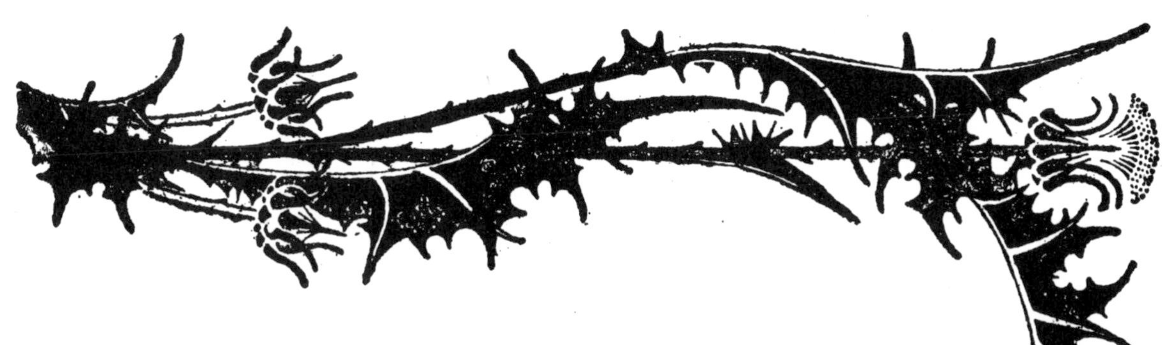

THE

B. E. F. TIMES.

WITH WHICH ARE INCORPORATED

The Wipers Times, The "New Church" Times, The Kemmel Times & The Somme-Times.

No 1. Vol 2. Wednesday, August 15th, 1917. Price 1 Franc.

CLOTH HALL, WIPERS.

Under Entirely New Management.

THE VENTILATION OF THIS THEATRE HAS BEEN ENTIRELY OVERHAULED DURING THE SUMMER MONTHS.

SPECIAL ATTRACTIONS.

—o—o—o—o—

Haig's Company in a Stirring Drama, Entitled:

PILKEM'S PROGRESS.

—o—o—o—o—

WILLIAM'S TROUPE:—

"THE COCKCHAFERS"

IN A HUMOUROUS KNOCKABOUT SCENE.

—o—o—o—o—

MANY OTHER ATTRACTIONS.

—o—o—o—o—

PRICES AS USUAL. BOOK EARLY.

WE HAVE A BOMB PROOF CELLAR IN THE EVENT OF AIR-RAIDS.

POILE AND CO.,

UNIVERSAL PROVIDERS.

THIS EMINENT FIRM HAS RECENTLY TAKEN OVER LARGER AND MORE LUXURIOUS PREMISES, AND HAS OPENED A NEW BRANCH.

WE CAN NOW SUPPLY ALL YOUR WANTS.

—o—o—o—o—

DO YOU WANT YOUR CROPS GATHERED? WE CAN HELP YOU.

—o—o—o—o—

BY YEARS OF CAREFUL ATTENTION TO BUSINESS, POLITENESS AND DILIGENCE WE HAVE BUILT UP A REPUTATION SECOND TO NONE.

—o—o—o—o—

OUR TRAVEL DEPARTMENT IS STILL OUR MOST POPULAR BRANCH, AND OUR PRINCIPAL FEATURE IS STILL AS MUCH IN DEMAND AS EVER.

—o—o—o—o—

"TEN DAYS IN BLIGHTY."

THE ROUND TRIP DOES NOT INCLUDE HOTEL EXPENSES, DRINKS, ETC., BUT A COMFORTABLE JOURNEY IS GUARANTEED.

ADDRESS :—KEW DOVECOTE.

THE

ZILLEBEKE FISHING & EXPLORATION CO.; LTD.

—o—o—o—

This Company has recently been formed for the purpose of acquiring the extensive fisheries in the district.

We propose to equip shortly a superb fleet of trawlers.

The district is free from the U Boat menace, and we hope to be able to supply all householders.

—o—o—o—

READ OUR BROCHURE :—

"FROM DITCH TO DUG-OUT."

" When in trenches you can wish
For nothing but a nice fresh fish."

—o—o—o—

Telegrams :— "Pioneers."

'Phone :— "42 and 59 Hop."

RABBITS!

RABBITS!!!

RABBITS!!!

—o—o—o—

NEW SEASON'S STOCK

HAS JUST ARRIVED, AND WE ARE DISPOSING OF THESE TASTY LITTLE BEASTS AT COST PRICE.

—o—o—o—

TRY THEM.

—o—o—o—

" Bully beef is but a habit,.
Try a tender young buck rabbit."

—o—o—o—

ADDRESS :—

BUNTER & CO.

SUPPLY VILLA.

THE

B. E. F. TIMES.

WITH WHICH ARE INCORPORATED

The Wipers Times, The "New Church" Times, The Kemmel Times & The Somme-Times.

No 1. Vol 2. Wednesday, August 15th, 1917. Price 1 Franc.

EDITORIAL.

WE must apologise to all our subscribers for the delay since our last issue. We are sure they will understand and forgive as the delay was due to an awkward providence and more war than is conducive to the steady production of a paper. What a lot has happened in the interim! Much to rejoice and plume ourselves about, but also many old chums to regret the loss of. That unfortunately must always be the way, but this time there seems to be more than a fair proportion of the old brigade. Some of these are mentioned in another part of the paper so we will leave the matter there. On the other hand we have to welcome others to the old Division, especially our new G.O.C. who achieved a speedy and lasting popularity. It could be no easy job to take up the mantle of "The Professor" who, through nearly two strenuous years, had led us from greenness to understanding. Much as we regret the loss of our old G.O C. we cannot grudge his departure and well merited honours. Also the loss is tempered by the arrival, in his successor, of one of the "Cognoscenti" There has been so much to write about since our last issue that one is rather at a loss where to begin. Hindenberg has won a long series of victories, (vide Official German news) and we have met with many repulses, (vide occupants of many well aired and commodious cages in the neighbourhood of Vimy, Messines and Vlamertinghe.) However the war goes on, and we are putting our faith on the journey of Ramsey Macdonald to

Stockholm ! ! ! We are afraid that this number may be rather a scratch one as there are so many counter issues. War is all very well in its way, but when it interferes with the publication of a journal it's a ——, well, let's turn to brighter subjects. Have any of you been on leave lately ? The Editor has just returned from thirty days of the best and brightest. A lot of the time he spent in London with the wind well up and a crick in the neck, but otherwise only filled with wonder at the bare-faced robbery which is rife. We should imagine that there are many people who will be sorry when the war is over and they don't all keep restaurants, We have had the opportunity lately of visiting the birthplace of our paper. One cannot notice any appreciable difference, and the neighbourhood is just as healthy ! We are glad to be able to announce that all previous numbers will be shortly available bound in book form, and purchasable at the modest price of 15 francs or thereabouts, through the enterprise of Mr, HERBERT JENKINS, publisher. At the present moment there's a church parade going on one side and a 'plane scrap on the other, so that this editorial must come to an untimely conclusion. We must ask all old contributors and also new comers to the Division to send along copy. A hearty welcome to all our new stars, and good luck to those who have left us.

THE EDITOR.

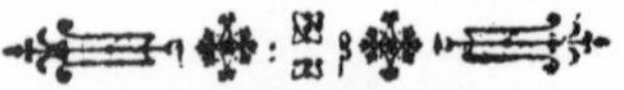

Don't sit up for the mine, Daddy ! don't sit up for the mine !
Let's go to our Chateau at Walton Heath, and to bed at half-past nine,
Mary can call us for zero hour, if she wakes us about 3·9,
We'll hear the big bang at 3·10, you see, so don't sit up for the mine.

SONG OF ANY INFANTRY BRIGADIER TO HIS MEN.

In my dug-out (where the plans are laid)
I sing this song to my Brigade.
You chaps who in a scrap have been
Will "compris" fully what I mean.
Just lately in the stunts you've struck,
You haven't had the best of luck.
You've had the kicks without the pence,
And always struck a stiffish fence.
You've had the mud: you've had the wet:
You've had the shells as well. And yet
You never grumble—just hold on
When all except your pluck has gone.
We know the cheery way you curse
When things are getting worse and worse,
Yet if I ask for further work,
There's not a dammed one here would shirk ;
The Higher Staff quite understand,
But know the old Division, and
They know that they have but to ask,
And you will carry out the task.
So I have pledged my knightly word
To stick it out until the Third.
And though I pledge it with remorse
I pledge it hopefully ; because
I know the stuff of which you're made,
I know the old "Umpteenth" Brigade.
I know you'll always play the game
(Although it is a b****y shame),
And so in tempest and in rain,
In shells and shells, and shells again,
Just understand (it's nothing new ?)
How proud I am of all of you.

WE ATTACK AT DAWN.

—:o:—

BY OUR SPECIAL CORRESPONDENT

Mr. Teech Bomas.

—:o:—

All was still as the first flush of dawn lit the sky. Then suddenly the atmosphere was riven by the crescendo chorus which leapt to meet the light as a bridegroom to his bride. The delicate mauve and claret of the dawning day was displaced by a frothy, and furious fandango of fire. The giant trogolythic ichnyosaurus crept fawning from their lairs, and gambolled their way to the line oblivions of anything that barred their passage. The disgruntled bosom of mother earth heaved with spasmodic writhings as the terrible tornado tore the trees. I was picking wallflowers in Glencorse Wood when all this happened, and even now the memory of that zero hour is with me. Having passed through several liberated villages, I stood on that historic spot and waited to put my watch right by the barrage. It came, and the world wilted. Then on came the gallant Esquimaux and Peruvians (I musn't mention anything English, it isn't "done,") and with a wild rush shattered Germany's grey-clad hosts. The while the guns thundered and boomed in hellish chorus across the riven bosom of Belgium, the wild flowers grew and the birds sang, revelling in hectic competition with their human rivals who figured in fantastic feats turning many a lark green with envy. Even the tanks, catching the atmosphere of excitement, threw cartwheels in an earnest endeavour to camouflage their real nature. Many parties of Huns were so surprised at their appearance that they offered them bird seed. In fact we attacked at dawn.

TEECH BOMAS.

ROADS.

Belgium, rain, and a sea of mud,
The first seven years are, they say, the worst;
The pavé roads when you're spitting blood,
And all you have is a priceless thirst.

—o—o—o—

From Café Belge down to Kruistraathoek
In the same old rain, and the same old din;
From Hell-fire Corner to Bellewarde Brook,
With the transport rattling on like sin.

—o—o—o—

We trod those roads in the days gone by
'Till we knew each brick, or shell-struck tree;
When the war was young, and our hopes ran high
That the summer would give us the victory.

—o—o—o—

Staggered along in the same old slush,
Dodging the crump-holes where one could;
Cursing all night, 'till the new-dawn's blush
Found us just flitting from Zouave Wood.

—o—o—o—

Much has been changed, but never the roads,
Each may be different yet each the same;
The same dammed pavé, the same dammed loads,
And fewer return by the road we came.

—o—o—o—

Maybe one day we'll forget the rain,
The mud and the filth of a Belgian scene;
But always in mem'ry I'll see again
Those roads with the stumps where the trees had been.

GREAT LABOUR MEETING AT DICKEBUSH.

—:o: —

Flamsey MacBonald in the Chair.

—:o:—

Last night, Flamsey MacBonald addressed a large and sympathetic audience at the Town Hall, Dickebush. Powerful support was given by Messrs. Grictor Vayson, A. Tenderson and a host of other hard (working) labourites. Mr. Mac Bonald commenced by saying that the war should be stopped (loud and unanimous cheering,) and said that if they only sent him to Christiania he would see to it. (A heckler here suggested that sending him to hell might help matters.) He said that he had the interests of the working man at heart. (Loud and unanimous cheers from Grictor Vayson.) When asked "Who the devil asked you to look after the working man, why not get on with a job yourself." Mr Flamsey only looked pained and surprised at the ingratitude of the working man who grudged him his self-appointed task of doing nothing at four hundred pounds a year. However, strong and vigorous speeches, which cut the usual amount of ice, followed in rapid succession from these eminent labourites. Mr. Grictor Vayson was just getting well away when a whizz bang fell within a couple of miles. As all present had every desire to avoid any harm happening to these modest delegates, a rush was made to the platform to safeguard them from danger. They, however, had already left, so that the citizens of Dickebush were prevented from wishing them God-speed.

BOIS DE RIAUMONT STAKES.

—:o:—

We have pleasure in recording the result of this classic event, which took place over the well-known course under rather trying conditions, in the spring of this year. At the same time we must apologise for its somewhat tardy appearance in print. The ante-post betting rather favoured "The Professor," but " Reggie was heavily supported at about a point more, and there was quite a lot of money for "Bill Buggan." This latter is a good looker but with—at this time— no public performances to his credit in this part of the world so the public were naturally shy about putting too much faith in the training reports. Punctually on schedule time the gate went up, and a magnificent start was witnessed. The three favourites got away in a bunch with a little fancied starter called "Sapper." The going was bad, but the pace was good, and it was anyone's race at the distance. "Reggie," however, here made a strong bid and came to the front, and although strongly challenged by "The Professor," won a good race by a neck. A length away came "Bill Buggan" going well, with "Sapper" fourth. They were greeted with loud cheers from their backers, but a prolonged fusilade of groans from the Hun bookmakers who had evidently lost a large packet on the event.

ROBIN HOODFELLOW.

One named Kaiser Bill, thought the world he could fill
With Kultur of his special making,
But after three years finds himself full of fears
For himself and his throne that is shaking.

CERTAIN
MAXIMS OF
HAFIZ—
FOR THE SOLDIER!

You fool, if you've joined the King's
Army; and want to be happy all day,
List well to the Maxims of Hafiz, these
words your poor father would say:

—o—o—o—

There are many good men in the Army,
Lord Kitchener and generals like that;
But your Q.M.'s the feller to bow to, he
sweeps all the rest off the mat.

—o—o—o—

Pick a servant, who's up to his business,
no matter a lean or a fat man,
Barabbas was but a beginner, compared
with the R.S.M.'s batman.

—o—o—o—

When you're marching, and fed-up, and
dirty; tho' you're thirsty and nearly
dead,
"Rinse your mouth, but don't swallow
the water!" mark well, what the
Adjutant said.—
I fill my Mark IV Water Bottle, with
Dewar's White Label, instead!—

—o—o—o—

My son, if you're thinking of trying the
old art of swinging the lead,
Just carefully pick out your victim, or
else you will find that instead,
The M.O. will do all the swinging, by
heaving F.P. at your head!

—o—o—o—

One talks about Heaven and Hades; but
I say "Verily—verily,
You may taste Heaven's nectar each
evening, if only the sergeant's T.T."

Pawn not your loot or your profits, but
if you're broke, wretched man,
The A.S.C.'s ready to purchase, all
genuine relics, it can
For that fine Prussian helmet, they'll
give you—a pot of nice strawberry jam.

—o—o—o—

When our Gunners are busily strafing, in
the neck you are sure to be caught,
But don't argue, my son, for no Gunner
admits, that his missiles fall short.

—o—o—o—

The way to get on in the Army, is to
wangle a place on the Staff;
For that's where they say things—and DO
them—and though the incredulous
laugh,
I'm inclined to believe it myself;—their
pay's not enough by a half!!!

R.M.O.

TO THE MEMORY OF

Lt.-Col. E. R. Mobbs, D.S.O.

Lt.-Col. H. W. Compton.

Lt.-Col. H.V.M. de la Fontaine, D.S.O.,

and those others who have left us lately.

CURLY SHELLOG AT THE FRONT.

—:o:—

[Ed. Note.—Of course everyone was at the great show, when Curly. the world famous dancer, appeared at Wipers, and, I am sure, they will be interested to read the following descriptive letter which she wrote to one of her American friends.]

Zero Time, 1917,
B.E.F. France.

Well, Polly, old pal, if you want to set up and take notice, and let excitement shake the rats from your hair, just start a coffin nail, glue yourself to a cushion and pipe your glimes on these here Fragments from France. Of all the hit-the sky, slip-a-leg stunts I've put over on these blarsted John Bulls, my Wipers debut takes the cake, and the Maiden's Dream Balloons they have out here can't float in the same class as my Success Bubble with a capital S and all the kudos attached. Of course, as you're no hearse for being awake, you've lamped the big journal stuff on the last push near Wipers, that tickled the Bosche to taking for the tall timbers off Pilkem Ridge. I s'pose when the high-brow pens get busy slinging ink on this war, they'll throw the bull, that this bit of Hun sticking was a piece out of the strategy basket, but you can plank np your diamond tiaras that that's out of the wrong pew. Just list to the bell of truth! I gave some of the dear old things, the band that a real screaming zizzler was coming to the dug-out dwellers as soon as they knocked kultur off Pilkem Ridge, and made the city of fallen bricks a fit place for a perfect ladv! The darlings fell just solid for this, so Fritz was bounced from the gallery without any rainchecks, and a trim little cloud-chaser bumped at my English bungalow door one day, to say the stage was set and the carriage waiting I didn't have tea, but I had experience that day! Eagles had nothing on us, with our three white wings, and as for speed—say, it made lightning look like slow freight. Going over London they was quite tumultuous, and sent up the cutest little white puffs of smoke that made a halo a mile or so below us. I'd always thot from the journal pipe dreamers that these was Archie guns for blasting the Zepps off the map but now I see they're only a token of welcome and esteem. We looped the loop. and took Boulogne like Ty. Cobb sliding for second base, where we hit a cove called AMLO He got fearful peevish at the kick off when I braced him for a drawing room on the Wipe s express, mumbled something about was I returning from leave. and where was my papers, but after flashing my moniker he squeezed a smile and like a 14th Street imitation of Chesterfield, crated me tor a box car, labelled 40 men and 8 horses. 'I didn't mind the men but those horses took up a lot of elbow room, Speed, on a returning leave train, gets about as much chance as a snowball in Hell, so I'll draw a veil on the car stuff. Just before my hair turned grey we ambled into old Pop. Here a pucker bunch of Red Bands met us, I was wise to it, that they are the real thing in Little Lord Fauntleroys who get elected to the Vermillion Band Fraternity by popular vote, and they wore their weight of crosses with some gentility. It sobbed a tear to hear they're soon to bust the scarlet crowd so's they con all get back to ths trenches where they feel more homelike. They jumped a new make of buzz wagons on me called the staff car. It's a bit like our Fords, only has a higher side and a larger body. We sure burnt gasoline, and them staff cars were more common than road lice [Ford cars] on Coney Island Boulevard on a Sunday afternoon. We teaed at Cafe Belge, on iron rations, and the cat's out wnen I says the bully beef only lost it's wreath to the bully band them Sherwood boys marched out. They'd planted my rest room at Shrapnel Corner, as that's the nearest to a graveyard quiet out here. The only things in abundance was sea shells known as Silent Percy's The boudoir was done mauve sandbags and the ceiling in a delicate shade of corrugated Iron that's all the rage out here. The only bug in the whiskey glass was the living pictures out of La Vie Parisienne, that fair made me blush, and a few little permanent inhabitants that took up an awful lot of attention for their size, But on to Wipers with it's duckboard stage and camouflage curtain, that's the disguise they use out here that'll make a hen look like a rooster or a 12in How like a dime cigar. Wipers is some town, and looks like some gang had been throwing bricks since Noah built the ark, or maybe it was a San Francisco earthquake they let out every morning for a ramble. Anyway a body what found two stones still stuck together gets a three weeks leave in Blighty, and you can't notice H.Q. losing sleep over the exodus. As to my part—modesty forbids, but the lid was off and none of 'em wore holes in their breeches from lack of interest. All I can say is, that that's where I sprung my top note in dances called the "Sludgy Mudgy Slide," and that sob song of mine entitled "My Little Mud Home in the Trench" Well, old girl, cheerio. More next week. A jam tin of love from

CURLY.

A POPULAR B.T.O. TO HIS MOUSTACHE.

—o—o—o—

Now, you are gone, I did not know before,
How I should miss you, when you came to pass.
Together, we have quaffed the Bottled Bass,
The Whiskey Cup, the Ale=for half a score
Of happy years, or haply even more.
And oft together, from a single glass,
The Wine of Life we sipped ; but now, alas,
For you, no more, this vintage, stewards pour.

—o—o—o—

Often, I touched, with trembling finger tips,
Your treasured form, your pulchritude, that lay
Quiescent, silent, beauteous, night and day ;
Or felt your fragrance pressed upon my lips.
But five short minutes in the barber's chair,
And you were gone—my upper lip is bare.

C.L.P.

ARMY TERMS AND THEIR DERIVATION.

—o—o—o—

G O:C.—Gold or carrots. Owes its origin to the gaudy colours affected.

—§ † §—

CAMOUFLAGE —From camel and flag, referring to the device adopted by this animal of tying a flag to its tail, and thus disguising itself as a ship of the desert. Hence—to deceive.

—§ † §—

A.P.M.—Awfully polite men. Originated in the politeness with which these people bandy airy persiflage with Transport Officers.

—§ † §—

T.O.—Ticked off. (See A.P.M.)

—§ † §—

M.L.O.—Medals and leave often. Reason obscure.

—§ † §—

TRENCH.—So called from the trenchant remarks from those inhabiting them.

—§ † §—

AREA COMMANDANT.—See dug out.

—§ † §—

ARCHIE.—So called after William Tell who shot so dexterously that he split the apple.

—§ † §—

DUG-OUT.—Of two kinds. The name originates in a habit of the early natives who excavated holes for themselves to avoid the slings and arrows of the enemy. Another kind is the erection in which Area Commandants dwell.

Our Short Story.

—o—o—o—

There once was a teetotal Q.M.

* * * * * * *

OUR SALE OR EXCHANGE COLUMN.

—:o:—

This branch has been established for the convenience of our subscribers and all small wants are advertised at a reasonable charge.

—o—o—o—

WANTED.—To rent for the winter season, DRY WARM DUG OUT. Must be commodious and in healthy locality; untroubled by hawkers and Huns. Good price offered for suitable residence. Apply.—Reggie, c/o of this paper.

FOR SALE.—TWO TANKS. Slightly soiled. Price moderate. Or would exchange for a pair of rabbits Apply.—41, Dammstrasse.

FOR SALE.—PLEASANT COUNTY ESTATE, situated in one of the nicest parts of Belgium. Heavily wooded. Has been shot over. Owner desirous of leaving. Apply. Feddup, Glencorse Wood.

FOR EXCHANCE.—TWO FIELD DRESSINGS, in good condition, and ONE IODINE AMPOULE (unused.) Would exchange for HATBAND and TABS (red or blue—the latter preferred.) Write.— Harassed, Canada Street.

GENTLEMAN, Young, in sixth form at Oxford and Cambridge Colleges, feels that his talents are wasted in the P.B.I. Would like a job cleaning the windows of a leave boat. Apply.—One Pip, Krab Krawl.

SEVERAL YOUNG GENTLEMEN, with University degrees (Heidelburg) would like to be taken as boarders in English country districts. Would do agriculture labour in exchange for lodging and keep. Apply—Fritz, Lens.

CRICKET.

—o—o—o—

BY OUR SPECIAL CORRESPONDENT

MR. F. B. PILSEN.

—o—

The pitch was the real thing for the spheriod when the Hoppers took the field. Old Sol was not in a kindly mood, but otherwise it was a good day for the King of Sports. The lads from the Midlands took first knock, and two of their stalwarts marched out into the arena to do battle with the champions of the Hop County. The latter's trundler got off the mark well, and a well-placed effort soon beat the guardians of the ash grove and shattered Number One's timber yard—one for three. The wielders of the willow were unable to get hold of the leather, and only notched 23 all told, Mr. Extras being responsible for the majority

Then it was the turn of the lads from Kent. Their skipper didn't cause the gentleman with the pad and pencil to develop writer's cramp, as he misjudged a cunningly delivered sphere from the opposing O.C, which spread-eagled his pegs. After this however, despite some good mixing by the lanky American expert, they managed to collect a good enough bunch, and the Notts and Jocks had a merry time chasing the elusive pillule. The tail wagged feebly however, and in the end the lads from the Strawberry County only clicked by three chips.

When the golden sun sets in the West,
And the sausages all go to roost,
Tho' the rain may be o'er,
We shall soon have some more,
And the Hun comes with bombs us to boost,
When the Archies should all be in bed,
They are kicking up Hell with a zest,
And the noise of the day,
Hasn't all passed away,
From my camouflaged tent in the West.

THROUGH PRUSSIAN PINCE-NEZ.

—o—o—o—

We reproduce below a few extracts from the Prussian papers which have fallen into our hands lately. They all tend to show the wilful misrepresentation of facts which is rife in the German Press.

The following is a free translation of an article in "Wurst und Sauerkraut," a leading Berlin daily :—"We have it on the best authority that the English are on their last legs. Our secret agents report that in many places the people are getting so thin that gratings in the streets are being carefully fenced off. Also that the Ladies' Grill in the House of Parliament is being closed, as this famous restaurant is so short of the tasty chops and steaks which delighted the hearts of the female English."

Following from "Die Schweinhund" :—"Our London agent reports that the last reserves of man power have already been eaten up by our brave field greys, and that the English pigs are calling up children now. He yesterday saw one of eight years in the abominable khaki. What can our brave airmen have been doing?

Following from "Die Potsdammerung" :—"Herr Von Tirpitz yesterday made a glorious speech praising our brave sailors. Our gallant matlows sing twice daily the Hymn of Hate, and we are sorry for the English Fleet if they ever should dare to tackle our men. That, as Herr Von Tirpitz said, is not to be expected as the cowards stay outside, and nothing can tempt them up the Kiel Canal. However our noble-never-to-be-despised sailors will put up with the disappointment, and sing the Hymn three times daily in future."

Following from "Die Schnitzel":—"The All High and Mightiest condescended to address his brave Pomeranians yesterday. He said: My brave-and-never-to-be-defeated-while-Wolff-and-I-are alive Pomeranians, once more you have a victory over the Pig-dog enemy gained. You waited till they nearly-up-to-you were, yet could they not catch you. I your War Lord say that you saviours of the Fatherland are. Your bread ration doubled-be-shall when our gallant U Boats bring us flour. Go now and beat the swine English again. I am your War Lord and the All Highest. Take my blessing and pull in your belts. I'm going to dine.'"

Sing of the joys of a transport man,
Who drives along with a gay "Hallo!"
Cracking his whip as he only can,
A smile and a joke as away they go.

—:o:—

His cap is jauntily placed on his head,
His clothes show the care of an old-time beau,
He hums to the tune that his mules' hooves tread,
His voice runs in dulcet tones and low.

—:o:—

With a load of duckboards he threads his way
Through the sylvan glades where the pavé runs,
And nothing can ruffle him night or day
As he brings up timber, or food for the guns.

—:o:—

Driving along on the smooth hard roads,
With never a jolt and never an oath,
Till at Hell Fire Corner he drops his loads,
And fondles his mules, for he loves them both.

—:o:—

Then homeward he wends his weary way
To the rose-decked villa, where he may sleep
Till night shall again give place to day,
And the angels above him their vigil keep.

MORE MUD THAN GLORY.

—o—o—o—

SCENE—Regent Street Tunnel. C.O. and Adjutant discovered sitting in recess.

C.O.—"Gawd! How this filthy place stinks." Adj. (trying to write)— 'Yes, sir." C.O—"Damn this water! It'll be over the tops of my boots directly." Adj.—"And I'm sure we shall all be getting trench feet." (Enter orderly hurriedly, perspiring and breathless.) Ord.—"Tunnel's just been blown in, sir, and the water's pouring in the hole." C.O.—"So that's it, is it?" Ord.—"Yes, sir." Adj.—"I'd better send for the Tunneller." (Shouts out some instructions.) (Exit Orderly.)

C.O.—"Some life, isn't it?" Adj.—"B- - - - -y." (Enter Bombing Officer very noisily and perspiring at every pore.) B.O.—"Have you heard the nooze?" C.O.—"What news you fool?" B.O.—"Why, the Germans have no shells!" C.O.—"What, no shells!" (Heard on the roof) Zip bang! Zip-bang! Zip bang! B.O. (humming to himself)—"La ta ta ta ta-" C.O.—"Shur-r-r-rup that blinking noise!" B.O.—Yes sir, shall I–" (Shouts of "gas" in the passages.) C.O.—"Where's my ruddy respirator?" Adj.—"Dammed if I know where mine is either!" (After much searching respirators are adjusted. After 5 minutes it is found to be a false alarm, and they are taken off again.) C.O.—"I can't stand these d- - -d gas-hats!" Adj.—"Nor can I." C.O.—"My nose is quite sore where the d- - -d thing pinches." Adj.—"And I've got a beastly headache!" C.O. (turning to B.O.) ' Just fetch the I.O., will you?" B.O.—"Yes sir." (Exit B.O., returning 2 minutes later with I.O.) C.O. (to I.O.)—"About this relief. Are you quite sure all the guides know their way and there will be no hitch?" I.O.—"Quite sure sir. They've all been over the course at least a dozen times." (At that moment the first relieving company is reported arriving.) I.O. (saluting)—' I'll go and see about the guides sir. It's now 8 p.m." C.O.—' And now for goodness sake let's have a glass of port or something. B.O.—"No port sir!" C.O.—"Well, some whisky?" B.O.—"No whisky, sir!" C.O.—"Well, what the devil have we got?" B.O.—"There's only well water left sir." C.O.—"Hell!" (Collapses, but is aroused by entry of C.O. and Adj. of incoming unit. Chorus of "Good evening" led by C.O.'s.)

C.O.—"Well, I'm afraid you will find this a pretty bloodsome spot!" C.O.I.U.—"Don't look up to much I must say, and what's this dreadful stench?" C.O.—"Oh dear! its no good worrying about that, its peculiar to the tunnel. C.O.I.U. (helplessly)—"Is it always here?" C.O.—"Always." C.O I.U.—"And the water?" C.O.—"And the water." C.O I.U.—"Where does one sleep?" C.O.—"One doesn't sleep." C.O.I.U.—"Got the right time?" C.O. (yawning)—"Oh!" it's about midnight." C.O.I.U.—"And no company reported clear yet?" C.O.–"Only the one that was in the tunnel." C.O.I.U.—"Still I suppose it's only a matter of another hour or two." C.O.—"Yes, our guides are top-hole." (Conversation lags, and one by one the party dozes off. They are awakened at 4 a.m. by the relief of B and C Companies being reported complete.) C.O.I.U.—"That only leaves A Coy." C.O.—"That's right." (They doze off again, and are aroused an hour later by I.O. of I.U., who reports that A Co. have returned, the guides having failed to find their objective.) C.O.—". . . !" (turning to C.O.I.U.) "I'm awfully sorry old chap." C.O.I.U.—Oh! that's all right. You are the ones to suffer by it." C.O.—"What's to be done?" C.O.I.U.—"Oh! we'll have a bit of breakfast whilst the I.O.'s go and fix this little show up. We'll have to chance it by daylight now." (Breakfast is served consisting of some slabs of cold bacon, and tea with a distinct flavouring of petrol.) C.O.I.U.—"I must apologise for the rotten breakfast." C.O.—"Lord! that's all right, I find it awfully hard to eat anything in this atmosphere. I expect you'll be the same in a day or two." (After breakfast they sit talking, and eventually at 10 a.m. the two I.O.'s enter and report relief of A Coy complete.) C.O.—"Thank Heaven! There's nothing more I can do for you, is there?" (starts collecting his paraphernalia.) C.O.I.U.—"No, thanks. Hope you'll have a quiet journey down. C.O.—"Thanks. I'm really awfully sorry about those rotten guides." C.O.I.U.—"Oh! that's quite all right." (Chorus of "Cheerioh's!") C.O. (to himself)—"I hope I never see this dammed place again." [EXIT.]

OUR SPLENDID NEW SERIAL.

—o—o—o—

FOR KING & COUNTRY.

—o—o—o—

A TALE OF THE GREAT WAR.

—o—o—o—

CHARACTERS :—

Major VERE DE BRETT — an A.P.M.
Col. CUSTANCE FITZGERALD— a M.L.O.
ARTHUR FITZGERALD — his son.
Miss VERA MARJORUMLEY — a W.A.A.C.
Miss SHEILA POPPING — her maid.
Sergt. LED SWINGER — at the Base.

Other characters will be introduced as the story proceeds.

—o—o—o—

CHAPTER I.

—o—

"NO Arthur," said old Colonel Custance Fitzgerald, as he sat in the abominable dug-out whence he conducted his arduous duties of Military Landing Officer, "I will NOT let you have any more money to spend in riotous living at Wipers; surely you realize we are at war, and with my life in daily or hourly peril I do not feel justified in encouraging your extravagence."

"Very well, father," said Arthur, "just give me one last thousand, and I promise you I will never worry you again."

"Rash youth! what would you do?"

"Oh! I don't care, a damm now," replied the reckless young man, "I'm going to join the R.T.O.'s!"

The old man's head fell on his arms, and sobs shook his form as he parted with the required thousand. When Arthur had left, the Colonel's old friend Major Vere de Brett, the dashing Ack Pip Emma, came in. Seeing the old man so dejected, he said, "Hullo Colonel! what's up?"

"It's Arthur," replied the old man with a hopeless gesture, "he's left me now, and is joining the 'R Tock O's.'"

"God!" ejaculated Brett, "can nothing be done to stop him?"

"Nothing," said the stricken old man, "he has gone for ever."

With a comforting remark, Brett left the poor old Colonel to his grief.

Meanwhile Arthur had jumped on a 'bus and, his mind fully made up to his mad course, presented himself at the office of the famous Corps. The officer in charge tried to point out the rashness of his wish but all to no purpose, and next day saw Arthur with the blue band adorning his hat, and the admiration of an excited populace.

Meanwhile what of Brett? Passing from the old man's dug-out, he pursued the perilous path to his own evil-smelling, dank hole, where amidst the shot and shell he pursued the duties of his office. He loved Vera Majorumley, who would have nothing to do with him as she loved Arthur. But he was not the man to be baulked.

(To be Continued.)

Two swift hours in a Pullman car
Aboard and afloat, and you're back again
In the land of the crump and the shooting star,
And you fight for a place in the old Pop. train,
Fifteen hours—rather more than less—
Of discomfort and boredom, and then you reach
(If you're lucky) your railhead, and then you guess
That some of the bloom is off the peach
Of ten days leave.

Correspondence.

To the Editor,
" B.E.F. Times."

Sir,

May I ask you to use your weight to obtain some special recognition for those, who like myself, enlisted almost at the outbreak of war, and have never yet been to the front line. Surely matryrs like ourselves who have had to put up with soft jobs in England or at the base in France deserve some special recognition to compensate for the weary months we have spent with yearning hearts while others had all the fun of the front line. It is only our deep sense of duty which has kept us from breaking our bonds and going up the line. Is it too much to expect that some permanent and distinguishing badge should be given us ?

Yours, faithfully,
" E. TERNAL LEDSWINGER."

—o—o—o—

To the Editor,
" B.E.F. Times."

Sir,

We request your assistance in bringing to the notice of the city-fathers the night noises which are going on in the district. As ratepayers we must protest against the increasing noisiness of a set of hooligans who operate chiefly during the night hours, and who seem to rely chiefly on fireworks to make a disturbance in an otherwise peaceful village. Surely householders should be granted some protection as the district is rapidly becoming uninhabitable owing to motor buses, etc., which pass in one unending stream day and night and the performances of the band of night hooligans.

Yours, faithfully.
" INDIGNANS."

LATE NEWS FROM THE RATION DUMP.

—o—o—o—

The Germans are short of shells.

—:o:—

The Pope is raising an army to come and stop the war.

—:o:—

We have the supremacy of the air—ESPECIALLY AT NIGHT.

—:o:—

The Germans have no guns.

—:o:—

We are going to dig-in, and wait till the Chinese are ready.

—:o:—

The Kaiser has been arrested by Hindenburg, and shot as a spy.

—:o:—

The Kiel Canal is closed to the public, as wheels are being put on the German Fleet to enable them to deal with the tanks. [This must be a canard, as no practical people would consider wheels necessary in Flanders.]

—:o:—

The Germans have no bombs.

ANSWERS TO
CORRESPONDENTS.

Owing to lack of space, answers to our numberless correspondents are unavoidably held over.

CAN YOU SKETCH?

Some of you may be able to draw corks.
Very few of you can draw any more money.
Probably some of you can draw sketches.

Here is a letter I have just received from a pupil at the front :—

"The other day by mischance I was left out in No Man's Land. I rapidly drew a picture with a piece of chalk of a tank going into action, and while the Huns were firing at this I succeeded in returning to the trenches unobserved "

COULD YOU HAVE DONE THIS?

—o—o—o—o—

SEND A COPY OF THE FOLLOWING ON A CHEQUE :—

Francs 500 - -

AND BY RETURN I WILL SEND YOU A HELPFUL CRITICISM AND MY FOURTEEN PROSPECTUSES.

PLEASE SIGN YOUR NAME IN THE BOTTOM RIGHT-HAND CORNER TO PREVENT MISTAKES.

CORPS CHRISTMAS CARD COMPANY.

THE HOOGE AND DISTRICT

TUNNEL & DUG-OUT

VACUUM CLEANING COMPANY.

—o—o—o—

WHY SUFFER FROM TRENCH FEET?
WHY RUN THE RISK OF PILES,
DIPHTHERIA & PERI-HEPATITIS.

We Can Help You!!!

—o—o—o—

WE GUARANTEE a well-drained, aired and ventilated Tunnel or Dug-out at reasonable cost.

WE are an entirely new firm and no tunnellers or R.E. are employed

Send six stamps when our illustrated booklet will be sent you free.

—o—o—o—

WE SPARE NO EXPENSE.

—o—o—o—

For a tunnel cool and sweet,
Write to us we're hard to beat.

Telegrams : HEDGE ST.

HAS IT EVER STRUCK YOU???

That water is a necessity, not only for the radiators of the Staff's cars, but for lots of other things.

Therefore ECONOMISE in it.

There is no need for you to drink it.

APPLY TO OUR

Mr. George Barrie.

He will not PROVIDE YOU with a BOOKLET (or anything else) FREE.

BUT :—He CAN provide you with the correct and PATRIOTIC drinks.

—o—o—o—

" Don't do anything that's risky,
Mix your water with some whisky."

—o—o—o—

Telegrams :— "Alcoholic."
Telephone :— " No. XXX Hop."

Printed and Published by
Sherwood, Forester & Co., Ltd.
B. E. F.

THE

B. E. F. TIMES.

WITH WHICH ARE INCORPORATED

The Wipers Times, The "New Church" Times,
The Kemmel Times & The Somme-Times.

No 2. Vol. 2. Saturday, September 8th, 1917. Price 1 Franc.

CLOTH HALL, WIPERS.

(Lifting Roof and Perfect Ventilation.)

THIS WEEK ONLY.

Grand New Revue Entitled:

"GOOD-BYE-EEE-E, WE MOS-COW."

INTRODUCING SELECTIONS FROM

"RIGALETGO."

AND

INCLUDING THE ENTIRE "BALLY RUSSE."

We hope to be able to announce a Return Visit of this Celebrated Company very shortly.

—o—o—o—o—

PRICES AS USUAL. BOOK EARLY.

SECOND AUTUMN

POLYGON RACE MEETING

THE FOLLOWING EVENTS WILL TAKE PLACE.

ZERO STAKES.
THE VON ARNIM PLATE.
HINDENBERG POINT-TO-POINT.
GHELUVELT GOBLET.
CROWN PRINCE'S PLATE.

—o—o—o—o—

STARTERS AND CLERKS OF THE COURSE:—
Messrs. PLUMER AND GOUGH.

—o—o—o—o—

MEMBERS TICKETS ISSUED FOR THE MEETING.
ENTRANCE TO BARBED WIRE ENCLOSURE FREE TO ALL TEUTONS
EXCELLENT TRAIN SERVICE. TRAINS NOW RUN RIGHT UP TO THE COURSE.

—o—o—o—o—

SECRETARIES: - KEW & CO.

TODD'S TRAVELLING

Kinematograph, Ltd.

—o—o—o—

PERFORMANCES NIGHTLY
(If the engine will go.)

—o—o—o—

THIS WEEK—

REGGIE VISITS PARIS.

A SCREAMING FARCE FEATURING THIS SERIO-COMIC IN A NEW ROLE (PARTLY CENSORED.)

—o—o—o—

Porky Plays Poker.

A TRAGEDY.

—o—o—o—

MANY OTHER THRILLING FILMS.

—o—o—o—

No Money Returned.

—o—o—o—

BOOK EARLY. PRICES AS USUAL

THE

WESTERN ADVANCE CO., HOOGE.

[D. HAIG, GENERAL MANAGER.]

—o—o—o—

Makes ADVANCES at SHORT NOTICE

UNDER PRIVATE ARRANGEMENT.

—o—o—o—

NO SECURITY.
SECRECY GUARANTEED.
PRINCIPAL REMAINING TILL END OF WAR.
AGENTS IN ALL CIVILISED COUNTRIES.

—o—o—o—

Wires—CUT. Phone—1918.
Code—Bab.

THE B. E. F. TIMES.

WITH WHICH ARE INCORPORATED

The Wipers Times, The "New Church" Times, The Kemmel Times & The Somme-Times.

No 2. Vol 2. Saturday, September 8th, 1917. Price 1 Franc.

EDITORIAL.

Oh, to be in Belgium,
Now that Winter's here!

BEFORE this appears in print it's more than likely that the weather will have gone round to May, but certainly at present it seems that Summer is a thing of the past. Anyway, Winter will certainly be with us before we've had time to dig up our thick underclothing from the spare kit dump, Winter! What memories that word conjures up. Brisk exhilarating walks over the snow-clad plains of Belgium. Oh, my sainted aunt! Most of our English contemporaries seem to fill their columns with reports of the doings of some people called Ramsay Macdonald, Grayson and others We should have thought that there would have been no difficulty in finding copy nowadays, and to chronicle the doings of a few nonentities seems to argue a lack of knowledge of what the people want to read about. However these penny dailies are generally very slow in feeling the public pulse. The whole B.E.F. will welcome with open arms the latest recruits to it's ranks in the shape of the W.A.A.C. The designers are to be congratulated on the attractive uniform, and the morale of the troops has gone up 100 per cent. (so has the candidature for a spell at the base.) We must again remind everyone that copy is necessary and ask them to send in.

THE EDITOR.

IF THE RAIN
AND
THE WAR
LAST.

The Summer had been long and cold,
And Intha Pink was growing old,
He stroked his hoary snow-white beard,
And gazed with eyes now long since bleared,
He scanned the waters deep and still,
And muttered grimly "Swelp me, Bill,
Unless 'Aunt Sally' heaves in sight,
We'll get no rations up to-night!"

—o—o—o—

"She's late," he said in husky tones,
From near his feet came strangled moans,
He peered below into the gloom,
And for a sodden form made room,
'Twas Atkins of the P.B.I.,
Who brought the news that Hooge was dry,
And 'less they steered a half-square right,
They'd get no rations up that night.

—o—o—o—

At last "Aunt Sally" hove in sight,
Old Intha hailed her with delight,
The rations soon were stowed inside.
And Atkins went to act as guide,
They steamed along at full six knots,
They dodged the shells, ignored the shots;
In fact the future seemed quite bright,
They'd get the rations there that night.

But stay, what means that sickening scrape,
That left them stranded and agape?
"Her bottom's out!" old Intha cried,
And with a tin of biscuits tried
To stem the stream that flowed between
Her riven planks, but soon 'twas seen
That nothing now could put her right,
They'd get no rations up to-night.

—o—o—o—

'Twas now all hands to save themselves
On biscuit tins with pick-axe helves,
They rowed away, yet paused to find
The reason of their fate unkind . . . .
The waters, tired of rising higher,
Uncovered the Cathedral spire!
Uncharted, it had caused their plight,
No rations reached the line that night.

JIM.

—:o:—

A hard little, scarred little terrier,
With a touch of the sheep-dog thrown in—
A mongrel—no matter,
There's no better ratter
In trenches or billet, than Jim.

—:o:—

A tough little, rough little beggar;
And merry, the eyes of him.
But no Tartar or Turk
Can do dirtier work
With an enemy rat, than Jim.

—:o:—

And when the light's done, and night's falling,
And the shadows are darkling and dim,
In my coat you will nuzzle
Your little pink muzzle
And growl in your dreams, little Jim,

R.M.O.

HOW THE MEN OF BLANKSHIRE BAFFLED THE BERLINERS.

—:o:—

BY OUR SPECIAL CORRESPONDENT
Mr. TEECH BOMAS.

—:o:—

It was indeed a stirring episode of war in all it's terror and magnitude of sound. I am allowed to chronicle the epic deeds of the men from Blankshire who met the Berliners and bilked them with bayonets. The scene of this historic encounter was—well I musn't tell you that. The terrific tornado had torn the trees (as described in my last) and the blighting blast had battered the bark, but nothing could daunt the men from Blankshire. On they came kicking footballs, and so completely puzzled the Potsdammers. With one last kick they were amongst them with the bayonet, and although the Berliners battled bravely for a while, they kamer-aded with the best. 600 burly Berliners was the bag, and filled to overflowing the already replete cages. Then the still of night fell on this homeric contest. The little field mice continued their inter-rupted life, the only evidence that remained of what had transpired being the trampled sward whose greenness was here and there besmirched with an ever crimsoning crimson, and the rotund bodies of Berliners who had been a bit slow in kamerading. The larks sang and the flowers burst into bloom as another episode ended. Yet not closed, as all these episodes are but one episode. and the baffled Berliners battling the Blank-shires is but typical of the events which, strung together, make the big offensive.

TEECH BOMAS.

WHAT A HOPE !

—o—o—o—

From Captain Bingham Jones, M.C ,

To Colonel Spanker,

Dear Siree,
I have the honour to request,
That you will do your very best,
To recommend, and strongly too,
This my appeal I put to you,
To ask the G.O.C. if he,
His heart will soften, just for me,
My plea is nothing very mighty,
For four long months I've not seen Blighty,
If he a little-leave will grant,
I'll go and see my wealthy aunt,
Who's lying on a bed of pain ;
And never will get up again,
At least the doctor's say that's so,
And so I think I ought to go,
For if I don't I'm on the rocks,
The same applies to Messrs. Cox.
I therefore hope he will not choose,
My application to refuse,
And incidently I'll add,
That when this "hoped-for" leave I've had,
My work will please the C.R.E.,
As well as charm the G.O.C.
I have the honour, sir, to be,
Your humble servant, O.C. "D."

The sausage was a high one,
The Hun began to shoot,
He sniped his best with 9·2,
And said, "Ach ! dies ist gut,"
The airmen saw the little game,
And swooped down on that Hun,
Now Fritz is where all Fritzes go,
But hasn't got a gun.

The shades of night were falling fast,
When up the muddy C.T. passed
A youth who bore, though looking glum,
A mighty gallon jar of rum.
Excelsior !

—§ † §—

" Try not to pass," the sergeant said,
" The blasted Hun might shoot you dead,
He's sniping near, he's shelling far,
Perhaps he'll hit that blooming jar !
So leave it 'ere."

—§ † §—

The youth moved on, no word spoke he
He wallowed up that old C.T.,
His visage grim showed pale in light
Where star shells glimmered through the night.
Excelsior !

—§ † §—

" Stay ! stay ! my lad," the corp'ril cried,
" Another who the Hun defied
He got a bullet through the 'tum,'
And broke his blooming jar of rum,
So go no more."

—§ † §—

The youth's sad face showed grim and pale,
He struggled on into the gale,
Passed whizz-bangs urgent in their flight
Where bullets pinged through deepest night,
And rain did pour.

" 'Ere ! Alfred, stop ! " the private hailed,
The sad youth's face but paled and paled,
" Don't try that trench, the bloomin' 'un
Is sweeping it with many a gun,
'E'll 'it the jar."

—§ † §—

" Ah ! stay me not," the youth replied,
" I must get there whate'er betide,
Though Hell may storm both near and far
I'll get there with this needed jar."
He strode some more.

—§ † §—

At last his goal appears in sight,
And blatant minnies rack the night,
He staggers to the Coy. H.Q.,
And to the precious jar he's true—
He still it bore.

—§ † §—

" Oh 'ell ! " the sergeant raging stormed,
Then to the job in hand he warmed,
He told that youth who proudly bore
The jar through all ! He told him more
And more and more.

—§ † §—

He told him all about his past,
His future, present, and at last
He paused for breath, he gasped and died,
And dying fell he down beside
An empty jar.

IT is with the greatest regret that we have to say "Good-bye" to one of the few remaining original members of the Division

This loss will be deeply felt by those who have served with him for so long a time, and who have known that his never-failing kindness and support were available at any moment. We wish him " Good Luck " wherever he may go, and ask him to accept our gratitude for the help and encouragement he has given us in many difficult moments.

OUR DIARY.

—o—o—o—

BY LIEUT. SAMUEL PEPYS.

TO-DAY, at 4 of the clock, we did arrive at our new billets, feeling very fatigued and with a touch of the megrims. When we had inspected our billets we had a lot more of the megrims. One tells us that the Huns have a practice of shooting in the surroundings, so that we are all of a windiness. Orders have come, so it is said, that we shall depart from here very soon and go down to the activities. We have all got the megrims. To-day, at 5 of the clock, I saw her Ladyship of Dickebush in the Park, and was much struck by her appearance. Woodbines are up one penny on the packet, which does perturb us. ere is also a rumour that the R.T.O. of Bath has not got a decoration in the new list. This is not understandable, and savours of a canard. The morrow a small party of us must take the coach at the toll gate at P 21 C 2·4, and go to reconnoitre the field of battle. This is a most unlikeable business, and I have the megrims worse, so that the leech has given me a potion. Sardines are up two pennies the tin, which is a scandal, it occurs to me that there may be much profits accruing to some persons. Anne has writ to say that the enemy has appeared in some balloon or ship which flies, and has thrown exploding missiles at London. This has disturbed me much, as the taxes will not allow of the provision of new clothes for Anne if she should spoil her present ones. There is a story that no rum issue will be made this night. We all have the megrims, and whisky is up 2 francs on the bottle. This is a terrible war. I must be astir betimes in the morning with my new gas-bag. It is of a poor pattern, and I am very envious of that of Captain Spanker, whose is of a better quality. As to-morrow is also bath parade, to bed at 9 of the clock, tired and with the megrims.

A few more Military Terms Defined.

—o—o—o—

R.T.O.—Rude to officers. A pleasing brusqueness marks their manner when dealing with officers who have the impertinence to come away from the line for a spot of leave. This is affected to emphasise the strain of their position.

—:o:—

E.F.C.—Every franc counts. Derived from the thrifty methods of those A men employed therein, who evidently think that miss not, want not—after the war.

—:o:—

DUDS.—These are of two kinds. A shell on impact failing to explode is called a dud. They are unhappily not as plentiful as the other kind, which often draws a big salary and explodes for no reason. These are plentiful away from the fighting area.

WITH APOLOGIES TO RUDYARD KIPLING.

—o—o—o—

When you're waiting for zero, to go o'er the top,
And yer mind gets a-wondering what you will stop,
Just go to yer bottle, and neck a wee drop,
Cos thinkin' ain't good for a soldier.

—:o:—

When the 'un starts a barrage and you've nowhere to go,
Don't wander round looking for dugouts and so,
Just flop where you happen to be, don't you know
Any 'ole's good enough for a soldier.

—:o:—

When yer click for a leave, and yer warrant's come through,
Don't waste any time thinking what you will do,
Just grab up yer pack, leg it quick fer Berloo,
Any leave's good enough for a soldier.

ANNE.

—:o:—

[An anticipation of what may be when the woman's army is in full swing.]

Anne, the Chemise Corporal (I never got further than that—I mean her name) was mildly intrigued, merely mildly as becoming to one bearing on her hearty bosom the ribbon of the Swan (and Edgar.)

The cause was the sudden arrival of the man driver of the G.S. wagon with fresh salmon coloured flashings from Divisional Laundry.

He was certainly un peu d'un oiseau, (thank God for the entente and the shilling dictionary) and then there was no army order against a member of the Woman's Auxiliary Army Corps talking to a man, so different from a winking officer.

The next time I go to G H.Q. (it will also be the first, but next carries more weight) will be to rake up the name of the cold hearted monster responsible for this order.

The man looked as if he might be worth taking over to the Q.M. Stores for tea with the Undies Sergeant. There was kept the dainty stock of Beauty Cream, Hinde's Curlers, Dress Improvers, Hair Food, Depilatory, Essence of Foxgloves, Skirts Divided, Lisle Stockings, Transformations all entered up ready to hand over as Trench Stores as there was talk of a relief by a new and nearly naked Division from Central Africa. Anyhow it would be a change for him from his own beastly dull place where they only had men's furnishings. He might like to have a look at the stock, and perhaps talk over things with her Q.M S. who was frightfully worried about transport because "Q." (with coral ear-rings instead of tabs) of the relieving Division said their only trench stores were cloths loin, white

The driver got out and saluted smartly, quite the little gentleman, asking her politely if she would care to read the newest "Mirror" serial, "What the Duchess liked and how," while he was off loading. The ice was broken. They could talk. Anne was pleased, she liked his teeth. and bore him off to unchlorinated tea with the Q.M.S., who at once plunged into the iniquities of the African "Q." His sympathy was immediate, the grievance might be redressed, and, while disclaiming any fear for himself or the B.E.F., he could not help worrying about wandering Walloons and the feeling of the local Y.M.C.A. Would he inspect the stores? He would. Did he like it ?. He did: Not for nothing had he spent many unfruitful years with Wm. Whiteley. He intended himself to universally provide on his own one dav: His tastes and knowledge were catholic: A woman's advice would be such a help. Anne was tickled at his ingenuousness: she was glad she had asked him in. But the Harlene Hair Instructor had a practice attack parade after tea, which Anne was on, so she had to bid him good-bye, and not to go over ten miles per hour through villages, and she would be glad when he came again, and yes she didn't mind a woodbine. thank you! There were happy times to come, jaunts by day in a pair-mule half-limber to the quaint old Hotel des Ramparts, where soul called to soul and vice versa and all that sort of thing, and still happier walks by night in the bombed area, where a strong right arm is such a protection to a slim waist against a long range gun or aerial bomb.

Ways and means discussed, revealed the strong silent man at his best when asked to show his pay-book, too completelely in love to contradict the feminine theory that if they were married their mutual separation allowances would be retained. A few days later two leave warrants arrived, one green, the usual political sop to Ireland, for the man, and the second puce for the little Chemise Corporal because no man ever knew the he meaning of the word.

The marriage ceremony was brief and in the later stages harmonious, as their bedroom was papered half in blue because he said it was the colour of her eyes, and the other half in red because she loved his ginger, a touching proof of the complete equality of the sexes.

I saw a miniature Anne some time ater smiling at me out of the advertisement pages in the "Sketch," displaying a fat little body, and telling all the world she lived on NESTLÉ'S FOOD. So Anne did something in the Great War, didn't she? What?

BLESS HER!

N. I.

TO A MARRAINE.

—o—o—o—

We are two bubbles in a glass of wine,
Smiling to one another, I and you,
Across the rosy sea, as if we knew,
That we should meet, some day, perhaps to dine
Together, at some Bacchanalian shrine.
Chamelion-like, the wine takes on a hue
More roseate; it smiles upon us two
In sympathy with this desire of mine.

—o—o—o—

We are two bubbles, floating in Life's glass,
Transparent, joyous, fragile, delicate,
Pulsing with life and hope, to-day, we seem;
And yet, to-morrow, it may come to pass,
That some unshaven, cruel lip of Fate
May burst this fairy bubble of my dream.

C.L.P.

AS OF OLD.

—o—o—o—

It came to pass in the year one thousand nine hundred and seventeen that DAVID, a captain of the Hittiteshire Regiment, did obtain a yellow parchment. And with this parchment he did cross the waters to the land of Berlighty. And during his sojourn in this land he did observe a woman bathing in the sea. And he found her exceedingly beautiful to gaze upon, so that he did ask of one "Who is this lady?" And they replied, "She is the wife of one Lieut. URIAH, of the Hittiteshires" And he did covet her so much that he despatched a messenger, even the buttons of her hotel, to her apartments, bearing his greetings and asking that she should break bread with him. Which she did. And it came to pass that the woman would not list to his pleading. Thereon he became exceeding wroth, until on the eleventh day he recrossed the waters and returned unto his men. And it came to pass even as he had wished that Lieut. URIAH was sent unto him to be an officer under him. Then became the heart of DAVID the captain glad. And it came to pass that certain elders became perturbed regarding a citadel in the land of Noman, and ordered the capture thereof. And even as DAVID the captain and URIAH his lieutenant were partaking of a mess of Makonokie and Rhum came a messenger bearing the tidings and instructions. And lo! the heart of DAVID was glad Then said he unto the lieutenant "Thou shalt take the forefront of the battle with thy platoon. Haste or the judgment of the Warofis will be upon thee." And URIAH did fill himself with Rhum, and likewise his platoon, and did sally forth. Then did the heavens awake, and the Amalekites did rage furiously having much wind, and with slings and outrageous weapons did hurl vigorously around. And it came to pass that DAVID, the captain, was standing at the door of his dug-out and did get a vertical gust. And the enemy did hurl a wizbhang with great violence, and did strike him on the nose, and he did die of it. So it came to pass that URIAH, the lieutenant, did return, having captured the citadel, and did find his captain dead. And he did become captain in his stead.

MORAL.—A sub. in a dug-out's worth two on the wire.

I'm a twenty-one years soldier, and I want to tell no lies,
But the job I'm now engaged on feeds me right up to the eyes.

—§ † §—

Before the war in days of old, I ran a little show
Hawkin' rags and bones at Wigan, why I left it I don't know.

—§ † §—

But I heard the bugles callin', and join up I felt I must,
Now I wish I'd let them bugles go on blowin' till they bust.

—§ † §—

I joined to fight the Germans, and I crossed the angry sea.
Now I pick up bits of paper in a Depot, marked " P.B."

—§ † §—

It's a bloomin' waste of money sendin' me across the foam
To pick up bits of paper, I could do that job at home.

—§ † §—

And the soldiers, think it funny, that's what fills my bitter cup,
For they chuck down bits of paper just to see me pick 'em up.

—§ † §—

They keep me in the Depot, 'cause I've got a nasty wheeze,
D.A.H., and bad bronchitis, and I'm groggy at the knees.

I tried to get some leave I did, I said my wife was dead,
They found I'd never had a wife, and I got crimed instead.

—§ † §—

I tried to go to Orsepital, I showed a wobbly knee,
I got what I expected, nnmber 9, and M and D.

—§ † §—

Last week they had a paper-chase, and all the Depots went ;
I had to follow up the 'ounds, and gather up the scent.

—§ † §—

On windy days they form a ring, and make a horse of me,
And back their bits of paper, ten to one against P.B.

—§ † §—

Once by mistake I found myself included in a draft,
The things that happened in the line have fairly turned me daft.

—§ † §—

I joined a working party going on up to the line,
The Hun he started shelling, so I thought I'd do a shine.

—§ † §—

I crawled into a drain-pipe to hide me from the Hun :
Then someone cried " Get out you fool, you're in a twelve-inch gun ! "

—§ † §—

I got back home—I don't know how—and saw the Batt. M.O.,
He passed me back again P.B., to where the sea winds blow.

—§ † §—

So here I am and here I'll stop ;. I'm bound to see it through,
I'll pick up bits of paper if my Country wants me to.

H. H. W.

There are many roads in Flanders, where the horses slide and fall,
There are roads of mud and pavé, that lead nowhere at all,
They are roads, that finish at our trench; the Germans hold the rest.
But of all the roads in Flanders, there is one, I know the best.
It's a great road, a straight road, a road that runs between
Two rows of broken poplars, that were young and strong and green.

—o—o—o—

You can trace it from old Poperinghe, through Vlamertinghe and Wipers ;
(It's a focus for Hun whiz-bangs and a paradise for snipers)
Pass the solid Ramparts, and the muddy moat you're then in,
The road I want to sing about—the road, that leads to Menin.
It's a great road, a straight road, a road that runs between
Two rows of broken poplars, that were young and strong and green.

—o—o—o—

It's a road, that's cursed by smokers; for you dare not show a light ;
It's a road, that's shunned by daytime ; and is mainly used by night,
But at dusk the silent troops come up, and limbers bring their loads
Of ammunition to the guns, that guard the Salient's roads.
It's a great road, a straight road, a road that runs between
Two rows of broken poplars, that were young and strong and green.

And for hours and days together, I have listened to the sound
Of German shrapnel overhead, while I was underground
In a damp and cheerless cellar, continually trying
To dress the wounded warriors, while comforting the dying
On that muddy road, that bloody road, that road that runs between
Two rows of broken poplars, that were young and strong and green.

R.M.O.

A POET'S DEDICATION.

—o—o—o—

'Tis you, that are the fount of Inspiration,
Creator of my verses, sonnets, songs ;
To you, all credit for these lines, belongs,
So, at your Shrine, I offer adoration
And dedicate to you this invocation.
For you, one wet and war-worn warrior longs,
Forgetful of all daily cares and wrongs,
In the delight of nightly expectation.

—o—o—o—

O Motive Force, that makes a soldier move
Great mountains of oppression from his soul ;
Let others sing about the varied goal
Of Great Ambition, Women, War and Love,
Such plaudits always leave me cold and dumb,
Only your charms, I praise, O Tot o Rum.

C.L.P.

SOMEWHERE IN—WIPERS.

—o—o—o—

By COCKLES TUMLEY.

—o—o—

(Our representative, Mr. COCKLES TUMLEY, has just paid a visit to the Front, and here describes his experiences in his inimitable manner.)

—o—

YOU can't imagine what I've seen. Neither can I! Stay, I will tell you.

I've worn a tin hat!

I've eaten a tin of bully beef!

I've talked with a general!

I won't tell you what he said, but you can take it from me THE WAR IS OVER.

I've been in the support line, which is much more dangerous than the first.

I've been in the reserve line, which is much more dangerous than the support.

I have been in Div. H.Q., which is more dangerous still.

And I have even been back to G.H.Q.

I have discussed the situation with the soldiers themselves. I can't tell you what they thought of it.

AND NOW FOR WHAT I HAVE LEARNT.

I have learnt that there's a lot of meat in a tin of bully. I have learnt that an army biscuit is a hard nut to crack. I have learnt that a tipping duckboard needs no push. I have learnt that Belgian beer wants a good deal of bush.

Every German prisoner I spoke to said the same thing. I can't tell you what it was, but THE WAR IS WON. To use one of our familiar slogans, I say "Watch the Q.M." I was having a talk with one of the Tommies who had answered the call of King and Country, and I asked him what he thought of it all. I can't tell you his answer, but it impressed me wonderfully. Well, I will write more next week when my head is clearer. I must go now and have my photo taken in a gas-bag and tin hat.

COCKLES TUMLEY.

AUNT ANNIE'S CORNER.

—o—o—o—

TENDER TALKS TO TINY TOTS.

—o—

MY Dear Lit-tle Tot-ties,

How have you been en-joy-ing your-selves all this time? Aunt Annie is very cross with you, as you have not written to her late-ly. This is very un-kind of you, as she brought you away from that nas-ty mud-dy place to the nice country. How-ever I know of the doings of some of you.

—:o:—

LIT-TLE Billy Buggan has got a nice new house and a great big piece of land to play on, so he will be able to have great fun with his lit-tle friend Reg-gie.

—:o:—

TOMMY Flint went to a nice dog show the other day. He has moved into the coun-try and says that there are no naughty boys over the way to throw stones at him. He has got a lit-tle Scotch friend staying with him.

—:o:—

PORKY and Jerry have been having a lot of games they tell me. I hope they have enjoyed themselves.

—:o:—

WE have got a lot of new Tot-ties who have joined our lit-tle cir-cle late-ly. They are all nice boys. I am sure we shall all be great friends, and play soldiers nicely together. Now that Xmas is coming we shall have a lot of parties. Won't that be nice Tot-ties? Lit-tle Jackie Shep-pard I think is going to give the first one.

—:o:—

Good-bye, Tot-ties,
Your Ev-er Lov-ing
AUNT ANNIE.

OUR SPLENDID NEW SERIAL.

—o—o—o—

FOR KING & COUNTRY.

—o—o—o—

A TALE OF THE GREAT WAR.

—o—o—o—

CHARACTERS :—

Major Vere de Brett — an A.P.M.
Col. Custance Fitzgerald — a M.L.O.
Arthur Fitzgerald — his son.
Miss Vera Marjorumley — a W.A.A.C.
Miss Sheila Popping — her maid.
Sergt. Led Swinger — at the Base.

Other characters will be introduced as the story proceeds.

—o—o—o—

CHAPTER 2.

—o—

BRETT let himself into his cheerless quarters by means of a latchkey which he carried suspended from a thick gold chain, and turning on the electric light hung up his cap, stick and spurs on the hall-stand. Passing through the dining room and library he entered his smoking room, and producing a key which he carried on the end of a thick platinum chain, unlocked the drink cabinet. Pouring himself out a treble whisky and Perrier he quickly enveloped same, and sank into a low armchair with a deep poetical sigh, and was soon lost in thought. His reverie however was to be short lived ɪr just as he was mixing his fifth drɪɴᴋ the front door bell was violently rung, and the sound of excited voices raised high in argument broke the stillness of the night. The Major, hastily emptying his glass, rushed hot-foot to the scene of the disturbance and flung open the door. There, in the darkness, three dim forms appeared to be struggling in mortal combat. Brett hiccoughed violently and so suddenly that the brawlers ceased their struggles and looked at him in astonishment.

" Who the Hell are you, and what the blazes do you want at this time of night?" demanded the A.P M. in the dulcet and courtly tones for which he was famous. " Please sir I've copped a spy," said a gruff voice which Brett recognised as that of his trusty Sergeant Led Swinger, " I found him at the corner of the communication trench where the poor old woman sits, behaving very suspicious like and talking to this 'ere gal." "Bring them all in," ordered Brett tersely.

Led Swinger did something with his foot, and a strange-looking individual sat down swiftly on the hall mat. He was a short thin man about 6 ft 5 ins in height and broad in proportion, clean shaven but for a long grey beard, heavy moustache and shaggy side whiskers. His shortly-cropped blonde hair hung in dark ringlets upon his greasy shoulders. His sun-burnt ruddy cheeks were pale with fright and exhaustion. He was dressed in an ill-fitting dinner jacket, dickey with blue celluloid collar and red tie attached, white flannel trousers, brown boots and a bowler hat. So strange a spectacle did he present that the Major rushed into the smoking room and hastily emptied the contents of the drink cabinet.

On returning to the hall he found the sergeant and the stranger had been joined by a slim and beautiful girl, dressed in the uniform of the W.A A.C., and heavily veiled. She was sobbing and wringing her hands.

" Who is this ?" demanded Brett.

" Oh Vere, don't you recognise me ?" sobbed the girl. tearing off her veil and exposing the lovely features of Vera Marjorumley.

" The Devil !—YOU ! ! " shrieked the Major, " what does this mean ?"

Only that Arthur disguised himself so as to be able to be with me, for as you know an officer in the R.T.O.'s is not allowed to talk to a W.A.A C. Oh save us, Vere, save us ! "

" Yes, save us, save us ! " echoed the gent on the mat, speaking for the first time in this chapter.

A dark and cunning look overspread the features of the A.P.M Here was his chance.

At that moment the gas alarm sounded.

(To be Continued.)

Correspondence.

To the Editor,
"B.E.F. Times."

Sir,

I shall be glad if you will spare a little space in your valuable paper to bring to the notice of your many readers the "Society for Providing Free Gin for Generals." This Society supplies a long felt want, and it's cause is entirely praiseworthy. "Jack" and "Tommy" have their rum provided by a benevolent government, what about our generals? "Gin for Generals" should be on everyone's lips during the coming months. We are holding a soirée and sale of work next Saturday at the "Crab and Horseshoe" Hotel, where all are invited: some of the best people are giving their services. A collection will be made after the proceedings, and a small toll will also be levied for exit. I shall also be glad to receive subscriptions through the post.

Yours, etc.,
J. I. N. CRAWL,
Hon. Sec. S.P.F.G.G.

ANSWERS TO
CORRESPONDENTS.

Owing to lack of space, answers to our numberless correspondents are still held over.

The Soldiers' Friend.

—o—o—o—

(With apologies to the "Daily Mail.")

—o—

MRS. P.—A soldier's pay ceases on the day on which he is killed.

—:o:—

WHISKY DISTILLER.—You should get total exemption, being engaged on work of national importance.

—:o:—

ANXIOUS WIFE. — Your separation allowance is probably correct. Your husband probably got a court-martial, and not a Field Marshal's job.

—:o:—

FLOSSIE.—Your husband had better consult his Regimental Medical Officer. He is sure to find him a very sympathetic person.

—:o:—

C 3.—As you say, total blindness should make you unfit for general service —appeal again.

—:o:—

"GUNNER."—No; "Sage Femme" has two meanings.

ONCE again it is necessary to say "Good-bye" to our G.O.C. Short though the time was that

was with us, yet in that time he had become popular with all ranks. We wish him the best of luck in the future. Also we take this opportunity of welcoming our new G.O.C ,

who will doubtless soon achieve the popularity enjoyed by his predecessors.

LITTLE WILLIE.—"When will our heaven-protected troops thrust back the hordes that seek to enter our sacred Vaterland, Papa?"

BIG WILLIE.—
"When their Rawlies cease from Goughing,
And their Plumers Byng no more."

An EPOCH-MAKING DISCOVERY.

THE HELPMAN MIND-TRAINING SYSTEM.

As approved by "John Bull."
Now used by Nineteen Field Marshals
Three Hundred Lieut.-Generals
Thousands of Officers
And over Ten Million Men.

SEE WHAT THEY SAY!

A Subaltern writes:—"My mind used to wander so much that I generally forgot what my balance at Cox's was. Since taking your course I have been reminded of it on several occasions."

This from a D.A.D.I W.T.:—"I used to be considered a dud. Now the D I.W.T. considers me his best officer, and I am down for the next medal he has to give away."

A Munition-worker:—"My income has gone up by 100 per cent."

"One who knows":—"I have had a letter printed in the *Daily Mirror*."

—o—o—o—o—

WRITE AT ONCE TO THE "HELPMAN INSTITUTE"

WHY???

SUFFER WITH YOUR FEET

—o—o—o—

IF YOU HAVE GOT

TRENCH FEET,
FLAT FEET,
Or COLD FEET.

WE CAN CURE YOU!
TRY OUR GUM-BOOTS THIGH·

—o—o—o—

NEW SEASON'S PATTERNS NOW IN STOCK
A SPECIAL NEW DEPARTURE.
FUR-LINED GUM BOOTS FOR GENERALS.

—o—o—o—

AGENTS: MESSRS. Q M. DADOS & CO,

—o—o—o—

"Soon will come the snow and sleet,
That's the stuff to spoil your feet!
If you do not want to die,
You must wear our gum-boots thigh."

MR. VENN'S VANITIES.

—o—o—o—

CHAT-BELTS

After the improved pattern invented by CAPTAIN SHINE.

PLAIN—100 FRANCS.
EMBROIDERED WITH YOUR REGIMENTAL BADGE, OR A PORTRAIT OF YOUR BEST GIRL—300 FRANCS.

—o—o—o—

VENN'S VESTS

IN WOOL, SILK, OR CORRUGATED IRON (FOR SNIPERS).

—o—o—o—

"If you want to look your best,
You must order a Venn's Yest."

Printed and Published by
Sherwood, Forester & Co., Ltd.
B. E. F.

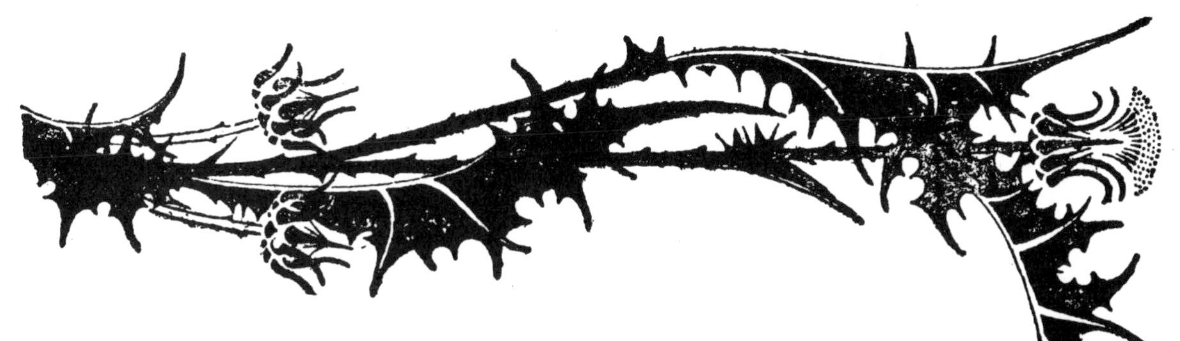

THE

B. E. F. TIMES.

WITH WHICH ARE INCORPORATED

The Wipers Times, The "New Church" Times, The Kemmel Times & The Somme-Times.

No 3. VOL. 2. Thursday, November 1st, 1917. PRICE 1 FRANC.

CLOTH HALL, WIPERS.

This Week—FOR ONE WEEK ONLY!!!

The Zepp. Troupe, "Tumblers."

—o—o—o—o—

WILHELM AND CO., PRESENT

Their Grand New Operas:

"GÖTTERDAMMERHAIG."

"FRITZ RAN AND I'M SOLD."

INTRODUCING THE FAMOUS IMPRESSARIO

MIKE HAYLISS

IN HIS LITTLE SONG ENTITLED;—

"HEIGHO! THE KIEL ROW."

PRICES AS USUAL. BOOK EARLY.

THE

GREAT ARMY PEACE MOVEMENT.

ENROL TO-DAY!!!

WE WANT PEACE!!!

ENROL TO-DAY!!!

—o—o—o—o—

THE SOCIETY has been formed with the object of insisting on PEACE at the EARLIEST POSSIBLE MOMENT.

—o—o—o—o—

YOU ARE ASKED TO HELP!

BIG ADVANCES IN THE CAUSE HAVE BEEN MADE THIS YEAR and we are holding a GREAT ANTI-WAR DEMONSTRATION at PASSCHENDAELE. All are welcome.

—o—o—o—o—

PRESIDENT:

D. HAIG, Esq.

—o—o—o—o—

SPEAKERS:

R. TILLERY and T. ATKINS.

WIPERS & DISTRICT GAS COMPANY.

—o—o—o—

ISSUE OF NEW STOCK.

—o—o—o—

Owing to the ever-increasing use of Gas in the neighbourhood of Wipers, the Company are increasing their plant to cope with the extra demand. They hope to be able to supply all (and more) than the consumers want.

The Company has Branch Offices at any Artillery Headquarters, where further information can be obtained.

Stock will be issued at 18*l* and 60*l*.

Rapid and regular delivery guaranteed.

WIPERS & DISTRICT GAS COY.

R. A. GUNNER, Secretary.

Poile's High-class Dairy Co., Ltd.

—o—o—o—

THIS COMPANY has lately opened a DAIRY, which is conducted on UP-TO-DATE and HYGIENIC PRINCIPLES, under the direct supervision of our Mr. ADAMS.

—o—o—o—

Purity Of Supply Guaranteed.

—o—o—o—

MILK DELIVERED 3 TIMES DAILY.

—o—o—o—

"Bring your cans and buy, buy, buy!
Jane's a well that's never dry."

—o—o—o—

Telegrams: "KEW."
Secretaries: POILE & CO.

THE B. E. F. TIMES.

WITH WHICH ARE INCORPORATED

The Wipers Times, The "New Church" Times, The Kemmel Times & The Somme-Times.

No 3. Vol. 2. Thursday, November 1st, 1917. Price 1 Franc.

EDITORIAL.

FROM the look of things it doesn't seem that our paper will run many more numbers before we have the "Special Double Potsdam Number." We wonder how the Huns have managed to bribe Mr. Jupiter Pluvius, he is certainly the only one who has never failed them yet. We are reluctantly compelled to inform our subscribers that unless greater assistance is forthcoming in the shape of copy we shall be compelled to shut down. Eighteen months ago and even up to a year ago members of the Division used to help us by sending along copy, which always came in useful, although most sent a covering letter speaking rather modestly of their attached "efforts." But nowadays it is a very different story, and we think only two members of the Division make an attempt at helping us along. It cannot be lack of ability, so that we must put it down to either laziness or lack of interest, and, if the latter, then the sooner we shut down the better. We must say that we think greater enthusiasm might be shown in the sporting side of Divisional life, and that Div. football contests might be arranged more often. It generally follows that those who play well together work well together, and with the present scope it should be easy to arrange a cup or medal contest throughout the Division. Much could be done by the appointment of one committee member by Brigades, and the necessary arrangements can be made very easily. We will ask everyone in the Division to write something and send it along within the next fortnight, so that we may have a "Grand Xmas Number." Write any old thing and send it along, it may not be used but it may be useful.

THE EDITOR.

THE BURNING QUESTION.

Three Tommies sat in a trench one day,
Discussing the war in the usual way,
They talked of the mud, and they talked of the Hun,
Of what was to do, and what had been done,
They talked about rum, and—'tis hard to believe—
They even found time to speak about leave,
But the point which they argued from post back to pillar
Was whether Notts County could beat Aston Villa.

—o—o—o—

The night sped away, and zero drew nigh,
Equipment made ready, all lips getting dry,
And watches consulted with each passing minute
Till five more to go, then 'twould find them all in it;
The word came along down the line to "get ready!"
The sergeants admonishing all to keep steady,
But out rang a voice getting shriller and shriller:
"I tell yer Notts County can beat Aston Villa!"

The Earth shook and swayed, and the barrage was on
As they leapt o'er the top with a rush, and were gone
Away into Hunland, through mud and through wire,
Stabbing and dragging themselves through the mire,
No time to heed those who are falling en route
Till, stopped by a strong point, they lay down to shoot,
Then through the din came a voice: "Say, Jack Miller!
I tell yer Notts County can beat Aston Villa."

—o—o—o—

The strong point has gone, and forward they press
Towards their objective, in number grown less
They reach it at last, and prepare to resist
The counter-attack which will come through the mist
Of the rain falling steadily; dig and hang on,
The word for support back to H.Q. has gone,
The air, charged with moment, grows stiller and stiller—
"Notts County's no earthly beside Aston Villa."

—o—o—o—

Two "Blighties," a struggle through mud to get back
To the old A.D.S. down a rough duck-board track,
A hasty field dressing, a ride in a car,
A wait in a C.C.S., then there they are:
Packed side by side in a clean Red Cross train,
Happy in hopes to see Blighty again,
Still, through the bandages, muffled, "Jack Miller,
I bet you Notts County can beat Aston Villa!"

HAIG HARRIES THE HUNS.

—:o:—

BY OUR SPECIAL CORRESPONDENT

Mr. TEECH BOMAS.

—:o:—

At break of day the hunters are about, and Haig's harriers hourly harry the Huns. What though the saturated bosom of mother earth is but a yielding morass which clasps mortals by the thighs, and makes every endeavour at progress one long struggle against nature in her vilest mood. The gallant umpty umpth went on gamely struggling through conditions which would have driven Napoleon to a headlong flight from the field of battle, crying as he went, "A horse! A horse! What's the good of one anyway." Yet the lads from ——— struggled on and gained the crest of the ridge. I could tell a tale of one aeroplane which gamely flew and scattered hundreds of generals, advancing to the attack in motor cars, although both its wings had been blown off in the gale I could tell you a tale of self-sacrifice surpassing anything in this or any other war, of how one man of the —shires stood on the shoulders of another to enable the third to climb on the shoulders of the top one and so reach the top of the mud and stop a counter attack. But why take up one deed when everything was epic. And so the battle rages, and Haig harries the Huns, though the heavens' rage and mother earth covers herself with Flanders vilest product. As I am going for my usual winter's tour to warmer climates after the end of Nov. there will be no more operations on a large scale to chronicle.

TEECH BOMAS.

OUR DIARY.

—o—o—o—

BY LIEUT. SAMUEL PEPYS.

—o—

On the Thursday of last week we did take up our residence in a new part of the trench. Tis a noisome place, and I am disgusted of it. The mud is of a terrifying stickiness, and I am feared for my breeches, which cost me one guinea at the Hope Brothers' establishment in Cheapside. Also I have spoiled my new coat on the barbed wire, which has grieved me, as it was of a good shape and fitting. Anne is also disturbing me much, as she is lavish in expenditure now, and writes me of coal which is now up 10/- the ton and potatoes, which I think she might forego, as they are of a great expense. One tells me that my old friend Major the Honourable Reginald is like to leave us. This grieves me, as to drink a stoop of ale with him was one of my few pleasures in this abominable country. It is raining with an intensity not to be believed, and our trench gets daily more unbearable. I think the Government should move in the matter, but one hears that they are taken up with other matters of lesser concern. Anne writes me that the enemy has again sent an airship to London, and has broken more windows. This is intolerable, and one must blame the Peelers. I did go to hear a speech on discipline yesterday, which did intrigue me mildly. It is said that Captain Hannay did throw a cricket ball 65 yards and did thus win many wagers. I saw the Countess of Kruisstraat in the Park yesterday, and was much impressed by her beauty and dressings. She was in the new style which is most becoming to her though I must tell Anne the mode would not suit her, as it is most expensive. As I must take a party out for the sandbagging, to bed at 7 of the clock, after a poor dinner, the Macconnochie being but of medium quality and not too hot.

FIVE MINUTES.

—o—o—o—

ZERO MINUS FIVE.—Two hours, we've been lying on the tape. Blondin's on a wire; and Niagara, the No Man's Land, we have to cross at Dawn. Our guns are busier than ever they have been before. See:—gigantic flashes of light; gigantic flashes of sound; a hundred hundred gigantic, jewelled hands rapidly running over the whole horizon, playing concerted Hell on the Harpsichord of Hate to an audience of terrified Teutons.

That is good. I must remember it, if I get out of this alive.

—o—o—o—

ZERO MINUS FOUR.—The music goes on. Starting off staccato, it has become forte, fortissimo, crescendo. I didn't think I could be sorry for those Huns. Not since they got my mate at Vimy. Well, Jim, old man, the Twenty-fourth is getting a bit of its own back to-day.

—o—o—o—

ZERO MINUS THREE.—That was a short one. Wonder why these Artillery blokes don't scrap their worn-out eighteen-pounders. God! There's another. Shrapnel too. Why, it's all along the line.

A big dump's been put up, somewhere back of Gheluvelt. Just in that dip, beyond the rise. Red fingers of flame, reflected in the window of the sky. There, chum, there—just below those shrapnel bursts. Look, straight where I am pointing.

—o—o—o—

ZERO MINUS TWO.—My mistake. It's the sun coming up. Phœbus they call it. And he'll be shining on Mary Matthews in her little cottage at home. What silly ideas to come into my head at a time like this!

ZERO MINUS ONE.—Here's the sergeant coming along. And the orficer, with him; a cool one he is, and the best one we've ever had in Beer Coy. Yes, sir, it is a bit cold this morning. What's that, serg'int?—Give them muckin' Fritzes, 'ell?—You bet, WE WILL!—

C.L.P.

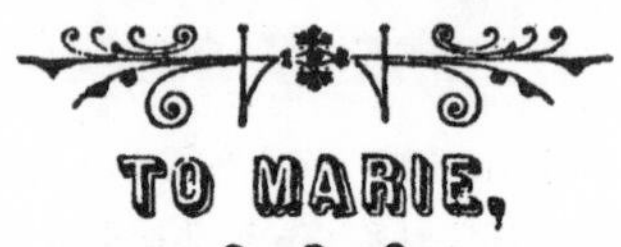

TO MARIE.

—o—o—o—

You were very shy and gentle, and your eyes were very blue,
And you didn't know (how could you?) what I had seen you do;
For I paid my bill, without a word, and went upon my way.
But this little recollection has diverted many a day.

—:o:—

My coat was hanging by the door, it's pockets gaping wide,
And I was dining far away—my table was beside
The long gilt-beaded mirror, and so, my fair Marie.
Although I did not try to yet I could not fail to see.

—:o:—

You sniffed, when serving potage, and I breathed a fervent wish,
That you wouldn't sneeze a second time upon my plate of fish.
My coat was very near you, and you had a cold I know,
For you snatched my handkerchief and took a surreptitious blow.

—:o:—

Your little nose was very red—I saw it in the glass—
I smiled—I smile again—you funny, fascinating lass.
You know, how people meet in France—we meet, we pay, we part:
But that day you stole my handkerchief, you stole into my heart.

R.M.O.

BASEBALL.

—o—o—o—

In special honour of the —th Division, its officers and men, there was arranged a match baseball game between two teams selected from the 12th Engineers (Railway) of the American Expeditionary Forces, played Sunday, October 21st.

The first team was made up of men selected from Companies B, C and E of that Regiment, and it was known as Headquarters Team, and the second team was selected from Detached Companies A, D and F, and were as follows :—

Headquarters' Team: Catcher—Baker, pitcher—Marquard, first base—Myers, second base—McOwen, third base—Ragland, short stop—Edmondson, left field—Lakers, right field—Reach, center field—Delan.

The Detached Companies' Team consisted of: Catcher—McGeehan, pitcher—Hinton, pitcher—Moss, first base—O'Brien, second base—Ritchey, third base—Barclay, short stop—McCarty, left field—Murphy, right field—Tate, center field—Sheftly.

The day selected was ideal for baseball. We were favoured by the attendance of generals, colonels, majors, and other officers from various units of the —th and —th Divisions. Three special trains were run on the light railways, handling personnel for attendance at the game. We were also favoured by the attendance of nursing sisters and officers connected with the —th and —th C.C.S.

One of the most enjoyable features of the game was the music furnished by the Sherwood Foresters Band of the —th Division, in its excellent rendition of music, before, during and after the game, and the Correspondent feels that they are entitled to special mention for their efforts in behalf of making the afternoon a complete success.

The game was called sharply at 2 p.m., and was a pitchers' battle between Marquard, of Illinois University and Hinton, of University of Arkansas, Hinton being relieved in the 5th inning and replaced by Moss of Company A. No runs were made until the first half of the 7th inning, when Murphy secured a walk stole 2nd and 3rd base and scored on a Texas Leaguer to short right field by Tate, which should have been handled by 2nd baseman McOwen. In the 9th inning the Headquarters' Team, after one man down, substituted Nig" Glenn as a pinch hitter, replacing Dolan in center field, who secured a two base hit to right field, went to third on a passed ball and scored on an infield tap by Lakers, which was badly handled by pitcher and 1st baseman, tieing the score in the last half of the 9th inning. Two extra innings were played without either side scoring, and game was called at the end of the 11th inning on account of darkness, score being 1 and 1, tie.

The feature of the game was the pitching of Marquard, who only gave up two hits and the high class work of pitcher Moss, who was only hit for three safe bingles. Hinton's work was very high grade, as they only secured two hits off him in two innings. The game was a splendid exhibition, replete with fine play in the field and light hitting, due to the masterful work of the pitchers of each side.

At the close of the game two selections were rendered by the Sherwood Foresters Band, thus ending a very enjoyable afternoon, which seemed to be thoroughly appreciated by all.

Sentry ! What of the night?
The sentry's answer I will not repeat,
Though short in words, 'twas with feeling replete,
It covered all he thought and more,
It covered all he'd thought before,
It covered all he might think yet
In years to come. For he was wet
And had no rum.

PRACTICAL PELMANISM PERSONIFIED.

—:o:—

I distinctly remember feeling for my right toe and putting it well between my my toothless gums; it sucked extraordinary good, and was a welcome change to my left thumb. This was while I was lying under a cabbage leaf in the kitchen garden at dawn just before the doctor came to find me, and put me in his black bag and take me into the house. As he showed me to my mother to ask if I would do, she murmured "Perfectly" (this was shortly before the introduction of the word "Priceless," or the sentence would have been completed.)

Still my existance was justified.

She fondled me deliciously before handing me over to a nurse, whom she addressed as Dinah. This name provided me with an opening for conversation of an attractive nature, and I suggested that she was doubtless called Dinah as a corruption of the Goddess Diana whom I reminded her was thought a good deal of by the Ephesians,

But Dinah had evidently never attended a school of languages. Her qualities were grossly undeveloped, or else she suffered from mind wandering or forgetfulness, as in reply she merely burbled at excruciatingly short intervals and with hideous reiteration, "Kootsie Koo," "Didums," "Rock-a-bye," "Bless'im."

I endured this with smouldering ill-humour for rather more than three and three-quarter hours when my tolerance became exhausted, and, with a concentration of will power, which I had held in leash only with the most infinite tact and determination not to interrupt a lady, I let forth yell upon yell, yell upon yell 71 per cent. cannibalistic, 29 per cent. Highland Flingy.

Strophe and anti-strophe, by jove, I gave it her, good and hot, no halt, no weakness, ding dong, hammer and tongs, crash bang, Sherwoods' Band ; pull out the Vox Humana? Did I not.

She "Rock-a-byed," I yelled: She "Kootsie kooed," I screamed: She "Didumsed," it was too much, I kicked, yes I regret to say I kicked, but it was a short lived triumph ; she countered painfully, and for the first time in my life, but by no means the last, my turnover beat all records: Gad! How hard her hand was. I decided to sleep to see if time would soften it.

I retired to a previously prepared position (what a lot of p's) admirably suited to the youthful temperament.

Awakening shortly, mentally refreshed and strengthed for the successful battle of life, I asked extremely explicitly for milk (not too much, for I am no bibber.) Dinah did not reason clearly, she did not even attempt to organise a cow; she was temporarily a student of the course of ill-requited love in the "Family Herald," not being bashful even then, or understating my bodily weakness, I concentrated and my worry was dissipated. She produced a bottle and gave me individual instruction through the tube, which rapidly afforded me a substantial rise in my tummy.

This was in progress when I was literally besieged by new relatives, eager applicants, among whom it was difficult at random to select the most representative. My clear reasoning however chose the unpaid acting lance-corporal Highlander ; on the whole he had the most to learn before he got his social advancement or financial betterment. As a whole these visitors did not impress me favourably, a drink is a great help to conviviality but they seemed a bit chilly towards my bottle. "Quot homines, tot sententiae," I murmured, but I did not see the point of talking for publication, and just let them rip a bit, ringing the changes on Dinah's preposterously limited vocabulary.

And while they were doing so I slumbered again.

* * * * * * *

And do you know, it's absolutely gospel! I remembered all this as soon as I had posted my cheque (33 per cent. discount) to the Pelham Institute, and remembered I was already a whole month's messing (Brigade too!) overdrawn at Cox.

28-9-17. *GRANDPA.*

THE WOOING OF EVANGELINE—

IN A SUPPORT LINE DUG-OUT.

—o—o—o—

Aloud, at nights, he will philosophise;
And squeaks his senile counsel all the day;
Pedantic lover, old and grim and grey,
He mingles love with wisdom, when he tries
To win his maid with sage remarks and wise.
And though I often drive the pair away,
They still return, and then I hear him say,
With many coughs, and splutterings, and sighs:

—o—o—o—

'The more I see of war, and all its woes,
The happier do I feel, Evangeline,
That you and I, dear heart, are not like those
Poor devils there, who have to fight, my Queen,
They have a rotten time, and Heaven knows,
We're better off, us rats:—
SOME PORK AND BEAN ?"

C.L.P.

WITH THE USUAL APOLOGIES.

—o—o—o—

If you can drink the beer the Belgians sell you,
And pay the price they ask with ne'er a grouse,
If you believe the tales that some will tell you,
And live in mud with ground sheet for a house,
If you can live on bully and a biscuit,
And thank your stars that you've a tot of rum,
Dodge whizzbangs with a grin, and as you risk it
Talk glibly of the pretty way they hum,
If you can flounder through a C.T. nightly
That's three-parts full of mud and filth and slime,
Bite back the oaths and keep your jaw shut tightly,
While inwardly you're cursing all the time,
If you can crawl through wire and crump-holes reeking
With feet of liquid mud, and keep your head
Turned always to the place which you are seeking,
Through dread of crying you will laugh instead,
If you can fight a week in Hell's own image,
And at the end just throw you down and grin,
When every bone you've got starts on a scrimmage,
And for a sleep you'd sell your soul within,
If you can clamber up with pick and shovel,
And turn your filthy crump hole to a trench,
When all inside you makes you itch to grovel,
And all you've had to feed on is a stench,
If you can hang on just because you're thinking
You haven't got one chance in ten to live,
So you will see it through, no use in blinking
And you're not going to take more than you give,
If you can grin at last when handing over,
And finish well what you had well begun,
And think a muddy ditch a bed of clover,
You'll be a soldier one day, then, my son.

Ten of the P.B.I. went to hold the line,
R.E. wanted a fatigue, and so there were nine.

Nine of the P.B.I. in the hand of Fate,
Pioneers demanded one, and then there were eight.

Eight of the P.B.I. sitting in the wet,
Tunnellers adopted one, and then there were "sept."

Seven of the P.B.I. one whose name was Wicks,
The M.G.C. demanded him, and then there were six.

Six of the P.B.I. clustered in the hive,
One joined the "Snipers," and then there were five.

Five of the P.B.I. lay them down to snore,
Someone had to go to school, and so there were four.

Four of the P.B.I., a dixey full of tea,
Then "Tock Emmas" wanted help, that left three.

Three of the P.B.I. wondering what to do,
The "Ack Pip Emma" came along, and that left two.

Two of the P.B.I. left to strafe the Hun,
One went to give a hand to "roads," so that left one.

One of the P.B.I. and a Lewis gun,
But no-one at the gum-boot store, and here my story's done.

Of ten gallant P.B.I. there's not one left, and so
The line is held both day and night by the P.B.C.O.

A LETTER FROM THE FRONT.

—:o:—

My Own, Dearest Sweetheart,—

I feel I cannot go on like this the uncertainty of it is driving me mad. Your letters hint but tell me nothing. Yet surely we should have no secrets after what has happened. At night I wake and my mind is one chaotic patchwork of questions, and yet no answer is possible. Can you imagine the suffering of this uncertainty. After those days together—what golden ones they were—this! To lie in a dug-out with a throbbing head, and the prey of any haphazard dread and uncertainty which may seize my disordered brain, Light of my life, remember all we have been to each other, that once your head has lain on my shoulder, and that your kiss has meant to me a paradise which had only perfect happiness and content, that your presence meant oblivion of the world and its meaner inhabitants, that your beauty left me stunned, yet satisfied that of the world I had seen its fairest flower, remember all this and in your next letter tell me, relieve my mind of this torturing anxiety which threatens the very foundations of my being, tell me, did you make that cake yourself?

Yours, to eternity,

HARRY.

Walking one day on a duckboard.
I was weary and ill at ease,
And my hands grasped vainly at nothing,
And the mud came up to my knees,
The duckboard began oscillating,
I knew that I had to go,
So I gave one wild and final plunge,
And fell in the mud below.

AS OF OLD.

—o—o—o—

And it came to pass that the King gathered together all his men, and his chariots, and his mules, and there was a great multitude gathered together, so that there was no blade of grass seen in the land. And one of the King's captains called WINDUP did send for his chief charoteer and did say unto him, "Bring unto me INTHA." Now INTHA was a man skilled in the learning of mules. And, lo, the chief charoteer brought INTHA unto WINDUP and did say unto him, "Lo, I have brought this man." And WINDUP spake and said, "It is given unto me to reward one man by sending him unto Blitee, a land flowing with milk and honey, and I have a good account of thee. Say, desirest thou to be the man chosen?" And INTHA answered him and said, "Not-arf," which being interpreted, means "Yea, verily." And WINDUP, the captain of the King's host, said unto him, "Go thou to the river Ancre, and bathe there, and put on clean raiment, and return unto me, and I will give thee a parchment." And INTHA did even as he was bid, and bathed himself in the river Ancre, and was clean. And he went unto the keeper of clean raiment, and received divers articles as white as snow. And when he had girded up his loins with clean raiment, he returned unto WINDUP, the King's captain, and said unto him, "Lo, I have done as my lord commanded." And WINDUP, the captain, said unto him, "Lo, take the parchment, and go thou to Blitee, and thou shalt return here in ten days. And if thou returnest not, then shalt thou suffer divers pain and penalties even the punishment of Effpy of the order one, and thy house also shall suffer." And it came to pass that INTHA took the parchment, and travelled unto Blitee and sojourned there for the space of ten days. Now there was much wine there. And it came to pass that INTHA had a great feast before returning unto his captain, and he drank of the wine until he got "Blotto," which being interpreted m ans, "Possessed of an evil spirit," and he returned not. And it came to pass that WINDUP, the King's captain, did send two men of his bodyguard to fetch INTHA. And they brought him. And WINDUP, the captain, said unto him, "Wherefore didst thou not return unto me, but sojourned in Blitee for many days?" And Intha answered him and said, "Lord I was sick" (and in this he spake the truth). And WINDUP said, "Wherefore then didst thou not go unto a man learned in such things, and obtain a parchment from him?" And INTHA answered him not. And WINDUP, the captain, was exceeding wroth, and commanded them to take INTHA outside and do unto him the punishment which had been commanded. And it came to pass as he had said, and INTHA did get a dose of Effpy of the number 1 order and was chastened.

THE LAST STRAW.

—o—o—o—

Hear now the howl of rage which rends
The skies from Nieuport to Lorraine,
Which wanders down the line, and ends
When breath has flown, and all are sane;
Blanched faces, furtive looks and eyes
Which show the horror felt by all,
And fury at the sacrilege
Holds every one of us in thrall.

—:o:—

And in each heart the certainty
That soon the deed reward shall find,
Just, swift and sure the payment be,
And we to pity all are blind;
He, with this infamy has topped
A list of crimes which e'er must irk us,
Who with a craven hand has dropped
A bomb in Piccadilly Circus.

TO-DAY'S GOSSIP.

BADGES OF RANK.—When an officer wears a trench coat it is impossible to tell what his rank is. However, I am told that a useful new regulation provides for the wearing of rank badges on the garment.—THE RAMBLER in the "Daily Mirror."

A FRIEND of mine, a Staff Officer of considerable rank, informs me that many misunderstandings arise through the difficulty of distinguishing between officers of G and Q Branches of the Staff during the dark hours of night. Some genius of the War Office has, however, introduced a new order whereby members of G side will in future wear bright red pyjamas and those of Q bright green ones, thus overcoming a really serious difficulty.

AN unpaid lance-corporal, in one of our famous Shetland regiments at the front, writes to me as follows:—"I was nearly court-martialed the other day for failing to salute an officer I met in the trenches one dark and foggy night." On making enquiries I am happy to inform my readers that a new regulation is being framed by the "powers that be," whereby officers in the forward area will in future have their rank stars illuminated by powerful electric lamps, the battery for same being carried in the pocket. Stars will be distinguished by white lamps, crowns by red lamps, and Generals and above will be known by a combination light green and dark ginger.

MUCH correspondence has reached me asking me to explain the meaning of the patches of many colours, shapes and sizes worn on the arms and backs of our brave lads home on leave from the front. I am told by "one who knows" that an illustrated guide book is shortly to be issued at the small figure of five shillings whereby Londoners and others will be able to understand and distinguish these mystic signs.

THE BABBLER.

MORT POUR LA FRANCE.

—o—o—o—

Many the graves that lie behind the line,
Scattered like shells upon a blood-stained strand,
Crosses and mounds, that eloquently stand
To mark a spot, that forms some hero's shrine.
And one, that nestles near a shattered pine,
Beside a war-wrecked wall, in barren land,
Is tended, daily, by a woman's hand,
Moistened by tears, that in her bright eyes shine.

—o—o—o—

But proud she was, and proud she still can be,
Lover and patriot, both, she proudly reads
His epitaph. It dries her tears to know,
That he has purchased immortality:—
"Mort pour la France." He filled his Country's needs,
And though he rests, for France he'd have it so.

OUR SPLENDID NEW SERIAL.

—o—o—o—

FOR KING & COUNTRY.

—o—o—o—

A TALE OF THE GREAT WAR.

—o—o—o—

CHARACTERS :—

Major Vere de Brett	— an A.P.M.
Col. Custance Fitzgerald	— a M.L.O.
Arthur Fitzgerald	— his son.
Miss Vera Marjorumley	— a W.A.A.C.
Miss Sheila Popping	— her maid.
Sergt. Led Swinger	— at the Base.

Other characters will be introduced as the story proceeds.

—o—o—o—

CHAPTER 3.

—o—

THE night was perfectly peaceful—the leaves were falling off the trees with a soft whirr—the late autumn moon was sinking to rest—and all nature was sleeping to rehabilitate itself to bear the stress of the coming winter. But, hark! what is this noise, heard at first faintly, but then with ever increasing clearness until with one terrific blast which rent the heavens and struck terror into the hearts of all our characters. Frantically Major Vere de Brett reached for his gas-helmet shrieking the time "Heavens! 'tis gas!" All the characters of this powerful serial followed his example, but alas! it was too late. The cloud rolled on with ever-increasing velocity, and one by one they were engulfed in the poisonous atmosphere which had been released by an unscrupulous and dishonourable foe. So we must leave them, with their bleaching features towards the heavens, and with Vera clasped tightly in the fast-stiffening arms of Arthur.

THE END.

[We regret the curtailment of our splendid serial, but the author has gone on leave. Anyway, we have it on the best local authority that it was the rottenest serial ever written.]

TO REGGIE.

—o—o—o—

So now at last you leave us!
Leave us with whom you've soldiered two long years,
Leave us with whom you've shared your hopes and fears,
St Eloi's mound and Wipers' mud-spread plain,
Then Loos and Vimy, sun and snow and rain,
The Somme and all it held for us and you,
Messines and Stirling Castle, friendship grew
With e'er a grin to smooth a troubled hour,
With sympathy and help if in your power;
And now you leave us, change must come we know,
And men must climb, for you we'd have it so;
In future days just think when feeling blue
Of those old pals who soldiered long with you,
Of happy days in spite of all the hell,
And know that we will always wish you well.

Correspondence.

To the Editor,
"B.E.F. Times."

Sir,

I am surprised and pained to see a letter in your valuable periodical advocating the issue of Gin to Generals. Sir, your correspondent must be most unpatriotic—he may even be a "Bolo." Those who have made a careful study of such problems have quite definitely proved that the minutest doses of alcohol poison the body for at least two days, and after the primary exhilaration, there is a reaction—particularly the morning after. Is it wise, sir, at a time like this to run the risk of making our generals too optimistic in the evening, and too depressed in the morning?

Yours Indignantly.
F. A. NATIC,
Hon. Sec. Little Stodgebury Temperance Association.

P S.—I might suggest that if our generals really need some stimulant, they might do worse than try a mixture in which I am interested—T.O. This cordial, which stimulates and cheers, but does not inebriate, was invented by me specially to meet the case of those who must have some stimulant, and any profits I make out of it will go towards furthering the campaigns of temperance—and T.O.

—o—o—o—

To the Editor,
"B.E.F. Times."

Sir,

I wish to draw your attention to the shameful way in which no mention is made of the glorious Manxman in this war. We hear about the glorious Anzacs and Canadians—English county troops, Scotch, Irish, Welsh, and so on, but I have yet to see the gallant lads from the Isle of Man mentioned. Sir, they have done their bit with the best, and it is a very galling business for them to feel that their pluck is unnoticed. Trusting that the publicity given to the matter by means of your widely read paper will remove the injustice.—I am,

Yours, etc.,
CALL HAINE.

BILGE VILLA, BUNKUM.

LATE NEWS FROM THE RATION DUMP.

—o—o—o—

Three submarines have been mined on the Menin Road. Crew of one captured.

—o—o—o—

The Swedes have declared war. Hence the shortage of turnips. Serious rumours that the Jamaicans are preparing for war and will cut off the rum issue.

—o—o—o—

The Germans have only 14 shells left.

—o—o—o—

Three flying pigs reached the Hun trenches. (This is probably an optimist rumour.)

—o—o—o—

The pay for men at the base is going to be doubled owing to the increased cost of living, and halved for those in the line as they are not in a position to spend it.

—o—o—o—

12 Zeppelins have been forced to descend, as we have discovered a new method of extracting gas from any distance.

ANSWERS TO
CORRESPONDENTS.

Owing to lack of space answers to our numberless correspondents are still held over.

PHOSGENE.

—o—o—o—

Private P. B—— writes as follows from "Somewhere in France."—

"SIR,—I feel I must write to thank you for all you have done for me. For several months I have been feeling off colour every morning, particularly on Saturdays. I suffered from headaches and sickness, and spots before the eyes, etc., and was always tired. I consulted several doctors, but all they did was give me M. & D., and I was always getting into trouble with my officers owing to my distressing malady. Finally I was put in the guard-room where I still am, and about the same time as this last extra burden fell on me I heard of PHOSGENE. I am pleased to say that I now wake up feeling fresh, and when I leave the guard-room I have hopes of very shortly feeling "fresher" still.

Yours, gratefully,
12307 Pte P. B——"

—o—o—o—

BUY A BOTTLE TO-DAY.
PHOSGENE COMPANY, FRANCE.

WELL-KNOWN SOCIETY LADY
TELLS YOU HOW TO

Cure Cold Feet.

—o—o—o—

"My husband was a famous Brevet Lance corporal, and while stationed in Africa was able to save the life of a Swateli who was being eaten by a camel This man told my husband (who was a famous Brevet Lance-corporal) the secret of the Swateli religion, which will not allow it's people to have colds anywhere except in their noses For the sake of my suffering fellow-creatures I am prepared to give away the secret that was given to my husband (who, I may say, was an exceedingly famous Brevet Lance-corporal) for the sum of ten Francs."

—o—o—o—

Write to-day to :—

MRS. FRIGIPED.

Mention This Paper.

SHE :—"AND DID YOU GET THE 5·9 HOW ?"

—o—o—o—

HE : —"Yes—it was a hot time while it lasted, and I had to get into the barrel for ten minutes on the way back with it, but fortunately I had some IVANHOE CIGARETTES in my valise, and the most unpleasant ten minutes soon pass with one of them between your lips, and you are thinking of the sweetest girl in the world."

—o—o—o—

IVANHOE CIGARETTES,

Hope Bros., & Co.,

ARE YOU SHORT?

OR DO YOU WISH TO

Enlarge Your Bust?

—o—o—o—

As long as you are not too short to send us a five-franc note—we can add a cubit to your stature or to your chest measurement.

Just write and tell us what you want and we can do you.

—o—o—o—

LORD B——, says :—"Six months ago I was rejected for the Boy Scouts owing to my poor physique—now I am commanding a battalion of the Guards."

—o—o—o—

"If you want to fill your bust,
Buy our stuff you simply must.
If you're troubled with your height,
Take our dope—you'll be all right."

—o—o—o—

WRITE TO :—

WINDUP & CO., FRANCE.

Printed and Published by
Sherwood, Forester & Co., Ltd.
B. E. F.

GRAND XMAS DOUBLE NUMBER.

THE

B. E. F. TIMES.

WITH WHICH ARE INCORPORATED

The Wipers Times, The "New Church" Times, The Kemmel Times & The Somme-Times,

No 4. Vol. 2 Tuesday, December 25th, 1917. Price 1 Franc.

CLOTH HALL, WIPERS.

(Best Ventilated Hall in the World.)

This Week, and for ONE WEEK ONLY.

MAUDE ALLENBY

IN HER FAMOUS SERIES OF EASTERN DANCES, INCLUDING THE

GAZA GLIDE,
BEERSHEBA BUNNY HUG and the
JERUSALEM JOSTLE.

—o—o—o—o—

OTHER ATTRACTIONS:

K. Rensky in his little Farce,
"IN AND OUT."

—o—o—o—o—

Southcliffe in his famous Impersonations:
1. JULIUS CÆSAR REFUSING the CROWN.

—o—o—o—o—

BOOK EARLY. PRICES AS USUAL.

HAVE YOU SEEN IT?
HAVE YOU SEEN IT??
HAVE YOU SEEN IT???

"THE WIPERS TIMES AND AFTER."

READ WHAT ALL THE LONDON TUBES SAY!!!—" Buy the Wipers Times, fill in your sugar card, and see life."
The dark days are with us, but whisky is not. You must have a tonic—write to JENKINS.
YOU WANT IT!

HE HAS IT!

Not whisky, of course, but an equally efficient tonic.

—o - o—o—o—

Its pages carefully avoid all reference to war, and recall the shaded peace of an English country lane, with the birds singing, and the cows plodding their serene way to the meadow where buttercups and daises grow in rich profusion. Where ever and anon the old village church bell rings out its dulcet notes, and the little flying pigs—Oh Heavens! I knew it was going to creep in somewhere—. . . . . .

However :—

If you care to join our ranks
Send to *Jenkins* fifteen francs.

—o—o—o—o—

HERBERT JENKINS & CO.,
3 York Street,
St James's, London, S.W.I.

—o—o—o—o—

N.B.—This is the only PUKKA advert we've ever had, and this is OWED for.

—o—o—o—o—

THE " EDITION DE LUXE " has been held up by a contretemps in the paper line. However, it will be ready very shortly, and will be sent to those who have ordered. Multiple orders will be cut down, as so many have been ordered but the number is restricted to 250. Preference will be given to the Division.—ED.

GRAND XMAS DOUBLE NUMBER.

THE B. E. F. TIMES.

WITH WHICH ARE INCORPORATED

The Wipers Times, The "New Church" Times, The Kemmel Times & The Somme-Times.

No 4. Vol. 2. Tuesday, December 25th, 1917. Price 1 Franc.

EDITORIAL.

HERE we are, knocking the Xmas number into shape again. It certainly does not seem to be twelve months since we were engaged on the same job, and yet quite a lot seems to have happened in the interval. By the time this number is published we shall have been running for two years and the first volume (containing first 15 numbers) should have made its bow to (let us hope) a kind and uncritical public. This Xmas we are more ambitious, and are making an effort to fill 20 pages, and the success of the venture must depend on how our wild appeals for copy are received by units. Of course it's quite likely that this war business may interfere with our plans and disturb the even tenor of our ways, so that our readers will understand, should the number contain less than the advertised 20 pages, that we have had to drop the pen for the sword, and go and liberate some more French villages, and thus fight the demon of oppression and barbarism, the last remaining relics of bestiality, brutality and Kultur. Should it come to this then indeed is the knell of Germanic despotism sounded, as the Sub-Editor is a holy terror at the end of a sword, and should once it be forced into his hand then Heaven help Hindenburg, as no one else could. However, there seems to be no alternative, and the Publisher has written home for a new pair of spurs and a mess canteen, so that he is evidently considering the necessity of taking an active part in the quarrel at no very distant date. However, one hopes that we may be allowed to have Xmas in peace. We cannot close without giving one and all the old greetings. Here's a Happy Xmas and New Year to you all, and may next Xmas see the whole damned business over. We are laying six to four on.

THE EDITOR.

A CHRISTMAS TALE.

—o—o—o—

ALFRED Higgins was a soldier. Officially he was No. 249,921, Pte. Higgins, A. His conduct sheet showed that he had usually been present when F.P. was handed out. On Christmas morning Alfred, with others, was holding the line. It was one of those Christmas mornings with which we have grown so familiar in this war. All was peace and goodwill. The gas gongs were chiming out their message of joy to all mankind, and the merry bark of the pip squeak, aided by the staccato cough of the how., combined to give the necessary impression of all being right with the world. Alfred had fallen into a deep reverie, when his sergeant approached him and said, "Alfred, have you had any rum?" Alfred moodily said "No." "Well," said the sergeant cheerily, handing him a canteen full, "have mine!"

* * * * * * *

When Alfred recovered, he found his hand being stroked by a "V.A.D." in a base hospital

OUR DIARY.

—o—o—o—

By LIEUT. SAMUEL PEPYS.

—o—

RUMOUR has come that our men have attacked the enemy with much vigour in Picardy, and have dealt grievously with him. This is of a good hearing, as last week he did annoy us much by throwing at us grenades of a great size, and again with some poisonous vapours. I did witness a game of hockey this last week, and was much amused at the efforts of many of the players, who did stop to cough frequently. The Countess of Cambrai was there, and all the beaux were much taken by her appearance, she being dressed in the latest mode and of Paris. Indeed, one does hear that there was fighting at Crockfords after dinner about her. I am glad Anne is not over in this country, otherwise it might give the most extravagant ideas to her, and there are many reasons that she is better in England. I took the coach with a merry party to A—— the other day, and we did enjoy ourselves much. All the young females of the town were to be seen, and one notices not too much of bashfulness. I am glad Anne is in England, as it is very wet in this country. Everything is of the most expensive, and soda is up one penny on the bottle, so that one must be careful. I did notice some strange soldiers this last week, and have been told they were from the Americas. They were of a goodly presence, but of a most ununderstandable language, talking, it seemed to me, much through the nose. As I must go on patrol soon to bed at 8 of the clock, in a bad mood and with the megrims, as I am wet and the rum did not come up to-night.

TO THOSE AT HOME.

Lift up your heads, O ye people, and be ye lifted up, ye everlasting grousers, and so will ye help in what is yet to do.

—o—o—o—

Ye who have given so freely nor counted cost,
Given of money and time ye could spare;
Give once again, give us what we would have the most,
Out of your confidence give us a share.

—o—o—o—

Though there be many whose faith ne'er can shaken be
Steadfast through all, be it good, be it ill,
Others whose faith veers with each wind alternately
Voicing, unheeding, their doubtings at will.

—o—o—o—

Yet every doubt that is whispered through heedlessness
Pulls twice its weight, and the harm still remains,
Going the rounds, growing rather to more than less,
Redoubling losses and carping at gains.

—o—o—o—

Lift up your heads, that in you our new strength we find,
Give of your faith as ye give of your gold,
Doubtings and fears all forgotten and left behind,
So shall ye help us most now, as of old,

—o—o—o—

Hush all the whisperers voicing in thoughtless way,
Reckoning little the harm that they do,
Steadfast in truth go ye onward from day to day,
Trusting in us and we trusting in you.

IN MY GARDEN.

—o—o—o—

WITH APOLOGIES TO THE "DAILY MIRROR,"

—o—

Although Crows' Feet are usually sown later in the season, in many sectors where a warm sunny border of light soil is available, the seed of this useful vegetable may, with advantage, be got in at this date.

—§ † §—

Where the soil is damp and heavy, an early planting of gooseberries is attended with some risk. This hardy perennial, being a strong grower, will quickly cover an unsightly patch of waste ground The best crops of this luscious fruit have been obtained when some support has been given by stakes.

—§ † §—

It must be remembered that the planting of Toffee-apples on the border of your neighbour's allotment will seriously interfere with the ripening of his gooseberries.

—§ † §—

By this time berms should be well covered with a luxuriant crop of Mustard and Cresol.

—§ † §—

That aggravating insect, the Phlying pig (sus maximus fossae) is particularly voracious just now, and can only be kept under by a liberal use of the vermoral sprayer. Should vermoral solution be unobtainable, an excellent substitute can be made by stirring a scoopful of chloride of lime in a tea-spoonful of water. This solution can be safely stored in water carts for an indefinite period.

ART. A. XERXES.

THE TOAST OF THE IRREPRESSIBLE.

The Colonel, the Major, the Adjutant, the whole of the Regiment's Mess
Were talking of Germans, of Ships, and of Things, of up-to-date War and the trouble it brings ;
And they wished they were back once more, to the slack, old days of the good Queen Bess ;

—o—o—o—

When Raleigh and Drake had manned their ships, and made the foemen run,
And returned, in a trice, to their worshipping home, scattering money and silvery foam,
The gifts of the seas, where their victories over Spanish fleets were won.

—o—o—o—

The Subaltern rose, a toast to propose:—" Why should we worry or grieve ;
And damn those silly old days," he said, as he shook his curly, precocious head,
" There are men like these, to-day, on the seas, to carry us home on leave.
So here's to the boat, where'er she float, that takes our soldiers over,
A health to the ship, that makes the trip, to Folkestone or to Dover."

—o—o—o—

And unafraid of the stir he made, he cried, " Don't think I'm silly—
Let the enemy gas us. and bomb us, and strafe ; we can give him as good as we get—not half !
If once a year, we can get out o' here, to the lights o' Piccadilly."

The Colonel recalled his familee ; and he wanted his leave once more.
The portrait, they say, of the Major's wench, hangs in his dugout in Canada Trench ;
And he couldn't guess, if she would say yes, next time, that he talked it o'er.

—o—o—o—

The Adjutant, Brown, wore a pessimist's frown—of " Private Affairs " he vaunted,
Of a moribund aunt, who was lingering still ; and a hope, that he'd head off the rest in her will.

—o—o—o—

But the Subaltern, bad, was a light-headed lad, and everyone knew what he wanted,
He was just a bit wild, and he beamed and he smiled, as he toasted the Leave Boat again ;
He sprang to his feet, and he stepped on the toe, of his most apoplectic and gouty C.O.
Whose remark does not matter—'twas drowned in the chattering Subaltern's ribald refrain
Of " Here's to the boat, where'er she float, that takes our soldiers over,
A health to the ship, that makes the trip to Folkestone or to Dover."

R.M.O.

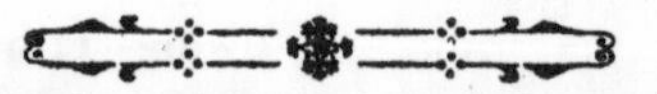

A SPLASH OF COLOUR.

In variegated colours, rich and new
Artists may dabble ; poets love to sing
Of dragon flies, with iridescent wing,
That dazzle with their brightness every hue
Of art ; of rainbows, in a drop of dew ;
Of butterflies, at morning, fluttering
Above the rarest flowers ; the priceless string
Of jewels. All are fair, but none will do.

—:o:—

For multicoloured metaphors, I grope
Climbing a long kaleidoscopic scale,
Striving to do you justice, but I fail.
Nor, in a sonnet, can I ever hope
To paint the incandescence of your voice—
Your language, R.S.M., is far too choice.

C.L.P.

OUR SPLENDID NEW SERIAL.

—o—o—o—

ZERO!

OR

"THE BOUND OF THE BASKERSHIRES."

—o—o—o—

ANOTHER HERLOCK SHOMES EPISODE.

—o—o—o—

CHARACTERS.:—

Maj.-General Wilfred Montmorency Duggout — A General.
Maj. Horace Malcolm Charles Frigiped Bassy — A Staff Officer.
Andrews — — His Chauffeur.
Anastasia Doubloy —An Estaminet Girl.
Marguerite — Waitress in a Restaurant.
Randolph Wunpip — — A Subaltern.
Capt. Martell — A Coy. Commander.
Herlock Shomes — The Great Detective.
Capt. Hotsam, R.A.M.C.—His Admirer.
Sergt. Sniffins — — Provost Sergeant.

W.A.A.C. and soldiers will be introduced as necessary.

—o—o—o—

CHAPTER 1.

—o—

NIGHT was fast closing in on Dickebusch when suddenly the door of an estaminet was flung open, and three figures emerged to be quickly swallowed up in the gathering gloom.

They were Sergeant Sniffins and two of his satellites, who had just been to see if Anastasia Doubloy was conforming with the regulations, and had destroyed the sugar card previously issued to her.

Hardly had they gone when a cry was heard and shouts for help. Figures came rapidly running from all sides, but too late. Captain Martell was gasping his last on the pavé with a hole in his windpipe. He just managed to gurgle "Cox 7 and 11!" e'er he threw himself back and died.

The crowd melted away in the darkness; and left one figure standing beside the corpse of Captain Martell. This was none other than our old friend Herlock Shomes, who had been looking for cigarette ends on the Dickebusch Road.

Hastily examining the surrounding country for clues, he crawled round on his hands and knees and made several small packages, sealing each, in an envelope. Then he carefully went through the pockets of Captain Martell, and disappeared into the night.

Meanwhile what of Anastasia? As it was after closing hours she had a full complement of military police, who were drinking and playing banker, pontoon, and other innocuous games. Only the quiet curses of the losers broke the stillness which was occasionally shattered as glasses hurtled across the room.

Suddenly the door was pushed open, and a man rushed in and broke the news of the murder of Captain Martell. All was instantly confusion as the M.P.'s returned to their posts, assuming an expression both grave and stern the while.

Anastasia was left alone, and closing the door she collapsed in a chair, and buried her face in her hands. Sobs shook her being.

WHY?

(Read next thrilling instalment.)

(To be Continued.)

LONG AGO.
BY GILBERT FRANKAU.

To-day, as we drank our wine,
Editor mine!
I thought of the early days,
Long ago;
When, new to soldier-ways,
We didn't know
That a G.O.C. was different from a third grade G.S.O.

—o—o—o—

I thought about Shoreham Camp—
Devilish damp!
Of the blue that he used to wear—
The recruit;
And the swears that he used to swear
When this "loot"
Took the early morning route march (only, then, we called it "root.";

—o—o—o—

Of our Div. as it used to be,
In K 3;
Of the faces of damn good chaps
One might meet
('Neath funny hard service caps)
On the street
Near the Hippodrome at Brighton with a piece of something sweet;

—o—o—o—

Of days when we all were green,
In 'fourteen;
Of tents that were bare of boards;
And the rain;
And the cockneys (as tight as lords).
In the train
Rolling home from week-end passes back to Shoreham Camp again;

Of drills that I used to drill
On the hill,
Rather bucked but deuced shy
At command,
'Neath the Sergeant-Major's eye,
Book-in-hand;
And of how the Buffs outswanked us with the first battalion band.

—o—o—o—

Lord, those other days they seem
Like a dream—
Movies flashed upon a screen
Long ago;
Like some half-remembered scene
From a show
That one went to half-seas-over and whose name one doesn't know.

—o—o—o—

Where are those days to-day?
Editor, say!
Where are those blue-clad men? . . .
I suppose
One meets with them now and then—
N.C.O.'s
With their Don C. Emma's scarlet faded to a washed-out rose.

—o—o—o—

Where are the lads who drank,
Full of swank,
In the halls of the Metropole?
Does one find
Here and there a cheery soul
To remind
Of the pegs we drank together and the girls we left behind?

—o—o—o—

What's the good in harking back
Along a track
That we travelled three years ago—
Rather more!
Let's wait till the last best "show";
Wipe the floor
With the Hun; take off our gum-boots, and return our guns to store;

Then, the fellows who took the job
At a bob
While the blighters who wouldn't fight
Grabbed the dough !)
Will have one great old night . . . .
And I know
That they'll talk till early morning of
"the days of long ago."

10/12/17.

???

—:o:—

Little things we want to know
Why messages by pigeon go ?
The eagle bird can fly as high
And C.O.'s dote on pigeon pie !

—:o:—

Why the man with one inch group
Joined the Ancient Archie Troupe ?
Surely it would raise a smile
If he grouped below a mile !

—:o:—

Why patrols with books to sign
Wander up and down the line ?
Surely flanks would safer be
If Fritz endorsed my 153 !

—:o:—

Why, although I've studied war
For a brace of years or more,
At present I can not secure
A case of Walker or of Dewar ?

—:o:—

Why—but stay ! I'm indiscreet,
Rushing in with careless feet
Where the angels fear to tread—
I nearly tried to pot "the red."

THE PERFECT LOVE.

——:o:——

[EXTRACT FROM LETTER FROM THE FRONT.—"Dearest, many thanks for parcel just received. Its contents were most welcome, especially the BACHELOR BUTTONS, as I had but five remaining buttons on my trousers . . . . .]

—o—o—o—

My Love loves me—'tis true—I cannot doubt her,
She is my own in word and thought and deed,
And though the leagues of space stretch out between us,
Her loving thought supplies my every need.

—o—o—o—

'Tis not the socks she sends that prove her passion,
Or layers of sweets so dear unto my taste,
'Tis not those fine delicious pies that win me
(Though I must own she makes a perfect paste).

—o—o—o—

'Tis not that there within each mighty parcel
I find cigars, both good and bad, galore—
Not e'en the witching weed hath pow'r to stir me,
Or cause my love to grow one whit the more.

—o—o—o—

Nor when I read the sweet and dainty missive
In which she tells her love so strong and true,
Do I, in fond and humble adoration,
Her photo kiss (as lovers ought to do).

—o—o—o—

Ah no ! Such things but prove a careless fancy
A love not of the heart, but of the lip ;
A PERFECT Love is mine—she always sends me
Bachelor Buttons with the "Bull-dog grip."

W.J.G.

HELP FOR THE HARASSED.

—o—o—o—

[A new series entitled "Help for the Harassed" is commencing in this number. This departure will, it is hoped, prove of assistance to many of our subscribers. The articles are by a Staff Officer of wide experience. We feel confident that if his methods are clearly studied, satisfaction is assured.]

—:o:—

THE OFFICIAL CONUNDRUM.

It is in dealing with this particular type of correspondence that Officers most usually fail.

We will assume a case and the resulting conundrum.

HARASSED ONE (ANY C.O.)

No. 1,005, Private W. Crook has been sent to a course (any old). He arrives minus his ground sheet.

THE RESULTING CONUNDRUM.

A full report is required from the Officer Commanding ——— of the circumstances in which No. 1005, Private W. Crook reported at ——— without a ground sheet.

It does not concern us to follow the snowball like career of this correspondence. Suffice it to say, a humble pencil written page from A.B., 152 has grown to an inspiring collection of type written documents by the time it reaches the P.B C.O.

The P.B. one makes enquiries, but finds with dismay that, long since, a "Blighty" has deprived him of Private W. Crook, also, no soul can give any information of the ground sheet.

Should my C.O. despair?

Certainly not! We will show him that it is to his advantage.

Why is this report required? Not from any grave concern with regard to Private Crook or his ground sheet.

Why then?

The reason is simply obvious. It is it order to test the C.O's literary ability.

For what reason?

So that his fitness for a Staff appointment may be judged.

Everything is favourable for the production of a masterpiece. A full report is demanded, no petty restrictions to cramp the style, no hard unwelcome facts to clip the wings of his fancy.

An Officer of little experience will damn his prospects by answering thus:—

"I regret that, owing to the lapse of time since Private Crook and ground sheet came unstuck, I am unable to produce any evidence which might tend to show the cause of separation."

This is not full, it shows no literary style, it will not please. On the contrary. The following report is one which will most certainly ensure either the coveted appointment or six months home duty under observation:—

Hd. Qrs.,

. . . . . I.B.

It is with mingled feelings that I take my pen (or pencil as the case may be); grief, on the one hand, that Private Crook should so far forget him self as to have been guilty of such conduct to the prejudice of good order and military discipline (A.A. Sec. 40) intense gratification on the other, that it is I, I alone, one among so many, who am deemed worthy to perform a task so momentous. But a report is required, a full report. That report shall be rendered cost what it may. In order to grasp the circumstances which led to the detachment of Private Crook from his ground sheet, it will be necessary to trace that unhappy soldier's career from his early childhood. This wayward soldier was once a child. Born of poor but dishonest parents, he received the baptismal name of William (to his intimates "Young

Bill"). From this onwards it is easy to trace his downfall until the culminating crime which resulted in the detachment from his ground sheet. When a youth, with life before him, his father entrusted him with a shilling and a jug. Did his father's thirst go unquenched? It did not, but Young Bill enjoyed the football match. To trace a long career of crime would take too much space, suffice it to say that his father eventually took him by the right ear to the nearest recruiting office, and here his military career commenced. "The boy is father to the man," and so we find him still a private after years of service. One day he, with others, was detailed to go over the top. He was entrusted with the care of the one prisoner captured on that occasion. Private Crook at once christened him "Fritz." In spite of every effort of the unfortunate Fritz to keep touch, Private Crook lost him. Poor Fritz, after long and anxious search, found at length a cage wherein to rest. Grievous to relate, it was the cage of another Division. I need say no more. My task is complete. I have the honour to submit these few lines, hoping they will find you as they leave me, in the best of health.

P.B. Lieut,-Col.,
Commanding . . . . .

It may possibly be remarked that no definite answer has been given to the enquiry.

Does any conundrum fiend, Official or otherwise, like the answer to be guessed first shot? Certainly not! it annoys him. It deprives him of the gratification of saying "Wrong, guess again," which in Official parlance will take this form:—

"The explanation given by the Officer Commanding . . . . is considered most unsatisfactory. A further report is required."

Remember the P.B.C.O. is out to please.

Red hair and freckles, legs beneath the lace
Of Sunday petticoats, long legs and slender,
That strength and leverage, oft-times, would lend her
In scaling trees ('tis true, without much grace,
But lots of skill) and wildly kick in space,
As she hung poised from topmost branches tender,
Before she dropped; whereafter she would mend her
Bedraggled hose, with grave unblushing face.

—o—o—o—

She speaks—a goddess tall and fair and stately—
"Why Jack, we haven't seen each other lately;
Not since you went to France." My sacred aunt!
Tempus et bellum omnia mutant;
But this their greatest change.—I scratch my napper,
Can this be Phyllis, that unholy flapper?

C.L.P.

Sing a song of Christmas!
Pockets full of slush,
Four and twenty P.B.I.
A dixey full of "mush,"
When that dixey opened
The Tommies said "Oh my!
It's beef to-day by way of change"
And then began to cry.

HOW IT IS DONE.

—o—o—o—

By Adsum.

—o—o—o—

To X Batt., Blankshire Regt.
S.C. 1009.—Please detail working party: 5 officers, 300 other ranks, to report to 2nd Lieut. ——, R.E., at 11 p.m., 26th inst., at Wapping Old Stairs AAA Lifebelts will be worn.
I. AMMITT, Capt.
Staff Capt. Nth Inf. Brigade.

—§ † §—

To H.Q., Nth Inf. Brigade.
A. 217.—Ref. S.C. 1009. Only 2 officers, 150 other ranks available owing to attack of German measles AAA Please say where lifebelts can be obtained.
B. SMART, Capt. & Adj.,
X Batt., Blankshire Regt.

—§ † §—

To X Batt., Blankshire Regt.
Reference my S.C. 1009 and your A 217, please state for information of this office why casualties due to enemy attack were not reported in accordance with A.R.O. 9992, A. 1/1/17, and memorandum of D.A.G. (Base) d 2/4/17 AAA Indent on D.A.D.O.S.
I. AMMITT, Capt.,
Staff Capt., Nth Inf. Brigade.

—§ † §—

To X Batt., Blankshire Regt.
O.O. 126.—Reference your Indent for 152 Belts, Life. Please state if B.O T. Pattern, M.A. III or M.A. III star required.
W E. GETTIT, D.A.D.O.S.,
—— Division.

—§ † §—

To D.A.D.O.S., —— Division.
A. 260.—Reference your O.O. 126, Belts, Life, B.O. Pattern III star required AAA Please hasten as these are urgently required.
B. SMART, Capt. & Adj.,
X Batt., Blankshire Regt.

—§ † §—

To X Batt., Blankshire Regt.
Reference A 260 and Indent 10,625. Please forward nominal roll and following particulars AAA Age and weight AAA Religion AAA Waist measurement AAA These are necessary before Belts, Life can be issued.
W. E. GETTIT, D.A.D.O.S.,
—— Division.

—§ † §—

To D.A.D.O S., —— Division.
Q.M. 60.—Reference Indent 10,625, Belt, Life AAA Nominal roll, etc., herewith AAA Please say when these will be available.
B. WARY, Lieut. & Q.M.,
X Batt., Blankshire Regt.

—§ † §—

To X Batt., Blankshire Regt.
S.C. 2060.—Cancel my S.C. 1009, and substitute 1 N. C.O., 6 men, report Brigade Headquarters, at 6 a.m., 27th inst. AAA Party to bring necessary material for scrubbing the Brigadier's terrier AAA
I. AMMITT, Capt.,
Staff Capt., Nth Inf. Brigade.

—§ † §—

Adjutant and Sergeant Major Xth Blankshire Regiment removed to nearest Field Ambulance.

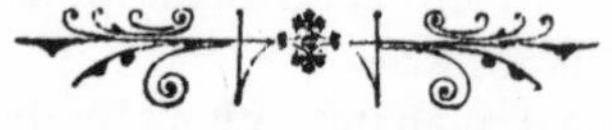

Love may laugh at bars and locks
And subs may go their wayward ways,
But dare they laugh at Mr. Cox
Now leave is up to fourteen days?

WHY NOT ?

—o—o—o—

We've had a play in ragtime, and we've
had a ragtime band,
We've had a ragtime army, and we've
had a ragtime land ;
But why not let us have what we have
never had before ?
Let's wade right in tomorrow and let's
have a ragtime war.

—:o:—

Let's carry up our duckboards to a
ragtime's jerky strains,
Let's whistle ragtime ditties while we're
bashing out Hun brains,
Let's introduce this melody in all we say
and do,
In our operation orders, and in all our
lies to Q.

—:o:—

Let us write O.O.'s to music, and the
red-hats can decide
The witching hour of zero to a dainty
Gaby Glide,
We'll take the fateful plunge, and when
we venture o'er the top,
We'll do it to a Turkey Trot or tuneful
Boston Hop.

—:o:—

We'll drink our S.R.D. to tune, and even
" chatting up "
Becomes a melody in rhyme if done to
" Dixie Pup,"
A bombing raid to "Old Kentuck"
would make a Fritzie smile,
He'd stop a bomb with pleasure to a
ragtime's mystic guile.

—:o:—

Can you see our giddy "Q" staff, as
they go up to the line,
Just walking round the trenches to the
air " Kentucky Mine,"
Gaily prancing down the duckboards, as
they tumble o'er a bucket,
To the quiet seducing strains of " My
Dear Home in Old Kentucket."

From Intelligence Summaries.

—:o:—

OPERATIONS.—At 1·2 a.m. a patrol of 1 O.R. left our wire where it was, and retired to his dug-out. No enemy was seen.

—o—o—o—

ARTILLERY.—1·10 p.m. to 2·3 p.m. Our front and support lines were heavily shelled with 303 inch shrapnel. No direct hits were obtained.

—o—o—o—

RIFLE AND M.G. FIRE.—Sniper suspected at A 29, Q 21 3/4, 4 1/8. (See Artillery above.

—o—o—o—

T.M 's.—Our H.T.M.'s fired one round rapid at suspected enemy Pigeon Emplacements.

—o—o—o—

MOVEMENT.—11·28 a.m. Man seen walking along pathway running E.S.W. from N.S.E. corner of M—— Wood. He was carrying a dark brown spherical object with a mottled surface, on a white disc. This seems to point to an early Christmas.

2·3 p.m.—Sentry with head and shoulders above parapet at B 73, h 19 1/4, 7 1/2. Our "heavies" were informed, and fired a concentration of 31 rounds at 8 p.m The sentry was enveloped by a cloud of dust and small stones. Our observer was hit by a flying tunic button, and after the shoot a boot and part of a rifle were seen lying about 30 yards from the point where the sentry had stood. A hit is claimed.

—o—o—o—

MISCELLANEOUS.—1·4 a.m. Two rockets emitting a pale black light were sent up in quick succession from M 19, n 50, 40. No action followed.

—o—o—o—

ENEMY'S ATTITUDE Distinctly hostile.

AS SEEN BY OTHERS.

—o—o—o—

DEAR MIKE.—

You asked me what is my impression of this war. Well, I don't know. From what the fellows tell me I guess I have not been to the war yet. The war must have been over before I came.

Now my impression of this show gained from pictures and stories before I came across the ocean was millions of men with guns constantly engaged in mortal combat, pieces of people flying into the air, field guns shooting as fast as they can, and dead men hanging on barb wire.

Not so, dear friend, MUD, that is the basis of this war. While just at present it is frozen hard and the walking and wheeling is good, we all know what is coming when it thaws. Sticking through this mud at various places you can see pieces of towns. These places are still inhabited, but not by the people who built them.

This is the closed season for aeroplane fighting, I know, for the planes that live on this side of the line fly at different hours than the German planes do when they come over for a visit. When a Bosche plane comes over, the others get out of the air so the Archies can have the whole sky to shoot into. I think our planes show good sense, but then shooting at a plane on the fly with an Archie is like shooting ducks with a rifle, it isn't done with much success. However, I hope to see a Bosche hit. I am a young man and have a healthy job, and this war may last a long time yet, so there is hope.

Now down on the earth things are different All over the landscape, hills, walls and bushes, in hollows and next to would-be-quiet dug outs are guns of various sizes. Every now and then the man who is boss of the gun finds that the ammunition is getting in the way, so they start the guns up and keep them going until the pile of shells is reduced to a handier size. This is usually done at night when you wish to sleep.

Of course somewhere out in front there are men armed and waiting for a fight. I know there must be, for I have seen them going out, and after a few days back they come. Now they must go somewhere to spend the time.

Out there there are trenches, one set for our men and another for the Bosche, with thick wire fences in front of them. In these wire fences are hidden gaps through which people can pass. Out in front the time passes slowly, and by way of amusement one side or the other will start out to get into the other trenches.

If they can find the hole in the wire they go on until they find the trench, and if in luck they may find someone about taking the air This man is brought back, and the score is one to nothing for the night. Fritz don't mind a little stunt like this but if those fellows happen to like the trench and stay there, Fritz, old boy, will bring on his gang and start a H— of a row. It seems a bit slow taking one man at a time like that, as there may be millions more. But it all helps to pass the time till Christmas, when the war is going to end. Only we don't know which Christmas.

H. DAVIS, M.O.R.C., U.S.A.

GOOD-BYE.

——:o:——

Farewell, my old and trusted friend,
For three long years of war! Ah me!
I've managed now and then to send
Upon your short and stunted key
A word or two.

—:o:—

Unprepossessing, small, and black,
No polished brass or ebonite
Adorn'd your square and ugly back,
(And yet you served me day or night)
Oh! D. Mark 3.

—:o:—

One fault, too garrulous by half,
(And through this you are now undone)
'Tis ordered by our gilded Staff
To pass you by, and use alone
A Fullerphone.

AS OF OLD.

—o—o—o—

AND it came to pass that divers men were needed to labour in the land, so that the King's hosts might journey to the Land of the Amalekites. And they sent for those skilled in the art of digging and delving, and said unto them "Go ye and prepare the way for us." And men to the number of fifty girded up their loins, and they took spades and weapons, and tin hats they took also. And one of them, by name SAPPA, the son of ARREB, did quake exceedingly when he heard the tumult that there was in the place, for the Amalekites did have an up-wind, and raged furiously. And it came to pass that SAPPA, the son of ARREB did say to his Captain "Lo, I am not afraid, but I am suffering from a palsy." And the Captain said unto him "Get thee back, and tell the leech what thou hast told me, and peradventure he will give thee a potion, which will drive out the palsy." And he went. And when he had come unto Rap, where the leech dwelt, he went in unto him and made much lamentation, and said, "Lo, thy servant is stricken with a palsy, and the blood is like water in my veins." And the leech said unto him "Beware, oh SAPPA, that thou deceivest me not." And SAPPA answered him and said "Lo, my speech is as the speech of babes and sucklings, and there is no guile in my tongue." Then did the leech make much examination, and he went away and thought for a space. And when he had come back he did write on the parchment N.Y.D., which being interpreted means "No you don't." and he gave unto SAPPA a potion of Kasteroil. And he sent a messenger to the Captain, and he said "1o the feet of SAPPA are cold, and it behoveth him to labour like Tumen, and peradventure he will not again suffer with a palsy. And the Captain tied SAPPA to the wheels of his chariot, and left him for a space. And then he said unto him, "Thou wilt now labour like Tumen, lest a worse thing befall thee." And SAPPA did as he was bid, and the palsy left him, and he was cured. And the fame of it went right through the King's hosts, as is written in the Second Book of Battorders.

AUNT ANNIE'S CORNER.

—o—o—o—

TENDER TALKS TO TINY TOTS.

—o—o—

MY DEAR TOT-TIES,

A ver-y hap-py X-mas to you all, and I hope you all en-joy the nice pres-ents that Sant a Claus brings you. Sant-a Claus has told me what some of you will find in your stock-ings. Lit-tle Wil-lie Poile is go-ing to get a tick-et col-lect-or's out-fit with green and yell-ow rail-way tick-ets. I hope he will be kind, and let the oth-er lit tle boys use them.

—:o:—

LIT TLE Al-fie Stalk-er has got a nice box of bricks, and a set of Mech-ano, and now he will be able to make some nice forts and things for his sold-iers.

—:o:—

LIT-TLE Fer-die Ad ams is get-ting a wool-ly lamb on a nice green stand, and a duck to float in his bath. Wouldn't you like to see him play ing with it?

—:o:—

BIL-LIE Tween-ey is go ing to have a box of paints, and I ex-pect he will have great fun with them; per-haps he will be ab-le to make a lot of things look dif-fer-ent from what they real-ly are, which would be very clev-er, would-n't it?

Your Lov-ing
AUNT ANNIE.

Forty-four Regimental Sergeant-Majors.

—o—o—o—

Sixty-three Unpaid Lance-Corporals.

—o—o—o—

TWENTY THOUSAND SANITARY MEN.

—o—o—o—

And one MEMBER of PARLIAMENT.

—o—o—o—

STARTLING STATISTICS OF HELPMANISM.

—o—o—o—

How many slats make a duckboard (a) before (b) after the trench fires are kept burning?

? ? ?

What does an "A" frame?

? ? ?

Why is a mouse when it spins?

? ? ?

Can you answer these simple questions without counting on your fingers, or referring to the D.R.O.?

? ? ?

If not, read on, it's YOUR money we want.

—o—o—o—

The Inestimable value of Helpmanism can best be gathered from a perusal of our brochure "Mime and Mummery," and the veracious verbosity of "Strewth," and both of these Epics will be sent free, gratis, and for nothing, to all whose incomes justify an enquiry into Our Modern Miracle (See Coupon ad fin).

Meanwhile we publish extracts from a few of the unsolicited testimonials which continue to pour in upon us night and day.

—o—o—o—

VERDICT OF A DISTINGUISHED STAFF OFFICER.

—:o:—

"LEAVE EVERY TWO MONTHS."

—:o:—

The first is from a Staff Officer, In The Field (near Boulogne). He says:—"When I first took over Staff duties I was timid, modest, and retiring; doing my own work myself and taking leave as it came, just like an ordinary Officer. After my first lesson in Helpmanism, I developed such a Personality that I obtained the assistance of two understudies and a Staff Learner; whilst after lesson three ('Passed to you for necessary action and return on completion please'), I expedited my office work to such an extent that I now get leave every two months without fail."

—o—o—o—

"THE UNBUSINESSLIKE QUARTER-BLOKE."

—:o:—

The next letter is from a Quartermaster, "Somehow in Somewhere," and speaks for itself:—"I feel it my duty as well as pleasure to draw your attention to the effects of Helpmanism on my career. When War broke out the Colonel treated me coldly, seldom standing me drinks and never lending me money (although I often asked him to). I made a bare living out of the men's clothing and rations, and could scarcely keep my R.Q.M.S. in rum. In fact I was known as the 'Unbusinesslike Quarter-Bloke.' Then one day I took to Helpmanism, and, after the first lesson, made a corner in Rations, Rum, and Rootie. I am now an A.Q.M.G., with a C.B., C.M.G., D.S.O. x (with bar), and pay super-tax on my War Loan."

FOREIGN ORDERS GAINED.

—:o:—

That this is by no means an exceptional case is shown by the next letter which is short but very pointed. In response to the query, "What have you gained from Helpmanism," a Private Soldier replies;—

A F.G.C.M. with F.P. (first class).
The Pip.
and
A Thick Ear.

—o—o—o—

A W.A.A.C. GIRL'S EXPERIENCE.

—:o:—

Women, too, profit by the Course as is shown by the following letter, one out of thousands, from a W.A.A.C. Girl in France:—"When first I joined the Army, I was so nervous that I used to BLUSH A MOST VIVID RED whenever the Adjutant spoke to me, though she is a nice girl if only she would do her hair properly and not ROUGE SO MUCH. Then A GREAT FRIEND OF MINE suggested Helpmanism as he had found it INVALUABLE and attributed his M.C., D.S.O., C.B., and O.M. to it as well as the PERFECT fit of his tunic, though he has to have ALL his hats made for him now, and so I tried the Course and after the FIRST LESSON I NEVER BLUSHED AGAIN. . . . .

—o—o—o—

"OFFICERS COME MILES TO LISTEN."

—:o:—

The Staff benefit immensely by the brain-work involved as is shown by the following letter from a typical Service Man:—"Before I underwent a Course of Helpmanism I was a Strong Silent Soldier, saying nothing and thinking less. After Four Lessons I could lecture on and off any subject for any length of time with the greatest of ease, and Officers now come miles in the rain to listen to me."

NOW, while you are convinced;
NOW, before you have time to think;
NOW, while your brain is palpitating;
FILL IN THE FORM BELOW.

—o—o—o—o—

IT'S YOUR MONEY WE WANT.

—o—o—o—o—

USE THIS COUPON

OR SEND US A BLANK CHEQUE.

(Advt)

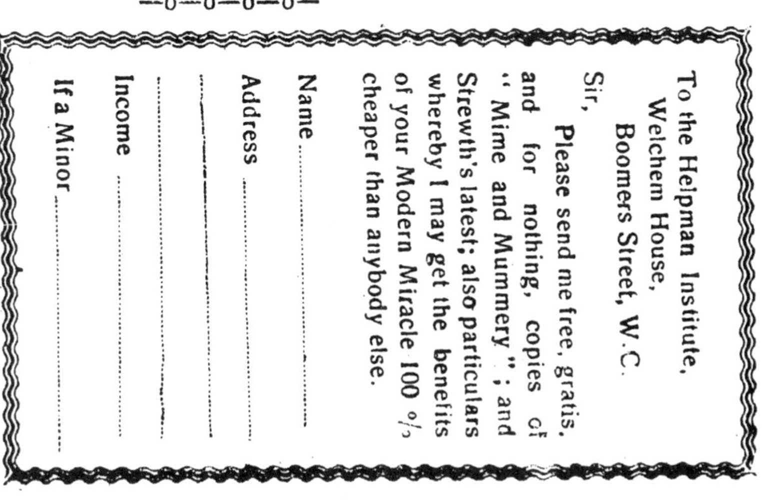

To the Helpman Institute,
Welchem House,
Boomers Street, W.C.

Sir,

Please send me free, gratis, and for nothing, copies of "Mime and Mummery"; and Strewth's latest; also particulars whereby I may get the benefits of your Modern Miracle 100 % cheaper than anybody else.

Name ....

Address ....

....

....

Income ....

If a Minor ....

Correspondence.

To the Editor,
"B.E.F. Times."

Sir,

I read in the papers that a star is being granted for the men who fought in 1914. As one of the earliest conscientious objectors (I discovered my conscience on August 5th, 1914) I must ask you to obtain for us some especial recognition. Surely you cannot but admire the struggle we have put up against the overstrong odds of a sensitive conscience, and that we have been defeated is no fault of ours. We trust that you will be able to help us in the matter.

I am, Sir,
Yours etc.,
ANASTASIUS DUNN,
Bowler Villa, Feltham.

To the Editor,
"B.E.F. Times."

Sir,

While waiting in a queue with my rum card the other night I was rudely approached by a sergeant, and told to "Getterlongoutervit." I protested, but eventually submitted to the hectoring importunities of one placed over me by a social upheaval. Surely this is not the spirit which will win the war, and I maintain that the sergeant had no right to speak to me in so unceremonious a manner, even if I HAD had one issue already, and merely taken my place in the queue on the chance that it might come off.

I am, Sir,
Yours etc.,
WILLIAM SHIFTER.

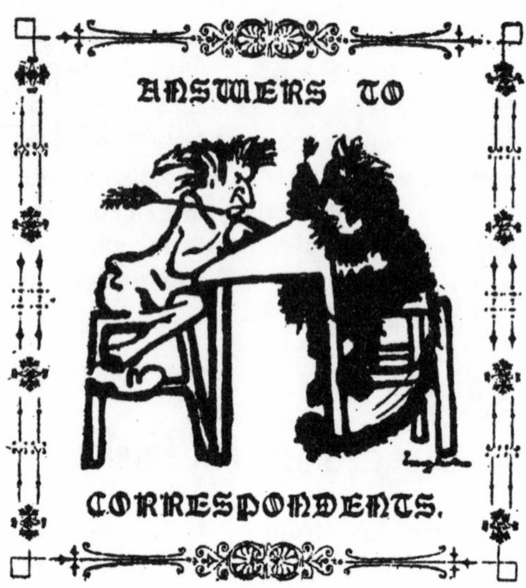
ANSWERS TO
CORRESPONDENTS.

TROUBLED, TOOTING BEC.—When you have filled up your sugar card truthfully and well, destroy it, and a new one will be issued next week.

—o—o—o—

ENQUIRER.—No. A policeman riding round the streets exhibiting a notice saying "Take Cover" is NOT encouraging your predatory instincts, but advising you to leg it for the nearest hole.

—o—o—o—

TOMMY.—Yes. If you hang your sock over the parapet on Xmas Eve you are likely to get something in it—or you—when you go to fetch it.

—o—o—o—

Owing to lack of space other answers to our numberless correspondents are unavoidably held over.

Will It Come Off?

—o—o—o—

HERE we have William Hohenzollern with a busted flush trying to choke off a crowd with a full house, and trying to do it "on tick" !!!

Remember the lads in the trenches!!

YOU want to give your brave defenders what THEY want!

YOU DON'T KNOW!

WE DO!

Let us send out a parcel for you. All you have to do is send us five, ten, or twenty shillings, and the name and address of your soldier boy—WE DO THE REST.

Our ten-shilling Xmas Box contains:

1 TIN COMPRESSED BEEF.
1 BOTTLE LIME JUICE.
1 PYJAMA CASE.
1 PAIR CARPET SLIPPERS.
1 UMBRELLA
1 TWO-POUND POT OF JAM (PLUM AND APPLE), AND
A NICE SOUVENIR FROM LONDON—A PIECE OF A.A. SHRAPNEL.

Messrs. SHORTONE & PASTUM.

MR. JERRY STICKET

BEGS TO ANNOUNCE THE OPENING OF A NEW COURSE OF LECTURES ON DEPORTMENT, etc.

—o—o—o—

HIS

First Lecture

WILL BE GIVEN ON

TUESDAY NEXT,

IN THE

Town Hall, Barnes.

—o—o—o—

SUBJECT:—

"HOW TO DO THE IMPOSSIBLE."

—o—o—o—

Fees for the Course of 6 Lectures 20frcs.
For each Lecture, 5frcs.

HAY & KEW,

AGENTS FOR TICKETS.

DANCING!!!

—o—o—o—

PROF. PORKY'S WEEKLY CLASSES.
COMPLETE MASTERY OF THE

HUNNY HUG

GUARANTEED IN TWO LESSONS.
LANCERS A SPECIALITY.

—o—o—o—

THE PROFESSOR WILL GIVE A PAS-SEUL EXPOSITION OF THE

Trench Tango

—o—o—o—

OTHER ITEMS WILL INCLUDE THE WELL-KNOWN DANSEUSE Signoretta

Aide C. Blochloë

IN HER INIMITABLE BACCHANALIAN REVEL.

—o—o—o—

ADMISSION:—The usual prices will be charged including war tax.

—o—o—o—

"If the FOX TROT you would learn,
Come and join our class at BURN."

—o—o—o—

Telephone: 69, JERRY

Printed and Published by
Sherwood, Forester & Co., Ltd.
B. E. F.

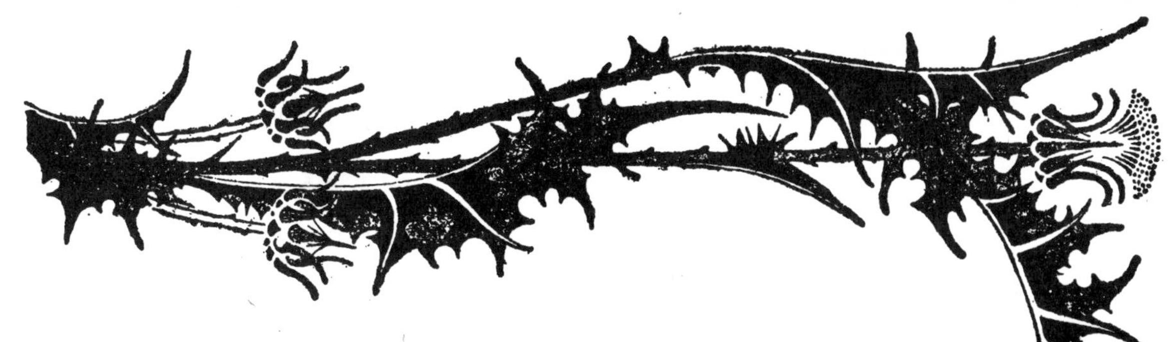

THE

B. E. F. TIMES.

WITH WHICH ARE INCORPORATED

The Wipers Times, The "New Church" Times, The Kemmel Times & The Somme-Times.

No 5. Vol. 2 Tuesday, January 22nd, 1918. Price 1 Franc.

CLOTH HALL, WIPERS

FOR ONE WEEK ONLY.

HERTLING AND CZERNIN,

FAMOUS BACK-CHAT COMEDIANS,

IN THEIR LITTLE SONG-SCENA, ENTITLED:—

"ALL THAT WE ASK IS A DOVE."

—o—o—o—o—

RORGE JOBEY

"I WAS WAITING IN A QUEUE AT KEW FOR CURIOS."

—o—o—o—o—

POSITIVELY THEIR LAST APPEARANCE.

"MARGER INE AND LEPINS" IN "THE DAYS' OF LONG AGO,"

A MOVING LITTLE TRAGEDY.

BOOK EARLY. PRICES AS USUAL.

THE OLD FIRM!

TWEN, TEFORTH AND CO.

Under Entirely New Management.

This Eminent Firm of General Merchants begs to announce to its Clients that, under the New Management, the following Additional Departments will be inaugurated :

THEATRE TICKET DEPARTMENT,
DANCING ACADEMY,
DAIRY DEPARTMENT and, a bit later,
FARMING AND SEEDS DEPARTMENTS.

—o—o—o—o—

" Like our friend, Sir Rosslyn Wemyss,
We are sound in all our schemyss."

—o—o—o—o—

We hope for the support which has been given so readily in the past, and every effort will be made to meet the wishes of clients.

Telephone, 20 lines : " 102, Museum."   Telegrams : " Hay and Kew."

GREAT SERIES OF LECTURES

WILL TAKE PLACE AT

"DEAD HUN FARM."

THE FOLLOWING HAVE PROMISED TO SPEAK :—

Sir SHETLAND STEDDES—Subject:
" What shall we do with our boys "

—o—o—o—o—

Mr. BARNES,
" The Labour-er- is worthy of his hire."

—o—o—o—o—

Mr. BENVER HAY,
" The blessings of Universal Peace."

—o—o—o—o—

Mrs. F. O. O. D. HUNTER,
On " Queues and their customs.'

—o—o—o—o—

NO SEATS RESERVED.

—o—o—o—o—

As there is likely to be a great demand for places, those who wish to hear these Lectures are advised to come early. Zero, 7.30 p.m. S.O.S , 10 p.m. Stretchers, 10 30 p.m.

THE B. E. F. TIMES.

WITH WHICH ARE INCORPORATED

The Wipers Times, The "New Church" Times
The Kemmel Times & The Somme-Times.

No 5. Vol. 2. Tuesday, January 22nd, 1918. Price 1 Franc.

EDITORIAL.

1918.

"SECONDS out of the Ring. Last round coming up." We have it on the best authority that William Hohenzollern has a little boat ready, with steam up, to cut it to Sweden. It came from the most reliable ration dump so naturally must be true. Up to now the luck has generally been with the Huns, but it looks as if it were going to leave them in the New Year. Anyway, we strongly advise Mr. Lloyd George and Sir Douglas Haig to get up and walk round their chairs three times. The sight of winter's white mantle always makes us feel poetic, but the thought of the future when the damned stuff melts restrains any rhapsodies on the subject. We have heard so many tales from Hunland about what he's going to do to us now that he has fixed Russia, that it makes us think he is trying to forget what WE are going to do to HIM. It is still our firm opinion that any Hun could be bought for a tin of bully and a slice of bread. Anyway, we feel inclined to get mixed up with the prophets Elijah, John the Baptist and Horatio Bottomley, and prophecy the general bust up of the Hun at no very remote date, say September next, provided all pull their weight. This proviso is necessary, and does not apply only to those not in khaki. So here's to 1918, a speedy finish and a job well done. Here's the best of luck to you all in the New Year, and a quiet thought and salutation to the memory of those stout lads who left us in the old.

THE EDITOR.

OUR DIARY.

—o—o—o—

By LIEUT. SAMUEL PEPYS.

—:o:—

THE Christmas festivities did pass off very well and with not too much hate, so that we were enabled to do full justice to the viands provided. Myself I did do much harm to the appearance of a roast goose, and next day did have the megrims of it. The soldiers did have an excellent repast. Anne writes to say that butter is up 6 pence the pound, so that I am afraid she will not get the new dress. We did have a game of hazard the other evening, and I was not in good trim losing several guineas to his Lordship of Ervilly who is of a most amazing fortune. It is a rumour that Mr. Jerry Sticket is giving a party at his country villa. I hope to go as these things intrigue me, and most of the quality are to be met there, but being near to the war one does not meet some people one does not want to meet. Yesterday I did meet the Vicountess of Villers in her chair, and was much taken with her, but the bloods did swarm round her that I got no more than a glance. Anne writes to say that she would like to come over—but I do not encourage her. We have much to do of the wiring, but the snow is a great hindrance and makes work much of a difficulty. To night I must take up a working party so that it will be late to bed—probably three of the morning. I must tell my man to leave out some rum.

A WINTER'S TALE.

—o—o—o—

(NOT SHAKESPEARE.)

—o—o—o—

There is an art, that does beguile our eyes,
When War's most hideous forms are all around,
I speak of that which we do now include
Inth' all-embracing term of 'Camouflage.'.
The poet sang, "things are not what they seem,"
In sooth 'tis so for men as trees appear,
And guns like nothing on this Earth; huts, tents,
And many other 'purtenance of War,
Are slashed with rainbow hues, and do outshine
The tiger's varied stripes, the leopard's spots.
The young aspiring sub. e'en learns, in schools,
How to deceive and trick the murd'rous Hun
With products of man's wit enough to 'maze
The Prince of all the Nether World, himself,
Who, eke a pastmaster, hath so appeared
A serpent, to our Eve in earliest days,
"A lion seeking whom he might devour,"
And other forms, as subtle, and more false.
And yet, man does but copy nature's task,
For she provides her brood with such deceits
The birds and beasts, the insects, in their haunts,
Like colouring do have, or do assume
Lest preying nature, "red in tooth and claw,"
Do extirpate the breed.
And Man, for his protection, hath applied
This art of Nature to the Art of War;
Perhaps he boasts his own transcendent power
And cries aloud. "I can myself surpass
These feats of Nature's might." Presumptious fool!
To thy vain boast, the skies an answer send,
Heaven's own perfect Camouflage of Snow.

C.W.T.

THOUGHTS.

I ain't no blooming Kipling, and I ne'er could be a Keats,
But I somehow sees a poem in whate'er I drinks and eats ;
When the night has fallen round me lovely verses seem to come,
As my thoughts in fancy linger on my evening tot of rum.

—o—o—o—

Oh! Naught in Heaven's pellucid heights
When shadows play in Very lights,
Can stem the fervent words which come
Whene'er the sergeant drinks our rum.

—o—o—o—

There's a poem in a biscuit, there's a poem in our tea,
In fact the blooming rations make a book of poetry ;
But to have the gift to find it and to understand it fully,
One must learn to look for Khayyam in a blooming tin of bully.

—o—o—o—

For all the wine you drink, the lips you press,
Will only land you in some blooming mess,
And fourteen days of F.P. No. 1 ;
But bully's bully, neither more or less.

—o—o—o—

You can have your blooming Shelley, Browning too, what did they know ?
They could only see a poem in the way the daisies grow ;
Had I got five francs to bet 'em then I'd very quickly risk it
That they couldn't find a poem in a blooming Army biscuit.

Hard is my lot, and hard is the world,
Hard are the shells day and night at us hurled,
Hard is the pavé, and hard is a stone,
But for hardness the biscuit's a class on its own.

S

TO THE AUTHORS OF Q 99065.

—o—o—o—

Brighter than tropic sunlight is the glare
Of the Brass Hats, of whom I speak ;
Redder than apples on the rustic cheek
Of winsome maidens, at the Country Fair,
The tabs and hat-bands, that these stalwarts wear ;
Rippling in wavelets, like some rapid creek ;
Or scented, smooth, immaculate and sleek,
The glossy beauty of their parted hair ;

—o—o—o—

Outrivalling the Cherry Blossom King,
Their boots, their belts, their buttons—everything
Most radiant. I dare not criticise
Their questions. And the foolscap query lies
Before my wondering gaze—I vainly strive
To answer their Q 99065.

C.L.P.

A Wail.

—o—o—o—

Life has many disappointments,
Days are never free from care,
For in spite of using ointments
Steadily I'm losing hair.

No gain to him, his labour unrequited,
His toil the sport of wind or wet or Hun;
No glory his in dredging or revetting
The sliding mud-banks of the danger zone.
He's met the wayward mind, the flights of fancy,
The change and chances of the battle plan,
And having gazed upon his work completed,
He's dug it up and done it all again.

—0—0—0—

He hunts the berm through tracts of devastation,
The wily A frame answers his demand,
His deftful fingers weave the concertina,
The giant elephant feeds from his hand,
The little ditto follows to his calling,
In apron wire he clothes the breastworks nude,
The everliving streams serve his direction;
He knows the standing slope of liquid mud.

—0—0—0—

He finds that duckboards can be used for firewood
He probes the mystery of the deepest sump,
And calculates to several points of figures
The daily fluctuations of his dump;
He soothes the corrugations of the iron,
Expanded metal bends to his behest;
He deals in wire both barbed and plain or binding,
You ask for what you want—he does the rest.

H.J.C.P.

THE PATRIOT.

—0—0—0—

THE other evening, as I was taking my usual walk before dinner by way of an appetizer, I saw someone off towards the Bosche lines digging in the ground. After a long and careful scrutiny it became evident that the man was alone, and from his bent shoulder and general air of weariness, I judged that he was old. Taking my six-shooter in one hand and courage in the other, I carefully stalked my prey and effected a capture. My joy was short-lived, for my man was a Tommy, old, and armed only with a spade. He had been digging holes in the ground, until that part of the field looked like a colander.

Now actions like these need explaining. The man was either exposing himself to a sniper's bullet in hope of ending all, or else there may be treason in this. Signals to aeroplanes or something.

On asking him what was his idea of digging shell holes in the fields so near the Bosche lines he said :—" Sir, it takes hundreds of men to get iron mined and treated. This iron is made into shells. These shells are then placed into costly guns or howitzers, and with the aid of a bag or two of cordite sent on the rest of their journey. All this costs money, two three or maybe five pounds a-piece, and the work of many people " The old man stopped and counted the holes he had dug eight in all. " You see, sir," he said, " I have saved my Government twenty to forty pounds, and if you had not interrupted me I would have saved it more, for that is all these shells are doing, digging holes, and I can do it cheaper."

I took the man's name and number, and reported the incident to the C.O. at mess that night. The poor old man was sent to Blighty by the Artillery M.O., who had heard the tale and diagnosed the case as " N.Y.D.—Mental."

But this winter, while you and I are out here in this country, in a little cottage in Yorkshire you might see our old friend with his people all about him, the fire burning brightly. In a corner there is a spade all cleaned and polished, and as the old man sees it there is a twinkle in his eye. While out here the Artillery M.O. is slowly writing on scraps of paper:" Mental—Query ? "

H. DAVIS.

D——
BY GILBERT FRANKAU.

[Being a plain statement of a disgusting crime wrought by the EDITOR of the "B.E.F. Times"; who ALTERED the last three lines of GILBERT FRANKAU's poem "Long Ago" in such a way as to make him appear guilty of writing false quantities.]

—o—o—o—

Waking, at noon, from nightmared slumber,
I found beside my bed,
Your special Christmas Double Number—
The which I duly read . . .
And wished that I were dead.

—o—o—o—

Since that there is within its pages
Which hurls my furious soul
From one rage into several rages;
And sends my self-control
Completely 'up the pole.'

—o—o—o—

So that I swear, with long black curses,
Never again to send
A single copy of my verses
To you . . . who ought to spend
Ten years in jail, my friend!

—o—o—o—

For you have had the nerve to "edit"
On some amazing plan,
The lines which GILBERT "dono dedit"—
And now, confound it, man,
Those lines don't even scan!

—o—o—o—

Had you forged cheques, committed arson,—
My clumsy Pioneer—
Rifled a church, or thrashed a parson,
Or—drunk on Belgian beer—
Sandbagged a Brigadier;

One might have found extenuation,
For these be minor crimes,
Compared with any alteration
Made by a "Wipers Times"
In GILBERT FRANKAU's rhymes:

—o—o—o—

For which black outrage, sin, and scandal
Do I here, publicly,
Brand you a metre-murdering Vandal,
And warn posterity:
"He dared to edit ME."

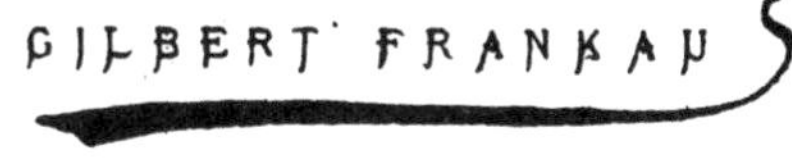
GILBERT FRANKAU

6/1/18.

IN JUSTIFICATION.

—o—o—o—

Dear GILBERT, once again we don—
To show our deep contrition—
Sackcloth and ashes. Hope is gone,
You hate our new rendition.

—:o:—

We know the fact we altered it
Calls for some explanation,
Although you're "nascitur non fit"
Yet we've a reputation.

—:o:—

The line we gently camouflaged
Presaged times alcoholic,
Right on our tend'rest corn you barged,
Our instincts are bucolic.

—:o:—

Nights wild and woolly you impute
To one, who seldom takes beer,
This imputation to refute
We'd "edit" WILLIAM SHAKESPEARE.

—:o:—

Yet now to calm a poet's soul—
And eke to get more "copy"—
We grovel in the ashes, coal,
And own our line WAS sloppy.

THE EDITOR.

MARTIALGIA.

—o—o—o—

THIS is a serious study. Let those who read be warned in time. If the flippant seek an effusion from an Expeditionary wag, let them call at Mr. TEECH BOMAS's next door; if the ribald desire an interview with a trench jester, let them consult Mr. PEPYS, two blocks further on.

This lecture treats of a new disease. Widespread as the world itself, it has affected all races, classes, creeds and colours. Nothing so common as Trench Feet, the delight of the Higher Command; nothing so limited as Shell Shock, the last endeavour of the unwilling. This disease is Martialgia, and after a two years sway, its characteristics are now recorded for the first time.

The incidence of the disease is mainly among males, between the ages of 17 and 45 years and it is extremely infectious at this period of life. A few women have been smitten with khaki fever. The existence of certain other ailments confer a certain amount of immunity; but instances have been reported at tribunals, where total blindness has been no bar to infection, and congenital idiots, the halt and the lame have all fallen victims to this disease.

The history of Martialgia is interesting. So far, the complaint has passed through three distinct epochs or epidemics; and it is expected that an Hibernian eruption will occur in the near future. In 1914 the first and most severe outbreak was recorded; and the symptoms then noted were a profuse discharge of martial fervour; whence the name, Martialgia.

In the second epidemic, which came to be known as Derby's Disease the pyrexia was not altogether of unknown origin, and the general symptoms were somewhat milder. The medical organisation for dealing with these cases was very effective, and patients were notified exactly when they were likely to become infected; and it was astonishing how many skilled munition-makers, who had regarded themselves as unlikely to catch the complaint, were admitted to the Recruiting Hospitals.

A noteworthy point about the third great epidemic, was the concurrent propagation of a new religion. In a medical thesis it would be out of place to touch on ecclesiastical subjects, more than to remark that its outstanding feature was hyperaesthesia of the conscience, associated with an affiction of the feet. At this period, all those who were smitten with Martialgia were speedily sent abroad on short sea voyages. And those who escaped the infection were isolated, and kept under observation in spacious and luxuriously appointed institutions, where baths and clean sheets were provided once a week; and hot water bottles were a nightly issue.

The symptomalology of the disease is varied. The majority of the patients—at any rate, in the early stage of the disease—have a sense of BIEN ÊTRE and are capable of performing prodigious tasks in the matter of laying duckboards and making roads. Later, however, they exhibit considerable malaise and some cases are fed up from the onset. A small number, of the plumbo-rotary type, become hypochondriacal and insist on constant medical attention, in spite of frequent M and D's. An occasional dose of the F.P. Mixture No. 1 has a marked effect in clearing up the introspective symptoms in these chronic cases.

As is the case with many other infectious fevers—typhoid and paratyphoid, variola and chicken pox, etc—there is a malignant and a benign form in Martialgia. The very large majority of cases fall in the first group and are further divided into sub groups, which are distinguished by initials, e.g. : R.A., R.E., P.B.I., etc. Each of these is subject to certain grave complications and dangers, and the mortality is extremely high.

The benign form is characterised by a roseolar eruption, which breaks out upon the forehead and clavicles. Sometimes the rash is green or blue, and the latter indicates an especially mild degree of infection. Such patients are robust and well nourished, and their mental state is one of exaltation, with a tendency to hilarity or boisterousness, which is not unnatural, as theie is practically no likelihood of a fatal termination to the benign or chromo-eruptive type of the disease.

The author is engaged on a more detailed article on Martialgia for the "B.M.J." and "Lancet," and those readers who are interested in the subject are referred to these medical journals for the further minutiae of the disease.

R.M.O.

Now William Hohenzollern, the King of all the Huns,
Had quite a lot of country and he also had six sons,
Of money too he'd plenty and a larder fully stocked—
In fact he'd all he wanted—so at grief and care he mocked.

Karl Baumberg lived in comfort with his frau and family,
His sons they numbered seven, and his daughters numbered three;
They'd just enough of everything and wished for nothing more,
(This happy time, you understand, was just before the war).

—0—0—0—

For reasons which they never knew Karl Baumberg's seven sons
Were quickly clad in suits of grey and labelled "food for guns,"
Two rot in mud near Wipers, and another at Verdun,
The Somme accounted for a brace, and Passchendaele for one.

—0—0—0—

The one remaining to old Karl is minus both his arms,
His fighting days are finished, and he's sick of war's alarms;
He grinds his teeth with fury, while old Karl hunts round for food,
And his mother freely curses both the Kaiser and his brood.

—0—0—0—

His one remaining sister (death has claimed the other two)
Out of water and a horse bone tries to make a dish of stew,
Comes a mandate "Our great Kaiser has another victory won
Fly your flags and cheer, by order, for the victory of Verdun."

—0—0—0—

Then old Karl, whose waking senses grasp a fact both strange and new,
That the victories are worthless if they bring no end in view,
And he curses Kaiser William who's the King of all the Huns,
But his frau is quietly sobbing for—the Kaiser has six sons.

A DAY IN REST.

—o—o—o—

All Officers will attend the Conference at the "Estaminet des Voyageurs" on the termination of operations.

—:o:—

DRAMATIS PERSONAE.

Director of Operations Major-General Baly.
Assistant of Operations Lieut. Col. Boil.
G.O.C. (Blue) — Brig. General Bone.
Umpire in Chief Lieut. Col. Bingham.
His Assistant — Captain Barris.
P.B.I.C.O. — Lieut.-Col. Bancock.
A Barmaid — — — Bessie.
A Bevy of Subalterns. — —

—:o:—

SCENE:

TAP-ROOM OF THE "ESTAMINET DES VOYAGEURS."

—:o:—

Opening Chorus of Subalterns.

—:o:—

We are weary, we are languid,
We are sore distressed,
What we want is not this rot, but
Beer and rest.

(Enter Bessie hurriedly.)

Bessie :—" Did you call, sirs ?

Bevy :—" Call? Good Lord, we shouted ! Bring buckets of beer."

(Exit Bessie coyly.)

Bevy :—" Ye Gods ! Some girl ! Thumbs up ! Bon for the troops ! I don't think ! I wonder ?"

(Enter red-hats and remainder of troupe Much tchunning and waving of arms.)

Baly :—" Good evening, gentlemen. Please sit down,"

Chorus :—" Good evening, sir."

Bone to Bancock (aside) —" Damned hot in here isn't it ? "

Bancock :—" Yes, I do feel rather thirsty."

(All seat themselves round the table.)

Baly :—" And now Col. Boil, will you read us the scheme ? "

Boil (blushing) begins :—" The enemy are retiring towards the Windyberg line, our troops are in hot pursuit. The Nth Division, full of enthusiasm and - —

(Enter Bessie bringing buckets.)

Baly, Boil and Bingham (in astonishment :—" Beer ? "

Bone and Bancock :—" A - - - h ! ! ! "

(Bevy giggle guiltily.)

Baly (badly baffled) :—" What is this ? "

Bessie (beaming) :—" Five francs please, sir."

Bingham (sternly) :—" Who ordered these ? " (indicating buckets.)

Bessie (bewildered, pointing at Barris) :—" I think it was 'im, sir ! "

Barris (blushing badly) :—" Please, sir, it wasn't me."

Bone : — " Your blushes belie you."

Barris :—" But really, sir, —"

Baly :—" Enough, that will do" (turning to Bessie) " we are busy here and have no time for these interruptions."

(Exit Bessie, looking daggers at Barris.)

Boil :— ' I forget where I'd got to."

Baly (looking at his watch and interrupting) :—" Oh ! Never mind, I think we all know the scheme, and it's getting late" (turning to Bancock) " Colonel Bancock, will you tell us what your dispositions were for the attack ? "

(Bancock gives the details required, and subsides with a sigh—Bone and Bingham voice their opinions in turn)

Baly :—" Has anyone else any remarks to make ? " (Turning to Barris) " You, for instance, as assistant umpire."

Barris (again blushing) :—" I ! Oh ! Ah ! Um ! I met a Staff Major from G.H Q. the other night, and he told me he thought the scheme was a good one."

Baly (coldly) :—" Most interesting, but hardly has any bearing on to-day's operations ! "

(Barris collapses.)

Baly (continuing) :— ' Well, gentleman, since we have all—— "

(Enter Bessie, wildly excited.)

Bessie (shrieking) :—" Oh ! Save us ! The Hun planes are here ! "

Boil (blanching) :—" Where ? Where?"

Bessie :—" Oh ! Everywhere. Can't somebody do something ? "

Chorus of Subalterns (in which Bone joins) :—" Rather ! "

(Bone hastily seizes Bessie, and commences stroking her hair.)

Bessie : — " Oh, sir ! I feel better now."

(Bombs are now heard bursting. Bancook bolts the beer, and the conference breaks up in confusion, leaving Bone master of the situation.)

K.R.

—o—

Life in the Army, you must know
Is hedged about with Regulation,
And I suppose it must be so
Although it causes much vexation;
We have to mind each P and Q
So that our conduct shall not jar,
But always be conforming to
K.R.

—o—o—o—

This volume we must know off pat,
With all its manifold restrictions
Of para this and para that,
Not wholly free from contradictions;
Each separate ruling we must note,
For all good soldiers always are
At any time prepared to quote
K.R.

—o—o—o—

It deals with every sort of case,
A most complete encyclopedia;
Its rules for every time and place
The soldier man may always read here;
Thus it will readily be seen
Why no excuses ever are
Accepted, when we contravene
K.R.

—o—o—o—

The powers who sit enthroned on high
Maintaining splendid isolation,
Draft an occasional A.C.I.
And publish it for information;
Yet is our Bible and our Creed,
Our Lodestone, and our Guiding Star
On which we model every deed
K.R.

—o—o—o—

O shades of Authors past and gone
Whose works we read with admiration,
Inspiring those who labour on
To toil of keenest emulation,
O peerless Lore, and priceless Myth,
Careers in Arms you'll sternly mar,
If they're not in accordance with
K.R.

MINOR KEY.

Another Wail.

—o—o—o—

Oh Mr. Cox! Oh Mr. Cox!
My heart you've nearly broken,
By telling me I'm on the rocks.
In words most harshly spoken.

—§ † §—

You say that I have overdrawn
A sum quite awe-inspiring,
If that were all I would not mourn,
Nor would I be perspiring.

—§ † §—

But to these awful words you add
A legend disconcerting,
In large black print, which makes me sad,
My tender feelings hurting.

—§ † §—

Your envelope, in words of fire,
Inscribed, "Buy War Bonds NOW!"
My dear old Cox just send a wire
And tell me, tell me, HOW?

BILL SHAKESPEARE.

It's a simple competition and hilariously funny,
Anyone can guess the Hidden Word, so pay your entrance money.
The terms are very easy and the prizes are unique.
You gather in the coupons—you can get one every week,
By sending ten and sixpence for a dozen weeks or so,
Then arrange the dozen coupons to spell out a word you know.
The prizes, seven in number, comprise some dainty things,
Each to bachelor or benedict unbounded pleasure brings,
They're quite unlike those ragged things of flannel thick or fine,
Your servant washes once a week and hangs upon the line,
That stretches from your dug-out to the Sergeant Major's door;
So send your ten and sixpence, boys, and then, a dozen more.
You mustn't wear the prize yourself, except perhaps on Sundays,
For think, they're seven boxes of Penn's dear delightful undies.

WHAT MIGHT HAVE BEEN.

—o—o—o—

THERE has been so much talk about poets produced by the War that I have lately given much thought to another side of the picture, and have wondered what would have happened if the War had coincided with several well-known poets. The following are a few of my deductions.

We will begin with Mr. W. Shakespeare, a poet who had a reputation, and flourished about the time of Queen Elizabeth. One can imagine him sitting in his dug-out near Hell-Fire Corner and writing thus :—

SCENE :—ESTAMINET AT DICKEBUSCH.

(ENTER TWO TOMMIES.)

TOMMY.—" Beer, mamselle, compree, what ? "

WAITRESS.—" Nutting doin'."

ATKINS.—" Narpoo ! Owell then get some old vang blang ! "

WAITRESS.—" No got it, m'sieur, you 'ave some vin rouge."

TOMMY.—" Alrite Bill, promenay out of this place,
We'll click at Café Belge for beer and cheese ;
This 'staminet's a dud. Alley—tout sweet ! "

ATKINS.—" Righto ! Cheero mamselle. Apree le guer ? "

(EXIT TOMMIES.)

Of course this is only a short example but space is limited.

Next we will take Craig, a poet who had a vogue in Surrey. The influence of War would have been felt by him thus :—

The Middlesex boys then took the field,
All full of knowing tricks ;
The blighted Hun he would not yield,
So they hit him for six.

Then take Browning, perhaps he might have felt the atmosphere thus :—

Teach me dearest Sergeant,
Don't look glum.
You may eat my bully,
Drink my rum.

—:o:—

Meet if you but ask it
Both desires,
Join a working party,
Put up wires.

—:o:—

And, where'er we be, dear,
Do fatigues ;
I am on F.P., dear,
Leagues and leagues.

Then again take a poet who had a reputation in Scotland, whether for poetry or some other vice is obscure. He naturally would have figured a Highlander in kilts. (I am not going to guarantee the spelling):—

O, Thamas is a wee puir body,
Thamas is a leear,
He draigl't a' his wee bit kilt,
Coming thro' the wire.

—:o:—

Gin a body meet our Thamas,
Thamas he can swear,
For he's draigl't a' his kilties
Coming thro' the wear.

This is easy, as you only have to alter the spelling of the word to make it fit. I could go on a long time, but this is the last page to be filled, and the Staff is waiting.

OUR SPLENDID NEW SERIAL.

—o—o—o—

ZERO!

OR

"THE BOUND OF THE BASKERSHIRES."

—o—o—o—

ANOTHER HERLOCK SHOMES EPISODE.

—o—o—o—

CHARACTERS :—

Maj. General Wilfred Montmorency Duggout — A General.
Maj Horace Malcolm Charles Frigiped Bassy — A Staff Officer.
Andrews — — His Chauffeur.
Anastasia Doubloy —An Estaminet Girl.
Marguerite – Waitress in a Restaurant.
Randolph Wunpip — — A Subaltern
Capt. Martell — A Coy Commander
Herlock Shomes — The Great Detective
Capt. Hotsam, R A M C.—His Admirer
Sergt. Sniffins — — Provost Sergeant

W.A.A.C. and soldiers will be intro duced as necessary

—o—o—o—

CHAPTER 2.

—o—

SOBS continued to shake the being of Anastasia. and so we will leave her and return to our friend Shomes.

On reaching his dug-out he dropped into a chair, and seizing his vermoral sprayer injected a good dose into his leg. Then picking up his banjo he began to play in an odd, disjointed manner. Suddenly the gas curtain was pulled aside and Hotsam entered. Throwing himself down on the bed he grabbed a tin of bully and a biscuit, and grunted —" Stop that damned row."

" My dear Hotsam," ejaculated Shomes. " You are unnerved. Music is absolutely essential for my brain, and I have a difficult problem on hand."

At the word problem Hotsam dropped the bully on the floor, and was immediately all attention.

" The case has some very interesting features, and I expect developments in a moment. In fact, I shouldn't be surprised if they are here now. You know my methods? Who is it we can hear coming up the duckboards ? "

Hotsam listened a moment, and said, "A runner."

" Wrong, my dear fellow," said Shomes. " Your powers of deduction are not very strong. It is a Staff Officer in a hurry. Heard him say, ' Which is the way to the line? Are they shelling ? ' And then when he fell off the duckboard he said, 'Bother.' " "Wonderful, Shomes." said Hotsam.

At that moment the gas curtain was violently wrenched aside, and a Staff Officer entered hastily. " Gad but the Hun is lively to-night " was his greeting, as he took a seat and a drink.

" Well," said Shomes. " What can I do for you ? "

" Have you got a drying room and a soup kitchen ?" said the Staff Officer.

" No," said Shomes.

" Then all is lost, and the murderer will get away undetected."

" Murderer," said Shomes. " What murderer ? "

" Come," said the Staff Officer and started off at a run.

Rapidly grasping the vermoral sprayer Shomes followed, accompanied by Hotsam. Shells fell rapidly some miles away, yet still they sped on in the opposite direction until they came to the estaminet at Dickebusch. Bursting open the door they rushed in

Anastasia was there rocking herself to and fro. Sobs shook her being.

WHY?

(Read next thrilling instalment.)

(To be Continued.)

Correspondence.

To the Editor,
"B.E.F. Times."

Sir,

The other day during my journey from London to here on returning from leave, I gave the matter considerable thought. The following are a few of the suggestions I should like to put forward. Whether it would not be shorter and more comfortable to go via New York, San Francisco, Japan, Brindisi and Genoa. Also why only allow eight persons in a compartment, surely twelve could get in. Of course we can have no quarrel with the arrangement that anyone who has been travelling in the "Train de Luxe" (better known as the "Flying Scotchman") for five or six days, is unable to get a drink, as it's always after hours when the train arrives anywhere. This is quite right, as it might lead to undue hilarity, and prevent the pessimism necessary to thoroughly enjoy the journey.

I am, Sir,
Yours, etc.,
VOYAGEUR.

—o—o—o—

To the Editor,
"B.E.F. Times."

Sir,

The other day while waiting in a beer queue at the "Foresters Arms," I noticed many who were certainly not fit to wait perhaps hours in the cold. It is a scandal that these poor weaklings should be allowed to run the risk of trench feet just for a spot of beer. Surely something can be done to stop it, as often I have to wait a long time before getting any beer, and sometimes it is finished before I can get my elbow on the counter. I appeal to you to use your influence to get something done in the matter.

Yours Faithfully,
A. SAPPER.

A Few Things We Really Want to Know.

—o—o—o—

Having heard so much of what "Labour" will allow the Army to do—whether it isn't time we heard what the Army will allow Labour to do?

? ? ?

Whether it wouldn't be beneficial if many people—including Labour leaders—followed Mr. LLOYD GEORGE'S lead, and read the "Wipers Times"?

? ? ?

Whether it might not give them a sense of proportion?

? ? ?

How much it would take to buy Turkey, lock, stock and barrel, at the present moment?

? ? ?

Whether the largely advertised Hun offensive hasn't put the wind up the Huns themselves more than anyone else? (With perhaps one exception.)

? ? ?

Whether the masses at home are not making an imaginary condition of food shortage themselves?

? ? ?

And why on earth they WANT margarine? (It's filthy stuff!)

ANSWERS TO
CORRESPONDENTS.

Owing to lack of space, answers to our numberless correspondents are unavoidably held over.

NO TRENCH COMPLETE WITHOUT ONE.

—o—o—o—

OUR NEW PATENT DEVICE.

"Kamooflage"

GUARANTEED TO BAFFLE THE ENEMY

—o—o—o—

Buy one and try.

—o—o—o—

A GRATEFUL CUSTOMER WRITES:—"Sometime ago I bought one of your "Kamooflages" for my trench. This has been so successful that the Huns have mistaken it for a Staff College, and refrained from shooting at it. My nights are now undisturbed You may use this as you like.—THREE PIPS."

—o—o—o—

Send for one at once.

—o—o—o—

Kamooflage & Co,

WYMEROO.

CAN YOU SKETCH?

—o—o—o—

Sketching is the latest fad of the Army, and many are coining millions out of their dud productions,

WHY DON'T YOU?

Copy any well-known picture in the National Gallery and send it along to me. (The copy not the picture, as you might get nabbed) I'll then tell you how bad it is. If it's hopeless I shall recommend one of my 100 guinea courses (payment in advance), after which I'll guarantee to get you taken up by "The Stybander." Also you might write a play

—o—o—o—

Write in all cases to

John Cassell's Art Academy,

LONDON

Telegraphic Address—"Perhaps."

DO YOU LIKE BALLOONING?

—o—o—o—

IF SO WRITE TO

"SAUSAGE," FRANCE,

AND ALL ARRANGEMENTS WILL BE MADE.

—o—o—o—

THIS FIRM IS FAMOUS FOR THE RAPIDITY OF ITS DESCENTS.

—o—o—o—

PARACHUTING A SPECIALITY.

—o—o—o—

SPLENDID SCENERY AND VIEW OF WAR TAKING PLACE IN THE DISTRICT.

o—o—o—

MOTOR TRIPS ARRANGED.

—o—o—o—

"In this awful pitch and toss age,
Don't omit to try a sausage."

—o—o—o—

Charges Moderate.

Can You Wait?

—o—o—o—

IF NOT, WHAT IS THE GOOD OF YOUR JOINING UP IN A QUEUE?

—o—o—o—

We Give Instructions.

—o—o—o—

5 GUINEA COURSE OF 6 LESSONS AFTER WHICH WE GUARANTEE YOU WILL BE ABLE TO WAIT ANYWHERE.

ALSO THERE'S A CHANCE OF "WAITING" TILL THE WAR'S OVER. THUS AVOIDING INQUISITIVE TRIBUNALS.

—o—o—o—

"If you're single and A 1,
Come and learn to wait, my son."

—o—o—o—

WRITE:—

Cuthbert & Slacker,

ENGLAND.

Printed and Published by
Sherwood, Forester & Co., Ltd.
B. E. F.

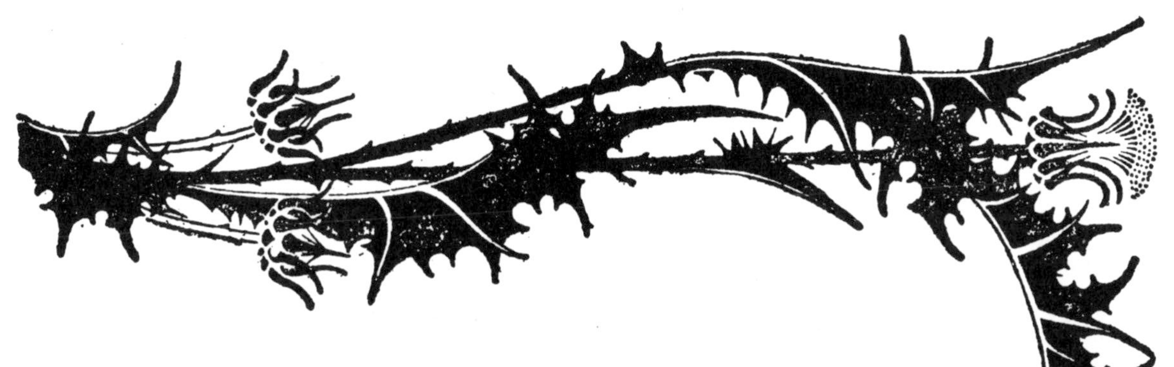

THE B. E. F. TIMES.

WITH WHICH ARE INCORPORATED

The Wipers Times, The "New Church" Times, The Kemmel Times & The Somme-Times.

No 6. Vol. 2. Tuesday, February 26th, 1918. Price 1 Franc.

CLOTH HALL, WIPERS.

THIS WEEK.

"RONDER"

THE CELEBRATED CARD MANIPULATOR AND ILLUSIONIST.
HAS PERFORMED BEFORE MOST OF THE CROWNED HEADS OF EUROPE.
"MEET FOR THE MILLION."

All Tricks will bear the closest scrutiny.

—o—o—o—o—

"THE WILLIES."

IN THEIR SONG SCENA,

"WE'LL PUT THE WIND UP IN THE WEST."

—o—o—o—o—

GEORGE LLOYD

AND MANY OTHER ATTRACTIONS.

—o—o—o—o—

BOOK EARLY. PRICES AS USUAL.

WHY??? LET THE HUNS WIN THE WAR AFTER THE WAR?

THEY ARE PREPARING BY MEANS OF A TRENCH UNIVERSITY. ALL RANKS CAN TAKE POST-GRADUATE COURSES, AND KEEP THEIR BRAINS ACTIVE, IN FACT,

THEY Are acquiring useful knowledge while,
YOU are only studying C.R.O., and similar periodicals. WHAT YOU WANT—and must have—is your own series of lectures.

—o—o—o—o—

TO THIS END——**US.**

—o—o—o—o—

MARCH 3rd.—" SHELLS. What they are. Their uses. How to find them. Having found them, how to use the field dressing, etc , etc."
By Professor W. I. Z. BANGS, R.A., etc.

MARCH 10th.—" ALCOHOL AND ITS TERRIBLE RAVAGES. With particular reference to the wicked issue of rum to the troops "
By Professor T. T. BILGE, H 2 O.
(THIS IS EXPECTED TO BE A VERY POPULAR LECTURE, AND TO AVOID DISAPPOINTMENT YOU SHOULD BOOK EARLY,)

MARCH 17th.—" THE GREAT WAR ; and how we won it every year until the Germans had no more reserves left."
By Professor HILLARY BULLOCK.

MARCH 24th.—" THE GERMAN AT HOME. His culture. Kindly Nature. Chivalry. Is he one of Nature's gentlemen ? Etc., etc."
By Professor RAMESES SNOWDEN.

—o—o—o—o—

THE ANGLO-AMERICAN UNIVERSITY EXTENSION LECTURE SYNDICATE, ACTIVE SERVICE BRANCH.

Secretary : S. U. M. NUTT. Telegrams : " WATAHOPE, B.E.F."

DO NOT READ THIS!!!

UNLESS YOU HAVE A GIRL AT HOME.

—o—o—o—o—

If you have, of course, you want to send her a souvenir. WE can supply just the tasty little thing you want Thousands to choose from :—

GERMAN SHOULDER STRAPS : 1/- each — — 10/- a dozen
DITTO, BLOODSTAINED : 1/6 each — — 15/ a dozen
SHELL HOLES, COMPLETE : 50/- each
DUCKBOARDS—ENGLISH : 5/- each
DITTO GERMAN : 10/- each
IRON CROSSES : 6d. a gross.

OUR SPECIALITY : BULLETS CAREFULLY FIXED IN BIBLES (FOR MAIDEN AUNTS) PHOTOGRAPHS (FOR FIANCEES.)

—o—o—o—o—

" To please your best girl, it is clear,
You must procure a souvenir."

—o—o—o—o—

SOUVENIR MANUFACTURING COMPANY, CAMBRAI.

THE B. E. F. TIMES.

WITH WHICH ARE INCORPORATED

The Wipers Times, The "New Church" Times, The Kemmel Times & The Somme-Times.

No 6. Vol. 2. Tuesday, February 26th, 1918. Price 1 Franc.

EDITORIAL.

WE almost feel inclined to commence our yearly song of Spring in this number, but remembering past seasons we refrain, and bottle it all up until our next, or next but one, number. The cognoscenti are using the warm spell to get some ploughing done, and there should be a reasonable chance that we are not the "spudless army" in the Summer. Anyway, we have got our farming experts detailed, and they are at present sorting the seed so that we run no risk of planting carrots upside down. The war seems to present the usual items of interest, and the Hun has rung his bell and blown his horn, since when he appears to have adopted the "you hit me first" attitude. Nations at war are very like individuals in a temper, but the Hun very much reminds one of a small boy with half-a-brick in his hand, and a large window near by. He'd love to do it if he could only be sure of getting away. We note many fresh innovations since our last number. Those who were soldiers before a certain date are getting a medal, others are getting more pay, and all are getting chevrons. How we've managed to sleep at night without chevrons all this time is one of the astounding features of the war. As a Tommy remarked when preparing to go over the top, "If only I'd got me bloomin' chevrings I'd die 'appy." Re the lesser but still interesting point of money, it is gratifying to see that the guileless sub will be able to adopt a more arrogant manner when talking to Mr. Cox. Our own feelings on the subject are rather mixed as we seem to be left out in the cold. However, we can at least draw pictures of how nice it would have been if we'd had all that money when we were subs. To paraphrise an old classic:

When we were subs,
When we were subs,
When we were subs together;
We drew but seven-and-six a day,
When we were subs together.

How ver, let the dead past bury its dead, Mr. Cox can afford to forgive and forget. Yet can we forget the furtive approach, the pleading eye and the plaintive request for a small overdraft, "only another tenner, I'm going over to-morrow." However, it is nice to have a lot of young Rothschilds for subs, and we elders can at least think we are mixing with "money." We are grateful for "copy" sent by newcomers to the Division, and extend them a welcome in real Oliver Twist style.

THE EDITOR.

THE BATTLE OF OXFORD STREET

BY "WOOLF."

Dear Germans list while I tell the tale
Of the awful battle in Oxford Street,
When the pavement shook, and the shops turned pale,
In the blood-bespatted—Oxford Street.

The crowds of people in fury fought,
For weapons they used all the food they'd bought;
Though the starving children of food went short,
Through the fearful battle of Oxford Street.

Mr. Selfridge fought with a leg of ham,
In the fearful battle of Oxford Street;
Snellgrove "stopped" a large pot of jam,
In the horrible battle of Oxford Street.
And a shock of fury rent the Heavens',
When Marshall walloped poor J. H. Evans
With a leg of mutton. All sixes and sevens
Were they in the battle of Oxford Street.

They fetched some Scotchmen from "Sheper Bush."
To quell the disturbance in Oxford Street;
And into the fight they did them push,
On that terrible day in Oxford Street.
Yet the Scotchmen straight from their mountains wild
In the "bush of Sheper," were not beguiled
To shoot. So in "Bailey" their arms are piled,
Through that awful battle in Oxford Street.

Now, my dear little Huns just believe my tale,
Of this ghastly battle in Oxford Street;
And in future for food and peace don't wail,
Remember the horrors of Oxford Street.
And if you're hungry and tired of war,
Remember that William has food galore,
And a nice soft job, so think twice before,
You fight like they did in Oxford Street.

OUR DIARY.

—o—o—o—

By Lieut. SAMUEL PEPYS.

—:o:—

THIS week there has been much of rumour but, as always, rumour is not of a reliability. They do say that the Hun will come at us in numbers. I do not believe it though at times his foolishness is unbelievable. I did go to a concert the other night and was much intrigued. We do hear of some high play at "C's." and of many guineas changing hands, in fact, it is said that young Prior has ruined himself, and that the house of Cox is in a very bad way thereby. Anne writes to say that she did fall in behind a lot of people for to buy sugar, and did wait five hours, then to find she was not in the right place, being indeed in some sort of singing hall. I did take the coach with some others yesterday, amongst them his Lordship of Argicore and the young heir of Temploo—we did go to A——. A most enjoyable day and the young females did show to much advantage. Anne presses me to come over here, but I think it not good for her to adventure it at this time with many strange engines of war in the seas. I did let her buy a new dress which was unfortunate, as now her Ladyship of Bulham has one of a later mode. There is much of the dancing now, in fact, it has become the fashion, and the quality is to be seen stepping it most nights at the club. In fact, it is rumoured that the G— himself did trip a measure, and his Lordship from the Highlands is a nightly adventurer. To-night I must take a party for the revetting so early to bed. My new man is of a poor intelligence, the dinner was bad, and the rum bottle had met with a misadventure on the way, so think I have the megrums.

What matter though the wily Hun
With bomb, and gas and many a gun
In futile fury, lashes out,
Don't wonder what it's all about—
"Stick it."

—o—o—o—

When soaked in mud, half dead with cold,
You curse that you're a soldier bold;
Don't heave your "A" frame through the night,
And, though it's wanted, travel light—
"Stick it."

—o—o—o—

Although it always seems your fate
To join a working party, mate,
Don't curse the sergeant, 'taint his show,
The work's to do, just grin and so—
"Stick it."

—o—o—o—

Though Belgium beer seems poor and thin,
And leaks the billet you are in;
When you are resting, some parade
Busts all the lovely plans you've made—
"Stick it."

—o—o—o—

Though shelled by day and bombed at night,
A shirt, though lively, dry, delight
When half-way there, you think your back
Must break, you're thirsty, grub you lack—
"Stick it."

—o—o—o—

As someone said, there's no road yet
But had an end, your grinders set
On this one thing, that if you grin
And carry on, we're sure to win—
"Stick it."

Time was when we knew what that infinite joy meant
The magic word "Leave" could inspire;
It was rest from our labours and change of employment,
It was all that the heart could desire.
How in "otium cum dignitate" we'd revel!
What freedom from sorrow and strife!
Our cares and our worries consigned to the Devil
'Twas life.

—o—o—o—

Having greeted our friends with a joyful emotion.
Like lovers who've plighted their troth.
We would give ourselves up with unfettered devotion
To Bacchus or Venus; or both;
We would bask as the ultimate Lords of Creation
In glances from maidens divine,
Or if in the mood we might pour a libation
Of wine.

—o—o—o—

We would lunch at the Club on the choicest of victuals
Set out in a tempting array,
Our life for the moment all beer and skittles,
With nothing to mar the display:
To our favourite tea-shop we'd certainly toddle
Forgetful of bullets and guns,
Entertaining fair damsels with intimate twaddle
And buns.

—o—o—o—

We would dine at the Berkeley, or Carlton, or Prince's,
Regaled upon wonderful fare,
With the zest the true Sybarite always evinces
On a menu selected with care;
Then a stall we would occupy, 'phoned up in haste for,
At the Gaiety, Lyric or New,
Or the Empire or Hippodrome if we've a taste for
Revue.

—o—o—o—

But alas! These good times are now finally ended,
'Tis Gilead without any balm
(I trust that the Censor will not be offended
And think I am spreading alarm),
At every turn there's some warlike injunction,
And now they are using the tanks
To squat in the squares of our cities, and function
As banks.

—o—o—o—

All food is controlled, and is eaten by order,
In rations minutely assigned:
The direst of penalties visit the hoarder;
He's imprisoned and heavily fined;
The food queues have tales which meander and wander
For miles where there's food to be had,
Defying all orders and driving Lord Rhondda
Quite mad.

—o—o—o—

If sugar is needed to sweeten existence
A card we must bear on our way,
Which states the amount that's required for subsistence—
One ounce and one seventh per day:
The gold of the Indies can purchase no butter,
No tea finds its way to the cup;
When we go to the butcher's we find that the shutter
Is up.

—o—o—o—

O then if we sigh with a ling'ring affection
For halcyon days that are gone.
If perchance we should pause for a moment's reflection
As time passes speedily on,
Don't imagine our thoughts of the pleasures departed
Can make us look glum or feel blue;
We still roar when the question comes.
"Are we downhearted?"
"Na Poo!"

MINOR KEY.

STAR-SPANGLED.

—o—o—o—

My Dear Mike.—

In my last letter I made a bum statement that this war must have been over before I dipped a hoof in this mud. You know these fellows were always telling me how cushy this front was, compared with some of the stuff they were up against before, so I doped it out that the show was off. But nix, the atmosphere is sultry with hunks of iron, and, at times, if you stick your dome out of your sleeping hole you will sure collect a wallop on your bean which is bad for the constitution. To alleviate the chances of this catastrophy they thatch us with a tin lid, which we fasten on our top-knobs with a strap under the food-grinder. I don't know whether this "coping" will stop Fritz's bouquets or not, but without it on, you sure feel the need of a good, active, paid-up, life insurance policy. I know they don't always stop them for these lads have an unpleasant habit of putting a perforated lid on the last bivouac of a Tommy, which same habit makes you resolve to let your hair grow longer for the added protection. Also, to proceed with the catalogue of innovations hatched by this row, let me give you a squint at our chest-protector. No, they are not made of red flannel to keep your chest warm as you might think, you wear them outside, belayed to your manly chest, and sticking out in front like a vestibule. I don't know what is in them, but at the start of a hike they are as light as airy nothing, but after pounding the itinerary for an hour or so, you take a look—see if some guy didn't slip a few hundred rounds of ·303 into it for transportation. Now wipe your eyeglasses and try to get my drift. This thing-a-my-bob is dope for the air like the chlorine is for the water. Some poet, I think it was Bill Shakespeare, said that "the air was free for man." Nix, not so, over here Fritz squirts stuff into the ozone which don't improve it none, a few whiffs and you are a gone gosling You know, like the skunks do in the States, only worse. Well, when Fritz starts his perfumery going, you start to count, and at each count you do something, only I forget what you do, but, anyhow, you wind up with your mug in a bag, and you suck on something like a nursing bottle, like when you was a little kid, only you don't get any milk. All the machine does is to unstick the air from Fritz's addition to it Oh yes, I just mentioned chlorine a while back. I will tell you about that. This outfit, over here, isn't on the water-wagon like our Army is, these lads can get beer and things, they buy them you know. Well, some bright guy thought that if the water was doctored up a bit, well, maybe more beer would be bought. Do you get me? Say, I got to cut out talking like that or the censor man will find another gob of ink to fresco my letter with again, and while I like the attention drawn, illustrations of a dark room at midnight don't add anything to the sense of the letter. Just one more word, when you come across you will cast your optics on some officers who stand very straight, and others who have the side elevation of a ? mark Don't slip a cog on the last guys like I did, they are not punk soldiers. These lads have been out in front and have bumped their brain-boxes often enough on the roof out here to make them curl up a bit. Well, kid, the hour is getting late, and while my Ingersoll bracelet has gone the way of all good time-meters I know it is time to hit the hay.

H. DAVIS.

Although you think you've had less rest than any other div.
In this, or any, army—ever had
And, taking over, draw the bow,
By this and that you try to show,
You've run the war for three long years
Come cheer up sonny, dry those tears—
You've not.

Though you have battled everywhere, and had most fearful loss;
Your div. is minus one, or less than that.
You say you've lost your thousands, but
Your figures you will find "all phut:"
Your pictured dream aside is tossed,
You talk of thousands you have lost—
You've not.

Although you think you do more work than any other div.
And criticise the crowd that you relieve;
Just weigh things up and you will see,
That all are treated equally.
You think that you, and you alone
Have made secure the line we own—
You've not.

The moral that I wish to point is not unkindly meant,
Though p'raps the point till now has been obscure;
Don't think that others get the cake
While you the roughest always take;
Remember when you so compare,
'Tis of YOUR team you're talking air—
So hot.

[We must apologise for this column, and know our readers will forgive us, as it was written by our T.O. Its presence in the paper is due to the interference of war with the liberty of the press.—ED.]

—o—o—o—

Little Tom Buffet,
Thought he would snuff it
When hit on the chest with a shell;
The shell was a dud-un
So all of a sudden
He rose and is now doing well.

—§ † §—

Ride a crocked horse
To Mobile, of course,
And see the old vet. standing there at a loss;
It may have big side-bones,
A splint or a sprain,
It's a ten to one shot if you see him again.

—§ † §—

Tommy found a little Hun,
With whom he had a tussle;
He fixed his bayonet on his gun,
And stuck it in his bussle.

—§ † §—

Bah, bah, Quarter, have you any rum?
Yes sir, yes sir, come! come! come!
A jar for the transport.
A jar for the Coy's
The rest is for the Q.M.
And all his merry boys.

—§ † §—

Dickory, dickory, dock,
I've had a terrible shock;
For a bit of a spree,
Fourteen days—F.P.,
Dickory, dickory, dock.

THE REVERSE.

—o—o—o—

HAVING seen in our last number what might have been the result had some of the old poets lived in these days, let us now see how delightful it would be if these same poets could influence the everyday language of war.

—:o:—

Take for instance a Tommy with a duckboard and a knowledge of Shakespeare. We can imagine him walking up the Menin Road and discoursing thus :—

TOMMY :

To be or not to be? That is the question.
Here's nature moulded by the hand of man,
To be a burden borne by his own fellow,
And placed again—a weight on nature's breast
To bear in turn he who had once it borne,
Thus ease his path to slay, or maim or take.
And yet methinks I'm wasting time, for here
Comes one whose voice has power to move the limbs
Of loit'rers.

SERG. : Nah then! Hop it quick or else,
You'll find some F.P. waiting you me lad.

TOMMY :

Oh! Soft-blown zephyrs flavoured well with rum,
Waft o'er me when I see the sergeant come.

(MOVES ON.)

—:o:—

Or again; take Zero hour and see the platoon officer throwing this off his chest :—

Awake! For see the barrage lifts at last,
Take up your bombs. For us the die is cast
Come all together, top the parapet,
This moment holds the present, future, past.
No time to waste, to think, or wonder how
A hasty shot, a hurried dig and thou,
Wilt either fix the Hun or he'll fix you,
And that is for the one who's fixed enow.

—:o:—

Or again imagine a Staff Officer with a fat job and love of Browning saying, as his car splashed you from head to foot with Belgium's Best :—

Take it, only take it,
  Where you will ;
I will go on foot, or
  Better still.

—o—o—o—

Jump in here beside me
  And just say,
Where you want to go to
  And you may.

—o—o—o—

We, if you desire it
  Will proceed
For a trip to Amiens,
  And a feed.

—o—o—o—

You may have the car, dear,
  Don't mind me.
I am but a red-hat,
  Don't you see.

—:o:—

Again! Take a sergeant with a raucous voice, and passion for Ella Wheeler Wilcox, and you might get something like this :—

Time flies. The swift hours hurry by,
You've yet to do your fatigew ;
No job of yours to reason why,
There ain't enough for me and you
Of this 'ere rum, So 'taint no good
Of cutting it in two.
And so I'll drink the lot—narpooed ;
The tin's for you.

—:o:—

If this principle was adopted throughout the Army it would make things much easier for us all, and take the rough edges off life in the trenches.

HEART TO HEART TALKS.

—o—o—o—

THE AREA COMMANDANT —ILLY AND THE TOWN MAJOR —IGNY.

—:o:—

A. C.—" Hullo—is that the Town Major."

T. M. (cursing beneath his breath) —" That fellow again! Yes, what can I do for you, old chap?"

A. C.—" I have just rung up to enquire if you have any accommodation left over there as— "

T. M.—" Accommodation! I have nothing to do with accommodation, It isn't my job."

A. C —" Wait a bit, old fellow. I was going to say that a coloured labour company has turned up here, and they're sitting about in the road waiting to be shown to their billlets. I havn't got any billets for them. Can you do anything?"

T. M.—" You know perfectly well the trouble I had to put up that stray Artillery Major last night, There isn't a ble sed rabbit hutch left here! And you talk to me about Labour Companies!"

A. C. (desperately).—" Well, what about those four empty Nissen huts, I saw over at your place this morning. They're not occupied "?

T. M.—" We've strict orders from Corps about those huts. They were built three months ago for a Cavalry Squadron of Engineers, and were to be kept until the owners turned up."

A. C.—' Well they haven't turned up —and these fellows must go somewhere."

T. M.—"My dear man—it simply can't be done. I should get hell about it. I might even lose my job."

A. C.—" And if I can't find room for these people I might lose mine. You don't seem to realize that. What about the Theatre? Is there anyone in there?"

T. M.—" It's full of stray cavalry officers looking for their units. You seem infernally anxious to saddle me with this damn Labour Campany. What about your Recreation Room, and that Adrian Hut you're so busy with just now. Can't you stow them away there for one night?"

A. C.—" I might conceivably put some of the men in the Recreation Hut even then there are four officers to be considered. Can you let me have any tents?"

T. M.—" No, afraid not! Three padres arrived this afternoon and collared my three remaining tents. I have a lot of canvases but no poles or pegs."

A. C.—" Curse! I have plenty of poles but no pegs. I really do think your sergeant, or whoever the idiot is who runs your show might at least see that he has complete tents and not bits of them."

T. M.—" Well if it comes to that, I think the corporal who bosses you might occasionally look at his accommodation map That Adrian hut—"

A. C.—" Is being built for a battalion mess. How do you suppose I could let a coloured labour people go trampling down the lawns, and hedges and things all round it. Besides half the B.E.F. arrives in motor cars every morning to inspect it. Where should I be then."

T M —' Well, I suggest that you give up temporarily one or two of the Nissen huts you occupy yourself. That'll still leave you a mess, a bedroom, a bathroom, study, reading room and a library, won't it?"

A C. (indignantly).—" That's an absolutely, unjustifiable insinuation, and your own nest wasn't feathered I remember without a fair amount of claim-jumping."

T. M.—" If you can't be more polite, I shall break off the conversation. I've done my level best to help you, and this is all the thanks—"

A. C.—" I shall write to Division about the lack of co-operation between Town Majors and Area Commandants, and say I think it desirable that the former's scope of duties should be much more limited."

Both together.—" Thanks, very much. Good bye "

The fate of the 756th Native Labour Company is left to the reader's vivid imagination.

AS OF OLD.

—o—o—o—

THEN the Lord of the King's hosts did summon his captains, and did say unto them :—" The King's enemies are ever against us, hiding in divers holes in the ground, and the King has commanded saying—' Go hence and bring ye me these evil men, and those ye cannot bring, slay ye, that mine enemies may cease from troubling me.' Therefore, send ye men to spy out the land, and, when all things are ready, we will smite them hip and thigh, so that their hearts may be turned into water, and of their dwellings we will not leave one pit prop upon another." So it came to pass that a patrol was sent out, and when they had spied out the land, they returned and told where the enemy was lying, and how one might come on him. And, at the appointed time, the captains of the King did summon the soldiers, and said unto them : " The enemies of the King lie over against ye—go then out therefore and smite them hip and thigh." And the soldiers answered and said, " Ubet ; we will give the —— —— ——"* And one of the King's officers—even the Kewem himself—prepared a feast for the soldiers, and much rhum, and they partook of it. And their hearts were made glad within them, and they cried, " where are the mangy blighters?" And, when the time came, all the King's archers let loose their arrows, and the catapult men, and the slingers did cast their stones, so that the air was thick with them, and the moon was darkened. And the soldiers did cross the Terra Nomanis, and did come unto the country where abode the enemies of the King, even the Boshites. And some they cast their boms at, and others did they smite with their weapons. And there was weeping and gnashing of teeth among the Boshites. And the soldiers went to the holes wherein the men were hid, and said, " come out of that you —— ——."* And when they did not come, they destroyed their dwellings about them. And when they had slain all the Boshites, they returned and brought with them much booty. And the King was glad in his heart, and said : ' Give unto the soldiers much rhum, and on the morrow I will send them to a land flowing with milk and honey where they may sojourn for the space of twenty-four hours. And they did, and the fame of the King's men was spread through all the land, even unto the dwelling-place of the King of the Boshites, and his heart was heavy within him.

Translators Note :—Unfortunately the manuscript is here illegible.

C———S JUNCTION.

—:o:—

C———s, where the Railway torturously twists,
I liken to some caravanserai ;
The Leave trains, crawling in, at break of day,
To caravans, approaching through the mists ;
One, with its load of lively optimists,
Laughing and joking, homeward-bound and gay ;
The other, bearing, on its weary way,
Its morbid freight of mournful pessimists.

—o—o—o—

And, as they wait for their respective trains,
Wayfarers from the line meet men from Blighty—
The gloomy one describes a vanished leave
And its delights. The other racks his brains
For ghastly tales of Hun offensives mighty,
To put the wind up poor old brother Steve !

C. L. P.

WHY NOT?

—o—o—o—

In war, as in many other things, there is so much that might be improved, and so many little inconveniences which might be done away with, if there were a better understanding on both sides. Take shelling for instance. Supposing a book of rules were drawn up by representatives of both parties, senders and receivers, something after this style,

1.—No shelling will take place between the hours of 11 p m., and 7 a.m.

2.—Parties wishing to shell will notify their opponents of tne exact hour and place to be shelled by sending over a dud T.M. at a stipulated spot with a note inside.

3.—Any sheller sending his obus into any H.Q. or dug-out will forfeit two turns.

4.—A shellee on being struck by his opponent will immediately retire from the contest.

5.—A sheller pulling or slicing outside the notified area will be disqualified.

6.—The winner of the contest will be the side obtaining the greatest number of hits in the notified area.

7.—Unlimited whisky to be supplied at the 19th hole by the losing side..

Then take raids. The freedom and haphazard methods employed by the modern raider should be curtailed in common fairness to the other side, and the following code would perhaps meet a few of the requirements.

1.—A large gong will be placed in a convenient place in "No Man's Land." This will be sounded half-an-hour before Zero, at the same time signalling by the number of beats which zone the raid will be carried out in.

2.—Gas must not be used until the reasons for the failure are being discussed.

3.—Anyone throwing a bomb down a dug-out, without sounding his horn, will will lose stroke and distance, and must go back and start again.

4.—A. party rushing wilfully into its own barrage will be instantly disqualified.

5.—Barbed wire must be treated as a hazard.

One might also formulate a few rules of etiquette to be observed in raids such as:

1.—Machine guns to be considered an unsporting article of defense, and a side found using them to be sent to Coventry.

2.—It is not considered good form to regale oneself in the other side's dug-outs unless your presence there is enforced.

The foregoing ideas are only rough and could be elaborated as desired. Any suggested codes from our readers on other spheres of warfare would be welcomed by us, and put before the proper authorities for necessary action.

IN A RECENTLY-VACATED HUN DUG-OUT (APRIL 1917.)

—o—o—o—

Oft have I scorned you; tapped you on my boot;
Reviled your bitterness; complained with ire
Your lack of name; wished that a worthy sire
Had fathered you, that you had been the fruit
Of Mr Dunbill's toil, A fickle brute
Am I, for now, I miss you and desire,
Only to see the sacred, scented fire,
Glow in your bowl, dear, juicy briar root.

—o—o—o—

These lines, I write, in pentametric measure,
'Midst German relics, loot and food and drink,
Arms and tobacco, bottles labelled Munich—
I spurn the lot, the only thing, I treasure,
Has been forgotten, left behind, I think,
Safe, in the pocket of my other tunic.

C. L. P.

OUR SPLENDID NEW SERIAL

—o—o—o—

ZERO!

OR

"THE BOUND OF THE BASKERSHIRES."

—o—o—o—

ANOTHER HERLOCK SHOMES EPISODE.

—o—o—o—

CHARACTERS :—

Maj.-General Wilfred Montmorency Duggout — A General.
Maj. Horace Malcolm Charles Frigiped Bassy — A Staff Officer
Andrews — — His Chauffeur.
Anastasia Doubloy —An Estaminet Girl
Marguerite — Waitress in a Restaurant.
Randolph Wunpip — — A Subaltern.
Capt. Martell — A Coy. Commander.
Herlock Shomes — The Great Detective
Capt. Hotsam, R.A.M.C —His Admirer
Sergt. Sniffins — — Provost Sergeant
W.A.A.C. and soldiers will be introduced as necessary.

—o—o—o—

CHAPTER 3.

—o—

WHILST the tragic scene described in our last chapter was being enacted, a gay throng was assembled at Headquarters, many leagues away, where a ball was in progress The orchestra had just struck up the opening bars of the next dance, a can-can ; asthmatic majors were picking their partners from the bevy of sweet and blushing young subalterns ; the drinkers were drinking noisily and swiftly at the bar ; the General was telling a few anecdotes to a small but admiring circle of his more intimate cronies ; when suddenly a perspiring and mud-bespatted dispatch-rider dashed into the room and handed to the General an envelope marked "URGENT. SECRET." Quickly tearing open the cover the General read the message, emitted a low groan, and turned a ghastly white. Seeing the agitated demeanour of their chief, the musicians, dancers and drinkers ceased their various occupations and crowded round the General. "Grave news, my friends" he cried. "Terrible news, listen," and holding the fateful message before him he read out. in a quaking and quivering voice, the following dreadful words : —"Capt Martell has been foully murdered in vicinity of front line AAA Am tracking down murderer with Shomes and Hotsam AAA Please send assistance to me at once to the Estaminet Dickebusch AAA Bassy AAA" Before the General had finished reading the last sentence the room had quickly, quietly and completely emptied, with but one exception, and shouts of "damn you that's my mess-cart," "leave my horse alone," "no, there's no more room in this car," were heard issuing from the darkness without. The General looked up and found that the only other occupant of the room was no other than Sec.-Lieut. Randolph Wunpip, V.C. (3 bars), D.S O. (5 bars), M.C., etc , etc., of the famous Baskershire Regt. "My good Wunpip," commenced the General "Say no more, sir." answered the gallant young officer, "I will go to Dickebusch." "My brave fellow, I will see that your action does not go unrewarded. Outside you will find my car. Take it and begone! Only do not forget your steel helmet, 120 rounds of ammunition and your iron ration Good-luck and God-speed," and the General's voice shook with emotion After two hours rapid driving Wunpip was in Dickebusch. Leaping from the car he thrust open the door of the estaminet where a strange scene met his astonished gaze. Upon the floor surrounded by many rum-jars, lay Bassy, insensible. Beside him knelt Hotsam vainly endeavouring to bring him too by pouring the contents of Shomes's vermoral sprayer down his throat. Shomes was standing before a mirror blacking his face with a piece of burnt cork. And Anastasia, poor Anastasia, was sitting on the floor, slowly rocking herself to and fro Sobs shook her being.

WHY?

(Read next thrilling instalment.)

(To be Continued.)

Correspondence.

To the Editor,
"B.E.F. Times."

Sir,

May I use your valuable space to urge on the authorities the necessity of doing something to stop the nightly disturbances. It is most annoying to the citizens of this peaceful village to have missiles, which explode with a loud detonation, thrown at them during the night hours. If nothing else can be done, surely four sausages could be hoisted holding, one at each corner, a large sheet. This would screen the moon if hoisted high enough, and thus deprive the night-hooligans of the required light to steer by. Surely, it should not be necessary for a peaceful citizen to point out methods to those highly-paid experts who are in authority.—I am, sir,

Yours faithfully,
"INDIGNANS."

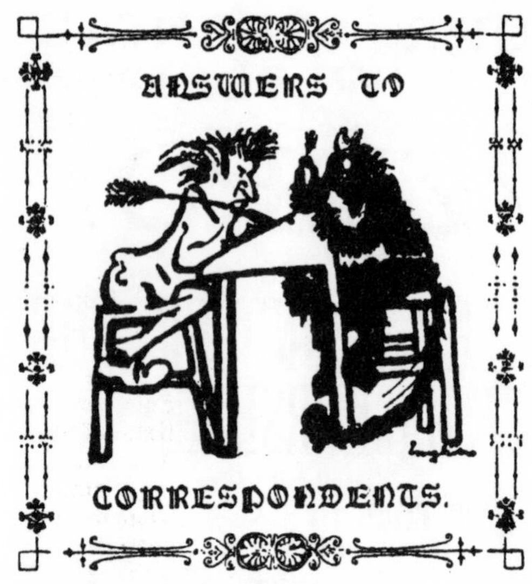
ANSWERS TO
CORRESPONDENTS.

JOHNNY SAVPA.—No.

Owing to pressure on our space, answers to our other correspondents are unavoidably held over.

MAMMOTH NEW "WHIZZ-BANG" COMPETITION.

CAN YOU READ THIS WELL-KNOWN PROVERB ?

L - - K B - F - R - Y - - L - - P

A PRIZE of 1,000,000 francs will be given for the first correct solution of the above.

In the event of no correct solution being received, a SPECIAL CONSOLATION PRIZE of 500,000 francs for the nearest attempt.

Subject to the following simple conditions :—

1.—The Editor's decision to be final.
2.—All attempts to be accompanied by a five-franc note.
3.—The prize will not be awarded unless there are at least a million competitors.

SUBS, WHAT DO YOU DO WITH YOUR MONEY?

—o—o—o—

BUY NATIONAL WAR BONDS!

—o—o—o—

Now that all Subalterns get about a million pounds a year, save for the future. Don't throw it away on leave, Amiens, and other fleeting pleasures.

—o—o—o—

SAVE FOR AFTER THE WAR.

—o—o—o—

Give a Standing Order to Your Bankers.

Do you value your manly beauty.

—o—o—o—

Prepare for the war after the war.

—o—o—o—

BLUSHING TAUGHT IN THREE LESSONS.

Don't soil your hands by throwing bombs, or soil your face with trench mud.

We supply all possible aids to manly perfecton, and preventatives for soiled skins.

Our patent bomb-tongs are in great demand. No more broken nails.

TRY OUR FAKEDULA FACE CREAM.

One application will fix any skin.

TRY IT ON YOUR MULES.

—o—o—o—

Royal Pinolia Coy.

HAZEBROUCK.

" HURRAH," they cry, as the quarter-master appears in the front line with the rations. " He's brought us some Kerona Kerona's to-night."

The glad cry is always heard from our brave lads at the front when they see " THE ONLY CIGAR."

—o—o—o—

Sold in two sizes and qualities.

THE BANGALORE 2000frcs. per box of 10
THE PITPROP — 4000frcs. per box of 10

—o—o—o—

" If you find they do not pull,
Never mind; they're Windigul."

—o—o—o—

THE "CABAJO" CIGAR CO.,

LONDON.

"SOMEWHERE ON SERVICE."

—o—o—o—

" DEAR AUNT.—

I have a shirt but no soap. Will you send me some, but please let it be Tights as the little darlings love it so.—Your loving nephew,

TOM."

This is only one letter selected at random from millions All our lads " somewhere on service" speak in glowing terms of " the finest soap in the world."

SEND THEM SOME.

—o—o—o—

TIGHTS OLD CAR SOAP.

—o—o—o—

COLLECT THE WRAPPERS AND WIN A PRIZE.

Printed and Published by
Sherwood, Forester & Co., Ltd.
B. E. F.

THE "BETTER TIMES."

WITH WHICH ARE INCORPORATED

The Wipers Times, The "New Church" Times,

The Kemmel Times, The Somme-Times,

& The B.E.F. Times.

No. 1. Vol. 1. November, 1918. Price 1 Franc.

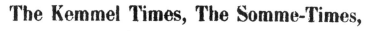

EUROPEAN THEATRE OF VARIETIES.

THIS WEEK AND TILL FURTHER NOTICE.

Professor FOCH & his Performing DOVE.

Signor Pleni Potentiario

WILL SING

"THE ONLY WAY"

AND

"THE END OF A PERFECT DAY."

WILLEM VAN HOHENZOLLERN

IN

"MY OLD DUTCH."

Book Early Prices as Usual.

Safe From Air Raids.

Paxone Boots.

The Footwear that gives PEACE to the Foot.

—o—o—o—

There is an ARMY OF OCCUPATION and an ARMY OF NO OCCUPATION.

MODEL 67, Frs. 42·40.

—o—o—o—

WHICHEVER ONE YOU'RE IN YOU NEED GOOD

RELIABLE MARCHING BOOTS.

NISSEN HUTS FOR SALE.

—o—o—o—

AS MOST OF THE BEST CAMPS ARE NOW CLOSED DOWN, WE ARE SELLING OFF NISSEN HUTS CHEAP.

—o—o—o—

COOL IN SUMMER!
COOLER IN WINTER!!

—o—o—o—

Medium Size—Frs. 450; with door Frs. 44 extra; with windows Frs. 58 extra. Three Special DRAUGHTPROOF Models, exceptionally rare—Frs. 920.

ADVERTISING PAYS.

—o—o—o—

Don't hide your light under a bushel. If you've got anything to say about yourself or

YOUR

WARES, COUGH IT UP!

BUT YOU NEED THE RIGHT MEDIUM.

"THE BETTER TIMES"

is read by all Englishmen in khaki, so send your ads. to us.

—o—o—o—

On the first glance you thought this was advertising a cough cure, but it isn't,

IT'S JUST TOUTING FOR "COPY."

PRUDENCE DICTATES that Insurance is a sound scheme.

—o—o—o—

OUR POLICIES MEET ALL CASES.

EXAMPLE:—A man 47 years old wants an annuity of 100 pounds payable when he becomes 93. All he has to do is to pay 19 pounds every six months until he becomes entitled to the Annuity.

EXAMPLE:—A man condemned to death wants to insure his life for 700 pounds. All he has to do is to pay 950 pounds in two instalments of 300 and 650. Write stating requirements to the

PRUDENCE ASSURANCE Co.,

Box 77. c/o "The Better Times."

THE

"BETTER TIMES."

WITH WHICH ARE INCORPORATED

The Wipers Times, The "New Church" Times, The Kemmel Times, The Somme-Times, & The B.E.F. Times.

No. 1. Vol. 1. November, 1918. Price 1 Franc.

EDITORIAL.

"ICI NOUS sommes encore!" As French that is probably rotten, but we have just found a complete outfit and are naturally jubilant that we can carry out our threat of carrying on a paper till the Hun is down and out. The old staff has rallied round us (with many regrettable vacancies), and Mr. Teech Bomas will retain his appointment at his previous enormous salary. Some new members have been enrolled, and we hope to receive the support accorded to the predecessors of the *Better Times*. With the present publication we are going to make an effort to reproduce illustrations As they will be hand engraved on wood-block, will intending artists please stick to line efforts. Our new paper is born in very different circumstances to the old *Wipers Times*, and it is strange that we should get our new outfit during an advance over the same country in which the old one was lost last March. We are the gainers by the exchange, as the new one is a much finer machine. Yet the old one held many memories for us, and we did not enthuse over losing it. Within four days of capturing the town where we found the new press we brought out an evening paper called the *Avesnes Advertiser*, although the Hun had done his best to prevent any effort at journalism by shifting all the type to his melting-station and filling the office with gas. However all the type is now in process of sorting, and we have a fine selection. The war itself needs no comment, and a few more efforts should bust the Hun completely. Anyway it seems pretty certain that everyone is out to finish the job properly, which is all very satisfactory. We hope that budding journalists will not wait to be asked to send along copy. Our letter box is open day and night, and the same fabulous rates will be paid for stuff used namely—copies of the paper.

The Editor.

"THE ORDERLY ROOM OF OTHER TIMES" SERIES.

—o—o—o—

NO. 1.—

THE SHAKESPEAREAN.

—:o:—

(Roberto, the C.O., discovered seated in a tent on the Plains of Burgundy. Gracio, his adjutant, is also present.)

Roberto.—Good Gracio, armed with parchment Army forms
To puzzle learned heads, and calm the storms
Brewed in the stewpot of stupidity,
Pray tell me if there any henchmen be
Who've broken Rules and Laws laid down by me
Sinning by Sloth or by Cupidity?

(There is a fanfare of trumpets without ; why? Lordie knows, but it's just Shakespearean.)

Gracio.—Roberto, Lord and Master. of the band
Of stalwarts fighting in this foreign land
For Rights of Little Nations,
There is indeed a scurvy henchman here
Who for his crime should pay a price as dear . . . . . .

Roberto.— . . . I'll make the computation!

(Gracio withdraws, reappearing presently followed by Stoutfellow, the Sergeant of the Troop, who drags with him Gohello, a scurvy poltroon with rusty bucklings, and unkempt mien.)

Sergeant.—O Sire! This knave 3945 Gohello
A lazy lout and illdisposed fellow,
Was still abed when all should be astir,
And snoring loud to wake the morning air
With sowlike trumpetings!

Roberto.—Ha, ha, poltroon, and hast thou aught to say
The falling hand of Justice now to stay?

(Gohello shakes his head)

Admitted then! So nothing now remains
Except to purge, to punish him with pains.

(Turns to Gohello)

Now and henceforth until thy day of death,
Each dreary morn until thy final breath,
Thou shalt arise before the first cock crows
Morn after morn until your Last Repose—
For Ever!

Gracio.—Take him hence, Stoutfellow. He has swooned.

(Exit Stoutfellow carrying Gohello.)

(Roberto sits on a tree-stump, picks up an alarm-clock and soliloquises.)

Roberto.—To rise or not to rise;
That is the question.
Whether 'tis nobler in the mind of man
To rise and watch the sun first climb the skies,
Or, (when thy varlet comes to waken thee) to turn
And grab that precious extra minute's sleep
So risk a spell of F.P. No. 1, ...
That is the question!

(Meditatively bites off a chunk of Cable Twist.)

Uneasy lies the head that wears a crown
But he who sleeps in crowns is e'en a clown;
A band of gold and jewels is all right
But only fools would wear them thro' the night;
Aye, there's the rub!

O.T

Should you happen choice to have
Would you be a Jugo-Slav?
Or, a disappointed cove, acknowledge you're a Czecho-Slovak!
Would you if you'd not a groat
Care to own yourself a Croat?
Fain would I be any one
Than to own myself a Hun!

A CLEVER WAR INVENTION.

—:o:—

THE PICKERING PATENT SHOVEL.

—:o:—

The acceptance of this remarkable invention shows how ready the Ministry of Munitions is to realise the value and ability of "something new."

The Pickering Patent Shovel is in reality the ordinary G.S. shovel with certain useful additions, ones, however, which make it *the* shovel par excellence for active service.

In the first place, there is a piece of emery paper 3 inches wide, wrapped round the handle 1 inch from the blade of the shovel. This is the Sharpener Plate, and is intended for section commanders to sharpen their pencils on, so that they can keep their section rolls up-to-date and a readable document.

On the back of the blade of the shovel is engraved a calendar for the year to enable N.C.O's and men to tell the date, and how long they will have to wait for leave.

Cleverly encased in the handle is a scraper to enable the user to scrape the mud off the calendar side of the shovel.

This scraper is also a tooth-pick (one end)—nail file (the other end.)

The weight of the whole ingenious device is only 15lbs. 3oz. heavier than the old G.S. shovel.

Mr. Pickering strangely enough is not a member of the Forces, but has a brother who is in a famous Labour Battalion now in France.

Mr. Pickering's hobbies, when he can spare a few moments from his laboratories and worksbops, are rat-catching (at which he is no mean performer), and cigarette-card collecting. He is only 5 short of the whole set of "Forest Flowers" which is to be found in that well-known brand of cigarettes—the "Aromatic Algy's."

War is full of quaint surprises,
Huns are never free from guile,
All the world—full of surmises
Watches William with a smile.

THE STUDENT'S CORNER.

(To be equipped for war is one thing; to be equipped for peace is another. When peace comes many new fields will be opened up, and for this reason a knowledge of languages will become almost an essential. Realising this, *The Better Times* has arranged to re-print in each issue a lesson from Hugo—Ivebeenovitch's "Russic Simplified," by arrangement with M. Ivebeenovitch. This is the first of the Lessons, and if at the end of 3 lessons you cannot vamp, your money will be refunded.)

LESSON 1.

ALPHABET:—The Alphabet is so simple that it needs no comment. There are only 94 characters, 96 of which are different. The chief difficulty lies in recognising the difference between [illegible] and [illegible]. The latter however is only used when following [illegible] which implies that the [illegible] is not to be sounded with the gutteral [illegible].

GRAMMAR.—This is very similar to English, inasmuch as all the monied people do not use it very much. Only poets, clergymen, and tutors use it, and therefore it is of little account.

FIRST CONVERSATION.

[illegible]—The parrot says.

[illegible]—The hussar talks to the parrot.

[illegible]§—Why? How? Who?

[illegible]—Is the brother of the hussar talking?

[illegible]—No, he is with the parrot of the Ambassador.

[illegible]—The Russic language is very simple.

[illegible]—The language of the parrot is like the Russic.

[illegible]—Only when he is angry.

[illegible]—The parrot of the hussar uses bad language to the aunt of the Ambassador.

[illegible]§—Why? (equiv: what for why, eh?)

[illegible]—Because it has to talk Russic in the garden of the aunt of the hussar

The day will come when even Mars is tired,
When obus slumber and no shot is fired,
When unashamed we'll don our bowler hats
And men shall dress complete, yea down to spats,
Then "what about it" you who find it hard
To hear unfettered comment from the bard.

—:o:—

The stars on this poetic sleeve are three,
That they're as many is *bonne chance* for me
Numbers there are who starred and likewise crowned,
Do tread the grateful and subservient ground
Some who by prowess lately proved in war,
May sport red 'tabs' and ribboned breasts galore.

—:o:—

When back returns the poise of other days,
When we shall tread the old, civilian ways,
Maybe we'll find that other honours count
Besides the ones with warfare for their fount
This bard may rise ere Phoebus rents the dark,.
To do the bidding of his whilem clerk!

—:o:—

Then may our colonels, yea, and majors too
Toil, while full privates tell them what to do
And subalterns shall see with glad surprise,
"Staff-wallers" working 'neath their watchful eyes.
Then may we hear, with withers quite unwrung,
"Promotion comes not only to the young."

—:o:—

All men shall reckon, when reigns commonsense,
That crowns and stars don't mean omniscience.
That somehow there are lots of things in life
Quite as important as the battle's strife
Consider, bard, the men you thus contemn,
How shall we e'er gain peace—except through them?

FAME: A TRUE STORY.

—o—o—o—

It was sometime in 1915 on a cold and windy day. Every now and again one of the few remaining walls in Ypres would collapse with a crash and a cloud of dust, sufficiently realistic to make the most hardened dweller in that delectable city jump a little.

Several of the party, which stood in little groups round the Menin Gate, were obviously ill at ease, either from a mistaken idea as to the origin of the noise and dust or because they knew that no one but a fool or an ignoramus stood by the Menin Gate any longer than could be avoided.

It was an imposing party of Brass-Hats and mingling with them one or two civilians, who looked particularly out of place in such warworn and desolate surroundings.

Presently one or two cave dwellers emerged from their quaint dwellings under the Ramparts, attracted by the unwonted sight of such a glittering throng, and marvelling at the temerity of the gilded ones in selecting such a particularly unhealthy spot at which to stand and talk.

One of them, braver than the others, approached, not without some diffidence, an A.D.C. who, wiser than the rest, was sheltering against the possible storm behind a corner of the Ramparts. "'Oos 'e?" he remarked, pointing over his shoulder to a tall commanding figure in khaki, wearing the gold embroidered hat of a general. "That's Lord Kitchener" replied the A.D.C.

The cave dweller whistled softly in petrified astonishment, and as he turned to give his pal the news remarked in a hoarse whisper: "Gawd strewth, ain't he like the cigarette cards!"

J.C.

Canada! Queen of the Western Snows,
Your fighters are peerless the journalist shows,
Though you kings and their kingdoms may shake
Leave us ah! leave us just *one* town to take.

THE CHRONICLES OF IZAWIT, THE SCRIBE.

—o—o—o—

AND it came to pass in the fifth year of the Great War that the Hosts of Attila were sore distressed, for the Avenging Hosts did draw nigh unto and press them hard.

And there came forth from the enemy certain who sought speech of the Commander of the Hosts, that he might stay the conflict.

And behold on the eleventh day of the eleventh month, even at the eleventh hour there fell a calm upon the land.

And being exceeding weary I fell asleep and dreamed, and in my dream the Commander of the Avenging Hosts did order his Armies by Companies, each one to go unto his own place.

Then went forward certain chosen men for to spy out the land and seek resting places for the mighty men of valour in the region unto which their faces are set!

And in my dream I saw that certain of the spies did draw nigh to the Gates of the Celestial City, and there did seek admittance of one Peter, the Mayjur of that Town. "Alas!" replied he, "I have not in my town so much room, no, not even as to swing a cat. For behold yesterday when it was even and I tarried with my friend the Artoco, a multitude of the tribe of Kew did arrive, strange men of ancient and venerable appearance and gross about the body, bearing with them much booty and stores of war, and speaking a strange tongue whereof the last words do appear to be the first. These did overcome my scribe and are even now in all my mansions great and small, and their booty doth cover the streets and courtyards. I have sent messengers in haste unto Korque, but methinks he tarrys by the way."

Then did I see the spies turn away exceeding sorrowful and betake themselves unto the Nether Regions.

Now in the Nether Regions there was Chaos such as there was not, no, not even in Gaul in the Great War in the month Mars; for Beelzebub, Prince of this Region had been so long absent serving his Imperial Master, that in that Region no Town Mayjur like unto Peter was to be found, those from Gaul not yet being come, for the chariots did overflow by reason of the multitude of the Artocoes and Ackpipemmas and their myrmidons who sought passage thither.

And many mansions did I see but each was taken—yea! and those of the most magnificent proportions—each was taken by a Kewem and at that I did not marvel, knowing these people and their habits.

But also did I see how the spies did wander throughout the length and breadth of the land seeking mansions and finding no room—no, not even for a single Bra-Sat, for behold on the lintel of every mansion and upon the gateways wherein beasts of burden were tethered there appeared a small papyrus whereon was inscribed:—

RESERVED FOR
THE SHERWOOD FORESTERS.

MORAL.—It's a wise unit that knows its own billeting area.

SOME HAVE FAME THRUST UPON THEM.

—o—o—o—

'Twas a sentry young on a lonely post
And he scanned the earth and sky,
When he was aware of a red tabbed throng
Which came a-trotting by.

—o—o—o—

Now the leading wight was a general old,
And the rest, some far, some nigh,
Came panting on in the deuce of a sweat;
The sentry wondered why.

—o—o—o—

But the general stopped and he spake these words,
"So you watch the earth and sky!
Do you know that the fate of an empire hangs
On just *your* watchful eye"

—o—o—o—

'Twas a grubby fist that the general grasped
"You'll be proud lad by and bye,
That you shook my hand on a summers day;
Your Corps Commander *I*.

—o—o—o—

When the sentry left to his lonely post,
He winked at the earth and sky,
Far off in the trenches a mile away,
Faint streaks of red flashed by.

EDITORIAL.

(Continued.)

OWING to the lapse of time between the beginning and end of setting up this number (a lapse which was unavoidable owing to the way Fritz hit the trail for the homeland) it has become necessary to add a few words, hence—*this*. Since writing and printing the Editorial page Fritz has turned it up, and our swords are going to be made into ploughshares or something of the sort. It seems a pity as the back end of the war was the best part we have struck so far, and we only had two months of it compared with three years of the muddy end of the stick. However everyone is heartily glad the ghastly affair is well over, and the future alone will show if there will ever be another number of this paper. The Editor and Sub-Editor send their congratulations to all members of the Division, particularly to the few who are original members and have followed the Division through all its vicissitudes. For those who are not with us, but lie in France and Belgium, our reverence and love be with them and they will never be forgotten. From September 14 to November '18 is a long span, and the old Division has seen many changes, luckily few for the worse. We are going to make an effort to keep the paper going till Peace is signed, sealed and delivered, and so we continue to pester all and sundry for copy.

The Editor.

EXTRACT FROM THE BOOK OF TOMAR-SAT-KINS.

—:o:—

And it came to pass at eleven hours of the eleventh day of the eleventh month there was silence throughout the Land of the Westernfront. And no one did loose a gun, no, not so much as a pip-squeak did go off. And the heart of Tomar-Sat-Kins was glad in him so that he did give praise saying "Wotto, no tarf, and the Land of Blighty shall know me *some* more." For he did know that the time of the Hunnites was come, and that peace would shortly come throughout the land.

THE FOREBODINGS OF A C.O.

—:o:—

"AND so most of us are, or shortly will be, out of work! Thrown on the mercies of a cruel hard world without the tender care of our foster-mothers, the corporals, sergeants, or whoever may have been *in loco parentis* during these years. Shall we all be able to resist the snares and temptations or will the guard room become, in memory, a desirable haven of rest, compared with the trouble which most of us will rush into."

It is thoughts such as these which are furrowing the brows and greying the hair of most Comm nding Officers. A Commanding Officer suddenly visualises his family thrown out of his fatherly care and into the snares and pitfalls which are waiting. Can you wonder at the pale and haggard look on his face? See the troubled eye, the furrowed brow, the greying temple. He gazes in the fire and pictures his Second-in-Command in the clutches of a Syren, his guileless Company Commanders stripped and broken by the first gang of crooks to meet them, his Adjutant in gaol for forgery, his Quartermaster in a home for incurable inebriates, his M.O. a drug fiend, his N.C.O.'s and men victims of harpies, crooks and other human vampires; all these, his children of the last four years he sees twisted, broken and writhing. His Subalterns, boys four years ago, plunged straight from school to war, and now to be plunged from war to the world.

Can you wonder that he shudders for them and his eye grows dim, and his mouth takes on a yearning droop. Pity him then,

"As a drooping lily"

aud mock not that age has gripped him 'Tis not the years that make his figure as a drooping lily, that make his face so pale and lined.

And so at last it's *fini* !
Can you understand the silence? Are you waiting for the barrage?
When the fateful hour of zero comes and you're "across the bags,"
Are your ears and senses straining for the vicious sound of shelling
When it's "down into a shell hole and God help the one who lags."

—:0:—

And now the Hun's "napooed"!
Can you forget those early days of undiluted hell?
That scared your soul and made you doubt your God.
When "Wipers" though a deadly rat-infested, muddy shell,
Seemed a Heaven when the mud of Hooge you trod.

—:0:—

And now "apres la guerre!"
For years you've heard that sentence tossed from taunting maid to man,
Heard it chanted right from Nieuport to Lorraine,
In a hovel up in Belgium when your soul was sick with war,
Or at Mazingarbe, Aubigny, or Avesnes.

—:0:—

"Oofs!! Compree, eggs?"
Will you e'er forget the jargon? Will these four years pass away
Till their memory is but an ugly dream?
Yet I would not lose the friends one found when life was less worth while
Than I had thought that life could ever seem.

—:0:—

"Hell! She's ditched!"
In the future years when dreaming of those nights along the roads.
When the rattle on the pavé drove you mad,
When you couldn't hear "it" coming, and the first thing that you knew
Was that Jim and George, your pals, had "got it bad."

"Curse this corner!"
Oh! that bloody reeking pavé round by Wipers and Potije
Where the corpses lined the sides, half hid in mud
Men and horses, and the litter of the stores they brought is spread
Through the night, while greedy Belgium laps up blood.

—:0:—

"Zero is at four!"
Loos, the Somme, Messines and Vimy, Passchendaele and Bourlon Wood,
The stink and bloody swelter of them all;
The acrid fumes of shelling, gas, and death, God send that we
May forget at least what we would not recall.

—:0:—

"Hostilities cease at 11 a.m.!"
Though these words marked hours which hist'ry well may hold divide the world
And the centuries in half by all they mean,
Yet our brains could not conceive it, and the Column plodded on—
You cannot blot out years as from a screen!

—:0:—

"Rations oop!"
When you're beat and wet and hungry, cold and don't care if you're dead.
Do you think that future hopes can ease the ache?
When you'd sell your soul for warmth, just want to sleep and sleep, and so
You just don't care a damn if you don't wake.

—:0:—

'Tis the small things make one's world up, and the greatest slither by,
'Tis "the canteen's closed" "late rations" make you curse;
What do emperors and empires going bust concern you when
The mud and rain and filth are getting worse?

—:0:—

"*Dis-miss!*"
Yet I think this lack of boasting and this calm, serene and still,
Mark a deeper sense of thankfulness and pride,
Pride—not in our own achievements, but in Britain and her fate
In our women, proved and tested, true and tried

THE SOLDIER'S FRIEND.

—o—o—o—

(In this column we will endeavour to cope with the problems that are troubling the soldiers.)

—o—o—o—

Private Stickit of Northampton writes :—

"Dear Sir.—I have been told that if a man has no work after the War, that the Government is going to pay him some money each week for a whole year. As I mean to have a long holiday after I am demobilised could I have a lump sum so as I could get married?"

—:o:—

Yes! Private Sticket, you will be able to have as much as you want. There will be a quarter-master's stores opened in every big town, and you will be able to obtain money on indent through the usual channels.

—:o:—

One Pip writes :—

"Dear Sir :—I was at the Front in 1914. Through all those awful months I stuck to my post and came through without a scratch. There were six of us at the Base, and we all managed to get through. We are writing to you to see if nothing can be done to stop these later fighters from wearing our Star"

"1914."

—:o:—

Well, "1914," we will exert our influence to stop an injustice being done.

—:o:—

Lce-Cpl. Jones (Buffs) writes :—

"Dear Sir.—I hear that the people who joined early are going to be demobilised first. I think this is very unjust. Surely those who joined first were much more eager to join the Army than we who were combed out later. As they were more eager to join, it must have been because they liked it. Therefore they should be demobilised much later than we who joined up reluctantly."

—:o:—

Yes! Jones. There's a lot in what you say, and we will put your view before the proper authorities.

—:o:—

Many answers are unavoidably held over owing to lack of space, but we will endeavour to answer them in our next issue

We are coming! We are coming!!
And the hour of peace is near,
Here we greet you with our homage,
And we bid you cease from fear.

—o—o—o—

You have drained your cup of anguish,
You have plumbed the depths of grief,
You have prayed each hopeless morning,
For the long-deferred relief.

—o—o—o—

We have marked with kindling spirit
All the traces of the beast,
And the Hun shall bear the branding
From "The Highest" to the least.

—o—o—o—

Brute in mind, and heart and body
He shall know the outcast's shame;
But the crowning of his Kultur
Is your curse upon his name.

—o—o—o—

Ruined homes and hearts nigh broken
Where the Boche has found his prey,
Left with only eyes to weep with,
Dear ones dead or far away.

—o—o—o—

For your sorrows take our pity,
For your dead accept our praise;
For the past of dire oppression,
Lo, we bring you brighter days.

—o—o—o—

Courage! you shall have your freedom
And your tears are not in vain.
For we bring you your deliv'rance
From your terror and your bane.

—o—o—o—

Count your woes a passing nightmare
Hideous, yet an evil trance.
From the welter of your trials
There shall rise a fairer France.

—o—o—o—

France, all fairer for your sorrows,
France, all nobler for your grief,
We are coming! We are coming!
And we bring you your relief.

THE PADRE.

RACING.

A SUCCESSFUL meeting was held on Wednesday, October 30th, under the aegis of the M.G. Battalion, and an interesting programme of five events was got through with commendable despatch. First-class weather conditions prevailed, and the course was thronged with the flower of the local chivalry The third race, which was the only open event, attracted a fair field, and about half-a-dozen animals eventually came under the starter's orders, all trained to the hour. The services of all the most famous jockeys had been secured, so the chances looked very open. As the time for the race drew near the excitement was intense, and I heard many large wagers freely offered and taken over the railings, every horse being well supported, though with slight preference possibly for Capt. Pincher's chestnut The gate eventually went up to a magnificent start. and there seemed little to choose between the bunch till the distance was reached, when the favourite with the Captain up drew clear, and won by about four lengths from Shid, who was using his whip. We hear on the best authority that the result was a big surprise to a certain clever division who had a real good thing to slip for this race. It is further rumoured that—anyway for the time being they've taken the knock.

The Band of the Coldstream Guards played delightful music on the lawn during the afternoon, and added to what everyone felt to be a delightful day.

Our Grand New Illustrated Feuilleton.

"VIRTUE WINS" OR THE 100-1 CHANCE.

A Tale of Adventure, Sacrifice and Love

BY

GOULD GARVICE.

CHARACTERS:—

Sir Marmaduke Cholmondeley Anstruther, K.O.B.E.—H.B.M's Ambassador to Japan.

Ambrose Archibald Anstruther—His Son, in love with

Sybil Clarissa Sutchapeach—Penniless, pretty but proud; who is also desired by

Rudolph Rugenoir—A dissolute gambler who wishes to marry for her money—

Estelie Pottsoudeau—A rich and handsome widow.

James Blink—Servant to Ambrose Anstruther

Silas Snitch—An ex burglar, under the thumb of Rugenoir.

Soames—Butler to the Anstruthers.

Steve Spring—A jockey with a heart of gold but a pitiful past.

Olga Otzstuphski—A crystal gazer, fortune teller and society leader.

—o—o—o—

CHAPTER 1.

—:o:—

"*Gloom only broken by the Milky way*"

THE night was black and the gloom was only broken by the Milky Way, which served to intensify the surrounding darkness. Suddenly the silence was shattered in a surprising manner.

"You lie! You dog!"

The angry voice rang out with a clarion cry and was followed by a shot, then a gurgle, then two gurgles, then—silence again.

Not for long however.

Once again—an earpiercing cry in a female voice, a cry for "Help!" then again a shot, then a gurgle, then two gurgles, then the clang of a shutting gate, then—silence. Who could it be? What could have happened? Why? Where? These questions rapidly flashed through the mind of Sir Marmaduke Anstruther as he was finishing his fourth bottle.

"*Clang of a shutting gate, then—silence.*"

(Olga blissfully unconscious of the victim's plight, meditatively dresses for dinner.)

Pressing the bell, it rang, and Soames the old butler appeared.

"Did you hear anything Soames?" queried the old baronet, his fine old figure a veritable question mark.

"No, Sir Anstruther! What was it?"

"I'm afraid something has happened," replied the baronet, "I distinctly heard a shot, followed by a rapid succession of gurgles, and then silence. What could it

Again, even as he spoke, a cry rang out and a shot echoed through the night. "Did you hear that, Soames?" said the baronet.

"No, sir!" said Soames.

"Then it must be as I feared," said the baronet, his aristocratic features taking on a look of sadness, "it's Arthur!" Leaning heavily on Soames' arm he tottered from the room.

As the door closed on his retreating figure a hand came round the heavy plush curtains—a strange wrinkled hand with nine fingers, all different. *WHOSE WAS THE HAND?*

(Read next thrilling instalment.)

(*Order Early.*)

(To be Continued.)

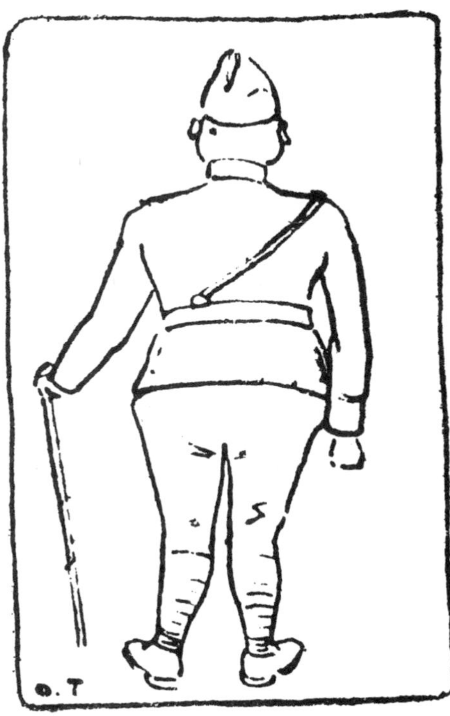

How the hours crept round the clock
Till we got our Yankee Doc.
Now the time slips gaily by,
List and I will tell you why!
When the war begins to bore us
Then our Yank joins in the chorus,
And (though p'raps not quite *de rigeur*)
Yet the ripples of his figure
As he yields to merriment
Makes us think the time well spent,
Sad must be the day and black
When we see our old Doc's back.

TOTTERING TO A FALL.

—:o:—

By TEECH BOMAS.

—:o:—

And so we broke through the line and the pride of Germany's colossal army was humbled to the dust. As I write the situation is liquid and I must tear round the battlefield several times more before I give a clear account of what has happened. I must tell you of how the North Southshires crossed the Canal. Every man was equipped with a pair of large springs under his feet. and a pair of wings strapped to his shoulders. At zero plus 5 the whole sprang on the bank and were carried over by these appliances, thus completely surprising the Huns. On they went in leaps and bounds, and in two hours the stream of prisoners began to pour in. I saw thousands myself and had I not been so busy I should have been able to see thousands more. Anyway, the vaunted Blindenburg line is shattered and we are through. I walked through Valenciennes this morning, and the Hun shells were still falling on every part of the town. I hurried through to the foremost battle-fronts although all inside me cried out to linger and study the condition of the town. I felt that I must be able to get you the latest situation so, having wired Foch that all was going well, on I went. Now I met Huns singly and in twos or threes putting up their hands. The most touching episodes occurred with the civilians who had been relieved by our advance. I was kissed on both cheeks by all and sundry, and although I was much embarrassed yet how could one stop these poor people. The situation is, as I repeat fluid, and until it sets it is impossible to tell you more. I am off to the battle again --I love it.

Teech Bomas.

There was a young man of Avesnes,
Took a stroll down a long shady lesnes,
He trod on a dud
Half hidden in mud ... *!
He never will do it agesnes.

LETTERS TO THE EDITOR.

—o—o—o—

To the Editor
The Better Times.
Sir,
Why shouldn't we who told our friends to enlist wear some modification of the 1914 Star? Surely our timely words were the cause of raising the first hundred thousand and ought to have some recognition.
Yours etc.,
CUTHBERT CUSHIJOBBE.
Dept. F
Ministry of Fancywork,
Hotel Velvet, W.C. 14

—o—o—o—

To the Editor.
Sir,
Your correspondence re the 1914 15 Star interests me very much I have never laughed so much since the day when father lost his false teeth overboard on the good ship *Angostura* in 1912.
Yours etc.,
A. E. G. BEAMS.

—o—o—o—

To the Editor.
Sir,
I didn't come out to France till 1918, and then managed to click for a job at the Base. Don't you think I ought to have the 1918 Star and Garter to show how clever I've been?
Yours etc.,
J. M. WANGLEUR,
A.P,O. 15.

—o—o—o—

To the Editor.
Sir,
I tried to enlist early in 1915 and was rejected on account of my teeth. I got a new set fitted at my own expense and managed to pass the doctor in June 1916 Surely there should be some sort of Star—say a 1915 16—for me! Or again, the "Spirit was willing but the Flesh (teeth) weak"; couldn't we wear a badge with that quotation engraved upon it?
Yours etc.,
O. MYE-MOLARS,
94th General Hospital,
France.

To the Editor.
Sir,
I do not agree with your correspondent Mr. Lettemnoe, who suggests that people should wear a placard on their backs stating their Army history. I suggest it should be on the front as well—or handier still—on properly fitted sandwich-boards.
Yours etc.,
A TRUE CONTEMTIBLE.

—o—o—o—

PRIZE MONEY.

To the Editor.
Sir,
I have been employed during the War on a mine-sweeper, and have swept up 47 mines. Taking the average value of a ship at 740,000 pounds, I have been the means of saving 740,000×47, viz.=34,780,000 pounds. Surely I ought to have at least 50 °/o of this?
Yours etc.
A LOYAL BRITON,
Grimsby.

STOP PRESS NEWS.

—o—o—o—

INTERNATIONAL HANDICAP RESULT.

—:o:—

John Bull : *DEAD*
Jonathan : *HEAT.*
Alphonse :
Also ran Fritz, Turco, and others.

—:o:—

S. P.—Even money Fritz
6/4 John Bull
3/1 Alphonse.

—:o:—

Jonathan was doubtful starter, and his number only went up at the last minute, but he came in with the leaders.

COPY THIS
CLEVER
DESIGN OF
ONE OF MY
PUPILS.

Can You Sketch? NO?

I CAN'T EITHER, BUT WRITE FOR MY ILLUSTRATED BOOKLET,

"HOW TO DRAW—ATTENTION, TEETH, Etc."

Pounds and pounds are made with the pen. One of my pupils uses his pen so well that he makes 1,000 pounds a month forging cheques.

A CLERGYMAN writes:—"Since taking your Drawing Course my lungs are much improved. Send another SIX BOTTLES." An ARTILLERY MAJOR writes:—"I find myself greatly benefited by your course. I can even draw fire."

DON'T PUT IT OFF TILL TO-MORROW!
WRITE TO-DAY!!

Particulars, Booklets, etc., from :—
PRINCIPAL, THE ART-TERIES, MARGATE.

LOOK!!!

—o—o—o—

POKER TAUGHT

(50 francs a Lesson.)

—o—o—o—

DON'T FAIL TO JOIN OUR POKER NIGHT CLUB. CLASSES NIGHTLY. 10.30 p.m. ENTRANCE FEE: 50 francs per Session.

—o—o—o—

A SIMPLE TESTIMONIAL.—"After six lessons of your excellent course I am able to play with Staff Officers, and take their money as easy as I can procure billets."
(Signed) *D. CANNY.*

—o—o—o—

APPLY:—ADAMS & SEEAREE, Ltd.
Telegraphic Address: "COUNTERS."

WE DO ALL KINDS OF

REMOVALS.

—o—o—o—

PROMPTITUDE AND THOROUGHNESS GUARANTEED.

—o—o—o—

APPLY:—BOSCH & Co., MOVERS,
Box No. 9, BERLIN,

Printed &
Published by
Sherwood, Forester &
Co., Ltd.
B.E.F.

Xmas, Peace and Final Number.

THE "BETTER TIMES."

WITH WHICH ARE INCORPORATED

The Wipers Times, The "New Church" Times,

The Kemmel Times, The Somme-Times,

& The B.E.F. Times.

No. 2. Vol. 1. December, 1918. Price 1 Franc.

EUROPEAN THEATRE OF VARIETIES.

THIS WEEK AND FOR ONE WEEK ONLY.

PLUMER AND CO,

IN THEIR SPECTACULAR DRAMA,

"THE CROSSING."

MAGNIFICENT SCENIC EFFECTS.

NO EXPENSE HAS BEEN SPARED TO ENABLE THIS PLAY TO BE STAGED.

ALSO

THE WESTMINSTER TROUPE

IN THEIR NEW SONG SCENA,

"OH PROMISE ME."

Book Early Prices as Usual.

ALL DISCORDANT NOISES HAVE BEEN REMOVED FROM THE NEIGHBOURHOOD.

HAVE A CUP OF

BOV-OX

(pronounced "Bov-Ox")

THE BEST BEEF TEA ON THE MARKET.

—o—o—o—

Many have tried to imitate us but have failed. Ask for BOV-OX and see that you get your change.

Our Trade Mark.

—o—o—o—

FROM ALL GROCERS, PROVISION DEALERS, IRONMONGERS, SHIP BREAKERS, ETC.

BO-VOX

(pronounced "Bo-Vox")

IS **THE** BEEF ESSENCE PAR EXCELLENCE.

—o—o—o—

Beware of imitators. There are several other beef essences, but none are "just as good." No—they are simply "just as bad."

"ALAS MY POOR BROTHER! HE IS THE TRADE MARK FOR OUR WRETCHED RIVAL FIRM 'BOV-OX.'

—o—o—o—

Remember, One BO-VOX Tablet will make a meal for 3 adults, so buy a package of 12 and have 19 good meals.

FROM ALL STATIONERS, ETC.

LOST, STOLEN OR STRAYED.

—o—o—o—

A Gent's Bicycle

JUST LIKE THIS ONE :—

Last seen wandering by itself on the main road to Lille.

Answers to the name of "GOVIE" (short for "Govern ment").

No questions asked of any-one who returns same within four weeks.

—o—o—o—

Owner. The Kennels. Cobrieux.

PRINCE ETHELBERT PIPE TOBACCO.

—o—o—o—

The real American product from Virginia.

—o—o—o

TALK NO. 1.—"There ain't no gaddam use of youse muts argufying alonga me about perfect pipe peace until you stuff some of this Prince Ethelbert Joyweed into the chimney of your pleasurepipe. Knock out that wet hay, that yellerbrown wool outer yer pipes and load up with the only tobacco—the angel-ammunition that would have kept Lucifer from revolting in Heaven.

He was one super gink, a mammoth mut to be without it—but you hombres, now that I've put you wise to it, you'd be *the Supreme Simps* of the world not to hustle hotfoot to the nearest store and get in your load of loveliness, *right now*."

Xmas, Peace and Final Number.

THE

"BETTER TIMES."

WITH WHICH ARE INCORPORATED

The Wipers Times, The "New Church" Times,

The Kemmel Times, The Somme-Times,

& The B.E.F. Times.

No. 2. Vol. 1. December, 1918. **Price 1 Franc.**

EDITORIAL.

" When this blooming war is over,
Oh! how happy we shall be;
When we get our civvy clothes on
No more soldiering for we."
(Expurgated Soldier's Song.)

ARE we? and shall we? The end of the War none of us will ever regret, but there will be a lot connected with the last four years that we shall miss. A lot of us can remember blue-clad mobs wandering (one cannot call it marching) down English lanes and streets singing the above. This was in the days before khaki was obtainable. And many of us can trace those same mobs through the various stages of camp, Aldershot, B.E.F., until to-day when we know them as soldiers, many of them veterans, beribboned, but still singing the same old grouse. We cannot say that the majority of us took to soldiering kindly, but now that it is all over and we shall soon " have our civvy clothes on," the reversion will be tinged with many regrets. One cannot but remark on the absolute apathy with which the end was received over here. England seems to have had a jollification, but here one saw nothing but a disinterested interest in passing events. Perhaps that was because the end came without the expected culminative crash, and the decisive battle was spread over many months, and so became an indefinite action and not a "show." Anyway though some may be sorry it's over, there is little doubt that the line men are *not*, as most of us have been cured of any little illusions we may have had about the pomp and glory of war, and know it for the vilest disaster that can befall mankind. We must apologise for the delay in issuing *No. 1 Better Times*. This was due to the nomadic existence we have been leading since the acquisition of the press which takes a day to set up and a day to take down, so that at least four days in one place are necessary before it's worth while unpacking. However, now we are established we hope to make our paper a weekly issue, and to print 1,000 copies. To do this more support must be forthcoming, and copy must roll in. So will Battn. Commanders and O's./C. units please do their best to make productive the shy and retiring subaltern. Cox will not be able to stand the strain of three month's peace warfare unless the time of subalterns is occupied by the less-expensive vices, poetry etc. If it could be done we should like to run a daily paper in conjunction, as we have the loan of another press. So will all the ex-journalists in the Div. please volunteer their services. This is our Xmas Number, and we take this opportunity of wishing all members of the Division a Merry Xmas, etc.

The Editor.

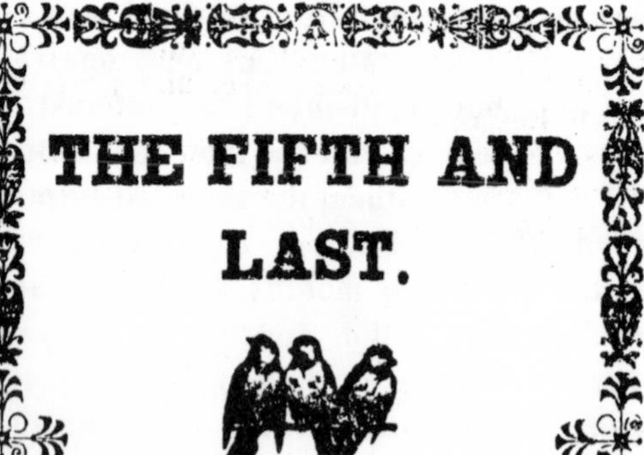
THE FIFTH AND
LAST.

In '14 when the war was young
By military ardour stung
We'd donned the khaki, and begun
To train for smashing up the Hun ;
Our tutors, though assuming lore
And dishing out wild tales of gore,
Knew just as much of war as we—
Which was *narpoo*, you must *compree*.

At 6 a.m. each winter's morn
The Front at Brighton looked forlorn
Yet not one tenth forlorn as we,
Who willy-nilly did P.T.
With mingled curses, sobs and groans
We dislocated all our bones,
Yet suffered gladly all that tosh
Thinking 'twould help to smash the "boche."

—o—o—o—

Our next Noël was passed in France,
At war by then we looked askance,
We'd sampled some of it at Loos
And for its charms had little use ;
We'd tried St Eloi and The Bluff
And thought the Huns uncouth and rough,
Yet things all panned out for the best
That Xmas Day found us "at rest."

—o—o—o—

The Natal Day of '16 found
Us back at Loos, the same old round
Of trenches, minnies, shells and mud,
Lord! how we'd got to hate the thud
Of shrieking hunks of metal, which
Just passed your ear and struck your ditch,
And to us all just then it seemed
This was not war of which we'd dreamed.

—o—o—o—

Another twelve months rolled away
Each month a year, each hour a day,
A plethora of blood and woe
The net result "in statu quo";
That Christmas Day itself we'd got
The soldier's dream—a cushy spot,
St Quentin just in front you'd find,
The old Somme battlefield behind.

—o—o—o—

By then we'd given up surmise
When peace would come and in what guise,
Nor wondered if it were the last
Noël which would at war be passed,
Just spared some breath to curse the Hun
For all he did, for all he'd done,
For all he yet might do, *àpres*
We'd celebrate our Christmas Day.

—o—o—o—

And now we've reached the last Noël
The job completely done and well,
We've done with mud and shells, and stench,
Hope ne'er again to see a trench,
No more to hear the crumps come in,
The whizzbang's shriek, the minnie's din,
The long last years have been well worth
If once again we've "Peace on Earth."

THE SITUATION IN RUSSIA.

—:o:—

From Our Special Correspondent.

—:o:—

AT great personal risk, which, however, is nothing to a correspondent such as myself, I have been able to obtain lucid details of the internal situation in Russia. I effected a landing upon the Murman Coast, the Navy kindly protecting me with a smoke barrage. I saw no Murmans when I arrived. They are, I understand, getting very rare, only 7 having been caught this year, the largest weighing 163 kopeks, 27 vodkas, after having been peeled. However, I digress.

To resume, I slipped a pair of sleighs on my feet, and ski-ed away as silently and swiftly as I was able. I was somewhat handicapped by the sleigh-bells, but I passed without comment and arrived at the town of Pschtvh (pronounced the same as the town with the same name in Galicia) at 6.30 a.m. on the 11th (Russian calender 11.30 a.m. on the 6th) and was surprised to find the factories as busy as ever.

In times of peace Pschtvh was a small bomb-manufacturing village, but at the outbreak of war, its resources having been exploited by the Romanoffs, it attained great importance, being one of the country seats of that sinister influence behind the throne—Rasputin, the peasant of Moujik. Before the war his financial interests in the bomb factories were colossal. He used his influence to compel the country to foster the bomb industry, and was always forcing bombs down the throats of the Duma, thus upsetting the Diet.

To continue, I found I had arrived just in time. I hailed a drosky driver and spoke to him in Russian. He was a poor stupid fellow. I struck him with my Bashi Bazouk and again addressed him in Russian. He was still unable to understand. The Russian educational system is the worst I have met. His ignorance handicapped me considerably. He was however able to speak English which enabled us to converse. He said that all drosky drivers had been abolished by the Soviet under the Gaming Act. He stated that I was just in time for the pogroms, and that there were a lot about. I accepted two roubles from him and went on, keeping to the outskirts of the town.

I was fortunate enough to come across a pogrom very quickly, and enticed it to me with a small piece of sturgeon which I always carry in my pocket in case of emergency. My heart went out to the little chap when I thought of the speed at which they had been exterminated. I stroked it for a while and it made no attempt to bite me. I should have liked to bring it away with me, but there—it might have led to my death, so I regretfully shot it and crept quietly out of the town.

I had just turned into the square when I ran into a large herd of Bolshevists. They were heaving Bolsh about all over the place. It was shocking to see how it was being wasted. A piece hit me in the face, and blood streamed down my cheeks, and I spat out some teeth. I at once realised that this had probably saved my life as I was not, until then, disguised. I therefore drew my beard from my pocket and slapped it on my face, drew my revolver from my hip and fired indiscriminately amongst the crowd. It was thus impossible to distinguish me from the Bolshevists, especially as I seized a lump of Bolsh and commenced heaving it. I shouted out coarse invectives in Russian, my pronounciation being rendered perfect by the absence of my teeth.

Passing as one of them I entered into conversation with one of their leaders. I said to him, "What is your opinion of the internal conditions in Russia." He was a simple fellow with simple ideas. He replied "Tshzv." I shot him and passed out into the night.

Thus you will see that the internal situation is still somewhat intricate. To-morrow I am going to Nijni Novgorod.

ALBERTA.

Scrap the pip-squeak, sixty pounders,
Six and eight inch, gun or how.,
Soon we'll be back playing rounders
Gone are all their uses now.
Pack away the good old sausage
Turn Tock Emmas into pans,
Now we're changed from war to school days
Even Wilhelm's changed to Hans.

A PAGE OF MINOR-KEY NOTES.

OUR SECOND TIME ON EARTH.

—:0:—

You know of the Phoenix, a wonderful bird,
And his powers I think you'll agree
Are a marvel; he rises from ashes, I've heard
Like Venus straight up from the Sea:
So we, though no powers supernatural we claim,
Have yet compassed a similar feat,
And out of the ashes enshrining our fame
Have arisen refreshed and complete.

We bade you a fond and touching farewell,
We wished you Good Luck and God-speed,
Our obsequies went off remarkably well,
Though the time was a sad one indeed:
But now we return to our labours once more,
And sadness is cast to the winds,
Throw open the wide Editorial Door,
Draw the curtains and pull up the blinds!

As the clown in the old-fashioned panto' appears,
And greets you with formula terse,
So we, bidding smiles take the place of your tears,
Send forth hearty greetings in verse:
Once more we emerge with a wave of the hand
Right into the glare of the limes,
And once more proclaim we are your's to command,
The Editor—*The Better Times.*

—o—o—o—

TRICOLOR.

—:0:—

Mid shriek and hiss of falling shell,
The torn Earth trembling, torture-riven,
God's face obscured, the World a Hell,
Man, like a puppet, onward driven,
On through the battle's smoke and roar,
Rushing with bayonet fixed, he saw
RED.

In quiet home of rest and peace,
Far from the conflict's blare and rattle,
Where wounds are healed and strivings cease,
For weary warriors worn by battle,
Mid sweet and smiling V.A.D.'s,
Waking from dreams of death, he sees
WHITE.

The time goes on, he leaves his cot
And hobbles round with aid of crutches,
The old familiar sights he'll spot,
The old familiar things he touches:
He little recks the scar he bears,
As taking his walks abroad, he wears
BLUE.

IN THE PINK.

—:0:—

Dear Father and Mother,
I hope and I pray,
(I'm writing in pencil, I've run out of ink)
That this letter finds you as it leaves me to-day
In the pink.

They told us to capture the Violet line,
Which we did after Zero, before you could wink,
Then we scuppered some Boches preparing to dine
In the pink.

Oh! Mabel's divine in the emerald green,
And Maudie in brown with the trimming of mink.
But Kitty for me is the absolute Queen
In the pink.

Some sigh for the scent of the lily or rose,
Mignonette or narcissus or orchid; I think
That the sweetest of perfumes will always repose
In the pink.

Some chivvy the fox in the ratcatcher kit,
Whilst others in black from publicity shrink,
But you'll come if you really intend to be IT
In the pink.

—o—o—o—

MEMORIES.

—:0:—

Do you remember, dearest, that day upon Hampstead Heath,
With the blue, blue sky above us, and the green, green grass beneath;
We talked of our love together,
Ah! sweet was the old refrain:
And then we talked of the weather,
And hoped that it wouldn't rain.

We strolled through the shady woodland, and down by the babbling stream,
While the birds in the trees above us kept murmuring love's young dream;
Our two hearts were one indeed, dear,
As we walked through the leafy glade,
And then we went off for a feed dear,
Of biscuits and lemonade.

When the beautiful time was ended, together we walked away,
As the shadows of night descended at the close of a summer's day;
We thought of the Summer Sun, love,
How brightly it shone for us,
And then we commenced to run, love,
To catch the last homeward bus.

R. W. M.

OUR SPECIAL REPORTER AT THE ARMISTICE TABLE.

—:o:—

Unparalleled Feat By Mr. TEECH BOMAS.

—:o:—

GREAT SCOOP BY "THE BETTER TIMES."

—:o:—

I AM cabling you here the true and inner history of what happened at the Armistice Table. I was present, camouflaged as a Spaniel and over heard the most momentous meeting in all history.

The scene was set in a rural glade. The birds were singing, although it was November, I don't know why but I must mention the fact—I always do.

Plunging into the smoke of the creeping barrage I was soon up to our foremost troops . . . . Cancel that last I've got the wrong number.

To resume, Autumn tints were quickly turning into Winter as I hid myself behind a tree and barked to be in keeping with my disguise. One could hear the boom of the guns, and one's heart ached to be back in the heart of the conflict. But duty is a stern mistress, and one cannot help thinking how many hearts have ached for the same reason during this concantenation of Herculean forces engaged in the death grapple. Stifling the almost irresistable desire to plunge back to the strife, I concentrated my attention on a blur of smoke just apparent in the West. Nearer it came and nearer, and eventually evolved itself into a train. Of course I knew what the train was, and where it would stop. (You know my methods, Editor?) No-one else knew, not even the driver. Suddenly the brakes screeched in answer to a sharp jerk at the communication cord and the train came to a standstill right opposite to my tree. I yelped with delight, and hurriedly dodging a lump of coal flung at me by the driver, was in time to see the dapper yet military figure of the Generalissimo descend from the wagon—I use the French-habit, you know!—rubbing his hands, and humming to himself that little air which he is famous for, he seated himself at the table. I prepared mys[elf] for a long wait, but nothing had b[een] left to chance, and shortly four perspiri[ng] allemands emerged from the jungle h[ard] right. The foremost approached a[nd] inquired, "Donnerwetter?"

"Ja, Monsieur," answered the gr[eat] man, "Beaucoup van Blang!"

"Ach, Himmel," cried the representati[ve] of fallen Germany, "Deutchland U[ber] Alles, napoo." So saying he fell in [a] swoon and his confreres carried on t[he] discussion without him.

Angrily striking the table Foch said [in] an imperative tone. "Armistice! Comp[ree?] Armistice? rien faisant."

"Verfluctes Kerl," cried the Huns [in] despair, "Armistice, napoo! Oh, hell!!"

With a sweep of the hand Foch affix[ed] his signature over a twopenny stamp, [the] others doing the same in rotation. Th[us] was I a privileged witness of one of t[he] most historical meetings in the worl[d's] history. Yelping with joy I threw off m[y] disguise. "The devil," cried Foch. "N[o] Monsieur," I replied, "Teech Bomas."

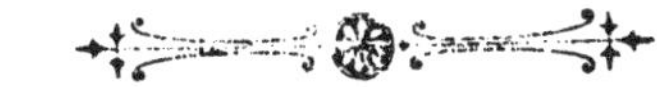

THE XMAS PRESENT.

—o—o—o—

German Plenipotentiary receives a "Special Peace-Signing" Fountain Pen.

"Good morning! I salute you as I rush up on my charger
Which is thoroughly and daily disinfected,
The impression I shall make will be proportionately larger
When a greater body-guard I have collected.
Now is your fly-trap grease-proof; are all my orders framed,
Have you put chloride of lime upon the ham,
Have your you-know-what's been thingummy and daily whatsernamed
But, by the way do you know who I am?

Chorus.—I'm General Sir Chloride H.K.L.M. Bunter, Bart.,
You'll have to say it slowly for a start,
You can write and tell your mother
Your father, sister, brother,
Your sons and daughters, uncles, aunts, and they can tell each other
That of all the Corps Commanders
Who command in France or Flanders,
You've never met one who is half as smart
Or so absolutely grand
As he who shakes your hand—
General Sir Chloride H.K.L.M Bunter, Bart.

—:o:—

Ah! now here a fly I notice, which is flat against my orders,
'Tis the cause of all the P.U.O. and similar disorders,
If it once gets on the meat
The result will be trench feet,
You must try and recollect the few suggestions I have made,
If you've read your C.R.O.
You certainly must know
That on no account will any fly be forward of Brigade,
Now get a piece of suet
Stick a pin or needle through it
And camouflage the front to look like jam,
He'll settle—exit fly
He'll see the point and die,
Are you sure you still remember who I am?

Chorus—I'm General Sir Chloride H.K.L.M. Bunter, Bart., *etc.*

Now let me see your transport, are your mules in good condition?
You must cheer them up if they're inclined to fret,
A blotting pad per head would be an excellent addition
To dry them if they ever start to sweat;
And now, when shoeing animals I'll tell you what to do,
You must always be as gentle as a lamb,
Just make the shoes of biscuit tins and stick them on with glue,
Farrier, do you know who I am?

Chorus.—I'm General Sir Chloride H.K.L.M. Bunter, Bart., *etc.*

—:o:—

And now we'll see the baths. Are you sure they're quite hygenic?
Does the band play when the men do their ablutions,
Are the pictures on the wall allegorical or scenic,
Are they well washed with bi-carbonate solutions,
Are you absolutely sure the men undress before immersion,
Do they dry themselves with bathmat, towel or soap,
If you'll dip their clothes in green cross gas you'll notice the desertion
Of all the lice. The men know me, I hope,

Chorus.—I'm General Sir Chloride H.K.L.M. Bunter, Bart, *etc.*

ALBERTA.

BON CHANCE.

—o—o—o—

As this is our last number the Editor and Sub-Editor would like to take this opportunity of thanking all those who have so kindly helped us with the paper. We had intended to carry on till we had all received the order of the bowler hat, but as most of the printing staff are miners and consequently going almost at once, it will be impossible to do any further numbers. To all of you the best wishes for Xmas and the future, and hearty thanks for your aid and support.

(*Signed*) F. J. ROBERTS, Editor
J. H. PEARSON, Sub-Editor.

THE LAY OF THE DUG-OUT.

When young and newly primed in lore
Of Army ways, and things pertaining
Which I must duly learn before
I'd find myself for France entraining,
My ardent soul sucked up each word
Let fall by those inured old heroes ;
No statement could be too absurd
If backed by one who'd fought Hereros.

—:o:—

" My lad," said one, " By Gad, you know, sir,
I won the War of 1880,
I swear by Gad that it was so, sir,
Had my friend Kitchener been matey
Not now I'd be a dug-out Major,
No! by Gad! no! 'tis Chief Commander
Of all the Forces, that I wager
If I would now but deign to pander."

—:o:—

Another cried " Why! At manœuvres
I've won the very highest praise !
'K' said to me: 'My dear old Stoovers
I wish I had you near always.'
'Twas this that made my C.O. jealous,
Assure you all of this I can,
Had I not always been so zealous
I'd now not be a *Capitan*."

—:o:—

Another howled with snorts and raging :
" I'm senior to everybody !
Yet here am I, though quickly ageing,
With but three pips!" ("Waiter! some toddy!")
"'Tis damned unfair. I was a gunner
For years that number six and thirty.
I used to shoot a fifty-tonner !"
(" More soda, if you please, dear Gertie !")

—:o:—

Yet was the cry of one and all
Of these old dug-outs, " Yes, by Gad. sir,
Just wait until we start the ball,
I'll show them who they might have had, sir!
Yet when they beg that I will take
A Batt., Brigade, and then Division,
With emphasis they cannot shake
I'll greet their offers with derision."

" There is not one of all the score
Of Generals leading our Divisions
But I could teach the art of war,
They cannot come to quick decisions.
Now if 'twere *me* who'd been appointed
As C. in-C. of all the Forces,
The Hun would soon have been disjointed
Things would have run their proper courses."

—:o:—

" And now they've the infernal cheek
To offer *me* ! By Gad, it's true, sir !
A paltry fifteen pounds a week,
And what d'you think they'd have me do, sir !
Me ! who am fit to take command
Of all the lot, on that I'll wager,
They offer *me*, you understand,
The job of Deputy Town Major!

—:o:—

" By Gad ! let England have a care
Or I'll send in my resignation,
And make 'em wonder how and where
They'll 'scape the consequent stagnation :
Yet for a week I'll deign to be
Town Major ! It does not alarm me,
I know full well that soon you'll see
They'll have to give to me an Army."

AT LAST.

—o—o—o—

"Our Cavalry have crossed the Rhine "—*Daily Paper*.

—:o:—

Our Cavalry have crossed the Rhine,
Ring out the bells with peal on peal,
Our Cavalry have crossed the Rhine,
Those words to all of us appeal ;
No blatant music-hall refrain
Or ill-timed boast of what we'd do
To smash the Kaiser and his train,
And then to " Wind a Watch Up " too.
Yet words which bridge four years of gloom
Which made us doubt the sun could shine,
Throughout the World the message boom :—
Our Cavalry have crossed the Rhine.

(In our last issue we published a reprint of Lesson 1 from Hugo Ivebeenovitch's "Russic Simplified," but even if you have missed that, it is such a simple tongue that Lesson 2 can be started first.)

—:o:—

LESSON 2.

NOUNS:—There are quite a number of nouns in the Russic language, but each one means something different. These can be sub-divided into three kinds Common Nouns, Proper Nouns, Improper Nouns.

COMMON NOUNS:—These are so awfully common that they need no discussion here. Besides who wants to know "common" nouns. Let us have the real top-notchers while we are about it. But, before passing, it is advisable for the student to notice that all nouns ending in ***s*** are feminine, and those ending ***ɟ*** are masculine—but words ending in ***uɐɯ*** have no sex at all. But that's their pidgin. Also notice that ***uɐɯ*** after words like ***ʎɐpllɐ*** and ***ɟɐɯɐɹ*** (these latter being of different genders) are kept as far apart as possible, otherwise they become Improper Nouns.

PROPER NOUNS:—These can be readily distinguished by the student, as they always look so nice and proper. They are generally chaperoned with a capital letter—as ***ɹɐɥɔ uɪlɔ, ɯnᴉƃlǝq***, i.e.—Charlie Chaplin, Belgium. Besides, as a general rule, the real Proper Nouns are always in by 9.30 p.m., and always say Grace before meals.

IMPROPER NOUNS:—***Ɐdɐɯu, ʞɔɐɹ***, which when freely translated mean . . . . . ("That will do. This is a family journal."—Editor.)

—:o:—

SECOND CONVERSATION.

ʇɐɔ ǝɥʇ ǝlqɐʇ ɯooɹ ɥɐɟ=The cat, the table, the bathroom, the loofah.

ɥʇ ʇɐɔ ǝɥʇ ʇɐ ɥɐɟ=Charles Chaplin throws the loofah at the cat.

ɥɯɐɥ ɹoʌI ɐɔ + ʇɐ=Thomas, Ivor, Ivan, Europe, America, Heaven, Hell.

ɹoʌI ǝɹ ɥʍ ʇɐ ɐs ɯoo ɐɟ ɐɹ§=Where is Iver? He is in the bathroom with the loofah of Thomas.

ɐɔ ʇ ɐ ǝ ɥɐɹ=Send the cat to America.

llǝɥ ɹ ɐɔ ɐɹ ɐɹ§="Hell," said the Ambassador, "where is the cat of the hussar?"

ʌI o ʇɐ ɐ ɐɔɐ ɯɐɹ=The cat of Ivan has eaten the loofah of the Ambassador.

ɔd . . o ɹɐɯ . . . ɐ ɐɹ + ɐɔɐ ɐɯ ɹɐɥ=Go! . . . Go to Europe! . . . Go to America, Heaven, Hell (as the case may be).

THE HORRORS OF PEACE.

—:o:—

We have had a good look at the horrors of war, and now we are undergoing another sort of frightfulness. What a life! Can anyone tell us of a nice war where we could get work and so save our remaining hair from an early greyness? 11·00 hours on the eleventh of November was zero hour, and the redhats attacked in mass. The barrage of paper fell right on our trenches, and mixed with the H.E was gas in enormous quantities. The supports were rushed into the orderly room in time to save the line from giving. Numbers are against us. Also the disposition of the enemy is much in his favour. His left flank rests on Education, and his right on recreation. He has carefully selected shock-masses of "Returns," and with these is rapidly undermining our morale. We are taking up a defensive position in various towns, and there we are going to hold on at all costs. Meanwhile we are drawing up a list of our "fourteen points," and these may form the basis of a suitable armistice. As I remarked before, if anyone knows of a *nice* war, or if one can be arranged, we hope we shall be allowed first call.

"THE ORDERLY ROOM OF OTHER TIMES" SERIES.

—o—o—o—

NO 2.— WITH THE IRONSIDES.

—o—o—o—

(Oliver Rumwell is discovered walking up and down with a spare mace in his hand, muttering "Bauble! Bauble!" Praise-the-Lord-Good-and-Plenty, his Adjutant, is chewing the end of a quill.)

P.L.G.P.—Wilt hear the case, Master?

Oliver (still preoccupied).—Bauble! Bauble!

P.L.G.P.—Master!...... Master wilt thou give ear to the case of one of your Ironsides, one Sing-Hymns-Loud-and-Lusty, who hath erred by lying long on his pallet.

Oliver (not listening).—Ugh?

P.L.G.P.—Master, a case.......er—a case of.......

Oliver (slightly interested).—What? A case of malted liquors? Well, keep two-thirds of it for ourselves, and distribute the remaining jars to......

P.L.G.P.—Nay, nay Master, a case of one of your troop who hath grievously sinned, insomuch as he hath lain long on his pallet when he should have been astir.

Oliver.—Let him be brought before me, Praise-the-Lord-Good-and-Plenty.

(P.L.G.P. exits, re-entering shortly followed by the Major-Sergeant of the troop, and the accused Sing-Hymns-Loud-and-Lusty. The accused is without his casque and girdle. The Major-Sergeant is a mighty man who carries a trusty broadsword and a well-worn Bible. He rejoices in the name of Strongitharm-and-Breath. He kisses the hilt of his broadsword as he approaches Oliver Rumwell.)

Strongitharm-etc.—Master! Master!

Oliver (scowls at accused).—So this is the Knave, this Sing-Hymns-Loud-and-Rusty?

Strongitharm-etc. — Nay Master, "Sing-Hymns-Loud-and-Lusty"—not Rusty, my master.

Oliver.—Names matter naught. He hath lain full long on his pallet, softening his bones in luxury. Hast any argument, sirrah, to defend thy indolence? Dost not know that to sing hymns loud and lusty, as thy name implies, does not suffice to make thee an Ironside? Dost not know that thou hast erred in not arising when the alarum did ring out? Well? Well? Thou who singest hymns so loud, wag now thy tongue in thine own defence if thou canst.

Sing-Hymns-Loud-etc.—Nay Master. I was heavy with sleep, and I admit the plaint.

Oliver.—'Tis well; thou givest the answer direct. For punishment thou shalt arise daily at the fourth hour for three score lunar months. Thou shalt then hie thee to the Forest and sing thy hymns louder and even lustier than of yore. That is all. Turn-about.

(Sing-Hymns-Loud-and-Lusty turns about, as also does Strongitharm-and-Breath. They start to march away; Strongitharm-and-Breath prods the accused with his broadsword saying fiercely the while, "Ha, sing! Sing now! Now!! Now!!!" Sing-Hymns-Loud-and-Lusty chants as follows.)

Sing-Hymns-Loud-etc. (singing):—

Yea who would not on bended knee
Praise the mighty powers that be,
And be an Ironside;
And be an Ironside!
To shave one's head and sharpen sword,
To rise betimes and be abroad,—
Yea, that's the Ironside!
Yea, that's the Ironside!!

O.T.

Our Grand New Illustrated Feuilleton.

"VIRTUE WINS" OR THE 100-1 CHANCE.

A Tale of Adventure, Sacrifice and Love
BY
GOULD GARVICE.

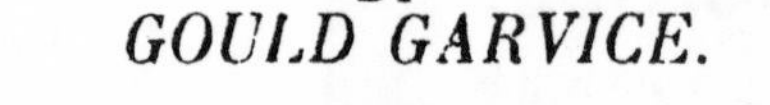

CHARACTERS :—

Sir Marmaduke Cholmondeley Anstruther, K.O.B.E.—H.B.M's Ambassador to Japan.

Ambrose Archibald Anstruther—His Son, in love with

Sybil Clarissa Sutchapeach—Penniless, pretty but proud ; who is also desired by

Rudolph Rugenoir—A dissolute gambler who wishes to marry for her money—

Estelle Pottsovdeau—A rich and handsome widow.

James Blink—Servant to Ambrose Anstruther

Silas Snitch—An ex-burglar, under the thumb of Rugenoir.

Soames—Butler to the Anstruthers.

Steve Spring—A jockey with a heart of gold but a pitiful past.

Olga Otzstuphski—A crystal gazer, fortune teller and society leader.

—o—o—o—

CHAPTER 2.

—:o:—

MEANWHILE in another place a very different scene was being enacted. In the flat of Ambrose Anstruther, Rudolph Rugenoir, dissolute gambler and rake, was running a crown and anchor board with great success. A score or so of young men dressed in the height of fashion were seated round the board, and their faces showed only too plainly that they were being very hard hit.

Pushing a roll of banknotes across the table Ambrose, his face flushed and his eyes shining with the delirium of gaming, cried "Another 100,000 pounds on red, damn you!"

"Hullo! Coming down to small bets now?" sneered Rudolph, as he spun the ball.

In silence they watched the little horses on which, although they knew it not, hung the lives of so many.

" Pair, Impair, Rouge et Noir!" chanted the croupier as the ball fell into the slot. With a groan of despair Ambrose pulled a revolver out of his pocket, and before anyone could stop him had stabbed Rugenoir to the heart then plunging the blade into his own breast. So perished the last of the Anstruthers and, by his hand, one of the most desperate characters in English social life—Rudolph Rugenoir.

"Olga, blissfully unconscious of the tragedy ...... prepares to retire for the night."

Meanwhile poor old Sir Marmaduke Anstruther was breathing his last, struck down by a sudden and painful malady. Round him were Sybil, Estelle, and Soames the faithful old butler.

His son Ambrose had been telegraphed for, as the news of his fate had not yet reached them. Estelle and Sybil were silently sobbing, and old Soames made no effort to conceal his sorrow. Suddenly Sir Marmaduke gave a gurgle and fell back dead.

Seeing that all was over, they gave way to uncontrolled grief and went down to tea.

Estelle Pottsovdeau eventually married and so did Sybil. Soames eventually died.

Let us take ourselves to yet another scene in this great tragedy.

A great express train is thundering along on its way to the racecourse. In one of the compartments are James Blink, Steve Spring, and Silas Snitch. They are immersed in a game of "Find the Lady" with two hospitable strangers who had allowed them to join in their game. Little they knew of the tragedy in which they were involved.

"'Ere y'are guv'nor!" said one of their fellow-players, "If yer don't pop it down yer carn't pick it up!" "Now yer see 'er and now yer don't!" exclaimed the other as the train plunged along on its eventful journey.

Suddenly the world seemed to upheave, and the whole atmosphere was rent by a terrific crash and roar of escaping steam, mingled with the shrieks of the dying and the dead.... "That's 'ard luck" exclaimed the fellow travellers of Snitch, Blink, and Spring as they lifted the mangled corpses of our three characters off the cards and picked up their money. Carefully examining them to see that no spark of life remained, the hospitable travellers went through their pockets and then left exclaiming sadly "Poor fellows, poor fellows!" and so ended in ignominy a scheme which was more far-reaching than any which has yet shaken our social fabric. Sybil and Estelle alone remain to live their lives, happy and prosperous in the love of their husbands and children. Thus is virtue vindicated on earth, and villany meets its due reward. Meanwhile Olga, blissfully unconscious of the tragedy in which she has been involved, prepares to retire for the night.

(THE END.)

(You see—it had to be finished in this number.—EDITOR.)

LETTERS TO THE EDITOR.

—o—o—o—

THE 1914 STAR:

To the Editor,
The Better Times.

Sir —I feel I cannot let this 1914 Star discussion pass without airing my little grievance. My husband has got the 1914 Star, and the red, white and blue ribbon clashes most horribly with my cerise blouse.

What can I do? I am most perplexed about it.

Am I to dye the blouse, dye the ribbon, or get a new husband?

Yours etc.,
A CONTEMPTIBLE'S WIFE.

9a Suburban Villas, Peckham.

—o—o—o—

To the Editor.

Sir.—My husband is a Corps Commander who has a very large number of decorations; in fact there is no more room left for any more ribbons.

It is rumoured that he is to be presented very soon with the O.B.E. and another Home and Colonial Order.

I propose therefore to make a flap, with ribbons on both sides. The flaps will bounce up and down as he walks, thus shewing either side alternately.

I thought this idea worth mentioning for the benefit of other worried wives of much decorated Corps Commanders.

Yours etc.,
INGENUITY.

27 Murkie Mansions, W.46.

—o—o—o—

To the Editor.

Sir.—Surely the practice of putting thrupennybits, silver charms, etc. in Christmas puddings ought to be stopped. Last Xmas I was dining with some friends and we, of course, had a Xmas pudding; but what do you think I got in my portion of pudding? A thrupennypiece, a 50 centime note (very dirty one), a Bosche cartridge, a piece of film 2·25 inches long, a cigar stump and 3 carpet tacks.

It is a dangerous practice as well as very insanitary. This view is endorsed by my doctor, who performed the operation afterwards.

Yours etc.,
WILLIAM WOOLFIT.

St Agnes' Convalescent Home
Seasyde super-Mare.

To the Editor.

Sir.—I think it is seasonable to bring to the notice of both young and old a new Christmas game I have invented. Anyone can play it; it is so simple. At present I call it "Stick-it-Girls," but perhaps some of your readers may be able to suggest a better name.

This is all it is: the ladies all go out of the room leaving the gentlemen to tie all their walking sticks and umbrellas together with a piece of short twine. One of the gentlemen goes to the door and says "Catchemquick!" whereupon the ladies rush in and untie the sticks. It is such fun, and merry peals of laughter always greet the lady who fails to say "Gallawalla" if she knocks a chair down in the rush.

Yours etc.,
B. F.

Lady Airbrane's Asylum for
Feeble Gentlefolk,
Chelmsford.

THE DEMOBILISATION
SMILE!

THIS EXCELLENT THRASHING MACHINE

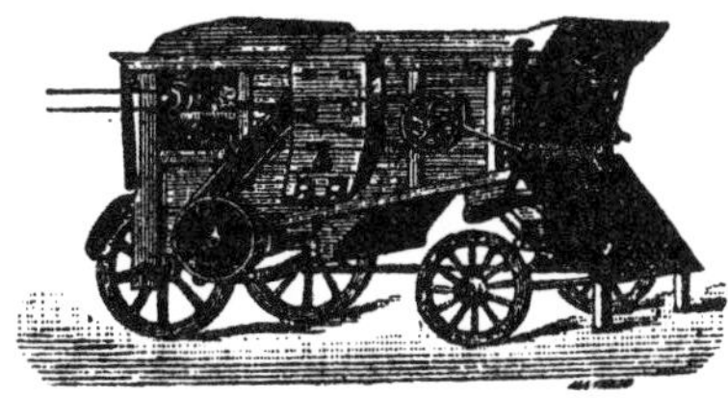

FOR SALE,

As Owner has no further use for it. He had it made to his own design in 1914 to be used in thrashing the Allies. Further comment is absolutely unnecessary.

—o—o—o—

APPLICATIONS DIRECT TO OWNER :—

K. A. ISER,
"The Retreat,"
Amer de Hollande,
Holland.

MAY I HAVE THE PLEASURE?

(I learnt it last Summah.)

With what alacrity she says "delighted" if you are a "HOP-SOGAY" student!!

—o—o—o—

"HOPSOGAY" must not be taken to be derived from the word "Hops," but "Hop."

—o—o—o—

Classes Every Evening: Evening Dress Optional (but no Army boots are allowed until after 9.30 p.m.)

—o—o—o—

"Come trip the Merry Legshake on the sward."
"Delighted! for you HOPSOGAY my lord."

GIVE HER A BOX OF "Meltz-Lykbuttah"!

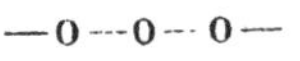

—o—o—o—

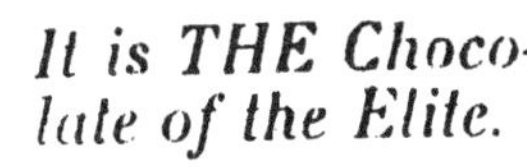

It is THE Chocolate of the Elite.

We did not get these Medals for nothing. We took these prizes by sheer merit. In fact we had three more once, but the authorities saw us taking them and told us to put them back.

"Meltz-Lykbuttah" just melts like butter. A Special Loaded Hatchet for breaking the sweetmeat is packed in every box.

BUY! BUY!! BUY!!!

—o—o—o—

I have a large consignment of bundles as per design. As I cannot tell from either the design or the commodity whether they are bundles of cigars or bundles of asparagus, I am offering them at seven bundles for a pound.

—o—o—o—

COME ON, RISK IT.

Printed &
Published by
Sherwood, Forester &
Co., Ltd.
B.E.F.

NOTES

N.B. *l* and *r* with page references denote left- and right-hand columns of type on the page

The Wipers Times 12 February 1916, No. 1, Vol. 1

Page NOTES

1*l* **Wipers Fish-Hook & Menin Railway:** A narrow-gauge railway from Ypres, through the Menin Gate to the front. The wagons were moved by mule, sometimes by hand.

1*r* **Hotel des Ramparts:** Certain dug-outs and casemates under the Ypres ramparts became well known for their hospitality and their more or less ample supply of whisky. The 'Hotel des Ramparts' was one of these and was probably the dug-out where the *Wipers Times* was produced. The 'hotel advertisements' were a somewhat wry comment on the standard of luxury offered by hotels in England through the columns of *The Times*.

2*r* **The Road to Ruin:** The Menin road (*see* Place Names). It was about 5,000 yards (or, as the 'advertisement' states, 15,000 feet) from the Menin Gate to the front line.

4*l* **Raise a wind:** Get the wind up (*see* Glossary).

5*r* **Carrier pigeons:** Used when other means of communication had broken down, carrier pigeons made a pleasant change from M & V (*see* Glossary) when they could be 'found'.

5*r* **The Fancies:** The 6th Divisional Concert Troupe which gave regular concerts in a makeshift theatre in Poperinghe. 'The concert troupe consisted of nine artistes and two girls. The latter were known as "Glycerine" and "Vaseline". One was a refugee from Lille, and the other was the daughter of an *estaminet* keeper at Armentières. The most priceless turn in the show was the singing of "I'm Gilbert the Filbert" by one of these wenches who could not speak English.' (F. C. Hitchcock, *Stand To* [London: Chivers 1965].)

Mr H. H. Morell writes of The Fancies: 'I saw them in Poperinghe and the stars were two buxom, bonny girls. They couldn't sing, act, etc. but who cared! They were well guarded and never seen off-stage.'

Every division had its own concert party which was provided with a hall or tent and given money for scenery and costumes. The names of some others were The Bow Bells, The Duds, The Follies, The Whizzbangs, and The Giddigoats.

6*r* **Oxford Street:** Oxford Street, Regent Street and the names of many other famous thoroughfares were given to particular trenches. These names were seldom permanent but changed in accordance with the home towns and counties of the troops occupying them. Oxford Street could well become Sauchiehall Street overnight and Unter den Linden on the following day.

7*r* **1 4 B 2–1:** A map reference.

8*l* **The Moat:** Part of the old defences of Ypres.

9*l* **Nunthorpe, Cox and Co.:** It is possible that Nunthorpe and Cox were officers responsible for the detection and dispersal of poison gas, as their names, which crop up frequently, are usually linked with chlorine. **Mist, East Wind** and **Frost** were conditions that favoured a German gas attack. From this and other advertisements and articles in the *Wipers Times* it also seems possible that Messrs Nunthorpe and Cox were in the habit of taking wagers for and against the probabilities of gas attacks at any particular time.

11*l* **Rhumatogen:** After 'Sanatogen' and 'Bynogen', two identical patent nostrums for the relief of 'nerves'. Rum mixed with tea (the way it was usually taken in the trenches) is here recommended as a cure for '**Wind up**' and '**Cold Feet**' (*see* Glossary).

11*r* **Hill 60:** *See* Place Names.

The Wipers Times 26 February 1916, No. 2, Vol. 1

PRINCIPAL WORLD EVENTS SINCE THE PREVIOUS ISSUE:

February 15 Fifth Battle of the Isonzo River (Italy) between Austrian and Italian armies begins.

21 Battle of Verdun begins.

25 Fort Douaumont (Verdun) stormed by German infantry.

NOTES

14*l* **Three Sisters Hun-Y:** The Bunny Sisters, a music hall act.

14*r* **Inferno:** D. W. Griffith's film *Intolerance* with '67,000 performers' was showing in London at the time.

Marley Taplin: The reference to Charlie Chaplin is unmistakable (*cf.* 'Piggles goes a Sniping' with 'Charley goes Gunning', *Wipers Times* 6 March 1916, p. 35). The meaning of the 'advertisement' is obscure for none of Chaplin's films bear a title resembling the above. His *Shoulder Arms* was made in 1918.

16*l* **Grafton Street:** A trench.

16*r* **The Denin Road:** The Menin Road.

17*r* **Kirsonner:** Rapahel Kirchner, a French artist who specialized in pictures of young women wearing the rather voluminous underwear of the day. The pictures were considered highly erotic and favoured by junior officers as decorations for the walls of dug-outs. Some were published in the London magazine *Sketch* as double page 'pull-outs' and may be considered to be the first 'pin-ups' (*cf.* 'Kirchner's naughtiest chromo', *Wipers Times* 6 March 1916, p. 30).

18 **Insurance Scheme:** Free life insurance was offered by many popular newspapers and magazines in exchange for 'regular orders'. The 'cover' offered was extremely limited; the *Daily Mail* offered £10,000 for death caused by Zeppelins.

18*l* **Belary Helloc:** Hilaire Belloc. He contributed regularly to the journal *Land and Water* always 'proving' that Germany did not possess enough guns, men or food to continue the war. Captain S. F. Naylor says that 'according to Belloc the war could never last another ten minutes. Unfortunately, the Germans didn't know this.' In 1916 a wit in the city of London published a small book entitled *What I Know About the War* by Hilaire Belloc, and distributed copies amongst his friends on the Stock Exchange. It contained only blank pages.

19*r* **Cockles Tumley:** Horatio Bottomley, financier, journalist and self-appointed champion of the British soldier. He contributed regularly to *John Bull* (which he had founded in 1906) and to the *Sunday Pictorial* which paid him the then enormous fee of £100 an article. He was acquitted on a charge of fraud in 1909, and made bankrupt in 1911. In 1922 he was sent to prison for seven years for fraud in spite of his threat to march on Westminster at the head of 50,000 ex-servicemen if he were prosecuted. The style of Cockles Tumley is a good imitation of that of Bottomley who, incidentally, would seldom write the word German or Germany, preferring instead, Germhun and Germhuny. Horatius Cocles was, of course, the Roman who traditionally held the Etruscans at the bridge over the Tiber.

21*r* **'East Wind':** The wind direction most favourable for a German gas attack.

21*r* **Mr Krump:** Crump (*see* Glossary).

The Wipers Times 6 March 1916, No. 3, Vol. 1

PRINCIPAL WORLD EVENTS

March 1 German extended submarine campaign starts.

NOTES

26 **Back Chat Comedians:** Not backchat. The reference, therefore, must be to 'chats' (*see* Glossary).

Mined: Mining, counter-mining and the consequent exploding of the galleries was a more or less constant activity along the edge of the Salient.

29*r* **Fox:** Cox and Company, the bankers responsible for keeping the accounts of many famous regiments, attracted the private accounts of many army officers. To Cox's premises in Craig's Court, London, came officers with the hope, alas not always realised, of cashing just one more cheque that would buy an evening's forgetfulness at *The Byng Boys*, *Chu Chin Chow*, or *The Maid of the Mountains.* Although no longer an Army agent, Cox's, who were amalgamated with Lloyds Bank in 1923, are still the paymasters to the Royal Air Force.

30*l* **Street Verbod te Wateren:** 'Commit no nuisance'.

30*l* **Are We as Offensive:** 'Are you as offensive as you might be?' was a frequent (and official) question from H.Q. to officers in the field (*c.f. The New Church Times* 22 May 1916, page 77). Norman Gladden relates that 'this policy of keeping the pot boiling at the front, by raids and stratagems, [was] designed by high authority to maintain an offensive spirit in the troops. While there was undoubtably something to be said for this policy, it was not one that the troops themselves wholeheartedly accepted!' (Norman Gladden, *Ypres 1917* [London: Kimber 1967].)

32*r* **Pennant and Tingle:** H. J. Tennant, Under Secretary of State for the War Office, and William Pringle, Liberal M.P. for Lanark, N.W.

34 **Staples:** Maples, the well-known London store.

35 **The Poplar:** Poplars, or what remained of them were, prolific in the Salient. Those that lined the much-used Menin Road provided an ideal target range for German artillery. Having previously registered their guns on each individual tree they were able to shell any particular point on the road with great ease and accuracy (*cf.* 'Road to Ruin', *Wipers Times* 12 February 1916, p. 2).

The Wipers Times 20 March 1916, No. 4, Vol. 2

PRINCIPAL WORLD EVENTS

March 9 Germany declares war on Portugal.
17 Fifth Battle of Isonzo ends.

NOTES

37 **Flammenwerfer:** *See* Glossary. The War Diary of the Sherwood Foresters records that on 11 March 1916, Captain Roberts 'proceeded to Camp . . . to witness a demonstration of a *Flammenwerfer* . . . but the machine did not work.' Thus 'guaranteed absolutely harmless'.

38 **Ferdy:** Franz Ferdinand, Emperor of Austria-Hungary.
Sultana: Mehmed V, Sultan of Turkey.

39*r* **Mr Shembertons Willing:** Pemberton Billing, Independent M.P. for Hertford and an active and constant critic of the government's war policies. He published a propaganda sheet, *The Vigilante*, in which he maintained that the Germans were deliberately fostering sexual perversions in England as a means of causing errors in the conduct of war. According to *The Vigilante* the Germans possessed a Black Book containing the names of 47,000 highly placed perverts that included most of the Cabinet as well as the Prime Minister himself! Billing joined the army in July 1916.

40*l* **Kew Gardens:** Q (*see* Glossary, G.Q.).

42*l* **Hordon Goose Farm:** Gordon House Farm (*see* Place Names).

43*r* **Fred Karno's Cavalry:** The A.S.C. (*see* Glossary).

45*l* **Fields of crosses:** 200,000 soldiers of the British Commonwealth lie buried within the area that was the 'immortal Salient'. Countless others died in hospitals behind the lines or in England as a result of wounds received there.

New Church Times 17 April 1916, No. 1, Vol. 1

PRINCIPAL WORLD EVENTS

(No events of major significance occurred during the period that elapsed between these two issues.)

NOTES

49 **He Didn't Want to Do it:** The name of a play running at the Prince of Wales Theatre, London in 1915.

50 **William O. N. Zollern:** Wilhelm Hohenzollern, Kaiser Wilhelm II.
William Junior: The German Crown Prince.

52*r* **The Mystery of 999:** Bottomley was a keen exponent of 'numerology'.

55*l* **Call Haine:** Sir Thomas Henry Hall Caine, novelist and journalist. He devoted his war-time activities to promoting Allied propaganda in the United States.

58*l* **Latest peace rumour:** The Crown Prince of Germany was reputed to possess a fabulous collection of jewels, paintings and antiques looted from the churches of France and Belgium.

59 **Are you going over the top?:** Very light-coloured riding breeches were fashionable among Army officers in France but they were quite unsuitable for 'going over the top' as the wearer was all too conspicuous and a ready target for snipers. It took several hundred casualties among junior officers before the authorities realised that the cause of the high casualty rate among platoon commanders was their uniform, and particularly their breeches.

59*l* **Bus Farm:** A ruined farm named after a derelict bus that lay nearby. The farm was in a comparatively sheltered position and was used by the troops as a place to stop and brew up tea.

The New Church Times 8 May 1916, No. 2, Vol. 1

PRINCIPAL WORLD EVENTS

April 24 Outbreak of Irish rebellion.
May 1 Collapse of Irish rebellion.

NOTES

61 **Mac Kensen:** Mackensen Farm, a German strong point near Pilkem.

62 **'Shell In':** After *Shell Out*, a popular play then running at London's Comedy Theatre.

Duddy Whizz-Bang: A 'dud' shell.

Hurla Shellog: A play on the name of the actress Shirley Kellogg.

Lewis Vickers: The Lewis and the Vickers guns were the two machine-guns in general use with the British army.

67*r* **The Right Barrel:** 'Sabretache', a gossip columnist in the *Tatler* wrongly credited the 6th Division with the production of the *Wipers Times*.

Eve: 'The Letters of Eve' was a regular illustrated feature in the *Tatler*. An example of its contents and style may be of interest: 'Can't help being just a wee bit bucked by it [the spring] can you, Betty? . . . no matter if we are dining and dancing or otherwise frivalling (sic), there's the rather aching thought of our own and all the other splendid men we've lost, or fear may get hurt or something in that Great Big Push we're all strung up to hear about that must be coming simply horridly soon now, I'm afraid . . . etc. etc. etc.'

68*l* **Mr Justice Starling:** Mr Justice Darling.

68*l* **Maurice Aviary:** Horace Avory, K.C.

70*l* **Carie Morelli:** Marie Corelli, a novelist.

71*r* **The 'Munque' Art Gallery:** This must refer to graffiti (*cf.* Munque Art Gallery 'advertisement', *Kemmel Times* 3 July 1916, p. 111, 'Telephone: "102 Knewd"'). Munque was a farm about two and a half miles N.N.E. of Neuve Eglise.

The New Church Times 22 May 1916, No. 3, Vol. 1

PRINCIPAL WORLD EVENTS

May 14 Austrian offensive in the Trentino begins.

NOTES

74 **Warm Woollens for War-worn Walloons:** Flag days, bazaars and fêtes were held regularly in England for such charities as the 'Help Roumania', 'French Wounded', 'Polish Victims', 'Russian Prisoners' and many other funds. The soldiers serving in the Salient felt, not unnaturally, that charity should begin at home. The appeal for warm woollens is a squib on the 'Belgian Boat Fund' (*cf.* Society for Providing Blue Body Belts for Bucolic Belgians, this issue p. 81). While charitable events in England were patronised by well-meaning society ladies, the 'local ladies' who street-vended for the *New Church Times* Flag Day were big guns in the literal sense.

Lady Ethel Fiveaye: was situated at map location 5A.

78*l* **Ruby N. Dares:** Ruby M. Ayres, a novelist.

78*r* **Tate's cube box:** Tate and Lyle's sugar.

79*l* **Der Deckungsoffizier:** Frankau here mistook *Deckungsoffizier* for the German word for 'junior officer'. In fact it means 'warrant officer' or 'non-commissioned officer'. Junior officers in the British army were advised by their superiors to 'Marry their platoons', i.e. to devote their entire care and attention to their commands to the exclusion of all else. A platoon consisted of about twenty-five men. Hence, 'Marital Martial Law!'.

Lord K-t-n-r: Lord Kitchener.

79*r* **Tiv:** The old Tivoli Theatre in the Strand.

82*r* **Red Lodge:** *See* Place Names.

83*r* **Daylight Saving Bill:** The Bill introducing 'British Summer Time' came into effect on 21 May 1916.

The New Church Times 29 May 1916, No. 4, Vol. 1

PRINCIPAL WORLD EVENTS

(No events of major significance occurred during the period that elapsed between these two issues.)

NOTES

85 **Willie Hozenzollern:** (i.e. Hohenzollers) The German Crown Prince William, always referred to by the British as Willy, usually 'Little Willie'.

Tewlies Troupe of Trick Tricyclists: Army bicyclists.

Meales Musical Mules: Army mules.

Beersons Bewildering Birds: Carrier pigeons.

91*l* **Blatchford:** A socialist politician who, in 1909, advised Lord Kitchener to prepare the nation for an Anglo-German war.

Willett: William Willett, champion of 'daylight saving'. He first advocated 'summer time' in 1907.

91*r* **Greys, Asquiths, McKennas:** Sir Edward Grey, Foreign Minister; Herbert Henry Asquith, Prime Minister; Reginald McKenna, Chancellor of the Exchequer.

Scandal of shells: On 31 December 1914, Sir John French, Commander of the B.E.F., laid down his shell requirements as: 50 rounds a day for 18-pounders; 40 rounds a day for 4·5-inch; 25 rounds per day for 4·7 inch. The actual number of rounds supplied to him throughout the first two years of the war was but a fraction of the above figures. In May 1915 the supply was: 11·0 rounds per gun per day for 18-pounders; 6·1 rounds per gun per day for 4·5-inch; 4·3 rounds per gun per day for 4.7 inch.

'These figures . . . speak for themselves,' wrote Lloyd George. 'The consequences of this deficiency were tragic for the troops who had to hold the line. . . . Throughout those months our men were being battered by the Germans without any effective means of retaliation. Retaliation meant protection. The Germans would have hesitated to open fire on our trenches had they known we could return shell for shell. But they knew too well that they could rain explosives on our poor fellows with practical impunity. And when we attacked, our advance was not supported by adequate artillery preparation or counter-battery work, and our men were held up by unbroken wire and there slaughtered by machine-guns. This calamity was due to the utter inadequacy of the preliminary bombardment. It was not the fault of our artillery; their guns were not heavy enough and their shell supply for heavy and light guns was not only painfully inadequate but inappropriate to the task, for it was mostly shrapnel.' (David Lloyd George, *War Memoirs*, Vol. i [London: Odhams Press 1938], p. 112 *et seq.*)

92*l* **Casement shipment:** In April 1916 Sir Roger Casement sailed from Germany to Ireland in a German submarine, accompanied by a vessel laden with arms and ammunition intended for the forthcoming Easter rising of the Irish. Casement was captured, brought to London, tried for treason and hanged on 3 August the same year.

92*r* **Billie Carleton:** A musical comedy actress.

93*r* **Glycerine:** A member of the 'Fancies' (*q.v.* Notes p. 5*r*).

97*l* **Skindles:** A riverside restaurant at Maidenhead, popular with junior officers.

Prince's: A London restaurant.

'Mr Manhatten': A musical comedy running in London.

98*r* **Art. Hillery's Hot Crumpets:** Artillery 'crumps' (*see* Glossary).

The Kemmel Times 3 July 1916, No. 1, Vol. 1

PRINCIPAL WORLD EVENTS

May 31 The two-day Battle of Jutland begins.
June 2 Fort Vaux (Verdun) stormed by German Infantry.

3 End of Austrian offensive in the Trentino.
4 The long-awaited Russian offensive begins.
16 Italian counter-offensive in the Trentino begins.
23 Fort Thiaumont (Verdun) stormed by German forces and taken after a heroic resistance. This date marks the limit of the German advance on Verdun.
30 Fort Thiaumont recaptured by French forces.
July 1 Battles of the Somme begin with the Battle of Albert.

NOTES

102 **Gas:** The 24th Division suffered a heavy gas attack (in three stages over a 10,000-foot front) while holding the line around Dranoutre on the night of 16–17 June 1916. Its casualties were 562 which included 95 dead. An intended assault by German infantry was foiled at the last moment when the wind changed and the gas blew back to the German trenches. The gas used on this occasion was probably chlorine which, when inhaled, could produce a long agonising death.

When the gas helmet was developed to afford complete protection against noxious vapours German chemists introduced a subtle dodge that increased the effectiveness of poisonous gasses. This was the introduction of 'stink' gas, so called from its intolerably disagreeable odour, which, although not in itself dangerous, caused vomiting. 'Stink' gas was mixed with poison gas with the result that men under attack were constrained to remove their gas helmets on account of the 'stink' which penetrated through them, and they then fell victims to the poison.

Twen Teforth: The 24th Division.

Eve at the Front: This undoubtedly refers to 'Eve' of the *Tatler* (*cf. New Church Times* 8 May 1916, p. 67) but the meaning is obscure. It was not unknown for celebrated ladies to visit the front but 'Eve' had yet to do so (*see* note p. 106*l*: 'The invitation also extends to Eve').

103*l* **Death of Lord Kitchener:** Lord Kitchener was drowned when H.M.S. *Hampshire* struck a mine off the Orkneys on 5 June 1916.

Naval Victory: The Battle of Jutland, fought 31 May – 1 July 1916.

105*l* **Teech Bomas:** William Beach Thomas, the *Daily Mail* war correspondent with the B.E.F. in France.

106*l* **Violet's Chronicle of Fashion:** A letter from the editor of the *Kemmel Times* to 'Sabretache' of the *Tatler* was published in that magazine on 31 May 1916. It reads: '. . . Glad you like our effort, which has provided us with a constant source of amusement and at "Wipers" with a very necessary counter-excitement. There is little going on over here, but I can assure you there's no need for cold feet. Old Fritz's frightfulness has now a big element of doubt behind it all. If it should ever happen that you take a run over, then we shall be delighted to see you and show you round the works. The invitation also extends to "Eve", who weekly delights us. By the way we are offering enormous salaries to a suitable young woman (or women) to run our "fashions" column. You might mention it.' 'Sabretache' mentioned it: 'There would appear to be an opening here for someone who can do "Fashions in the Fire", or "Frocks and Shocks", or something like that.' In the *Tatler* of 5 July 1916 he wrote: 'Our friends on the *New Church Times* (late *Wipers Times*) have, one is glad to learn, managed to collect a lady correspondent through the medium of a note published in this column. The editor of that famous journal was, so we learn, absolutely overwhelmed with applications, and when here on leave not very long ago arranged to hold an inspection parade of the candidates. The name of the successful competitor is in the possession of the writer but for the sake of the *New Church Times's* editor's future safety it is not going to be divulged.' The identity of Violet remains a mystery.

107*l* **Tock Twenty-seven Beer:** T 27 B: a map reference.

107*r* **I. Beer:** I.B. (*see* Glossary).

109*l* **Von Tirpitz:** Grand Admiral von Tirpitz, Secretary of State for the German Imperial Navy until his fall from power in March 1915. He had no control over the war at sea at the time of the Battle of Jutland. There are a number of references in various issues of the *Wipers Times* to Tirpitz's alleged habit of 'driving nails into his statue'. A large iron statue of Von Tirpitz known as 'The Iron Tirpitz' stood in Wilhelmshaven until 1918 but how and why the Grand Admiral drove nails into it cannot be ascertained. According to the Northcliffe press of the day members of the German High Command were guilty of every atrocity from child murder to cannibalism, and the 'statue' story may have been that von Tirpitz practised witchcraft.

The Somme Times 31 July 1916, No. 1, Vol. 1

PRINCIPAL WORLD EVENTS

July 3 Battle of Baranovichi (Russia) begins.
7 David Lloyd George succeeds Lord Kitchener as Secretary of State for War.
14 Battle of Bazentin (Somme) begins.
15 Battle of Delville Wood (Somme) begins.
23 Battle of Pozières Ridge (Somme) begins.

NOTES

113 **The Three Lorelei:** Three blonde 'sirens'. Lorelei is a rock in the River Rhine which gives a remarkable echo. The story is that a maiden threw herself into the Rhine in despair over a faithless lover and became a siren whose voice lured fishermen to destruction.

114 **Albert-Pozieres-Bapaume Circuit:** The British line of attack during the Battle of the Somme, June–September 1916.
Enrico Walthallo: Possibly Oberleutnant Franz Walther, a German submarine commander.

117*l* **X.I.B.:** 10th Infantry Battalion.

117*r* **A jar enfolds:** Rum!

118*l* **Eve, Blanche and Phrynette:** Blanche and Phrynette were the *Bystander*'s and the *Sketch*'s versions of the *Tatler*'s 'Eve'. Phrynette wrote a weekly column called 'Letters to Lonely Soldiers'.

The B.E.F. Times 1 December 1916, No. 1, Vol. 1

PRINCIPAL WORLD EVENTS

August	4	Battle of Rumani (Sinai) begins.
		Sixth Battle of Isonzo begins.
	27	Roumania declares war on Austria–Hungary.
	28	Germany declares war on Roumania.
		Italy declares war on Germany.
	30	Turkey declares war on Roumania.
	31	Battle of Verdun ends.
September	1	Bulgaria declares war on Roumania.
	3	Battle of Guillemont (Somme) begins.
	9	Battle of Ginchy (Somme).
	14	Seventh Battle of Isonzo begins.
	15	Battle of Flers-Courcelette (Somme) begins; tanks in action for the first time.
	25	Battle of Morval (Somme) begins.
	26	Battle of Thiepval Ridge (Somme) begins.
October	1	Battle of Transloy Ridge (Somme) begins.
		Battle of the Ancre Heights (Somme) begins.
	9	Eighth Battle of Isonzo begins.
	24	'First Offensive Battle' of Verdun begins.
		Fort Douaumont recaptured by French forces.
	31	Ninth Battle of Isonzo begins.
November	1	Fort Vaux (Verdun) retaken by French forces.
	11	Battle of the Ancre.
		Battles of the Somme (1916) end.
	23	Greece declares war on Germany and Bulgaria.

125 **Hullo Tanko:** *Hullo Tango*, a revue, was produced at the London Hippodrome in 1913. The title song was still popular in 1916. Tanks were first used in battle on 15 September 1916. Roberts makes many references to London's theatrical world and the fact that the war brought it record business does not seem to have concerned him. It certainly concerned Siegfried Sassoon who wrote ('Blighters', July 1916):

> I'd like to see a Tank come down the stalls,
> Lurching to rag-time tunes or 'Home Sweet Home',
> And there'd be no more jokes in Music Halls
> To mock the riddled corpses round Bapaume.

125 **'No Treating':** Under an Order in Council passed in July 1915 it became a legal offence in Great Britain to 'treat' a person to an alcoholic drink in a licensed premises.

126 **L.B.M.L. Railway:** Lille, Bailleul, Menin Light Railway.

128*r* **'Eskimo' return:** Officers in the line were frequently required to supply statistical 'returns' concerning details which they considered trivial and time-wasting – how many men of Irish nationality? how many with a knowledge of ironmongery or bus-conducting? how many could speak Swahili? For a reason that is obvious these questionnaires became known as 'Eskimo returns' (*cf. B.E.F. Times* 5 March 1917, 'R. the Returns', p. 179).

130*r* **Tirpy and Falky:** Grand Admiral von Tirpitz and General von Falkenhayn, Chief of the German General Staff.

132*l* **Cloridy Lyme:** Chloride of lime was used extensively in the forward area to disinfect and deodorise. It even found its way into the men's tea.

132*l* **Quality Street:** A trench.

135 **Jarrie and Cames:** Carrie and James (?), probably Quartermasters.

The B.E.F. Times 25 December 1916, No. 2, Vol. 1

PRINCIPAL WORLD EVENTS

December 1 Battle of the Arges (Roumania) begins.
4 Asquith resigns as British Premier.
6 Bucharest capitulates to German forces.
7 Lloyd George becomes British Premier.
9 War Cabinet formed in Great Britain.
11 Lloyd George's coalition ministry formed in Great Britain.
18 'First Offensive Battle' of Verdun ends.

137 **L – – – –:** Loos or Lillers (?).

Bethmaniano: Herr von Bethman-Hollweg, the then Imperial Chancellor of Germany. In December 1916 the Germans were campaigning for peace and their efforts were supported by President Woodrow Wilson. In a note addressed to all the belligerent powers Wilson shocked the Allies by stating that the objects of both sides were 'virtually the same'.

138 **Lillies Lecture Hall:** On 9 December 1916, a lecture was given to officers of the 24th Division in the town hall of Lillers. The subject was 'The German Army' and the lecturer was Colonel W. L. O. Twiss who in the 'advertisement' becomes 'Mr Hiteof Bliss'. The height of bliss was *not* a state into which junior officers were transported when attending lectures on military tactics.

Furs, Tarmy and Co.: First Army.

'Vermorlet': Vermoral (*see* Glossary) and 'Sparklet', the latter being a patent device for making soda-water.

139*r* **Extra pat of butter:** A Board of Trade Order came into force on 18 December 1916, limiting all hotel and restaurant meals to three courses; on the same day the Military C.-in-C. of the London district required hotels and restaurants (on pain of being placed 'out-of-bounds' to all ranks) to limit the price of meals to members of the military forces as follows:

Lunch	3s-6d.	(17½p)
Tea	1s-6d.	(7½p)
Dinner	5s-6d.	(27½p)
Supper	3s-6d.	(17½p)

This was to 'check unnecessary extravagance'. On 18 November 1916 *The Times* had reported rises in teashop prices. 'Bread and butter is now 2½d (1p), while the slices are appreciably thinner. Steak puddings have risen from 5d (2p) to 6d (2½p). Two poached eggs on toast cost 11d (4½p). A small sandwich costs 3d (1½p).

145*l* **Tempora Mutantur:** Times change.

151 **The Bing Bangs:** *The Byng Boys*, a revue running in London.

The Westminster Troupe in All Change Here: In December 1916 Lloyd George succeeded Asquith as Prime Minister and converted the cabinet into a small war executive supported by new ministries for the control of food, shipping, labour, pensions and air. The more important departments were headed by experts instead of politicians.

The B.E.F. Times 20 January 1917, No. 3, Vol. 1

PRINCIPAL WORLD EVENTS

January 9 Battle of Kut begins.

NOTES

153 **Inn Dent and Dados:** Indent (to) Deputy Assistant Director of Ordinance Services.

154 **'Tickling Fritz':** Tickler (*see* Glossary).

154 **Crassier:** A slag-heap.

155*r* **Dis-ing, chases, furniture:** Printing terms.

156*l* **Whiskey will shortly be 'na-poo':** A temperance society, the 'Strength of Britain Movement' was promoting an intensive campaign to introduce 'prohibition' into Great Britain. According to the society the demon drink was responsible for all the reverses suffered by the Allies. 'Since the war began,' said one of its half-page advertisements in the national press, 'alcohol has wasted enough food to last the nation 100 days . . . 4,000,000 tons of coal . . . and £400,000,000 of the people's money.' An anti-drink petition organised in 1916 collected the support of over 1,000 distinguished personages including eight admirals, eight generals and a host of politicians (*see* Glossary, Napoo).

158*r* **Tenth Avenue:** A trench.

160*l* **Indian Corps:** Indian troops served in the trenches of France and Belgium throughout the war.

163*r* **The Siegesallee:** An avenue in Berlin adorned along its length with groups of statuary representing the Hohenzollerns. It was not in Potsdam as 'Kurly Kertin' states.

Kurly Kertin: D. Thomas Curtin, an American journalist. He was commissioned by Lord Northcliffe to contribute a series of articles to *The Times* and managed to spend ten months in Germany by posing as anti-British (*cf.* 'Tuckis Shurtin' *B.E.F. Times* 10 April 1917, No. 5, p. 196).

167 **Doctor Shaveling:** The Medical Officer to the Battalion was Lieutenant Aveling. The rest of this 'advertisement' is a mystery.

The B.E.F. Times 5 March 1917, No. 4, Vol. 1

PRINCIPAL WORLD EVENTS

February 1 German 'unrestricted submarine warfare' begins.
3 United States of America sever diplomatic relations with Germany.

NOTES

169 **The Maude Troupe:** Lieutenant-General Sir Stanley Maude, commanding the 13th Division in Mesopotamia, advanced on Baghdad during February and March 1917. The city was occupied by the British on 11 March.

Enver: Pasha Enver, Turkish Minister of War.

'Willie's Turkey': A reference to the Turkish-German Union, formed on 17 February 1916.

170 **Sports Meeting:** The division was in training at the time of this issue as can be seen from the 'list of events'.

173*l* **General Capper:** General Sir John Capper, commander of the 24th Division October 1915 – May 1917.

173*r* **Movie-King:** Gilbert Frankau was in Italy promoting British war films.

179*l* **Pediculi:** Lice.

179*r* **V for the Vices:** A reference to a spate of letters to *The Times* bewailing the 'temptations' that beset British soldiers in France and Belgium.

183*r* **Senators Glee Party:** America broke off diplomatic relations with Germany on 3 February 1917.

Devonport: Viscount Devonport, founder of a grocery empire, was appointed first Food Controller in November 1916.

The B.E.F. Times 10 April 1917, No. 5, Vol. 1

PRINCIPAL WORLD EVENTS

March	11	Baghdad occupied by British forces.
	12	Russian Revolution begins.
	14	German retreat from the Somme to the Hindenburg Line begins.
	15	Tsar of Russia abdicates.
	26	First Battle of Gaza begins
April	6	U.S.A. declares war on Germany.
	9	Battles of Arras (1917) begin with Battle of Vimy Ridge.

NOTES

185 **Duma:** The Russian Parliament.

Rodzi: President of the Duma.

Teddy: Theodore Roosevelt, President of the United States, September 1901 – March 1909. When the United States entered the war in April 1917, Roosevelt offered to raise a division of volunteers and to lead them into battle himself.

Murray: General Sir Archibald Murray, Commander of the British forces in Egypt.

186 **Cruise of the Catch-a-Lot:** This appears to be a reference to the Battle of Jutland, fought nearly a year before this 'advertisement' appeared. (From *The Cruise of the Cachalot* by F. T. Bullen.)

The Drink Habit: A satire on an advertisement that appeared regularly in the London newspapers. Needless to say, it is the complete opposite of the original.

189*r* **Arma Virumque Cano:** 'To arms and the man I sing' (Virgil's *Aeneid*, C.1).

191*l* **Sursum Caudasi:** Tails up. 'Tails up and stick it!', an enlivenment exchanged by officers in the line.

193*l* **Der Tag:** The day of victory, from Lissauer's 'Hymn of Hate' (*see* Glossary):

> In the Captain's Mess, in the banquet-hall
> Sat feasting the officers, one and all,
> Like a sabre-blow, like the swing of a sail,
> One seized his glass held high to hail:
> Sharp-snapped like the stroke of a rudder's play
> Spoke three words only: 'To the Day!'

Louvain: A town in Belgium from which came the first reports of German 'frightfulness'.

194*l* **Bully-Barlin Stakes:** Bully and Barlin were two villages north of Arras and on the front line. The 'events' refer, presumably, to activity in the area at the time.

Admiral Jellicue: Admiral Jellicoe, then First Sea Lord.

196*l* **Tuckis Shurtin:** Thomas Curtin (*cf. B.E.F. Times* 20 January 1917, p. 163).

199*r* **Emo's 'Fruity Ports':** Eno's Fruit Salts.

The B.E.F. Times 15 August 1917, No. 1, Vol. 2

PRINCIPAL WORLD EVENTS

April	10	Bulgaria severs diplomatic relations with U.S.A.
	11	Brazil severs diplomatic relations with Germany.
	13	Bolivia severs diplomatic relations with Germany.
	16	French offensive begins with Second Battle of the Aisne.
	17	'Battle of the Hills' (Champagne) begins.
		Second Battle of Gaza begins.
	20	French offensive checked.
		Turkey severs diplomatic relations with U.S.A.
	23	Second Battle of the Scarpe (Arras) begins.
	28	Battle of Arleux (Arras).
May	2	Third Battle of the Scarpe begins.
		Battle of Bullecourt begins.
	5	Battle of the Vardar (Macedonia) begins.
	12	Tenth Battle of Isonzo begins.
June	7	Battle of Messines begins.
	14	Battle of Messines ends.
	25	First contingent of U.S. troops arrives in France.
	29	Russian summer offensive begins.

July 18 German counter-offensive begins on the eastern front with the Battle of East Galicia.

31 Battles of Ypres (1917) begin with Battle of Pilkem Ridge.

August 14 China declares war on Germany and Austria-Hungary.

NOTES

201 **William's Troupe: 'The Cockchafers':** The German Guard Fusilier Regiment known as the 'Maikafers' (May Beetles). They were the military pets of the Kaiser who – for a reason unexplained – sent them a little packet containing a live cockchafer every first of May.

202*r* **Rabbits:** The food shortage of 1917–1918 resulted in an enormous slaughter of rabbits and large quantities of them found their way to the Western Front (rabbit fur collars became quite a fashion amongst British officers in France). **Supply Villa** must be the local ration dump and **Bunter** (Hunter?) the regimental quartermaster.

203*r* **The journey of Ramsay Macdonald to Stockholm:** In July 1917, the Labour leader, Ramsey Macdonald, together with Arthur Henderson, a Labour member of the Cabinet, travelled to Paris to attend a secret meeting of the Stockholm International Peace Conference, an unofficial 'peace conference' of international socialists which included some German delegates. This meeting was a preliminary to a larger function to take place in Stockholm. Macdonald and Henderson never reached Stockholm for the National Seamen and Firemen's Union, none other, decided that no British ship would carry British delegates to the conference.

Punch's comment on the affair expressed mass opinion in Britain: 'The real voice of Labour is not that of the delegates who want to go to the International Socialist Conference at Stockholm to talk to Fritz, but of Tommy, who, after a short "leaf", goes cheerfully (sic) back to France to fight him. And the fomentors of class hatred will not find much support from the "men in blue" [i.e. hospital 'blue' worn by the wounded].'

204*l* **Wind well up and a crick in the neck:** An apt and expressive reference to the German air raids on London.

206*l* **Flamsey Macdonald:** Ramsay Macdonald.

Grictor Vayson: Victor Grayson, elected socialist M.P. for Colne Valley in 1907. He took to drink and was expelled from the House of Commons in 1910. He joined the army as a private soldier in 1915 and was wounded in October 1917. In 1920 he disappeared from a London hotel, leaving all his luggage behind and was never heard of again.

A. Tenderson: Arthur Henderson. At the time of this issue he had just resigned from the war Cabinet as a result of the 'Stockholm scandal'.

207*r* **To the memory:** The 24th Division suffered heavy casualties in the great battles that were fought in the Salient in 1917. In the first month of the fighting (April) its losses were 73 officers (27 killed) and 1,191 other ranks (272 killed).

208*l* **Curly Shellog:** Shirley Kellog, a variety artiste who was appearing with Harry Tate in *Razzle Dazzle*, first produced at the Empire Theatre, Leicester Square, in 1916.

214*r* **The Pope is raising an army:** On 1 August 1917, Pope Benedict XV addressed a plea for peace 'to the heads of the Belligerent Peoples'.

The Chinese: A large Chinese labour force, recruited by the British, was employed behind the lines in France and Belgium.

The B.E.F. Times 8 September 1917, No. 2, Vol. 2

PRINCIPAL WORLD EVENTS

August	15	Battle of Hill 70 (Lens) begins.
	16	Battle of Langemarck (Ypres) begins.
	17	Eleventh Battle of the Isonzo begins.
	20	'Second Offensive Battle' of Verdun begins.
September	1	Battle of Riga begins.

NOTES

217 **'Rigaletgo':** Riga let go. The Russian city of Riga was surrendered to the Germans on 3 September 1917.

218 **Polygon:** A village in Belgium and the scene of much fighting in August–October 1917. The Battle of Polygon Wood began on 16 September 1917.

Von Arnim: General Sixt von Arnim, Commander of German 4th Army Corps.

221*l* **Kicking footballs:** British infantry were known to have kicked footballs amongst themselves during daylight attacks.

224*l* **Swan (and Edgar):** The famous London department store.

226*l* **The P.B.:** O.R.'s who were unfit for the forward area but not ill enough to be sent home were often given light duties to perform in the Permanent Base of the division.

230*r* **The Soldiers' Friend:** The *Daily Mail* styled itself thus.

'When their Rawlies, etc': General Rawlinson, commanding 4th British Army; General Gough, commanding 5th British Army; Field-Marshal Lord Plumer, Commander of British Forces in France; General Byng, Commander of 3rd British Army.

231 **The Helpman Mind-Training System:** Pelmanism, a much advertised 'mind-training' course. The 'Pelman Institute' claimed that forty-one generals, eight admirals and ten thousand officers and men were Pelman trained. It claimed

also that it was to be nationalised by the government 'so that everyone would take the course and the war would soon be won' (*cf.* 'Helpmanism', ***B.E.F. Times*** 25 December 1917, p. 264).

The B.E.F. Times 1 November 1917, No. 3, Vol. 2

PRINCIPAL WORLD EVENTS

September	20	Battle of Menin Road Ridge (Ypres) begins.
	26	Battle of Polygon Wood (Ypres) begins.
October	4	Battle of Broodseinde (Ypres) begins.
	9	Battle of Poelcapelle (Ypres) begins.
	12	First Battle of Passchendaele (Ypres) begins.
	23	Battle of La Malmaison begins.
	24	Twelfth Battle of the Isonzo begins.
	26	Brazil declares war on Germany. Second Battle of Passchendaele begins.
	27	Third Battle of Gaza begins.

NOTES

233 **Gotterdammerhaig:** A double joke. *Gotterdammerung*, the opera by Richard Wagner, becomes 'God Damn Haig'. It also appeared from events that the 'Twilight of the Gods' was at hand at last.

Fritz ran and I'm sold: *Tristan and Isolde*, another Wagner opera.

Mike Hayliss: Georg Michaelis, German Chancellor, July–August 1917. His fall was the result of the 'row' which followed a minor mutiny on board a German battleship at Kiel.

235*l* **Jupiter Pluvius:** The God of Rain. The Flanders battles of 1917 were fought in almost continual torrential rain.

237*r* **The Peelers:** Nineteenth-century slang for the police, founded by Sir Robert Peel in 1829.

238*l* **Blondin's on a wire:** Blondin, a famous tight-rope walker, crossed the Niagara Falls on a high-wire.

238*r* **Beer Coy:** B Company.

243*l* **Effpy:** F.P. (*see* Glossary).

243*r* **A bomb in Piccadilly Circus:** The bomb referred to did not drop in Piccadilly Circus but near to the Ritz Hotel. Twenty-one people were killed and seventy injured in the incident, which occurred on 24 September 1917.

247*l* **Ivanhoe Cigarettes:** A satire on the 'She and he' dialogues featured in newspaper advertisements for Kenilworth cigarettes (2s 6d [12½p] per 100).

The B.E.F. Times 25 December 1917, No. 4, Vol. 2

PRINCIPAL WORLD EVENTS

November	20	Battle of Cambrai begins.
	30	German counter-attacks at Cambrai begin.
December	2	Suspension of hostilities between the Russian and German armies.
	6	Hostilities between Roumania and the Central Powers suspended.
	7	Truce between Russia and Central Powers comes into official operation.
	8	All hostilities on Eastern Front suspended.
	9	Jerusalem surrenders to British forces.

NOTES

249 **Maude Allenby:** Lieutenant-General Maude and General Allenby, commander of the Egyptian Expeditionary Force. Beersheba, Gaza and Jerusalem were captured by the British in October, November, and December 1917, respectively.

K. Rensky: M. Kerensky, head of the provisional coalition government, formed in October 1917, that followed the Russian revolution. His ministry was short-lived, for after a struggle for power with Lenin he fled on 7 November 1917.

Southcliffe: Lord Northcliffe who, by 1917, had risen to the post of Minister for Air.

250 **'Wipers Times and after':** Herbert Jenkins & Company published a facsimile edition of all the *Wipers Times* numbers up to November 1917.

256*r* **Don C. Emma:** The Distinguished Conduct Medal, the ribbon of which is scarlet.

257*l* **One inch group:** In marksmanship, the ability to group several shots within a circle one inch in diameter.

261*l* **Gaby Glide, Turkey Trot, etc.:** Titles of rag-time tunes popular at the time.

262*r* **H. Davis:** Because of the shortage of medical officers in the British Army, a number of American doctors were seconded to the British forces in 1917. Davis was one of these and served with the Sherwood Foresters. He was a very courageous officer who carried on work for several days after being wounded in March 1918.

263*l* **Arree:** R.E. (*see* Glossary).

264*l* **Mime and Mummery; Strewth:** *Mind and Memory* and *Truth*, two books published by the Pelman Institute (*cf. B.E.F. Times* 8 September 1917, p. 231).

265 **Use this coupon:** The Pelman enrolment form was invariably printed 'sideways' in *The Times*. The real address was Wenham House, Bloomsbury Street.

267 **Shortone & Pastum:** A double joke. Fortnum and Mason's, the London store, and 'short one and paste them' – shells from one's own artillery which fell short ('short ones') were liable to 'paste' one's own trenches.

267*l* **Hay & Kew:** A.Q. (Assistant Quartermaster).

267*r* **Hunny Hug:** A dance called the 'Bunny Hug' was popular at the time.

The B.E.F. Times 22 January 1918, No. 5, Vol. 2

PRINCIPAL WORLD EVENTS

(No events of major significance occurred during the period that elapsed between these two issues.)

NOTES

269 **Hertling and Czernin:** Count Hertling, German Chancellor from November 1918, and Count Ottokar Czernin, Minister of Foreign Affairs in Austria-Hungary. In January 1918 they replied to Woodrow Wilson's 'fourteen points' in separate speeches.

Rorge Jobey: George Robey, a well-known English comedian then appearing at the London Hippodrome.

Margerine and Lepins: Possibly bread and margarine (lepins – *le pain*?).

270 **Sir Rosslyn Wemyss:** Then First Sea Lord. To him was mainly due the dramatic exploit of Zeebrugge.

'Dead Hun Farm': (*cf.* Dead Cow Farm).

270 **Sir Shetland Steddes:** Sir Eric Geddes, appointed First Lord of the Admiralty in July 1917.

Mr Barnes: G. N. Barnes, Labour M.P. for the Blackfriars division of Glasgow and a member of the war Cabinet.

Benver Hay: Pasha Enver (formally Enver Bey), Turkish Minister for War.

272*l* **Ervilly** and **Villers:** Two villages near Roisel.

The B.E.F. Times 26 February 1918, No. 6, Vol. 2

PRINCIPAL WORLD EVENTS

February 18 Armistice terminates on Russian front, hostilities resumed by German armies.

NOTES

285 **'Ronder':** Lord Rhondda (D. A. Thomas), appointed Food Controller in June 1917. He was instrumental in the introduction of ration cards in January 1918.

286 **Trench University:** With the end of the war in sight a number of postal degree courses were being advertised in the British press.

Hillary Bullock: Hilaire Belloc again.

Rameses Snowden: Ramsay Macdonald and Philip Snowden, Labour M.P. and pacifist. The latter was an active champion of conscientious objectors and was not admired by serving soldiers.

286 **Bullets carefully fixed in bibles:** In Britain, everybody knew someone whose soldier relative had been miraculously preserved when a bullet was stopped by a bible kept in the breast pocket. As a result, soldiers on the Western Front could be embarrassed by the number of pocket bibles they received from well-meaning relatives.

295*l* **Kewem:** Q.M. (Quartermaster).

295*r* **C _ _ _ _ s: Junction:** Calais, the main transit port for the B.E.F.

296*r* **Mr Dunbill:** Dunhill, maker of tobacco pipes.

299*r* **Tights old car soap:** Wright's Coal Tar Soap. The 'little darlings' referred to are, of course, lice.

The Better Times November 1918, No. 1, Vol. 1

PRINCIPAL WORLD EVENTS

March	3	Peace signed between Russia and Central Powers, Bulgaria and Turkey at Brest-Litovsk.
	21	First Battles of Somme (1918), opening with Battle of St Quentin, begin the great German offensive in the west.
	24	First Battle of Bapaume.
	27	Battle of Rosières (Somme).
	28	First Battle of Arras.
April	5	Battle of the Ancre (Somme)
	9	Battles of the Lys begin.
	10	Battle of Messines (1918) begins.
	14	General Foch appointed Commander-in-Chief of the Allied armies in France.
	23	Blocking raid by British navy on Ostend and Zeebrugge.
May	27	Battle of the Aisne (1918) begins.
	31	German forces reach the Marne.
July	15	Fourth Battle of Champagne begins.
	18	Battle of the Marne (1918) begins.
August	8	Battle of Amiens begins.
	13	Czechoslovakia declares war on Germany.
	18	British advance into Flanders begins.
	21	Second Battle of the Somme (1918) begins with Battle of Albert.
	26	Second Battle of Arras (1918) begins.
September	12	Battle of St Mihiel.
		Battles of the Hindenburg Line begin.
	26	Battle of Champagne and Argonne begins.
	27	Battle of Canal du Nord begins.
	28	Battle of the Flanders Ridges begins.
		Battle of Ypres (1918) begins.

	29	Battle of St Quentin Canal begins.
October	1	Damascus taken by British and Arab forces.
	4	German and Austro–Hungarian governments send notes to President Wilson proposing an armistice.
	8	Battle of Cambrai (1918) begins.
	27	Austrian government asks Italy for an armistice.
	30	Armistice between Turkey and Entente Powers signed.
	31	Revolutions break out in Vienna and Budapest.
November	3	Armistice signed between Austria–Hungary and the Entente Powers. Mutiny breaks out in the German Fleet at Kiel.
	4	Battle of the Sambre.
	6	Rethal taken by French forces. Sedan taken by United States forces.
	9	Revolution in Berlin.
	10	The Kaiser flees to Holland.
	11	Armistice signed between the Allies and Germany. Mons retaken by British forces. Hostilities on the Western Front cease at 11 a.m.
	12	Emperor of Austria abdicates.

NOTES

301 **Professor Foch:** Field Marshal Ferdinand Foch, Commander-in-Chief of the Allied Armies in France at the time of the Armistice. He conducted the negotiations and dictated the terms of the Armistice, 8–11 November 1918.

My Old Dutch: The Kaiser, having announced his intention of abdicating on 10 November, fled to Holland on the same day.

302*l* **Paxone Boots:** (*Pax* = peace), Saxone, the shoe merchants.

Army of no Occupation: A reference to the fears of unemployment on demobilisation which were later justified.

Advertising Pays: An imitation of an advertisement for Ware's cough mixture.

302*r* **Prudence Assurance:** Prudential Insurance Company.

303*l* **'Ici Nous Sommes Encore':** After the popular song 'Here we are Again'. The allied armies in France had by this time reoccupied all the territory lost to the Germans in 1914.

306*l* **Whilem:** A misprint for 'whilom' – one-time.

307*l* **Kew:** Q. (*see* Glossary, G.Q.).

307*l* **Speaking a strange tongue:** e.g. 'Boots, gum, thigh, pairs, one'.

307*r* **Bra-Sat:** Brass-hat (*see* Glossary).

308*l* **Tomar-Sat-Kins:** Tommy Atkins.

310*l* **One-Pip:** A second lieutenant.

310*r* **Star:** The 1914–1915 Star, a medal awarded to all members of the forces who served between August 1914 and March 1915.

The Better Times December 1918, No. 2, Vol. 1

PRINCIPAL WORLD EVENTS

November 14 Hostilities in East Africa cease.
19 Metz occupied by French forces.
21 German High Seas Fleet arrives at Rosyth, *en route* for internment.
24 British and United States troops reach the German border.
25 Strasbourg occupied by French Forces.
December 12 British troops cross the Rhine at Cologne.

NOTES

317 **Plumer and Co:** The British 2nd Army, commanded by Field Marshal Plumer, crossed the Rhine and occupied the Cologne bridgehead on 12 December 1918.

318 **Bov-Ox and Bo-Vox:** Oxo and Bovril, two similar brands of meat essence.

319*l* **Blue-clad mobs:** Recruits to 'Kitchener's Army' in 1914 were issued with blue uniforms because of a shortage of khaki material.

323*r* **Rien faisant:** Nothing doing. Foch refused to discuss terms with the German representatives at the Armistice meeting but insisted on immediate and total capitulation.

Verfluctes Kerl: Accursed fellow!

324*r* **Miners:** Coal miners were given priority of demobilisation.

326r **'Fourteen points':** In January 1918, President Wilson drew up 'the only possible programme' for peace. It was contained in fourteen paragraphs.

327*l* **Ironsides:** The name given to Cromwell's soldiers after the Battle of Marston Moor.

Casque and Girdle: Hat and belt. A soldier 'on a charge' was stripped of these items before appearing before his commanding officer.

327*r* **Have you voted yet?:** Polling for the 1918 general election took place on 14 December and the result was announced on 30 December, the delay being due to the soldier's postal vote. It was a triumph for the mainly Liberal and Conservative coalition party. The landslide against Labour was largely due to popular reaction against the activities of 'Ramsay Macdonald and Co. during the war.

328 **Gould Garvice:** Nathaniel Gould and Charles Garvice. Gould wrote about 130 novels on horse-racing; Garvice wrote romances.

330*l* **A Contemptible:** The B.E.F. in France in 1914 was styled 'The Old Contemptibles' after the Kaiser referred to it as 'French's contemptible little army'.

GLOSSARY

A.A. Army Acts.

A.A. Assistant Adjutant.

A.A.A. Used in signalling to indicate the end of a sentence.

A.B. Army Book; a pay book carried by all ranks.

A.C. Area Commander.

A.C.I. Army Council Instructions.

Acquittance Rolls Army Pay Sheets.

Ack Emma A.M. (*ante meridiern*) (Signalese).

Ack Pip Emma A.P.M. (Signalese) *See* **A.P.M.**

A.D.C. Aide-de-Camp.

A.D.M.S. Assistant Director of Medical Services.

Adrian hut A hut of French pattern that widened at floor level to provide extra space.

A.D.S. Advanced Dressing Station.

A.D.V.S. Assistant Director of Veterinary Services.

A.F.G.C.M. (?) F.G.C.M. = Field General Court Martial.

'A' frame A frame in the form of an inverted letter 'A'. They were fitted into the bottoms of flooded trenches and planks were placed along the cross-pieces to form platforms above the water or mud. When needed they were brought up by incoming troops, one to a man.

Ally Sloper *See* **A.S.C.**

A.M.L.O. Assistant Military Landing Officer.

Ancient Archie An anti-aircraft Gun.

A.O. Army Order.

A.P.M. Assistant Provost Marshal. An officer of the Military Police equivalent to a Chief Constable. He was the terror of junior officers and was sometimes known as 'A permanent malingerer'.

Apres la guerre Eric Partridge tells us* that 'Après la guerre' carried two connotations for the soldier: it was used jokingly for the indefinite and remote future, e.g. 'When will you marry me? – Oh, après la guerre,' or 'When's the Colonel coming up the line? – Après la guerre'. The phrase was also part of a song sung to the tune of 'The Bridges of Paris':

* Eric Partridge and John Brody, *Songs and Slang of the British Soldier* (O.U.P. 1931).

Après la guerre finis,
Soldat Anglais parti;
Mam'selle Fransay boko pleuray,
Après la guerre finis.

Après la guerre finis
Soldat Anglais parti;
Mademoiselle in the family way,
Après la guerre finis.

Apron wire Wire used to construct an 'apron' – a type of fence laid along the front of a trench.

A.Q.M.G. Assistant Quartermaster General.

Archie An anti-aircraft gun; anti-aircraft fire (*cf.* **Ancient Archie**).

Archied Hit by anti-aircraft fire.

A.R.T.O.C.O. Area Railway Transport Office Commanding Officer.

A.S.C. Army Service Corps. Also known as 'Ally Sloper's Cavalry', after a children's comic character, and as the Army Safety Corps. Also Aunt Sally's Cavalry—thus a ration truck became an Aunt Sally.

Aunt Sally *See* **A.S.C.**

Bachelor Buttons A patent button that could be affixed to a garment without needle and thread and consequently much favoured by private soldiers. They were advertised as possessing a 'bull-dog grip'.

Baron Army Commander.

Batt Battalion.

Beer Coy 'B' Company (Signalese).

B.E.F. British Expeditionary Force.

Berloo Bailleul (*see* Place Names).

Berm The ledge between the trench and the parapet formed during excavation. Sometimes used for storing bombs, signals, etc.

Blighty Soldiers' slang for England or home.

Blighty one A wound that secured return to England.

B.M. Brigade Major.

B.M.J. *British Medical Journal.*

Bolo A spy. After Bolo Pasha, a notorious and impudent German agent active in France during the Great War. He was well supplied with money by the Germans and used it to corrupt the defeatist faction in France. He was executed in April 1918.

Bouncing Bertha Big Bertha: a term used to describe any large German gun – of which there were many varieties.

Brass hat A high-ranking officer.

B.T.O. Battalion Transport Officer.

Bully	Bully-beef, i.e. corned beef.
Cage hotels	Prison camps.
C.B.	Companion of the Bath.
C.C.S.	Casualty Clearing Station.
C.G.I.	Corrugated Galvanised Iron.
Charlie Chaplin	A moustache in the style of that worn by the famous comedian. It was favoured by British Infantry officers but, by unwritten law, forbidden to other ranks.
Chats	Lice.
C.H.Q.	Company Headquarters.
Click	To strike up a chance acquaintance with a member of the opposite sex. One could also 'click a leave' or 'click a guard'.
C.M.G.	Companion of the order of St Michael and St George.
Coal box	The shellburst of a heavy shell because of its blacks moke (*cf.* **Johnson**).
Cold feet, to have	To flinch through fear; to back out of a duty through fear. To show signs of alarm that might, in those robust days, be taken for cowardice. Not to be confused with 'wind up' (*q.v.*).
Concertina wire	A defensive wire used by the French. It was not barbed but possessed the power of 'whipping back' and coiling around anyone who disturbed it.
Counterstrafe	*See* **Strafe**.
C.R.E.	Commander Royal Engineers.
C.R.E.	Corps Supplies from R.E.'s (*q.v.*).
Crimed	To be put on a charge.
C.R.O.	Corps Routine Orders.
Crows feet	A Caltrop, i.e. a many-spiked device thrown on the ground to maim horses.
Crump	The burst of a 5·9-inch shell.
C.T.	Communication trench.
Cuthbert	A man who stayed at home in an easy job. In particular, an officer posted at the War Office.
D.A.A.	Deputy Assistant Adjutant.
D.A.D.I.W.T.	Deputy Assistant Director of Inland Water Transport Service.
D.A.D.O.S.	Deputy Assistant Director Ordinance Services.
D.A.G.	Deputy Adjutant General.
D.A.H.	Disordered Action of the Heart.
D.A.Q.M.G.	Deputy Assistant Quartermaster General.
D.C.C.	Divisional Comic Cuts. The nickname given to communiqués and reports from Divisional Headquarters.
Derby's Disease	'Derby men' were recruited under a voluntary scheme instituted by Lord Derby before conscription became compulsory in March

1916. 'Derby men' were invited to enlist in the army and serve one day (for which they were paid 2s 9d [13p]). They were then 'lent back' to their civilian employers to await recall to the colours according to age and occupation groups as and when needed.

Dido Rum.

D.I.W.T. Director of Inland Water Transport Service.

D Mark 3 A Field Telephone comprising handset, buzzer, key, etc., connected by D3 wire to a similar set (*cf.* **Fullerphone**).

Don C Emma D.C.M. The Distinguished Service Medal (Signalese).

D.R.L.S. Despatch-Rider Letter Service.

D.R.O. Divisional Routine Order; also Divisional Records Office.

D.S.O. Distinguished Service Order.

Duckboard A narrow, slatted path of wood laid over wet and muddy ground

D5 wire A later type of telephone wire (*cf.* **D Mark 3**).

E.F.C. Expeditionary Force Canteen. A canteen set up behind the lines for the sale of foodstuffs and liquid refreshments. They could be either 'wet' or 'dry' but were usually the latter.

Effpy *See* F.P.

Elephant A hut built of rounded sheets of corrugated iron, often without floorboards. Also dug-outs constructed with corrugated iron.

Eliza A long-range shell.

Fatigew Army pronunciation of 'fatigue' – the extra-professional duties of a private soldier.

Firework display A heavy night bombardment (from either side) usually accompanied by red, white, green and blue lights.

Five-nine A 5·9-inch gun.

Flammenwerfer A flame thrower. First used by the Germans at Hooge (*see* Place Names) on 30 July 1915, the *Flammenwerfer* was a steel cylinder filled with inflammable liquid and fitted with a long steel nozzle that projected a jet of flame some twenty yards long. It was first used by the British in August 1917. Its main effectiveness was in the terror it inspired even at a distance but it had great practical value in 'mopping up' enemy dug-outs which it did by burning alive any unfortunate occupants. Its invention by the Germans was hailed by the Allies as a typical instance of 'Hun frightfulness'. Compared with the frightfulness of our modern engines of war the *Flammenwerfer* is as it is described in the *Wipers Times* issue of 20 March1916: 'A natty little toy'.

Flying pigs German trench mortar bombs of about 10-inch diameter. Also known as 'oil cans'.

F.M. Field Marshal.

F.P. No. 1 Field Punishment No. 1. This comprised tying the defaulter to a gun-wheel for one hour in the morning and one hour in the afternoon. In the period under review the guns might be needed at any moment and although it was not unknown to tie a man to a gun in action, the C.O. would, for humanitarian reasons, arrange for the F.P. to be inflicted when the battalion was out of line. The defaulter would then be lashed to a fence. The rest of the punishment was severe pack drill.

Frigiped Cold Feet (*q.v.*).

Fullerphone An improved telegraph apparatus invented by a General Fuller. Conversation, both spoken and telegraphic, on a 'D Mark 3' (*q.v.*) could be picked up by enemy listening-in posts behind their lines. The Fullerphone consisted of two circuits, one carrying direct current providing a continuous buzz, the other supplying an alternating current that carried Morse code signals. The German listeners could only pick up the buzz. The Fullerphone could not be used for speech.

Funk hole A dug-out. A funk wallah was an officer who, when in the line, seldom, if ever, left his dug-out; such men were extremely rare.

G. General Staff (*cf.* **G. & Q.**).

G. & Q. The headquarters of a division were commanded by a Major General attended by two aides-de-camp of whom the senior was the Camp Commandant. Under the General the work was divided into two parts. Operations, or the business of actual fighting, fell to three General Staff Officers known as G.S.O. (*q.v.*) 1, 2 and 3, or the 'G side'. Maintenance and discipline of the troops was the responsibility of the Assistant Adjutant and the Quartermaster-General with various assistants and deputies. This was the 'Q side'.

Gas bag An early type of gas helmet (*see* **P.H.G.**). Later applied to all types of gas mask.

Geese Portuguese soldiers; also known as 'Pork and Beans'.

G.H.Q. General Headquarters.

G.O.C. General Officer Commanding (or in command).

Goer, a A shell passing overhead.

Gooseberries Near-spherical entanglements of barbed wire.

Grand-pa (or Grand-ma) A 12-inch gun.

Green Cross gas Mustard gas, so called after the green cross painted on the gas cylinder.

G.R.O. General Routine Order.

G.S. General Service. G.S. wagon; G.S. hammer, etc.

G.S.O. General Staff Officer, or Office.

Haig Field Marshal Douglas Haig, Commander-in-Chief of the B.E.F. from December 1915.

Hairy, a A horse or mule.

H.B.M. His Britannic Majesty.

H.E. High Explosive.

Hindenburg Line The German line of defence which issued from the original defences near Arras and ran back some twelve miles to Queant and thence west of Cambrai towards St Quentin. It was supported by several switches, or loops, which served as a second line. It was evacuated by the Germans in October 1918. Its official (German) name was Siegfried Line.

How A Howitzer.

H.Q. Headquarters.

Hymn of Hate An anti-British song composed by one Herr Ernst Lissauer on the outbreak of the war, that became very popular in Germany. Of its fifty lines, the last are typical:

French and Russians they matter not,
A blow for a blow, a shot for a shot,
We fight the battle with bronze and steel.
And the time that is coming Peace will seal.
You will we hate with a lasting hate,
We will never forgo our hate,
Hate by the water and hate by the land,
Hate of the head and hate of the hand,
Hate of the hammer and hate of the crown,
Hate of seventy millions, choking down.
We love as one, we hate as one,
We have one foe, and one alone –
ENGLAND!*

All Germany went wild over the 'Hymn of Hate'. It was taught in the schools and sung in the trenches. A German artillery bombardment was known by the British as a 'hymn of hate' (*cf.* Notes, p. 193*l*).

I.B. Infantry Brigade.

In the pink Letters from private soldiers frequently ended 'hoping this finds you as it leaves me at present in the pink'.

I.O. Infantry Officer.

Johnson Another name for a 'Coal box' (*q.v.*) after the negro pugilist, Jack Johnson. 'A shout, a scream, a roar' is an accurate description of the delivery and explosion of a 'Johnson'.

K.R. King's Regulations.

* This translation first appeared in the *New York Times*

Lead swinging Malingering.

L.I. Light Infantry.

M & V diet Maconochie's tinned rations consisting of meat and vegetables.

Maconochie's Suppliers of tinned food to the army.

M.C. Military Cross.

M & D Medicine and Duty, i.e. a dose of No. 9 (*q.v.*) or other medicine and back to work.

Megrim The English word for 'migraine'.

M.G. Machine Gun.

M.G.C. Machine Gun Corps.

M.G.O. Master-General of Ordinance.

Minnie A German trench mortar – *Minenwerfer*, bomb thrower (*cf.* **Flying Pig**).

M.L.O. Military Liaison Officer.

M.O. Medical Officer.

Morning hate The artillery on both sides opened fire regularly at dawn and dusk, these being the times that an infantry attack could be expected. These bombardments were known by the British as the 'morning hate' and the 'evening hate' (*cf.* **'Hymn of Hate'**).

Mustard gas By far the most effective poison gas used in the War. Its effects on the eyes, throat and lungs were devastating and it continued to give off potent vapour for a considerable period. It possessed an unfortunate tendency to remain in unsuspected pockets in shell-holes which would be dispersed by later gunfire. It might then drift into a trench – friendly or otherwise – when it was least expected.

Napoo or Narpoo From the French, 'Il n'y en a plus' – there is no more. The word was later applied to mean 'there is none' – thus 'Napoo rum', no rum; and again, 'napood' i.e. dead. ('So I jumps into this shell-'ole and there's twelve Bosch there, all dead 'cept one. So I says to 'im, "You're a lucky b.........., ain't yer?" and I napooed 'im.') The word was also used for 'No' or 'Not good enough' (*see B.E.F. Times*, Monday 5 March 1917, p. 181, col. 2, '"You no tell" said Madeline "and I give you beer." "Narpoo!"'). Also 'no more' in a different sense (*see Better Times*, December 1918, p. 323, col. 2, '"Ach Himmel . . . Deutschland Uber Alles, napoo."').

N.C.O. Non-Commissioned Officer.

No bon No good, useless.

No. 9 A purgative pill handed out by the Medical Officer more or less indiscriminately to the entire sick parade and in particular to men classified M & D (*q.v.*) and N.Y.D. (*q.v.*). It was also known as 'the star of the movies'.

N.Y.D. Not Yet Diagnosed. In other words keep this man working. (Colloquial: Not Yet Dead.)

O.B.E. Order of the British Empire.

Obus A howitzer shell.

O.C. Coy Officer in command of a company.

O.M. Order of Merit.

On the wire Killed in action. Also 'present whereabouts unknown' (not necessarily a casualty).

O.O. Orderly Officer.

O.P. Observation Post.

O pip O.P. (*q.v.*) (Signalese).

O.R. Other Ranks.

Over the top, to go To climb over the top of the parapet into 'no man's land' in an attack, or raid, on the enemy line.

Pavé The stone-paved surface of roads in Belgium and France.

P.B. Permanent Base.

P.B.C.O. Poor Bloody Commanding Officer, a development of P.B.I. (*q.v.*).

P.B.I. Poor Bloody Infantry. Applicable to Infantry Officers as well as privates.

Pediculi Lice.

P.H.G. helmet Phenate-Hexamine Goggle Helmet. An early respirator comprising a felt hood with eye-pieces, the felt impregnated with chemicals.

Phosgene Carbonyl Chloride. An extremely poisonous gas used in both cloud-gas and shell-gas attacks. It has a nauseating, choking smell and affects the heart and lungs.

Piou-piou A French soldier.

Picket A pointed stake driven into the ground to support barbed-wire entanglements. Later pickets were corkscrew-shaped iron stakes that could be driven in without noise.

Pimple A hill.

Pineapple A Mills pattern hand grenade.

Pip squeak A rifle grenade or a small gas shell.

Pit props Used to support dug-outs, shelters etc.

Plug Street Ploegsteert (*see* Place Names).

P.M. Provost Marshal.

Pomegranate A type of hand grenade.

Pop Poperinghe (*see* Place Names).

Professor A senior Army Officer.

P.U.O. Pyrexia of uncertain origin, more often called 'Trench Fever'. Also: Placed Under Observation.

Pumpkin A type of mortar bomb.

Q. *See* **G. & Q.**

Q.M.G.	Quartermaster-General.
R.A.P.	Regimental Aid Post.
R.B.	Rifle Brigade.
R.E.	Royal Engineers. *The Salient* (another Ypres trench magazine, but one that was printed in England) said that the R.E.'s were 'otherwise known as the "Press Gang". Isolated members of thir Corps have been known to imprison large numbers of othes regiments and act as taskmasters to them in making dug-outs and roads. Troops get into the habit of instinctively taking cover from all Engineers.'
Red tab	A Staff Officer.
Revetting	Strengthening the walls of trenches or parapets with stakes or sandbags.
Revetting maul	A type of sledgehammer used for facing trenches and parapets.
R.F.A.	Royal Field Artillery.
R.M.O.	Regimental Medical Officer.
Roger	A poison gas cylinder; also Rum.
Rootie (or Rooty)	Bread; from Urdu, *roti.*
R.Q.M.S.	Regimental Quartermaster-Sergeant.
R.T.O.	Railway Transport Officer. Eric Partridge tells us that: 'The duty of the R.T.O. was to direct the transport of troop movements and to assist soldiers who were returning to their units from leave. He seldom cared where his charges went so long as they passed out of his sphere of influence so "returning soldiers" might easily and deliberately spend a week or more in short railway trips, a delightful holiday rich with new scenes and an air of personal freedom otherwise unknown to the Army. You caught the wrong train, or at least missed the right one, and then persuaded the R.T.O. to date-stamp your pass, so that the Town Major [*see* T.M.] would give you a night's billet and a day's rations.'*
Rum jar	Trench mortar bomb (also, of course, a jar for containing rum).
S.A.A.	Small Arms Ammunition.
Sap	A covered trench or a narrow communication trench.
Sapper	A private of the Royal Engineers. Originally, a soldier employed in working at saps, the building of fortifications, etc.
Sausage	A 'sausage-shaped' observation balloon more often referred to as a 'maiden's prayer' but not, needless to say, in the pages of the *Wipers Times.*
Shell shock	Derangement of the nervous system to a greater or lesser degree resulting from exposure to shell explosions at close quarters.
Shooting gallery	The Front Line.

* Partridge and Brody, *Songs and Slang of the British Soldier.*

Short one, a A shell from artillery that fell near to or on its own lines.

Silent Percy Any large, long-range gun, the report of which could not be heard on the receiving end. Also known as a 'rubber gun'.

Sniperscope A contraption fitted onto a sniper's rifle that allowed it to be fired without the marksman exposing himself. A periscope was also attached to enable the rifleman to aim. In most places in the front line it meant instant death to expose one's head.

Sniping plate A shield with eye-slots used by snipers.

S.P. Sniper's Post.

Stand to Stand to arms – a period of about an hour at daybreak and at dusk when the parapet was fully manned, this being the time when an enemy attack was most likely to occur. The call to 'stand to' also preceded the operation of 'going over the top' (*cf.* **over the top**).

Stokes gun A trench mortar of the type invented by Sir Frederick Stokes, K.B.E.

Strafe To fire upon with rifle or artillery. From the German battle cry, '*Gott Strafe England*' (God punish England). The morning (or evening) hate (*q.v.*) was also known as the morning (or evening) strafe.

Sub Sub-Lieutenant.

Tape Tapes laid down before the front line to mark the starting line for an attack, or to mark the routes across ground which, as a result of continual bombardment, had no recognisable features.

Tickler Jam, so called after a brand name for a jam supplied to the army. Jam tins were made into improvised bombs which were also called 'ticklers' – a grim pun. In times of shortage, 'tickler' was eaten with anything and it was always good currency in an *estaminet*.

Tina Probably a member of the W.A.A.C. (*q.v.*) who ran the local E.F.C. (*q.v.*).

T.M. Town Major – an officer permanently stationed in a town or village and responsible for billeting passing parties of troops; also trench mortar.

T.O. Transport Officer.

Tock Emma T.M. (*q.v.*) (Signalese).

Toffee apple A German hand grenade so called because of its throwing stick

Toughs, the The 'Old Toughs' – name given to the Royal Dublin Fusiliers.

Traverse A barrier; e.g. a parapet of earth thrown up across a line of enemy fire as a defence or to prevent enfilading fire.

Trench feet A painful affliction of the feet caused through long exposure to damp and cold. It was a technical offence to be afflicted by trench feet although there is no record of any man being 'crimed' for the misdemeanour.

Two-in-Command The Second in Command.

V.A.D. Voluntary Aid Detachments comprising trained nurses who volunteered for service in hospitals abroad.

Vermoral sprayer Ordinary garden syringes issued to the army to dispel poison gas, bad smells, etc. They were filled with diluted Creoline to combat flies and bad odours and with a solution of Hypo Soda to deal with gas.

Very lights Lights fired from special pistols and used in night-signalling or for illuminating the enemy's position. Named after the inventor, Samuel W. Very.

W.A.A.C. Women's Auxiliary Army Corps. Formed in February 1917 to relieve the Army of some of its non-combatant work. Its members served in France as motor drivers, technicians, cooks, tailors, etc.

Walla or **wallah** Chap; from the Hindustani.

Wind safe A wind blowing in a direction unsuitable for German gas attacks

Wind up Fear – but not to be confused with 'cold feet' (*q.v.*). Partridge says that 'to *have the wind up* implied no disgrace, and could be mentioned in conversation, although usually in the past tense'.*

Windy *See* **Wind up.**

Windyberg Line, the The Hindenburg Line (*cf.* **Wind up**).

Woodbines A brand of cigarette.

W.P. Weather Permitting.

Yellow parchment A leave pass.

Zig zag Intoxicated. Partridge reports that the following was actually heard in a Belgian shop near the line: '"Marie, ally promenade ce suir?" – "Non, pas ce soir" (Interlude of blandishments). "Ah! moi ally estaminet, revinir zig-zag, si vous no promenade."'†

* Partridge and Brody, *Songs and Slang of the British Soldier.*

† Partridge and Brody, *op. cit.*

LIST OF PLACE NAMES

Albert A town in the Somme *département* of France. It was captured by the Germans in March 1918 and recaptured by the British the following August.

Ancre, River A river that rises south of Bapaume and flows to the Somme. It gave its name to a battle fought in November 1916.

Avesnes Town in the French *département* of the Nord, 13 miles east of Cambrai.

Bailleul A town in the French *département* of the Nord, 19 miles N.W. of Lille. It was the scene of many German attacks during April 1918 and was almost obliterated by a terrible bombardment before being taken by the Germans on 15 April 1918.

Bapaume A town in the Pas de Calais *département* of France, it was captured by the British in March 1917, by the Germans in March 1918 and, finally, by the British in August 1918.

Bellewarde Brook Bellewarde Bec, a brook running into Bellewarde Lake.

Bellewarde Lake A lake just north of Hooge.

Bourlon Wood A wood outside the village of Bourlon, west of Cambrai.

Boesinghe A small town N.W. of Ypres where the British right joined the French left. The town, with its beautiful chateau, was completely flattened.

Bulford Camp A training camp near Neuve Eglise named after a famous military camp on Salisbury Plain.

Clonmel Copse A little copse two miles east of Zillebeke.

Contalmaison A village near La Boisselle (*q.v.*).

Crump Farm Most of the many farms in the Salient had ceased to exist. The sites were renamed by British soldiers; hence Argyle Farm, Shell Trap Farm, and Kultur Farm (after the Kaiser's threat to bring German culture to the rest of Europe).

Culvert, The A culvert passing under the Menin Road and the railway a quarter of a mile west of Hooge. It was used as a dug-out.

Dawson's Corner A road junction two and a half miles N.W. of Ypres.

Dead Cow Farm A farm lying two and a quarter miles due east of Neuve Eglise. It was so named by the British because of the presence for a time of a number of cows' carcasses.

Dead Dog Farm A ruined farm two and a half miles south of Ypres.

Dickebushe Pond The *Etang de Dickbusch*, a large lake near the village of Dickbusch, three miles S.W. of Ypres.

Douave River A river in Belgium which passes about six miles south of Ypres.

Dranoutre A village S.W. of Kemmel.

Fish-Hook Most of the villages surrounding Ypres had names ending with 'hoek'. Fish-hook, presumably, was the English pronunciation of one of these villages and, again presumably, it lay between Ypres and Menin (*Wipers Times*, 12 February, p.1). Neither modern nor contemporary gazetteers of the area show any village with a name resembling 'Fish-Hook', the nearest being Westhoek, a village three miles east of Ypres.

Fleurbaix A village S.W. of Armentières.

Fosse Wood The remains of a wood nearly two miles S.E. of Zillebeke.

Gheluvelt A village on the Menin Road, four miles E.S.E. of Ypres, completely razed to the ground in the first German offensive of 1914. From November 1917 to April 1918 the German front line ran through the village and it was retaken by the British in October 1918.

Glencourse Wood A wood on a hill four miles east of Ypres. It changed hands a number of times and was finally taken by the Australians in September 1917.

Gordon Farm A farm situated three miles S.S.W. of Ypres.

Gordon House A farm situated about half a mile south of Hell Fire Corner.

Guillemont A ruined village standing on a high ridge dominating the surrounding countryside. It was very heavily fortified by the Germans but taken by the British, 3 September 1916.

Half-Way House A ruin of a house between Zillebeke and Hell Fire Corner.

Haubourdin A ruined hamlet on the Neuve Eglise Road.

Hazebrouck Town in French *département* of the Nord, twenty-eight miles W.N.W. of Lille.

Hell Fire Corner A point on the Ypres–Menin Road where it was joined by the road to Potijze and where it was crossed by the Ypres–Roulers Railway. It was under fire almost continuously.

Hill 60 Hills were named after their height in metres. Hill 60 was a small hill some 150 yards wide by 250 yards long, standing a few miles from Ypres. It commanded the flat countryside surrounding it and as a consequence it was of immense importance. So constant and so fierce were the battles to possess this terrible hill that it took a strong stomach to penetrate the surface of its ground. Within Hill 60 was a veritable warren of tunnels, both British and German, and the grave of many a tunneller. It was not unknown for British and German miners to break in on each other under Hill 60, there to engage in hand-to-hand fighting with pick and shovel.

Hollebeke A village four miles south of Ypres. It was in German hands until it was captured by the British in the advance of 1917.

Hooge A tiny hamlet on the Menin Road, two and a half miles east of Ypres. Completely obliterated early in the war, Hooge was looked upon as the worst section in the whole of the Salient being continuously subject to shell-fire, machine-gun fire and gas. The British cemetery at Hooge contains some 2,000 graves.

Kemmel A village near Ploegsteert, six miles S.W. of Ypres. There were fierce battles in front of Kemmel in April 1915. It was taken by the Germans on 25 April in spite of a heroic defence by the British.

La Boisselle A French village on the Albert–Bapaume Road.

Lille Gate A gate through the Ypres fortifications on the Lille–Ypres road.

Locre A village N.W. of Dranoutre and about six and a half miles S.W. of Ypres.

Locrehof A farm near Locre (*q.v.*).

Loos A mining village in northern France and the scene of a great battle during the Allied offensive in the Autumn of 1915.

Mackenson Farm A farm situated two and a half miles north of Ypres.

Mazingarbe Town in Pas de Calais *département* of France, five miles S.E. of Bethune.

Menin A Belgium town on the left bank of the River Lys. It was in German hands until the great Allied advance of 1918.

Menin Gate The gate through the Ypres fortifications on the Menin Road.

Meteren A village S.W. of Dranoutre. It fell to the German advance of April 1918 and was recaptured by the British in July 1918.

Neuve Eglise A village about eight miles S.S.W. of Ypres, standing on an important cross-roads. It was the scene of much fighting during the battles of April 1918.

Passchendaele A wood and village seven miles E.N.E. of Ypres. In October 1916 Passchendaele was attacked by British and Canadian troops and was the subject of prolonged and furious fighting. During the battle von Hindenburg ordered: 'Passchendaele must be held at all costs and retaken if lost.' It was taken by the Canadians and held until April 1918. It was finally taken by the Belgian Army in September 1918.

Pilkem A village on a ridge three miles north of Ypres. It was taken by the Germans in April 1915 and recaptured by the British in July 1917.

Ploegstreet A Belgian town near the French border, eleven miles N.W. of Lille.

Poperinghe A small town seven miles west of Ypres. Although subject to occasional shellfire, it became a rest centre for the British. Here it was that the Rev. P. B. (Tubby) Clayton established Toc H (Talbot House) in memory of his friend Gilbert Talbot, a subaltern who was killed while leading his men in an attack near Hooge. The Hotel Skindles in Poperinghe was a favourite with British officers.

Potijze A hamlet on the Ypres–Zonnebeke road.

Pozieres A village in France, fiercely fought over in the battle of the Somme, July–August 1916.

Railway Wood The remains of a wood near Hooge and two miles east of Ypres. Like all other woods on the edge of the Salient it was reduced to a clump of shattered stumps. Three N.C.O.'s and eight men were buried alive while tunnelling near Railway Wood.

Red Lodge This could have been at any number of places. There was a Red Chateau near Wytschaete, a Red Cottage near Messines and a Red House (or the remains of one) three miles east of Ypres.

Reninghelst A village seven miles S.W. of Ypres.

Rossignol A common with some small woods E.S.E. of Ypres. It was heavily fortified with concrete 'pillboxes' by the Germans. Rossignol was also the name of a village five miles S.W. of Ypres.

St Quentin A town in northern France and the scene of much fighting. It was finally captured by the Allies in October 1918.

Sanctuary Wood A wood south of Hooge and the scene of continual fighting which soon reduced it to a few stumps of tree trunks. It changed hands several times during the course of the war and being under constant shellfire it was never a sanctuary for either side.

Spanbroekmolen The site of a mine exploded by the British near Hill 60 (*q.v.*) on 7 June 1917.

Spree A river in Prussia.

Trones Wood A wood near La Boisselle (*q.v.*).

Vimy Ridge A ridge of ground, 476 feet high, near Vimy, a village N.N.E. of Arras. Attacked unsuccessfully by the French in 1915 and finally taken by the Canadians after bitter fighting in August–September 1918.

Vlamertinghe Village west of Ypres, it suffered many heavy bombardments.

Wulverghem A village eight and a half miles south of Ypres.

Zillebeke A village S.E. of Ypres.

Zillebeke Lake A lake near the village of Zillebeke and the scene of many attacks from both sides in the 2nd and 3rd battles of Ypres.

Zouve Wood A small wood south of Hooge.

APPENDIX

24th DIVISION

Order of Battle, 1914-1918

Dates	INFANTRY		Mounted Troops	ARTILLERY						Engineers	Signal Service	Pioneers	M.G. Units	Field Ambulances	Mobile Vety. Secn.	Divnl. Emplnt. Coy.	Divnl. Train
	Brigades	Battalions and attached Units		Field Artillery			Trench Mortar Bties.		Divnl. Ammn. Coln.	Field Cos.	Divnl. Signal Coy.						
				Brigades	Batteries	Bde. Ammn. Colns.	Medium	Heavy									
1914 October (England)	71st ... 72nd ... 73rd ...	9/Norf., 9/Suff., 8/Bedf., 11/Essex 8/Queen's, 8/Buffs, 9/E. Surr., 8/R.W.K. 12/R.F., 9/R. Suss., 7/Northn., 13/Middx.	24th Div. Cyclist Coy.[1]	CVI[2] .... CVII[2] .... CVIII[2] ...... CIX (H.)[2] ...	A, B, C, D A, B, C, D A, B, C, D A (H.), B (H.), C (H.), D (H.)	CVI B.A.C. CVII B.A.C. CVIII B.A.C. CIX (H.) B.A.C.	...	...	24th D.A.C.	91st[3] 92nd[4]	24th	...	...	72nd 73rd 74th	36th[5]	...	24th[6]
1915 September (France)	71st[7] ... 72nd ... 73rd ...	9/Norf., 9/Suff., 8/Bedf., 11/Essex 8/Queen's, 8/Buffs,[8] 9/E.Surr., 8/R.W.K. 12/R.F.,[9] 9/R. Suss., 7/Northn., 13/Middx.	A Sqdn.[10] 1/R. Glasgow Yeo. 24th Div. Cyclist Coy.[11]	CVI[12] .... CVII[13] ...... CVIII[14] ...... CIX (H.)[15] ...	A, B, C, D A, B, C, D A, B, C, D A (H.), B (H.), C (H.), D (H.)	CVI B.A.C. CVII B.A.C. CVIII B.A.C. CIX (H.) B.A.C.	...	...	24th D.A.C.	103rd[16] 104th[16] 129th[17]	24th	12/Sher. For.[18] (P.)	...	72nd 73rd 74th	36th	...	24th
1916 June (France)	17th[19] ... 72nd ... 73rd ...	8/Buffs,[8] 1/R.F., 12/R.F.,[9] 3/R.B.; 17th Bde. M.G. Coy.;[20] 17th T.M.Bty.[21] 8/Queen's, 9/E. Surr., 8/R.W.K., 1/N. Staff.;[22] 72nd Bde. M.G. Coy.;[20] 72nd T.M. Bty.[21] 9/R. Suss., 7/Northn., 13/Middx., 2/Leins.;[23] 73rd Bde. M.G. Coy.;[20] 73rd T.M. Bty.[21]	...	CVI[12; 24] ...... CVII[13; 25] ... CVIII[14; 26] ... CIX[15; 27]	A, B, C; D (H.) A, B, C; D (H.) A, B, C; D (H.) A, B, C	...[30]	X.24[28] Y.24[28] Z.24[28]	V.24[29]	24th D.A.C.[30]	103rd 104th 129th	24th	12/Sher. For. (P.)	...	72nd 73rd 74th	36th	...	24th
1917 June (France)	17th ... 72nd ... 73rd ...	8/Buffs,[31] 1/R.F., 12/R.F.,[32] 3/R.B.; 17th M.G. Coy.;[39] 17th T.M. Bty. 8/Queen's,[33] 9/E. Surr., 8/R.W.K., 1/N Staff.; 72nd M.G. Coy.;[39] 72nd T.M. Bty. 9/R. Suss., 7/Northn., 13/Middx., 2/Leins.;[34] 73rd M.G. Coy.;[39] 73rd T.M. Bty.	...	CVI[24] .... CVII[25]	A, B, C; D (H.) A, B, C; D (H.)	...	X.24 Y.24 Z.24[35]	V.24[36]	24th D.A.C.	103rd 104th 129th	24th	12/Sher. For. (P.)	191st M.G. Coy.[37]	72nd 73rd 74th	36th	224th[38]	24th

1918 March (France)	17th ... 72nd ... 73rd ...	8/Queen's,[33] 1/R.F., 3/R.B.; 17th T.M. Bty. 9/E. Surr., 8/R.W.K., 1/N. Staff.; 72nd T.M. Bty. 9/R. Suss., 7/Northn., 13/Middx.; 73rd T.M. Bty.	...	CVI .... CVII	A, B, C; D (H.) A, B, C; D (H.)	...	X.24 Y.24	...	24th D.A.C.	103rd 104th 129th	24th	12/ Sher. For. (P.)	No. 24 Bn., M.G.C.[39]	72nd 73rd 74th	36th	224th	24th

NOTES

[1] Coy. was formed by 15/2/15 and concentrated at Henfield on 17/2/15.

[2] In Jany., 1915, the Bdes. were organized as 4-battery brigades; the Bties. were 4-gun batteries, and were lettered—A, B, C, D—in each Brigade.

[3] In Jany., 1915, 91st Fd. Coy. was transferred to 15th Div. at Bordon.

[4] In Jany., 1915, 92nd Fd. Coy. was transferred to 18th Div.

[5] Joined Div. at Blackdown on 25/6/15.

[6] Train consisted of 194, 195, 196, and 197 Cos., A.S.C.

[7] On 11/10/15 the Bde. was transferred to the 6th Div., in exchange for 17th Bde. (see note 19).

[8] On 18/10/15 Bn. was transferred from 72nd Bde. to 17th Bde.

[9] On 12/10/15 Bn. was transferred from 73rd Bde. to 17th Bde.

[10] Sqdn. joined Div. at Blackdown on 30/6/15. Sqdn. disembkd. at le Havre on 1/9/15, left Div. on 29/4/16, was attached to 2nd Cav. Div. from 30/4–14/5/16, and on 21/5/16 Sqdn. joined V Corps Cav. Regt.

[11] Coy. disembkd. at le Havre on 31/8/15, left Div. on 29/4/16, was attached to 2nd Cav. Div. from 30/4–17/5/16, and on 18/5/16 Coy. joined V Corps Cyclist Bn.

[12] On 13/5/16 D Bty. left and became A/CIX; and A (H.)/CIX joined CVI and became D (H.)/CVI.

[13] On 13/5/16 D. Bty. left and became B/CIX; and D (H.)/CIX joined CVII and became D (H.)/CVII.

[14] On 13/5/16 D Bty. left and became C/CIX; and B (H.)/CIX joined CVIII and became D (H.)/CVIII.

[15] On 3/12/15 C (H.) left CIX (H.) and became C (H.)/CXXXI (H.), 2nd Cdn. Div., on 7/12/15. On 13/5/16 CIX was reorganized. A (H.), B (H.), and D (H.) left CIX and became D (H.)/CVI, D (H.)/CVIII, and D (H.)/CVII; and D/CVI D/CVII, and D/CVIII joined CIX and became A, B, C/CIX

[16] In Feb., 1915, 103rd and 104th Fd. Cos. joined from 33rd Div., to replace 91st and 32nd Fd. Cos. (see notes 3 and 4).

[17] 129th Fd. Coy. joined before 7/4/15.

[18] Bn. (from Army Troops) was attached to Div. before March 1915; and by 7/4/15 Bn. was converted into 24th Div. Pioneer Bn.

[19] On 14/10/15, 17th Bde. (1/R.F., 1/N. Staff., 2/Leins. 3/R.B., and 2/Lond.) was transferred from 6th Div. and joined 24th Div., to replace 71st Bde. (see note 7). 2/Lond. left 17th Bde. on 9/2/16 (see General Notes).

[20] M.G. Cos. were formed and joined Bdes. as follows:—
17th—formed in the Bde. on 17/1/16, at Poperinghe;
72nd—formed at Grantham; disembkd. at le Havre on 11/3/16, and joined Bde. at Ouderdom on 14/3/16;
73rd—mobilized at Grantham on 22/2/16; disembkd. at le Havre on 11/3/16, and joined Bde. at Ouderdom on 14/3/16.

[21] T.M. Bties. were formed in the Bdes.:—
17th—17/1 by 22/3/16, 17/2 by April, 1916, and they became 17th T.M. Bty. by 26/7/16;
72nd—72/1 joined Bde. on 11/3/16, 72/2 was formed on 10/4/16, and they became 72nd T. M. Bty. on 19/7/16;
73rd—73/1 by 17/3/16, 72/2 by 24/5/16, and they became 73rd T.M. Bty. on 15/6/16.

[22] On 18/10/15 Bn. was transferred from 17th Bde. to 72nd Bde.

[23] On 19/10/15 Bn. was transferred from 17th Bde. to 73rd Bde.

[24] On 3/10/16 A & R. Sec. B/CIX joined CVI: R. Sec. A/CIX made up A, L. Sec. A/CIX made up B, and R. Sec. B/CIX made up C/CVI to 6, 18-pdrs. each. On 27/1/17, 1 sec. C (H.)/CVIII joined and made up D (H.)/CVI to 6 hows.

[25] On 3/10/16 L. Sec. B & C/CIX joined CVII: L. Sec. B/CIX made up A, R. Sec. C/CIX made up B, and L. Sec. C/CIX made up C/CVII to 6, 18-pdrs. each. On 27/1/17, 1 sec. C (H.)/CVIII joined and made up D (H.)/CVII to 6 hows.

[26] On 3/10/16 A Bty. was broken up: R. Sec. A made up C and L. Sec. A made up B to 6, 18-pdrs. each. On 8/10/16, 522 (H.) Bty.—4, 4.5" H.—joined Bde. from England and became A (H.); on 13/10/16. C. Bty. was redesignated A and A (H.) became C (H.)/CVIII. On 27/1/17 CVIII became an A.F.A. Bde.: C (H.) left and was broken up to make up D (H.)/CVI and D (H.)/CVII to 6 hows. each; C/XCVI (6, 18-pdrs.) joined from 21st Div. and became C/CVIII; and 1 sec. D (H.)/XCVI also joined and made up D (H.)/CVIII to 6 hows.

[27] On 3/10/16 CIX was broken up: A Bty. and R. Sec. B were transferred to CVI, and L. Sec. B and C Bty. to CVII, they were then allotted by secs. to make up the 18-pdr. Bties. of CVI and CVII to 6 guns each (notes 24 and 25).

[28] The 3 Medium T.M. Bties. were formed by 30/4/16.

[29] V joined by 30/7/16.

[30] B.A.C.s were abolished and the D.A.C. was reorganized on 13/5/16.

[31] Between 8–13/2/18 Bn. was drafted to 1/Buffs (6th Div.), 6/Buffs (12th Div.), and VII Corps Rft. Camp. On 13/2/18 Bn. was disbanded.

[32] Between 2–13/2/18 Bn. was drafted to 1/R.F. (17th Bde.), 10/R.F. (37th Div.), 11/R.F. (18th Div.), and VII Corps Rft. Camp. On 13/2/18 Bn. was disbanded.

[33] On 7/2/18 Bn. was transferred to 17th Bde.

[34] On 1/2/18 Bn. left 24th Div. and joined 47th Bde., 16th Div., on 2/2/18.

[35] In Febry., 1918, Z was absorbed by X and Y Medium T.M. Bties.

[36] In Febry., 1918, V H.T.M. Bty. was transferred to Corps Troops.

[37] Coy. disembkd. at le Havre on 13/12/16 and joined Div. on 15/12/16 at Noeux les Mines.

[38] Coy. joined Div. on 24/5/17.

[39] Bn. was formed on 5/3/18, and consisted of 17th, 72nd, 73rd, and 191st M.G. Cos.

ORDER OF BATTLE, GENERAL NOTES

The following Units also served with the 24th Division:—

ARTILLERY:—522 (H.) Bty., R.F.A. (4, 4·5″ hows.), disembkd. at le Havre on 4/10/16 and joined CVIII on 8/10/16 (see note 26).

24th (New) Heavy Bty., R.G.A.* (4, 60-pdrs.), was raised for the 24th Div. and served with the Div. at Mytchett Camp from 12/6–27/8/15. 24th (New) Heavy Battery was redesignated 130th Heavy Battery, and on 9/10/15 joined XXXV Heavy Artillery Brigade (on formation) at Charlton. 130th Heavy Battery embkd. at Southampton on 7/2/16, disembkd. at Alexandria on 20/2/16; returned to France in April 1916, disembkd. at Marseille on 14/4/16, and joined XXI H.A.G. on 12/5/16.

13th Division Ammn. Coln., was attached in England from 3/7–6/8/15.

INFANTRY:—

11/R. Warwick., was attached in England from before March 1915 to 9/4/15. Bn. then joined 112th Bde., 37th Div., and served with 37th Div. until Bn. was disbanded in Feb., 1918.

13/R.F., was attached in England from before March 1915 to 9/4/15. Bn. then joined 111th Bde., 37th Div., and served with 37th Div. until Bn. was disbanded in Feb., 1918.

12/Sher. For., was attached in England from before March, 1915. In April 1915, Bn. was converted into Divnl. Pioneer Bn. (note 18).

1/2/London, joined 24th Div. in France on 14/10/15, with 17th Inf. Bde. (note 19). On 9/2/16 Bn. left Div. and joined 169th Bde., 56th Div., on 10/2/16.

MACHINE GUNS:—No. 3 Motor-Machine-Gun Battery, served with the Div. from 30/10–23/11/15, and the Bty. was then transferred to 3rd Div.

OTHER UNITS:— 13th Division Train, was attached in England from 3/7–20/8/15. On 16/11/15 the Train became 28th Div. Train.

41st Sanitary Section, joined Div. at Blackdown on Friday, 20/8/15 and disembkd. at le Havre on 2/9/15. The Section left the Div. on 5/4/17 and took over No. 6 Sanitary Area, First Army.

* 24th Heavy Battery, R.G.A. (4, 60-pdrs.) was serving with the 6th Division at the outbreak of the Great War; and in September 1914 24th Heavy Battery went to France with the 6th Division.

24th Division Motor Ambce. Workshop, joined Div. in England, disembkd. at Rouen on 31/8/15, rejoined Div. on 7/9/15, and in April 1916 the Workshop was transferred to and absorbed by 24th Div. Supply Column.

On 13/2/18 the reorganization of the 24th Division on a 9-battalion basis was completed; and on 4/3/18 the pioneer battalion (12/Sher. For.) was reorganized on a 3-company basis.

24th DIVISION

List of Staff Officers

G.O.C.

19 September, 1914 ... ... Major-General Sir J. G. RAMSAY.
3 October, 1915 ... ... Major-General J. E. CAPPER.
12 May, 1917 ... ... Br.-Gen. H. C. SHEPPARD (acting).
18 May, 1917 ... ... Major-General L. J. BOLS.
12 September, 1917 ... ... Br.-Gen. E. S. HOARE NAIRNE (acting).
15 September, 1917 ... ... Major-General A. C. DALY.

G.S.O. 1.

17 Sept., 1914...Lt.-Col. C. F. HEYWORTH-SAVAGE (tempy.).
11 Jan., 1915...Major Sir W. A. I. KAY, Bt. (acting).
16 May, 1915...Lt.-Col. C. G. STEWART.
23 Feb., 1916...Lt.-Col. Sir W.A. I. KAY, [Bt.
9 Nov., 1916...Captain H. BOYD-ROCHFORT (acting).
1 Dec., 1916...Lt.-Col. Sir W.A. I. KAY, [Bt.
5 Oct., 1917...Lt.-Col. H. C. MAITLAND-MAKGILL-CRICHTON.
31 Jan., 1918...Lt.-Col. J. H. MACKENZIE.
26 Aug., 1918...Major C. G. LING (acting).
27 Aug., 1918...Lt.-Col. C. M. LONGMORE.

A.-A. and Q.-M.-G.

7 Oct., 1914...Captain J. H. LLOYD (acting).
10 Oct., 1914...Colonel H. T. KENNY.
28 Sept., 1915...Lt.-Col. J. F. I. H. DOYLE.
24 Dec., 1917...Lt.-Col. E. V. D. RIDDELL.
14 April, 1918...Lt.-Col. Hon R. H. COLLINS.

B.-G., R.A.

9 Nov., 1914...Br.-Gen. Sir G. V. THOMAS, Bt.
26 Oct., 1915...Br.-Gen. L. M. PHILPOTTS (killed, 8/9/16).
8 Sept., 1916...Lt.-Col. D. R. COATES (acting).
11 Sept., 1916...Br.-Gen. H. C. SHEPPARD.
5 Sept., 1917...Br.-Gen. E. S. HOARE NAIRNE.
22 Mar., 1918...Lt.-Col. D. W. L. SPILLER (acting).
24 Mar., 1918...Lt.-Col. W. STIRLING (acting).
27 Mar., 1918...Br.-Gen. E. S. HOARE NAIRNE.*
26 Oct., 1918...Br.-Gen. H. G. LLOYD.

C.R.E.

14 Oct., 1914...Lt.-Col. H. E. G. CLAYTON.
25 July, 1915...Lt.-Col. A. J. CRAVEN.
12 Feb., 1917...Major C. N. RIVERS-MOORE (acting).
4 Mar., 1917...Lt.-Col. A. J. CRAVEN.
2 April, 1917...Major F. P. HEATH (acting).
4 April, 1917...Lt.-Col. T. T. BEHRENS.
24 Aug., 1917...Major J. H. PRIOR (acting).
4 Sept., 1917...Lt.-Col. A. D. WALKER (killed, 26/3/18).
26 Mar., 1918...Major J. H. PRIOR (tempy.).
1 April, 1918...Lt.-Col. J. H. PRIOR

24th DIVISION

List of Engagements

1915

25 and 26 September **Battle of Loos** [XI Corps, First Army].

1916

30 April ... ... **Wulverghem** (German Gas Attack) [V Corps, Second Army].

BATTLES OF THE SOMME

11–22 Aug.; and 31 Aug.–2 Sept. **Battle of Delville Wood** [XIII Corps, until m/n., 16/17; then XIV Corps; and from 31/8, XV Corps, Fourth Army].
3–5 September ... ... **Battle of Guillemont** [XV Corps, Fourth Army].

* Br.-Gen. E. S. Hoare Nairne acted from 22–24 March, 1918, as B.-G., R. A.,of the 50th (Northumbrian) Division; and on 25 and 26 March, 1918, as B.-G., R.A., of the 8th Division.

1917

BATTLES OF ARRAS

9–14 April ... ... **Battle of Vimy Ridge** [I Corps, First Army].
7–14 June ... ... **Battle of Messines** [X Corps, Second Army].

31 July–13 Sept. **BATTLES OF YPRES**

31 July–2 Aug. ... **Battle of Pilckem Ridge** [II Corps, Fifth Army].
16–18 August ... ... **Battle of Langemarck** [II Corps, Fifth Army].

BATTLE OF CAMBRAI

30 Nov.–3 Dec. ... **The German Counter-Attacks** [VII Corps, Third Army].

1918

FIRST BATTLES OF THE SOMME

21–23 March ... ... **Battle of St Quentin** [XIX Corps, Fifth Army].
24 and 25 March ... **Actions at the Somme Crossings** [XIX Corps, Fifth Army].
26 and 27 March ... **Battle of Rosieres** [XIX Corps, Fifth Army].
4 April ... ... **Battle of the Avre** [XIX Corps, Fourth Army].

THE ADVANCE TO VICTORY
BATTLES OF THE HINDENBURG LINE

8 and 9 October ... **Battle of Cambrai** [XVII Corps, Third Army].
9–12 October ... **Pursuit to the Selle** [XVII Corps, Third Army].

THE FINAL ADVANCE IN PICARDY

4 November ... ... **Battle of the Sambre** [XVII Corps, Third Army].
5–7 November ... ... **Passage of the Grande Honnelle** [XVII Corps, Third Army].

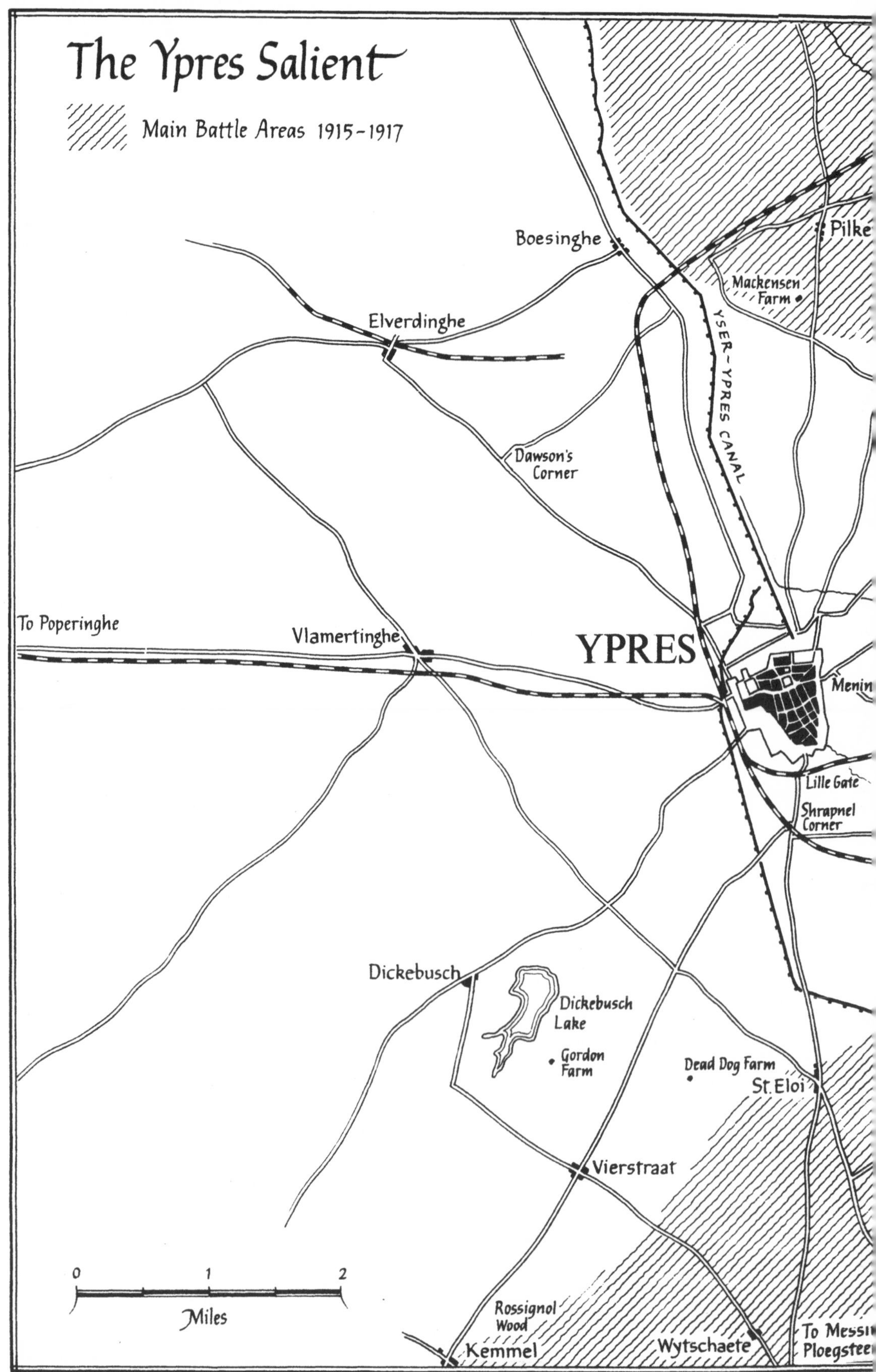

The Ypres Salient
Main Battle Areas 1915–1917
Boesinghe
Pilke
Mackensen Farm
Elverdinghe
YSER–YPRES CANAL
Dawson's Corner
To Poperinghe
Vlamertinghe
YPRES
Menin
Lille Gate
Shrapnel Corner
Dickebusch
Dickebusch Lake
Gordon Farm
Dead Dog Farm
St. Eloi
Vierstraat
0
1
2
Miles
Rossignol Wood
Kemmel
Wytschaete
To Messi
Ploegstee